Lecture Notes in Computer Science

Lecture Notes in Artificial Intelligence 14857

The series Lecture Notes in Artificial Intelligence (LNAI) was established in 1988 as a topical subseries of LNCS devoted to artificial intelligence.

The series publishes state-of-the-art research results at a high level. As with the LNCS mother series, the mission of the series is to serve the international R & D community by providing an invaluable service, mainly focused on the publication of conference and workshop proceedings and postproceedings.

Héctor Quintián · Emilio Corchado ·
Alicia Troncoso Lora · Hilde Pérez García ·
Esteban Jove Pérez · José Luis Calvo Rolle ·
Francisco Javier Martínez de Pisón ·
Pablo García Bringas ·
Francisco Martínez Álvarez · Álvaro Herrero ·
Paolo Fosci
Editors

Hybrid Artificial Intelligent Systems

19th International Conference, HAIS 2024
Salamanca, Spain, October 9–11, 2024
Proceedings, Part I

Springer

Editors
Héctor Quintián
University of A Coruña - CITIC
Ferrol, La Coruña, Spain

Emilio Corchado
University of Salamanca
Salamanca, Spain

Alicia Troncoso Lora
Pablo de Olavide University
Seville, Spain

Hilde Pérez García
University of León
León, Spain

Esteban Jove Pérez
University of A Coruña - CITIC
Ferrol, La Coruña, Spain

José Luis Calvo Rolle
University of A Coruña - CITIC
Ferrol, La Coruña, Spain

Francisco Javier Martínez de Pisón
University of La Rioja
Logroño, La Rioja, Spain

Pablo García Bringas
University of Deusto Avda
Bilbao, Spain

Francisco Martínez Álvarez
Pablo de Olavide University
Seville, Spain

Álvaro Herrero
University of Burgos
Burgos, Spain

Paolo Fosci
University of Bergamo
Bergamo, Bergamo, Italy

ISSN 0302-9743 ISSN 1611-3349 (electronic)
Lecture Notes in Artificial Intelligence
ISBN 978-3-031-74182-1 ISBN 978-3-031-74183-8 (eBook)
https://doi.org/10.1007/978-3-031-74183-8

LNCS Sublibrary: SL7 – Artificial Intelligence

This Springer imprint is published by the registered company Springer Nature Switzerland AG
The registered company address is: Gewerbestrasse 11, 6330 Cham, Switzerland

Preface

This volume of Lecture Notes in Artificial Intelligence (LNAI) includes accepted papers presented at the 19th International Conference on Hybrid Artificial Intelligence Systems (HAIS 2024), held in the beautiful city of Salamanca, Spain, in October 2024.

HAIS has become a unique, established, and broad interdisciplinary forum for researchers and practitioners who are involved in developing and applying symbolic and sub-symbolic techniques aimed at the construction of highly robust and reliable problem-solving techniques and achieving the most relevant progress in this field.

The hybridization of intelligent techniques, coming from different computational intelligence areas, has become popular because of the growing awareness that such combinations frequently perform better than the individual techniques such as neurocomputing, fuzzy systems, rough sets, evolutionary algorithms, agents and multiagent systems, and so on.

Practical experience has indicated that hybrid intelligence techniques might help solve some challenging real-world problems. In a hybrid intelligence system, a synergistic combination of multiple techniques is used to build an efficient solution to deal with a particular problem. This is, thus, the setting of the HAIS conference series, and its increasing success is proof of the vitality of this exciting field.

The HAIS 2024 International Program Committee selected 52 papers, which are published in these conference proceedings, yielding an acceptance ratio of about 46%.

The selection of papers was extremely rigorous to maintain the high quality of the conference and we would like to thank the Program Committee for their hard work in the reviewing process. This process is very important in creating a conference of high standard and the HAIS conference would not exist without their help.

The large number of submissions is certainly not only a testimony to the vitality and attractiveness of the field but an indicator of the interest in the HAIS conferences themselves.

HAIS 2024 enjoyed outstanding keynote speeches by distinguished guest speakers: Ajith Abraham of Bennett University (India) and Paulo Leitão of Polytechnic Institute of Bragança (Portugal).

HAIS 2024 has teamed up with "Neurocomputing" (Elsevier) and "Logic Journal of the IGPL" (Oxford University Press) for a suite of special issues, including selected papers from HAIS 2024.

Particular thanks go as well to the conference's main sponsors, Startup Olé, the CIBER-OLÉ project (within the National Cybersecurity Industry Promotion Program, framed within the INCIBE Emprende program and financed by INCIBE and the University of Salamanca), BISITE research group at the University of Salamanca, CTC research group at the University of A Coruña, and the University of Salamanca. They jointly contributed in an active and constructive manner to the success of this initiative.

We want to thank all the contributing authors, members of the Program Committee, and the Local Organizing Committee for their hard and highly valuable work. Their work helped to contribute to the success of the HAIS 2024 event.

We thank the staff of Springer for their help and collaboration during this demanding publication project.

October 2024

Héctor Quintián
Emilio Corchado
Alicia Troncoso Lora
Hilde Pérez García
Esteban Jove
José Luis Calvo Rolle
Francisco Javier Martínez de Pisón
Pablo García Bringas
Francisco Martínez Álvarez
Álvaro Herrero Cosío
Paolo Fosci

Organization

General Chair

Emilio Corchado	University of Salamanca, Spain

International Advisory Committee

Ajith Abraham	Machine Intelligence Research Labs, Europe
Antonio Bahamonde	University of Oviedo, Spain
Andre de Carvalho	University of São Paulo, Brazil
Sung-Bae Cho	Yonsei University, South Korea
Juan M. Corchado	University of Salamanca, Spain
José R. Dorronsoro	Autonomous University of Madrid, Spain
Michael Gabbay	Kings College London, UK
Ali A. Ghorbani	UNB, Canada
Mark A. Girolami	University of Glasgow, UK
Manuel Graña	University of the Basque Country, Spain
Petro Gopych	Universal Power Systems USA-Ukraine LLC, Ukraine
Jon G. Hall	Open University, UK
Francisco Herrera	University of Granada, Spain
César Hervás-Martínez	University of Córdoba, Spain
Tom Heskes	Radboud University Nijmegen, Netherlands
Dusan Husek	Academy of Sciences of the Czech Republic, Czech Republic
Lakhmi Jain	University of South Australia, Australia
Samuel Kaski	Helsinki University of Technology, Finland
Daniel A. Keim	University Konstanz, Germany
Marios Polycarpou	University of Cyprus, Cyprus
Witold Pedrycz	University of Alberta, Canada
Xin Yao	University of Birmingham, UK
Hujun Yin	University of Manchester, UK
Michał Woźniak	Wrocław University of Technology, Poland
Aditya Ghose	University of Wollongong, Australia
Ashraf Saad	Georgia Southern University - Armstrong Campus, USA

Fanny Klett	German Workforce Advanced Distributed Learning Partnership Laboratory, Germany
Paulo Novais	Universidade do Minho, Portugal
Rajkumar Roy	EPSRC Centre for Innovative Manufacturing in Through-Life Engineering Services, UK
Amy Neustein	Linguistic Technology Systems, USA
Jaydip Sen	Tata Consultancy Services Ltd., India

Program Committee Chairs

Héctor Quintián	University of A Coruña, Spain
Emilio Corchado	University of Salamanca, Spain
Alicia Troncoso Lora	Pablo de Olavide University, Spain
Hilde Pérez García	University of León, Spain
Esteban Jove	University of A Coruña, Spain
José Luis Calvo Rolle	University of A Coruña, Spain
Francisco Javier Martínez de Pisón	University of La Rioja, Spain
Pablo García Bringas	University of Deusto, Spain
Francisco Martínez Álvarez	Pablo de Olavide University, Spain
Álvaro Herrero Cosío	University of Burgos, Spain
Paolo Fosci	University of Bergamo, Italy

Program Committee

Alfredo Cuzzocrea	University of Calabria, Italy
Álvaro Michelena Grandío	University of A Coruña, Spain
Anca Andreica	Babeş-Bolyai University, Romania
Angel Arroyo	University of Burgos, Spain
Antonio Díaz-Longueira	University of A Coruña, Spain
Antonio Dourado	University of Coimbra, Portugal
Antonio Jesús Díaz Honrubia	Polytechnic University of Madrid, Spain
Arkadiusz Kowalski	Wrocław University of Technology, Poland
Borja Sanz	University of Deusto, Spain
Carlos Carrascosa	Universidad Politécnica de Valencia, Spain
Carlos Pereira	ISEC, Portugal
Darius Galis	West University of Timisoara, Romania
David Iclanzan	Sapientia University, Romania
Diego P. Ruiz	University of Granada, Spain
Dragan Simic	University of Novi Sad, Serbia
Eiji Uchino	Yamaguchi University, Japan

Eneko Osaba	TECNALIA Research & Innovation, Spain
Enol García González	University of Oviedo, Spain
Enrique De La Cal Marín	University of Oviedo, Spain
Enrique Onieva	University of Deusto, Spain
Esteban Jove	University of A Coruña, Spain
Federico Divina	Pablo de Olavide University, Spain
Fermin Segovia	University of Granada, Spain
Fernando Moncada Martins	University of Oviedo, Spain
Francisco Javier Martínez de Pisón Ascacíbar	University of La Rioja, Spain
Francisco Martínez-Álvarez	Universidad Pablo de Olavide, Spain
Francisco Zayas-Gato	University of A Coruña, Spain
Georgios Dounias	University of the Aegean, Greece
Giorgio Fumera	University of Cagliari, Italy
Giuseppe Psaila	University of Bergamo, Italy
Gloria Cerasela Crisan	"Vasile Alecsandri" University of Bacau, Romania
Héctor Quintián	University of A Coruña, Spain
Hugo Sanjurjo-González	University of Deusto, Spain
Ignacio Turias	University of Cádiz, Spain
Igor Santos-Grueiro	HP Labs, UK
Ioannis Hatzilygeroudis	University of Patras, Greece
Javier De Lope	Polytechnic University of Madrid, Spain
Jorge García-Gutiérrez	University of Seville, Spain
Jose Alfredo Ferreira Costa	UFRN, Brazil
José Aveleira Mata	Research Institute of Applied Sciences in Cybersecurity, Spain
Jose Divasón	University of La Rioja, Spain
Jose Dorronsoro	Autonomous University of Madrid, Spain
Jose Garcia Rodriguez	University of Alicante, Spain
Jose Luis Calvo-Rolle	University of A Coruña, Spain
José Luis Casteleiro-Roca	University of A Coruña, Spain
José Luis Verdegay	University of Granada, Spain
Jose M. Molina	University Carlos III of Madrid, Spain
Jose Manuel Lopez-Guede	University of the Basque Country, Spain
José María Armingol	University Carlos III of Madrid, Spain
José Ramón Villar	University of Oviedo, Spain
Juan Humberto Sossa Azuela	CIC-IPN, Mexico
Juan J. Gude	University of Deusto, Spain
Juan Pavón	Complutense University of Madrid, Spain
Lidia Sánchez-González	University of León, Spain
Manuel Castejón-Limas	University of León, Spain

Manuel Graña	University of the Basque Country, Spain
Manuel Rubiños Trelles	University of A Coruña, Spain
Mario Villar	University of Oviedo, Spain
Marta María Álvarez Crespo	University of A Coruña, Spain
Míriam Timiraos Díaz	University of A Coruña, Spain
Nuño Basurto	University of Burgos, Spain
Ovidiu Cosma	Technical University Cluj Napoca, Romania
Paula M. Castro	University of A Coruña, Spain
Paula Patricia Arcano Bea	University of A Coruña, Spain
Peter Rockett	University of Sheffield, UK
Petrica Pop	Technical University of Cluj-Napoca, Romania
Qing Tan	Athabasca University, Canada
Robert Burduk	Wrocław University of Science and Technology, Poland
Sean Holden	University of Cambridge, UK
Theodore Pachidis	International Hellenic University, Greece
Urszula Stanczyk	Silesian University of Technology, Poland

Organizing Committee Chairs

Emilio Corchado	University of Salamanca, Spain
Héctor Quintián	University of A Coruña, Spain

Organizing Committee

José Luis Calvo Rolle	University of A Coruña, Spain
Esteban Jove	University of A Coruña, Spain
José Luis Casteleiro Roca	University of A Coruña, Spain
Francisco Zayas Gato	University of A Coruña, Spain
Álvaro Michelena	University of A Coruña, Spain
Míriam Timiraos Díaz	University of A Coruña, Spain
Antonio Javier Díaz Longueira	University of A Coruña, Spain
Paula Patricia Arcano Bea	University of A Coruña, Spain
Manuel Rubiños Trelles	University of A Coruña, Spain
Marta María Álvarez Crespo	University of A Coruña, Spain

Contents – Part I

Biomedical Applications

Contents – Part II

HAIS Applications

HAIS Energy Applications

Image and Text Processing

Biomedical Applicatons

Surface EMG Profiling in Parkinson's Disease: Advancing Severity Assessment with GCN-SVM

Daniel Cieślak[1,3](✉), Barbara Szyca[1], Michalina Razik[1], Liwia Florkiewicz[1], Anna Prus[2], Hubert Lis[2], Kinga Grzęda[1], Weronika Bajko[2], Helena Kamieniecka[2], Weronika Matwiejuk[2], Inga Rozumowicz[2], Wiktoria Ziembakowska[2], and Mariusz Kaczmarek[1]

[1] Gdańsk University of Technology, Gdańsk, Poland
milab.weti@student.pg.edu.pl
[2] Medical University of Gdańsk, Gdańsk, Poland
[3] IDEAS NCBR, Warsaw, Poland

Abstract. Parkinson's disease (PD) poses challenges in diagnosis and monitoring due to its progressive nature and complex symptoms. This study introduces a novel approach utilizing surface electromyography (sEMG) to objectively assess PD severity, focusing on the biceps brachii muscle. Initial analysis of sEMG data from five PD patients and five healthy controls revealed significant neuromuscular differences. A traditional Support Vector Machine (SVM) model achieved up to 83% accuracy, while enhancements with a Graph Convolutional Network-Support Vector Machine (GCN-SVM) model increased accuracy to 92%. Despite the preliminary nature of these results, the study outlines a detailed experimental methodology for future research with larger cohorts to validate these findings and integrate the approach into clinical practice. The proposed approach holds promise for advancing PD severity assessment and improving patient care in Parkinson's disease management.

Keywords: EMG · sEMG · Parkinson's disease · wearables · GCN-SVM

1 Introduction

Parkinson's disease (PD) is a progressive neurological disorder affecting a significant portion of the elderly population globally [4]. Marked by debilitating motor symptoms such as tremors, stiffness, bradykinesia, and postural instability, PD significantly impairs daily activities and reduces quality of life [9]. The disease's progressive nature and complex symptomatology present substantial challenges in its diagnosis and management. Although the Unified Parkinson's Disease Rating Scale (UPDRS) is employed to assess PD severity, its subjective and time-consuming nature in detecting early-stage symptoms are notable limitations [5]. In light of these challenges, wearable sensors, particularly surface electromyography (sEMG), offer promising solutions for objective PD assessment by providing detailed insights into neuromuscular function [6]. Previous studies have highlighted sEMG's effectiveness in evaluating motor symptoms and monitoring disease progression in PD patients, as reviewed in the *Related Work* section.

H. Quintián et al. (Eds.): HAIS 2024, LNAI 14857, pp. 3–15, 2025.
https://doi.org/10.1007/978-3-031-74183-8_1

This study aims to develop and validate a novel sEMG-based methodology for objectively assessing PD severity, focusing on the biceps brachii muscle. By analyzing both linear and nonlinear sEMG parameters, we seek to identify neuromuscular differences between PD patients and healthy controls. Furthermore, we propose a Graph Convolutional Network-Support Vector Machine (GCN-SVM) model designed to achieve better and more reliable results on small data samples compared to classical methods.

This research contributes in two fundamental ways: firstly, by introducing a detailed and novel sEMG-based methodology for the objective evaluation of PD severity, emphasizing the analysis of both linear and nonlinear sEMG parameters. Secondly, through the introduction of the GCN-SVM model, which exhibits significant advancements in classification accuracy over traditional SVM approaches, particularly noteworthy given the constraints typically associated with pilot studies involving limited data. Despite the small sample size, our preliminary results indicate that the GCN-SVM model significantly enhances the accuracy and reliability of PD severity assessments. This innovative approach addresses the limitations of existing subjective tools and has the potential to improve clinical practices by providing a more individualized approach to therapy and enhancing PD management.

Subsequent sections provide detailed descriptions of the study cohort, experimental hardware configurations, and measurement protocols within the *Methods* section. Furthermore, this section discusses the data analysis techniques employed. The *Results* section presents comprehensive findings from the comparative analysis and performance evaluations of the proposed models. Finally, the *Conclusion* section provides a comprehensive summary of our findings along with the recommendations for future research to advance sEMG-based methodologies in Parkinson's disease assessment.

2 Related Work

Advanced methods are crucial for accurate diagnosis and monitoring of Parkinson's disease. The integration of technology, particularly wearable sensors, has shown promise in enhancing clinical assessments and treatment strategies. This study builds upon previous research that has utilized sEMG to evaluate motor symptoms and disease progression in PD patients:

Fundaro et al. [1] compared sEMG recordings in healthy individuals and PD patients, finding significant correlations between sEMG findings and Parkinson Fatigue Scale (PFS) scores. They gathered demographic and clinical data, ensuring consistent L-DOPA dosage for at least two weeks before the experiment. The protocol included three types of movements.The study found significant correlations between sEMG findings and both PFS and UPDRS scores but no discernible difference in muscle strength between the groups.

Kleinholdermann et al. [5] developed a non-invasive method for assessing motor symptoms in 45 PD patients using sEMG from a wristband. Patients performed a tapping task at five-second intervals. The study found a correlation coefficient of 0.739 between sEMG activity and UPDRS scores, indicating the potential utility of sEMG features in predicting medication adjustments, particularly in telemedicine applications.

Meigal et al. [6] compared linear and nonlinear sEMG parameters across healthy young individuals, healthy elderly participants, and PD patients. The study revealed that RMS (Root Mean Square) increased with load in all groups, while MDF (Mean Frequency) showed a significant increase only in the PD group. Nonlinear parameters exhibited notable differences between the PD and control groups, especially without additional load. Significant correlations were established between novel sEMG parameters and UPDRS scores, highlighting the potential of these nonlinear parameters in assessing motor symptoms and disease severity in PD patients.

In recent years, Support Vector Machines (SVM) have been widely utilized in various medical applications, including Parkinson's disease assessment. SVMs have shown effectiveness in classifying and predicting disease severity based on different data modalities [7]. SVMs have been particularly valuable in handling small datasets and achieving high accuracy in disease prediction tasks [7]. However, the traditional SVM model may face limitations in capturing complex relationships within the data, especially in scenarios with limited sample sizes.

On the other hand, Graph Convolutional Networks (GCN) have emerged as a powerful tool for learning from graph-structured data, offering the ability to capture intricate relationships and dependencies within the data [8]. GCNs have been successfully applied in various domains, including brain disease diagnosis [8]. Introduced a framework that employed GCN to explore deeper relationships for improved disease prediction [8]. GCNs have the advantage of aggregating information from neighboring nodes in a graph, enabling the model to capture local graph structures and identify patterns effectively [8]. In the context of PD assessment, GCNs can enhance the classification accuracy by leveraging the graph-based representations of sEMG data, which may contain complex interdependencies that traditional models like SVMs may struggle to capture.

The integration of GCN with SVM, as seen in the GCN-SVM model proposed in this study, represents a novel approach that combines the strengths of both methods. By leveraging the graph-based representation capabilities of GCNs and the classification power of SVMs, the GCN-SVM model aims to provide more accurate and reliable assessments of PD severity based on sEMG data [8].

3 Methods

In this section, we provide a comprehensive description of the study cohort, detailing the measurement methodology employed and outlining the approach used for data analysis. This study was approved by the Ethics Committee of Gdańsk University of Technology. All subjects gave their written informed consent before participating.

3.1 Study Cohort

The study included five PD patients and five healthy controls. PD patients were recruited from the Association for People with Parkinson's Disease and Brain Degenerative Diseases and their Caretakers 'Park On' in Gdańsk, Poland. Inclusion criteria were prior PD diagnosis; exclusion criteria included other motor function-affecting diseases, pacemakers, metal implants, and recent upper limb injuries. The study group demographics and clinical characteristics are summarized in Table 1. Disease duration refers to the length of time since the individual was diagnosed with Parkinson's disease. Medication duration, in the context of Parkinson's disease, refers to the length of time the patient has been taking medications specifically prescribed to manage their Parkinson's symptoms. The control group was selected to match the age distribution of the PD group, ensuring comparability, as shown in Table 2.

Table 1. Characteristics of the study group.

PD Patient	Age	Gender	BMI	Disease duration (years)	Medication duration (years)
1	76	F	23,8	4	3
2	64	M	22,3	12	12
3	84	M	17	5	3
4	73	F	24,2	6	6
5	72	F	21,9	7	7

Table 2. Characteristics of the control group.

Subject	Age	Gender	BMI
1	67	M	26.60
2	71	M	31.46
3	71	M	24.91
4	64	M	29.38
5	80	M	33.00

3.2 Hardware

The measuring device employed in our study utilizes the Myoware 2.0 Muscle Sensor [3], designed for assessing the electric voltage associated with muscular contraction. This sensor interfaces with gel Ag/AgCl electrodes that comply with ANSI/AAMI EC12 standard for disposal ECG electrodes [2]. The electrodes were positioned bilaterally on the skin surface to capture electrical signals from the biceps brachii muscle, as illustrated in Fig. 1.

The non-invasive methodological approach minimizes participant discomfort and preserves skin integrity. Signal acquisition is done via jumper wires connecting the sensor to an ESP32 board, which uses Bluetooth v4.2 for wireless data transmission. The system, powered by a 5V power bank, avoids signal interference issues common with PC power sources. The Myoware Sensor converts analog muscle activity signals into digital data, reflecting muscle contraction characteristics like amplitude, frequency, and waveform shape. Data is sent to a mobile device, then transferred to a computer for generating voltage-muscle time dependency graphs, offering insights into muscle activity patterns over time.

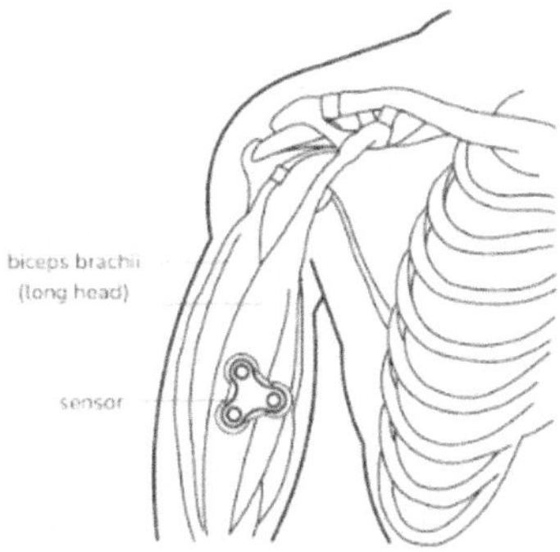

Fig. 1. Placement of the electrode on the biceps muscle.

3.3 Measurement Procedure

To collect sEMG data, we devised a measurement procedure enabling the comparison of muscle activity between healthy individuals (control group) and subjects with Parkinson's disease (study group). The procedure includes three stages:

1. The first stage involves measuring the resting activity of the biceps muscle for 30 s.
2. The second stage involves a 30-s measurement where participants hold a 2 kg weight. The arm is positioned with the elbow bent at a 90-degree angle, close to the body, and the forearm parallel to the floor. This posture induces an isometric contraction, allowing assessment of muscle activity under load.
3. The final stage requires participants to perform alternating arm flexion and extension with the 2 kg weight at 5-s intervals. This dynamic movement pattern assesses muscle activity during functional tasks that mimic daily activities.

To ensure consistent timing and initiation of measurements, the servo mechanism was utilized. This mechanism, placed in participants' hands, generates vibrations to signal the start and end of each measurement stage. Additionally, messages printed with timestamps during each stage facilitate data processing synchronization. Before each stage begins, participants receive three servo vibrations as a readiness confirmation. The measurement itself starts and stops with a single vibration, and each interval within the stage is also marked by a vibration signal.

The servo mechanism was integral to our protocol, ensuring standardized timing cues and minimizing variability in data collection. By providing clear signals to participants and autonomously managing measurement initiation, the servo mechanism enhanced the reliability and accuracy of our sEMG data, crucial for comparisons between healthy individuals and those with Parkinson's disease.

3.4 Data Processing

Python was used for EMG data analysis, leveraging libraries such as Pandas, NumPy, SciPy, Matplotlib, and Seaborn. The analysis process included data collection, cleaning, feature extraction, visualization, and model evaluation to ensure data integrity and quality.

Data Collection and Cleaning.
The initial phase of the data processing pipeline involved the collection and cleaning of acquired sEMG data, stored in CSV files. These files contained recordings from both healthy individuals and subjects diagnosed with Parkinson's disease, including timestamps and muscle activity values measured in Arbitrary Units (AU). To ensure the integrity and quality of the data, validation checks were performed during the collection process. This involved confirming the absence of outliers and ensuring continuous sampling intervals. Any measurements that fell outside the expected range were either corrected or the measurement was repeated, ensuring the completeness and accuracy of the dataset.

Subsequently, the collected data were systematically organized into distinct folders based on the health condition of the subjects (PD or healthy). The example of an acquired sEMG signal is shown in Fig. 2. The signal has five marked segments that represent different phases of muscle activity: Segment 1 - Relaxation Phase; Segment 2 - Preparation for Contraction; Segment 3 - Maintenance of Contraction; Segment 4 - Preparation for Repetitions; Segment 5 - Execution of Repetitions.

In the figure, the x-axis represents time in seconds (s), while the y-axis denotes the result in Arbitrary Units (AU), reflecting the muscle activity level recorded by the sEMG sensor. Segment 1 shows the muscle in a relaxed state with minimal activity. Segment 2 indicates a slight increase in muscle activity as the participant prepares for contraction. Segment 3 captures sustained muscle activity while holding a 2 kg weight, indicated by increased and stable sEMG signals. Segment 4 involves a brief preparatory period before performing repetitive movements, with a slight drop in muscle activity. Segment 5 shows periodic spikes in the sEMG signal as the participants perform alternating arm flexion and extension.

Further categorization was done by hand dominance (left or right). Specific segments of data corresponding to the exercise phases (1, 3, and 5) were isolated for detailed analysis. This structured approach facilitated a streamlined and efficient data processing workflow.

Feature Extraction.
Various statistical features were extracted from the sEMG signals to facilitate the analysis. Key features included Root Mean Square (RMS), Median Frequency (MDF), Mean Frequency, Variance, Skewness, Kurtosis, Standard Deviation (SD), Percentage of Recurrence (REC), Percentage of Determinism (DET), Sample Entropy (SampEn), and Correlation Dimension (CD). These features were chosen based on their established relevance in the literature for characterizing neuromuscular activity.

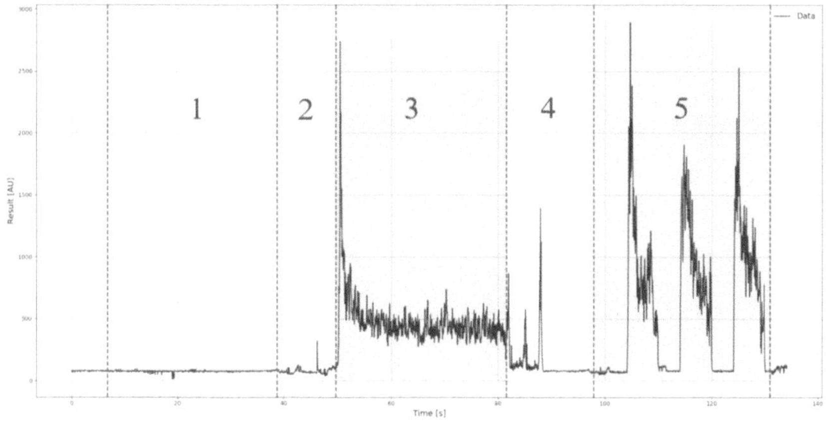

Fig. 2. Example of an sEMG signal with marked segments.

RMS was calculated to provide a measure of the signal's amplitude, while MDF and Mean Frequency offered insights into the frequency characteristics of the sEMG signals. Variance, Skewness, and Kurtosis described the statistical distribution of the signal values, highlighting their spread, asymmetry, and peakedness, respectively. SD was used to quantify the dispersion of the signal data points. REC and DET, derived from recurrence quantification analysis, provided information on the repeating patterns within the sEMG signals, which is critical for understanding muscle activity regularity. SampEn quantified the complexity and irregularity of the signals, with higher values indicating more complex muscle activation patterns. CD measured the signal's complexity in terms of fractal dimensions.

The extraction process ensured that these features were consistently calculated across all samples, facilitating a reliable comparison between healthy individuals and PD patients. This comprehensive feature set enabled a detailed analysis of the neuromuscular differences between the two groups, providing a robust basis for subsequent model training and evaluation.

3.5 GCN-SVM Architecture and Implementation

The GCN-SVM model effectively combines GCN and SVM to classify Parkinson's disease using sEMG data. The process involves detailed data preprocessing, feature extraction, and graph construction, as shown in Table. 3. The GCN model, with its layered architecture, captures complex relationships in the data, leading to improved classification performance. Training and evaluation involve cross-entropy loss, Adam optimization, and extensive cross-validation to credibility.

Table 3. Detailed GCN-SVM Model Architecture.

Stage	Description	Details
Feature Calculation	Extract statistical features from sEMG signals	RMS, MDF, Mean Frequency, Variance, Skewness, Kurtosis, Max, Min, Range. Fourier Transform (FFT) used for frequency domain features
Data Loading	Load and clean sEMG data from CSV files	Label data for 'healthy' and 'PD' groups. Separate by hand (left/right) and patient segments. Standardize features using StandardScaler
Graph Construction	Create a KNN graph to represent relationships between data points	Use kneighbors_graph to construct the graph. Convert adjacency matrix to edge indices
GCN Model Architecture	Graph Convolutional Network layers for feature processing	GCNConv Layer 1: Initial graph convolution. ReLU Activation: Introduces non-linearity. Dropout Layer: Regularization. GCNConv Layer 2: Second graph convolution. ReLU Activation: Non-linearity. Dropout Layer: Regularization. GCNConv Layer 3: Final graph convolution. Log Softmax: Output classification
Model Initialization	Initialize model, optimizer, and loss function	Model initialized with 16 hidden channels and 2 output channels. Adam optimizer with learning rate of 0.01. Cross-entropy loss (NLLLoss)
Training	Train the model with the training dataset	Perform forward and backward passes. Update model weights using optimizer. Train for 50 epochs
Cross-Validation	Evaluate model performance using cross-validation	Stratified K-Fold cross-validation to assess model performance on different subsets
Testing	Evaluate the trained model on a test dataset	Assess model accuracy, generate confusion matrices, and create classification reports

(*continued*)

Table 3. (*continued*)

Stage	Description	Details
Data Dimensions	Various dimensions of data and model inputs	Feature Dimensions: 9 (RMS, MDF, MeanFreq, Variance, Skewness, Kurtosis, Max, Min, Range). Hidden Channels: 16. Output Channels: 2 (Healthy/PD)
Performance Metrics	Metrics to evaluate model performance	Accuracy, F1-Score, Precision, Confusion Matrix

4 Results

The results section presents a detailed analysis of the collected sEMG data, comparing the neuromuscular characteristics between Parkinson's disease patients and healthy controls. Additionally, it evaluates the performance of the proposed Graph Convolutional Network-Support Vector Machine (GCN-SVM) model in accurately classifying PD severity based on the extracted features.

4.1 Linear and Non-Linear sEMG Parameters

The analysis identified several key sEMG parameters, both linear and non-linear. Among the linear parameters, Median Frequency (MDF) showed stability across samples, making it a critical metric for distinguishing between healthy and PD-affected muscles. MDF demonstrated variability in frequency domain characteristics, reflecting notable differences between groups. Mean Frequency values hovered around zero, indicating a balanced frequency distribution essential for reliable comparative analysis. Root Mean Square (RMS) had a mean of 503.08 (SD = 491.26, range = 12.84 to 2548.65), indicating a wide range of values.

Non-linear parameters also showed significant variability. Skewness had a mean of 2.47 (SD = 3.53, range = -4.52 to 19.85), while Kurtosis had a mean of 24.83 (SD = 65.38, range = -1.57 to 426.37). Sample Entropy (SampEn) highlighted the complexity and irregularity of EMG signals, with higher values indicating more complex muscle activation patterns typical in PD. Our study corroborates the findings of Meigal et al. [6], showing similar trends in RMS and MDF with higher values in the PD group. Table 4 summarizes the statistical characteristics of the features calculated from the EMG signals.

The presented results contribute to understanding the diverse characteristics of sEMG signals in both healthy individuals and those with Parkinson's disease, emphasizing the importance of considering a broad range of muscle activities and conditions in such studies [6]. The classification model's effectiveness in distinguishing between healthy individuals and those with Parkinson's disease was evaluated across different data subsets (Table 5).

Table 4. Statistical characteristics (PD vs Healthy)

Feature	Mean		Std		Min		Max	
	PD vs Healthy		PD vs Healthy		PD vs Healthy		PD vs Healthy	
RMS	503.08	466.99	491.26	322.04	12.84	27.64	2548.65	961.53
MDF	7.69	6.87	1.91	3.27	0.31	0.31	9.75	9.75
MeanFreq	-0.004	-0.002	0.006	0.006	-0.24	-0.014	0.00	0.004
Skewness	2.47	2.69	3.53	4.05	-4.52	-4.52	19.85	10.17
Kurtosis	24.83	11.59	65.38	43.89	-1.57	-0.84	426.37	117.03
SD	244.71	239.39	237.57	199.52	2.02	2.02	1192.09	658.09
REC	0.032	0.048	0.048	0.065	0.003	0.003	0.2	0.2
DET	0.255	0.077	1.285	0.089	0.00	0.00	10.239	0.27
SampEn	0.898	0.684	0.614	0.512	0.044	0.044	2.306	1.76
CD	1.29	1.06	0.56	0.64	0.00	0.00	2.09	2.107

Table 5. Classification model performance for the complete dataset, right hand data, and left hand data.

Metric	Complete dataset	Right hand data	Left hand data
Cross-Validation Scores	[0.772, 0.777, 0.766, 0.774, 0.773]	[0.784, 0.846, 0.825, 0.835, 0.828]	[0.811, 0.806, 0.802, 0.804, 0.804]
Confusion Matrix	[[3519, 830], [1005, 2877]]	[[1863, 282], [410, 1553]]	[[1755, 422], [379, 1567]]
F1-Score (Healthy)	0.79	0.84	0.81
F1-Score (PD)	0.76	0.82	0.80
Accuracy	0.78	0.83	0.81
Macro Avg F1-Score	0.78	0.83	0.81
Weighted Avg Precision	0.78	0.83	0.81

The discrepancies in the number of samples between the right hand, left hand, and the complete dataset arise from the nature of the data collection process. Each participant had multiple measurements taken, resulting in several samples per user. The numbers reflect the total measurements taken for each hand separately. In contrast, the complete dataset combines all measurements from both arms.

These results indicate that the classification model performs better with the right-hand data compared to the left-hand data and the complete dataset, as evidenced by higher cross-validation scores and F1-scores.

4.2 GCN-SVM Classification Effectiveness of sEMG in PD Assessment

The effectiveness of the GCN-SVM classification model in distinguishing between healthy individuals and those with Parkinson's disease was evaluated across different subsets of the data (Table 6). Despite being based on a small sample size, these preliminary results show promising accuracy and reliability, significantly better than the classic SVM. Graph statistics provide insights into the structural properties of the graphs used in the GCN model. Key statistics include an average degree of approximately 9.964 across all folds, indicating robust connectivity; an average centrality value consistently at 0.000303, suggesting uniform centrality across nodes; and a high average clustering coefficient of 0.991021, reflecting strong clustering and implying that nodes form tight-knit groups.

Table 6. GCN-SVM model performance for the complete dataset

Metric	Healthy vs PD subjects
Cross-Validation Scores	[0.843, 0.931, 0.937, 0.949, 0.946]
Confusion Matrix	[[4003. 346], [302. 3578]]
F1-Score (Healthy)	0.93
F1-Score (PD)	0.91
Accuracy	0.92
Macro Avg F1-Score	0.92
Weighted Avg Precision	0.93

The GCN-SVM model significantly outperforms the traditional SVM model in classifying healthy individuals and those with Parkinson's disease. The GCN-SVM achieved a higher accuracy (**0.92 vs. 0.78**), improved F1-scores (**0.93 vs. 0.79** for healthy, **0.91 vs. 0.76** for PD), and better precision. The enhanced performance of GCN-SVM can be attributed to its ability to capture complex relationships and dependencies within the sEMG data through graph-based representations.

In the "Cross-Validation Scores" row, accuracy is used as the primary metric, defined as the ratio of correct predictions to the total number of test examples, expressed as a percentage or fraction. The process involves 5-fold cross-validation with StratifiedKFold, ensuring class proportions are maintained across folds. The data is divided into five equal parts, and in each iteration, the model is trained on four parts and tested on one part. This is repeated five times with different test folds. Individual fold results are recorded, and the final cross-validation result is the average accuracy across all folds. This simplicity and intuitiveness make accuracy an ideal metric for reporting.

5 Conclusion and Future Works

This study introduced a novel approach utilizing surface electromyography for objectively assessing Parkinson's disease severity, focusing on the biceps brachii muscle. By analyzing both linear and nonlinear sEMG parameters, significant neuromuscular differences between PD patients and healthy controls were identified. The findings underscored the utility of sEMG as a non-invasive tool for precise PD severity assessment, particularly when combined with advanced machine learning techniques.

Key linear parameters such as Median Frequency exhibited stability across samples. Non-linear parameters (Skewness and Kurtosis) demonstrated variability, highlighting their role in capturing the complexity of muscle activation patterns. Moreover, the study proposed and evaluated a GCN-SVM model, which outperformed traditional SVM approaches, particularly in scenarios with limited data samples. The GCN-SVM model achieved higher accuracy, improved F1-scores, and superior precision by effectively modeling the intricate relationships within sEMG data through graph-based representations. Future research directions should prioritize validating these findings with larger, diverse cohorts to enhance the robustness and generalizability of the proposed methodology. Such efforts will further refine sEMG-based assessments, potentially paving the way for personalized therapeutic strategies and improving overall patient care in PD management.

In conclusion, the integration of sEMG with advanced machine learning methodologies represents a significant advancement in Parkinson's disease research, offering nuanced insights into motor dysfunction and laying the foundation for tailored therapeutic interventions aimed at optimizing patient outcomes.

Acknowledgments. This study was made possible by the invaluable support of The Association for People with Parkinson's Disease, Degenerative Brain Disorders, and Caregivers - 'Park On' in Gdańsk. Additionally, the research was supported by the Dean of the Faculty of ETI, benefiting the Medical Intelligence Laboratory.

References

1. Fundaró, C., Gazzoni, M., Pinna, G., Dallocchio, C., Rainoldi, A., & Casale, R.: Is fatigue a muscular phenomenon in Parkinson's disease? Implications for rehabilitation. Eur. J. Phys. Rehabil. Med., 57 (2021). https://doi.org/10.23736/S1973-9087.21.06621-1
2. Fannin. ECG Catalogue (2024). Retrieved 30 Apr 2024, from https://www.fannin.eu/wp-content/uploads/2018/06/ECG-Catalogue.pdf
3. MyoWare. Technical Specifications: Muscle Sensor (2024). Retrieved 22 Apr 2024. https://myoware.com/products/technical-specifications/#muscle-sensor
4. World Health Organization. Parkinson disease (2024). Retrieved 22 Apr 2024. https://www.who.int/news-room/fact-sheets/detail/parkinson-disease
5. Kleinholdermann, U., Wullstein, M., Pedrosa, D.: Prediction of motor Unified Parkinson's Disease Rating Scale scores in patients with Parkinson's disease using surface electromyography. Clin. Neurophysiol. **132**(7), 1708–1713 (2021). https://doi.org/10.1016/j.clinph.2021.01.031

6. Meigal, A.I., Rissanen, S., Tarvainen, M.P., Karjalainen, P.A., Airaksinen, O.: Novel parameters of surface EMG in patients with Parkinson's disease and healthy young and old controls. J. Electromyogr. Kinesiol. **19**(3), e206–e213 (2009). https://doi.org/10.1016/j.jelekin.2008.02.008
7. Mudawi, N.: Developing a model for Parkinson's disease detection using machine learning algorithms. Comput. Mater. Continua **79**(3), 4945–4962 (2024). https://doi.org/10.32604/cmc.2024.048967
8. Zhou, H., Zhang, D.: Graph-in-graph convolutional networks for brain disease diagnosis. In: Proceedings of the IEEE International Conference on Image Processing (2021). https://doi.org/10.1109/icip42928.2021.9506259
9. Martignon, C., et al.: Evidence that neuromuscular fatigue is not a dogma in patients with Parkinson's disease. Med. Sci. Sports Exerc. **54**(2), 247–257 (2021). https://doi.org/10.1249/mss.0000000000002791

Batch-Balancing Improvement with Data Augmentation Techniques for Clinical Electroencephalographic Data

David Fernández-Madera González[1], Fernando Moncada Martins[1,3](✉), Víctor M. González[1,3], José R. Villar[2,3], Beatriz García López[4], and Ana Isabel Gómez-Menéndez[4]

[1] Electrical Engineering Department, University of Oviedo, Gijón, Spain
{uo277577,uo245868,vmsuarez}@uniovi.es
[2] Computer Science Department, University of Oviedo, Oviedo, Spain
villarjose@uniovi.es
[3] Biomedical Engineering Center, University of Oviedo, Oviedo, Spain
[4] Clinical Neurophysiology Department, Burgos University Hospital, Burgos, Spain
{bgarcialo,agomm}@saludcastillayleon.es

Abstract. Photosensitivity is a neurophysiological condition in which the brain produces epileptic discharges, known as Photoparoxysmal Responses, as a reaction to light flashes which may lead to seizures. The standardized diagnosis procedure consists of stimulating the patient with a flashing light while Electroencephalography records their brain activity until one of these epileptic reactions occurs, which causes a scarcity of such phenomena in the recordings that, added to the low prevalence of this condition, generates an extremely imbalanced dataset which decreases the performance of automatic detection using Deep Learning techniques. This research proposes applying two different Data Augmentation techniques in the Data Generator phase of a Convolutional Neural Network to create synthetic paroxysmal instances and balance each input batch independently. Various network architectures are also tested. Results obtained from these experiments concluded that both DA techniques are equivalent in performance, but could not outperform previous experiments. This project is being developed with patients from Burgos University Hospital, Spain.

This research has been funded by the Spanish Ministry of Economics and Industry –grant PID2020-112726RB-I00–, the Spanish Research Agency –grant PID2023-146257OB-I00–, Missions Science and Innovation project MIG-20211008 (INMERBOT), and by the Ministry of Science and Innovation under CERVERA Excellence Network project CER-20211003 (IBERUS). Also, by Principado de Asturias, grant SV-PA-21-AYUD/2021/50994, and by the Council of Gijón through the University Institute of Industrial Technology of Asturias grants SV-21-GIJON-1-19, SV-22-GIJON-1-19, SV-22-GIJON-1-22, and SV-23-GIJON-1-09. G. Finally, this research has also been funded by Fundación Universidad de Oviedo grants FUO-23-008 and FUO-22-450.

H. Quintián et al. (Eds.): HAIS 2024, LNAI 14857, pp. 16–28, 2025.
https://doi.org/10.1007/978-3-031-74183-8_2

Keywords: Photosensitivity · Epilepsy · Electroencephalography · EEG · Photoparoxysmal Response · PPR · Deep Learning · Data Augmentation

1 Introduction

Electroencephalography (EEG) is a clinical technique used for measuring the brain electrical activity of a person by placing electrodes in different brain regions and recording the electrical signals over time, thus creating a multivariate time-series (or univariate if only one electrode is used). Since it can be applied in a non-invasive way using caps or helmets, it is the most widely used tool for diagnosing and monitoring different neurological disorders, like photosensitivity.

This condition is defined as an abnormal brain reaction to certain visual stimuli –such as flashing lights or visual patterns– in the form of epileptic activity. The international standardized clinical protocol used in hospitals to diagnose photosensitivity is called Intermittent Photic Stimulation (IPS) [19] and it consists of stimulating the patient with a flashing white light at different standard frequencies while recording their brain activity via EEG: when a photosensitive person reacts to a flash of light, the epileptic response is called Photoparoxysmal Response (PPR) [20].

The study published in [21] proposes a theoretical PPR classification that eventually became the standard. It divides PPRs into four groups depending on their intensity and their spread to different brain regions:

- Type-1: spikes in the occipital region.
- Type-2: spikes followed by a biphasic slow wave in occipital and parietal regions.
- Type-3: spikes followed by a biphasic slow wave in occipital and parietal regions, spreading to frontal regions.
- Type-4: generalized poly-spikes and waves.

The diagnosis protocol is applied in two phases: the first one increases the stimulation frequency from the minimum value (1 Hz) to the maximum value (50–60 Hz); the second one follows the inverse sequence, starting from the maximum frequency and decreasing it until the minimum value. Each phase ends when the last stimulation is applied or when a PPR is triggered at any given frequency, so the goal is to determine at which frequency range the patient shows PPRs. Each flashing frequency is tested with eyes open and closed, and a resting step is applied between different frequencies. Currently, the analysis of the EEG recordings and the detection of PPRs is performed visually, which takes time, effort, and concentration, especially when performed during the stimulation process. Moreover, PPR waveforms and morphologies mix between types and vary between patients or even sessions from the same patient because they depend on other clinical factors such as medical treatment, sleep quality, or time of day. All these reasons make PPR detection and classification difficult.

This research is a continuation of [12], where an ad-hoc Data Augmentation (DA) technique was applied to increase the number of PPR instances and balance the training and test sets before performing the classification with Machine Learning (ML) algorithms. Now, we propose the use of the same ad-hoc DA method, along with a new one, as part of a CNN model through a Data Generator layer that applies one of both methods to each batch of input data after introducing them into the models, balancing the input batches instead of the whole sets. The goals are I) to compare which DA technique produces more suitable data; and II) to analyze the effects of applying DA before or after introducing the data into the models.

The structure of this study is as follows: the next section (Sect. 2) presents the existing automatic detection of epileptic activity state-of-art, as well as the evolution of our research through our previous studies; Sect. 3 describes both DA techniques used in this research and the usage of the Data Generator layer, while the dataset and the details of the experiments are included in Sect. 4. Finally, the results are shown in Sect. 5 along with their analysis; and the final conclusions are gathered in Sect. 6.

2 Related Work

Although DL models were originally created to address image-processing problems due to the high complexity of that type of data, in the last few years they have been gaining a significant presence in the time-series processing field [7], being one of the multiple applications for the detection, prediction, and classification of epileptic seizures, like Long Short-Term Memory Network in [2] or a combination of an autoencoder and a neural network proposed by [1]. Convolutional Neural Networks (CNN) are the most popular DL models and have been used in various ways: [17] combined it with a wrist-band wearable, the creation of a visual mapping of the brain activity in [5], or to reduce the limitations of spectrograms by using Phase Space Reconstruction in [6]. These are some examples of recent publications that focused on a topic that continues under research after several decades now, proving that the analysis of epileptic seizures is a recurrent field of study that is far from being completely solved [14].

Due to their complexity, DL techniques are able to perform more effective analysis of complex patterns present in EEG signals than ML but, in exchange, they require a higher amount of training data to do so. This consolidates a major issue to be addressed specifically in the medical field, where clinical data are restricted, limited, and often heavily imbalanced. In these cases when not enough real data is available, one solution is to artificially create synthetic minority-class samples maintaining as much resemblance as possible to the real data. Data Augmentation (DA) was initially designed for image-processing tasks to address the need for data, but it has also started to be tested in time-series tasks as a consequence of DL becoming more important in this field. DA encompasses procedures from simple operations over real samples –like Slicing, Scaling, Warping, or Jittering– to complex DL networks that learn samples and produce new ones

–like autoencoders or Generative models– [8]. DA has already been applied to clinical data such as fall detection in [3], ECG classification improvement in [9], sleep stage classification in one-channel EEG in [4] or epileptic seizure analysis in [15].

Nevertheless, to our best knowledge, automatic PPR detection has not been fully addressed yet. There are some previous studies, like [10] which proposed a spectral analysis by computing the Discrete Fourier Transform to EEG segments prior to the triggering of a PPR in order to predict the epileptic response while applying the IPS protocol, or the analysis of high-frequency oscillations as a response to a flashing stimulation different from IPS in [16].

Our previous work regarding automatic PPR detection started using simple ML techniques: in [13] we proposed a combination of two versions of KNN –a one-class version as an anomaly detection and a two-class version to distinguish PPRs from the detected anomalies–; then different ML algorithms were tested in [11] to classify EEG fragments previously clustered using K-Means, being this the first attempt to address the imbalance problem in a simple way; and finally, the methods that showed the best results were tested again with a more balanced dataset after applying an ad-hoc DA technique to create synthetic PPRs in [12].

3 Data Augmentation Techniques

DA is a process that aims to increase the generalization capacity of a DL model by improving the balance of the dataset. For this purpose, new synthetic instances of the minority class are artificially created from real data to reassemble their real behavior as much as possible. In this way, the model can learn and, thus, better recognize the features and patterns of such class, decreasing overfitting.

This research compares the effects of two DA techniques on the automatic PPR detection performance. The first one (***BasicDA***) is a new proposal that consists of the application of basic time-series distortion operations [8] on real PPR segments to modify them and to increase the variability of data. This set of transformations includes scaling (modification of amplitude), warping (expansions and contractions in amplitude or time), permutation (rearranging of segments), and flipping or rotation (changing of the angle of the series). These transformations are applied over each of the 19 signals from one PPR instance to generate 19 new signals of a synthetic instance. Nevertheless, after experimentation, only two of those operations were included in this research since they were the only ones that allowed to maintain the highest possible realism concerning the original data:

– Time Warping: modifying the time dimension by shrinking some intervals and expanding others, always starting and ending at the same samples. A cubic spline curve following a Gaussian distribution is created to perform a soft deformation of the signal timestamps (see Fig. 1b).

- Jittering: adding white noise to the signal following a Gaussian distribution (see Fig. 1c). It is widely used to increase the generalization capabilities of neural networks.

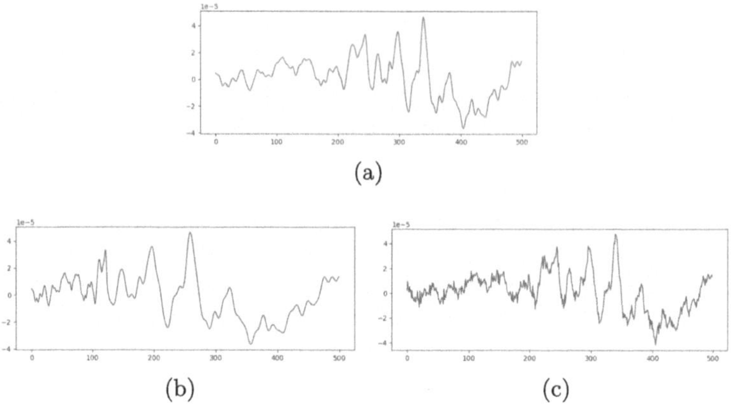

Fig. 1. Examples of new EEG segments after applying each basic DA operation: **(a)** shows the original PPR segment from one EEG channel and the same segment after Time Warping **(b)**, and Jittering **(c)**.

The second method was proposed in previous research [12]. In that case, an ad-hoc DA procedure (***Ad-hocDA***) was specifically designed to maintain the real data's clinical behaviour in the synthetic segments. This technique consisted of applying permutation over segments extracted from two different PPR instances. After randomly selecting two parent windows that showed similar morphology (A and B), they were divided into equally length subsegments depending on the number of N cut-points (the size of the resulting subsegments being 19 x $\frac{500}{N+1}$ size). Then, the $N+1$ subsegments from both parents were mixed in an alternate way –A_1, B_2, A_3, ... – to create the child as represented in Fig. 2, with one channel as an example. Weighted interpolation is computed in the cut-points to ensure the EEG signal continuity.

4 Material and Methods

This section explains the dataset used for this research (Sec.4.1), the preprocessing operations (Sec.4.2) and the details of the designed experiments (Sec.4.3). The models were implemented in Python.

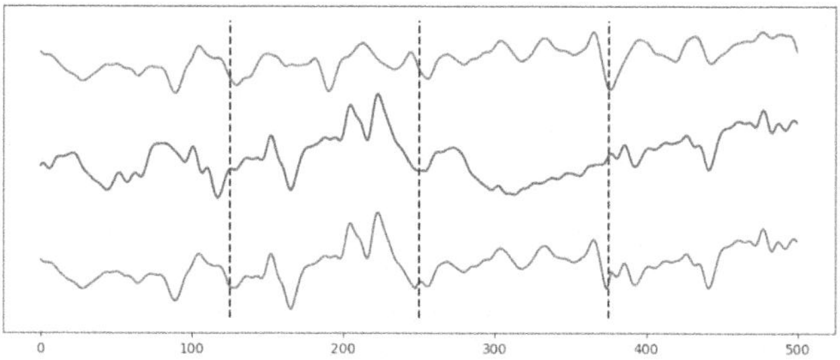

Fig. 2. Example of new child PPR segment (**green** (Color figure online)) created by alternately mixing two randomly selected parent PPR segments (**blue and red**) from only one EEG channel divided into four subsegments.

4.1 Dataset Description

The dataset used for this research was recorded, annotated, and anonymized by the clinical neurophysiologist from Burgos University Hospital using their medical equipment: Natus Nicolet v44 for EEG recording and Natus Neuroworks9 for EEG visualization, annotation and marking. The dataset is formed by 10 anonymized EEG recordings from 10 different photosensitive patients during an IPS session, resulting in 3-to-5-minute continuous recordings. The EEG was recorded at a sampling rate of 500 Hz from 19 electrodes –each electrode generating an independent time-series of the brain activity produced in the corresponding region– placed according to the 10–20 standardized system [18] (see Fig. 3). The neurophysiologists performed a visual analysis of the recordings and manually marked every PPR that was triggered during each session.

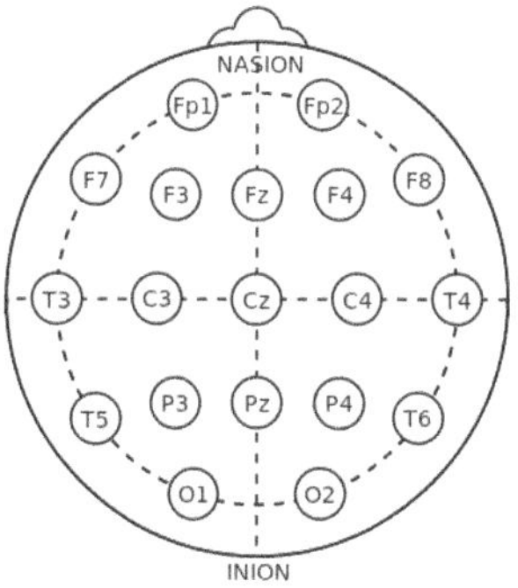

Fig. 3. Position of the 19 electrodes following the 10–20 international standardized system. The *Nasion* is located at the center of the frontonasal area, and the *Inion* is located at the center of the back of the neck.

4.2 Pre-Processing

All EEG recordings were preprocessed by removing the average component and filtering using a Notch filter at 50 Hz to remove power-supply effects plus a band-pass 5th-order Butterworth filter in the range of 1 to 50 Hz. Then, a sliding window was used to divide the recordings into 1-second-length windows with 90% overlapping, generating instances of size 19x500. By using the marks and annotations, each window was manually labelled into two classes: **"PPR"** and **"non-PPR"** activity. As can be seen, the proportion of instances forming the dataset presents an extreme imbalance problem between the two classes, which can be addressed with the DA approach:

- Total number of EEG windows: 29,190
  - Number of non-PPR windows: 27,968 (**95.81%**)
  - Number of PPR windows: 1,222 (**4.19%**)

The application of the sliding window resulted in the creation of four different types of PPR windows depending on the location of this activity within the window: PPR instances that are cut after the onset of the epileptic activity (Fig. 4a), the ones that are cut before the offset (Fig. 4b), PPR windows whose limits are after the onset and before the offset, so they are fully-covered by PPR activity due to its large duration (Fig. 4c), and the ones that include both onset and offset due to its short duration (Fig. 4d).

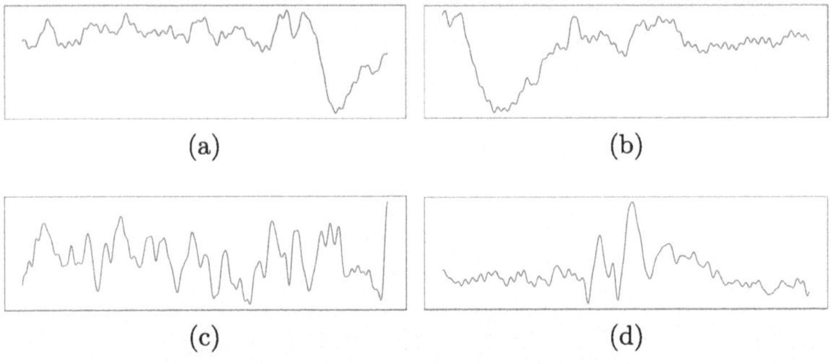

Fig. 4. Four different types of PPR windows depending on the location of the PPR activity within the instance: **(a)** shows only the onset; **(b)** shows only the offset; **(c)** does not include either the onset or the offset; and **(d)** includes both onset and offset.

Because of the different nature of these windows regarding the epileptic PPR activity, the separation of the PPR instances into these four groups is necessary when applying ***Ad-hocDA***, where the two real PPR parents that are mixed to create one synthetic PPR window must be extracted from the same group to maintain the original nature; randomly mixing two PPR windows with different types of activity may result in unrealistic PPR instances with discontinued epileptic activity, or no event at all. Given the need for respecting this division, it is maintained during the whole process to ensure the proportion of the different groups.

4.3 Experimentation Set-Up

Following a 10-fold Cross-Validation scheme, PPR and non-PPR classes are shuffled so the dataset can be divided into folds that retain the same class proportion. Then, a training set is created with 9 folds (thus, containing 90% of the instances of each class), while the unused fold formed by the remaining 10% of each class data is used as the test set. In both sets, the PPR class also maintains the proportion of each type of PPR window.

In previous research [12], ***Ad-hocDA*** was applied in each fold to improve the balance of the sets; however, in this study, both DA techniques are executed during the batch creation by the Data Generator. This component is in charge of receiving the whole set of instances and splitting it into multiple input batches that are used to feed the model, making the data processing easier and less resource-consuming. In this experiment, this element implements the DA procedure when generating the batches to increase its size and improve its balance before feeding it into the model. Given a desired batch size L as a parameter, the Data Generator first extracts real non-PPR and PPR instances from the current fold to fill up to $50\% * L$ and $20\% * L$ of the batch, respectively; PPR instances are extracted with replacement from each of the 4 groups to maintain their proportion. Then, the DA step is executed to create as many synthetic PPR instances from all groups as needed to fill the remaining $30\% * L$, also preserving their ratio.

BasicDA and ***Ad-hocDA*** are applied independently in two different executions. On the one hand, the different operations included in ***BasicDA*** are randomly applied to achieve an even higher level of variety: I) only time-warping, II) only jittering, or III) time-warping and jittering; on the other hand, ***Ad-hocDA*** was configured to split the parent windows using 3 cut-points, thus creating 4 subsegments of size 19x125 to mix them alternately.

Previous research demonstrated that simple ML methods achieved promising results in PPR detection. However, these methods have likely reached their maximum performance. Consequently, the evaluation of more complex DL models for time-series data has been proposed. Thus, three simple CNN architectures were tested due to their high suitability in pattern recognition, which can help detect the PPR epileptic waveforms. The first one (**CNN1**) was formed by three 1D-Convolutional layers of 8, 16, and 32 filters and 4, 3, and 2 kernel sizes respectively, all applying the ReLU activation function and followed by a MaxPooling layer. After that, a Flatten layer is included before the output layer. The input layer was configured to apply the personalized Data Generator that executes one DA strategy, and the output layer was a 1-neuron Dense layer that applied the Sigmoid function to classify the instance as PPR or non-PPR. For the second and third architectures (**CNN2** and **CNN3**), one less layer and one more layer were tested respectively: in the former, the last 1D-Convolutional layer from **CNN1** was removed, while an additional 1D-Convolutional layer of 64 filters and a kernel size of 2, and its corresponding MaxPooling layer, were added as the last Convolutional block before the Flatten layer in the latter. In all architectures, convolution was applied with stride 1 and no padding, and all Max Pooling layers used a window size of 2. Each model was tested twice, applying each of the DA strategies at a time: in the end, this study conducted six experiments. All the models were trained during 5 epochs using the Adam algorithm with the learning rate set at 0.001 as the optimizer and the Binary Crossentropy as the loss function.

5 Results and Discussion

To evaluate the performance of the PPR detection in all six experiments, Accuracy (ACC), Sensitivity ($SENS$), and Specificity ($SPEC$) metrics were employed, and the results obtained are gathered in Table 1. These metrics are widely used in the medical diagnosis field since the rates of positive and negative correctly detected are extremely important information in the evaluation of a clinical test. On the one hand, regarding **CNN1**, results obtained with both DA techniques are very similar, so a hypothesis test is applied to check if the results belong to the same distribution and thus are equivalent. The null hypothesis could not be rejected, which means that no DA method is better and both are equivalent. In the case of **CNN2**, ***BasicDA*** achieved better ACC and SPEC values, while ***AdhocDA*** showed better SENS. However, when applying the hypothesis test, both also belonged to the same distribution. Finally, the results obtained in **CNN3** when using **BasicDA** showed that the classifier could not distinguish PPR from the non-PPR class in most folds. On the other hand, when comparing the different architectures, removing and adding one more layer resulted in worse results when using **BasicDA**, while it reached the best results with the first configuration, so no confirmation about which method is better can be made. Moreover, compared to the previous study in [12], both, these architectures and the current design of the DA step, could not outperform previous results where ACC and SPEC values were around 98% and SENS reached 85%, all of them with higher robustness.

Table 1. PPR detection results achieved for each fold by the six experiments: three CNN architectures applying each DA strategy. The mean, the median, and the Standard Deviation (StD) are calculated for each experiment.

	BasicDA								
	CNN1			CNN2			CNN3		
P_i	ACC	SENS	SPEC	ACC	SENS	SPEC	ACC	SENS	SPEC
P_1	0.7426	0.4180	0.7568	0.8876	0.1393	0.9202	0.9582	0.0000	1.0000
P_2	0.9705	0.5410	0.9893	0.9794	0.5574	0.9979	0.9582	0.0000	1.0000
P_3	0.8780	0.6885	0.8863	0.9178	0.8934	0.9188	0.9582	0.0000	1.0000
P_4	0.8807	0.5902	0.8934	0.9054	0.7213	0.9134	0.9582	0.0000	1.0000
P_5	0.9136	0.6967	0.9231	0.9633	0.4754	0.9846	0.9582	0.0000	1.0000
P_6	0.8221	0.7377	0.8258	0.7748	0.2459	0.7979	0.9582	0.0000	1.0000
P_7	0.9722	0.7459	0.9821	0.9757	0.4180	1.0000	0.9582	0.0000	1.0000
P_8	0.8266	0.9672	0.8205	0.7481	0.9672	0.7386	0.8766	0.2623	0.9034
P_9	0.7824	0.9918	0.7732	0.8643	0.8770	0.8637	0.6056	0.7213	0.6005
P_{10}	0.7228	0.9754	0.7117	0.9020	0.8361	0.9049	0.7519	0.6066	0.7582
Mean	0.8512	0.7352	0.8562	0.8918	0.6131	0.9040	0.8941	0.1590	0.9262
Median	0.8523	0.7172	0.8560	0.9037	0.6393	0.9161	0.9582	0.0000	1.0000
StD	0.0874	0.1945	0.0944	0.0788	0.2895	0.0852	0.1214	0.2797	0.1386
	Ad-hocDA								
	CNN1			CNN2			CNN3		
P_i	ACC	SENS	SPEC	ACC	SENS	SPEC	ACC	SENS	SPEC
P_1	0.7457	0.3983	0.7604	0.8157	0.3475	0.8355	0.7134	0.5434	0.7210
P_2	0.9612	0.5847	0.9771	0.9763	0.6102	0.9918	0.9794	0.6354	0.9939
P_3	0.8329	0.6271	0.8416	0.9403	0.6186	0.9539	0.9019	0.7203	0.9095
P_4	0.8394	0.5254	0.8526	0.9417	0.6271	0.9549	0.8421	0.7542	0.8459
P_5	0.8518	0.7881	0.8544	0.8795	0.8814	0.8795	0.9403	0.6864	0.9510
P_6	0.7093	0.8390	0.7039	0.6633	0.8814	0.6541	0.8315	0.8475	0.8308
P_7	0.9653	0.7119	0.9760	0.9698	0.8983	0.9728	0.9701	0.7203	0.9808
P_8	0.7097	0.8305	0.7046	0.6249	0.8898	0.6137	0.9238	0.6441	0.9356
P_9	0.8016	0.8305	0.8004	0.7097	0.9068	0.7014	0.6095	0.9746	0.5941
P_{10}	0.8113	0.7373	0.8144	0.7714	0.8305	0.7690	0.6616	0.9153	0.6509
Mean	0.8228	0.6873	0.8285	0.8293	0.7492	0.8327	0.8374	0.7441	0.8413
Median	0.8221	0.7246	0.8280	0.8476	0.8559	0.8575	0.8720	0.7203	0.8777
StD	0.0900	0.1495	0.0953	0.1316	0.1889	0.1406	0.1325	0.1334	0.1415

6 Conclusions and Future Work

This research proposes the application of two different DA techniques to improve the balance of the input batches introduced into the CNN classifier. The first one, **BasicDA**, applies basic time-series modifications such as jittering, time-warping, or both to real instances; while the second one, **Ad-hocDA**, creates new instances by mixing sub-segments from two random instances. These methods are applied to the data as part of the Data Generator layer, which is the one in charge of forming the input batch, so each batch introduced into the model is perfectly balanced. To test these techniques, three CNN architectures are tested using 3, 2, and 4 convolutional layers. Results show that all the models performed very similarly well in most cases and, after executing a test hypothesis, it can be concluded that all results belong to the same distribution, so all the models are equivalent and no one can be selected as best.

For future work, the imbalance problem will be approached in two different ways: using Generative models to create synthetic data and improve the dataset, and testing Anomaly Detection techniques in time-series to detect these abnormal instances that form the minority class directly.

Author contributions. David Fernández-Madera González, Fernando Moncada Martins, Víctor M. González, and José R. Villar designed the methodology and experiments, and executed all technical and computer work. They all wrote the paper. Clinical specialists Beatriz García López and Ana Isabel Gómez-Menéndez collected the data at Burgos University Hospital. They looked for suitable EEG recordings from photosensitive patients with an appropriate amount of PPRs, and anonymized them.

Ethical Approval. The study was conducted in accordance with the Declaration of Helsinki and approved by the Ethics Committee of the University Hospital of Burgos (Protocol Code CEIm2467, 23 February 2021). Informed consent was obtained from all subjects involved in the study. Written informed consent was obtained from the patients to publish this paper.

References

1. Abdelhameed, A., Bayoumi, M.: A deep learning approach for automatic seizure detection in children with epilepsy. Front. Comput. Neurosci. **15**, 29 (2021). https://doi.org/10.3389/fncom.2021.650050
2. Chakrabarti, S., Swetapadma, A., Pattnaik, P.K.: A channel independent generalized seizure detection method for pediatric epileptic seizures. Comput. Methods and Programs in Biomed. **209**, 106335 (2021). https://doi.org/10.1016/j.cmpb.2021.106335, https://linkinghub.elsevier.com/retrieve/pii/S0169260721004090
3. García, E., Villar, M., Fáñez, M., Villar, J.R., de la Cal, E., Cho, S.B.: Towards effective detection of elderly falls with CNN-LSTM neural networks. Neurocomputing **500**, 231–240 (2022). https://doi.org/10.1016/j.neucom.2021.06.102, https://www.sciencedirect.com/science/article/pii/S0925231222006440
4. He, Z., et al.: Single-channel EEG sleep staging based on data augmentation and cross-subject discrepancy alleviation. Comput. Biol. Med. **149**, 106044 (2022). 10.1016/j.compbiomed.2022.106044, https://www.sciencedirect.com/science/article/pii/S0010482522007612
5. Hossain, M.S., Amin, S.U., Alsulaiman, M., Muhammad, G.: Applying deep learning for epilepsy seizure detection and brain mapping visualization. ACM Trans.

Multimedia Comput. Commun. Appl. **15**(1s) (2019). https://doi.org/10.1145/3241056.
6. Ibrahim, F.E., et al.: Deep-learning-based seizure detection and prediction from electroencephalography signals. Int. J. Numer. Methods Biomed. Eng. **38**(6), e3573 (2022). https://doi.org/10.1002/cnm.3573, https://onlinelibrary.wiley.com/doi/abs/10.1002/cnm.3573
7. Ismail Fawaz, H., Forestier, G., Weber, J., Idoumghar, L., Muller, P.A.: Transfer learning for time series classification. In: 2018 IEEE International Conference on Big Data (Big Data), pp. 1367–1376 (2018). https://doi.org/10.1109/BigData.2018.8621990
8. Iwana, B.K., Uchida, S.: An empirical survey of data augmentation for time series classification with neural networks. PLoS ONE **16**(7) (2021). https://doi.org/10.1371/journal.pone.0254841
9. Jacaruso, L.C.: Accuracy improvement for fully convolutional networks via selective augmentation with applications to electrocardiogram data. Inf. Med. Unlocked **26**, 100729 (2021). 10.1016/j.imu.2021.100729, https://www.sciencedirect.com/science/article/pii/S2352914821002082
10. Kalitzin, S., Parra, J., Velis, D., Lopes da Silva, F.: Enhancement of phase clustering in the EEG/MEG gamma frequency band anticipates transitions to paroxysmal epileptiform activity in epileptic patients with know visual sensitivity. IEEE Trans. Bio-med. Eng. **49**, 1279–86 (2002). https://doi.org/10.1109/TBME.2002.804593
11. Martins, F.M., González, V.M., García, B., Álvarez, V., Villar, J.R.: A comparison of machine learning techniques for the detection o type-4 photoparoxysmal responses in electroencephalographic signals. In: Hybrid Artificial Intelligent Systems, pp. 3–13. Springer International Publishing, Cham (2022). https://doi.org/10.1007/978-3-031-15471-3_1
12. Martins, F.M., Suárez, V.M.G., Flecha, J.R.V., López, B.G.: Data augmentation effects on highly imbalanced EEG datasets for automatic detection of photoparoxysmal responses. Sensors **23**(4) (2023). https://doi.org/10.3390/s23042312, https://www.mdpi.com/1424-8220/23/4/2312
13. Moncada, F., et al.: Virtual reality and machine learning in the automatic photoparoxysmal response detection. Neural Comput. Appl. **35**(8), 5643–5659 (2022). https://doi.org/10.1007/s00521-022-06940-z
14. Rasheed, K., et al.: Machine learning for predicting epileptic seizures using EEG signals: a review. IEEE Rev. Biomed. Eng. **14**, 139–155 (2021). https://doi.org/10.1109/RBME.2020.3008792
15. Shu, K., Zhao, Y., Wu, L., Liu, A., Qian, R., Chen, X.: Data augmentation for seizure prediction with generative diffusion model (2023)
16. Strigaro, G., Gori, B., Varrasi, C., Fleetwood, T., Cantello, G., Cantello, R.: Flash-evoked high-frequency EEG oscillations in photosensitive epilepsies. Epilepsy Res. **172**, 106597 (2021). https://doi.org/10.1016/j.eplepsyres.2021.106597, https://linkinghub.elsevier.com/retrieve/pii/S0920121121000504
17. Tang, J., et al.: Seizure detection using wearable sensors and machine learning: setting a benchmark. Epilepsia **62**(8), 1807–1819 (2021). 10.1111/epi.16967, https://onlinelibrary.wiley.com/doi/abs/10.1111/epi.16967
18. International Federation of Clinical Neurophysiology: Report of the committee on methods of clinical examination in electroencephalography. Electroencephalogr. Clin. Neurophysiol. **10**(2) (1958). https://doi.org/10.1016/0013-4694(58)90053-1
19. Trenité, D.G.N., Binnie, C.D., Harding, G.F., Wilkins, A.: Photic stimulation: Standardization of screening methods. Epilepsia **40**(9) (1999). https://doi.org/10.1111/j.1528-1157.1999.tb00911.x

20. Trenité, D.K.N.: Photosensitivity in epilepsy. Electrophisiological and clinical correlates. Acta Neurol. Scand. Suppl. **125**, 3–149 (1989)
21. Waltz, S., Christen, H.J., Doose, H.: The different patterns of the photoparoxysmal response - a genetic study. Electroencephalogr. Clin. Neurophysiol. **83**(2) (1992). https://doi.org/10.1016/0013-4694(92)90027-F

The Third Codon Nucleotide's Role in Genetic Recombination Within SARS-CoV-2 Spike Protein: A Pilot Study

Ana Guerrero-Tamayo[1(✉)], Borja Sanz Urquijo[1], Isabel Olivares[2], María-Dolores Moragues Tosantos[3], Concepción Casado[2], and Iker Pastor-López[1]

[1] Faculty of Engineering - University of Deusto, Avenida de las Universidades, 24, 48007 Bilbao, Biscay, Spain
ana.guerrero@deusto.es

[2] National Microbiology Center (NMC) - Instituto de Salud Carlos III (ISCIII), Ctra. de Pozuelo, 28, 28222 Majadahonda, Madrid, Spain

[3] Faculty of Medicine and Nursing, University of the Basque Country UPV/EHU, Barrio Sarriena s/n, 48940 Leioa, Biscay, Spain

Abstract. Genetic recombination is a key mechanism of viral evolution in coronaviruses. In the case of SARS-CoV-2, the Spike protein (S) is a crucial genomic region where multiple recombination events have occurred. Previous research identified mathematical signatures associated with the recombinant feature in HIV-1. Based on evidence from experiments on SARS-CoV-2 unrelated to the present study, we hypothesized a relationship between a mathematical signature associated with the recombinant feature and arithmetic series with a ratio of 6 (nucleotide periodicity) in the S protein. We conducted a pilot study analyzing arithmetic series with a ratio of 6 in recombinant S proteins, finding a high presence of Thymine in series with an initial position multiple of 3. This pattern was not observed in other proteins like M and N. Repeating the process with non-recombinant sequences, we detected a similar pattern, although common nucleotides differed significantly between both sets. In this pilot study, we identified mathematical patterns associated with genetic recombination, specifically related to the third codon nucleotides. Our methodology was alignment-free and with minimal computational consumption. Our findings suggested the existence of mathematical signatures in the genome, especially in the encoded information of third codon nucleotides. Considering the diversity of perspectives and levels of information when reading and interpreting the genome may be necessary, acknowledging the existence of multiple layers of data and their interpretation.

Keywords: SARS-CoV-2 · Genetic Recombination · Third Codon Nucleotide · Third Nucleotide · Triplet · Mathematical Pattern · Mathematical Signature

University of Deusto - Research Training Grants Program.

H. Quintián et al. (Eds.): HAIS 2024, LNAI 14857, pp. 29–40, 2025.
https://doi.org/10.1007/978-3-031-74183-8_3

1 Introduction

Severe Acute Respiratory Syndrome Coronavirus 2 (SARS-CoV-2) emerged as a novel coronavirus in late 2019, swiftly escalating into a global pandemic [1]. Its remarkable contagiousness significantly fueled the tragic impact of Coronavirus Disease 2019 (COVID-19). The spectrum of SARS-CoV-2 symptoms ranges from mild respiratory ailments to severe pneumonia, and in some instances, fatality [11]. Since the onset of the pandemic, numerous variants have emerged, each possessing distinct evolutionary traits that contribute to heightened transmissibility or increased resistance to vaccines.

A critical mechanism driving viral evolution in coronaviruses is genetic recombination, where genetic material from different strains or viruses is combined, providing the resulting virus with competitive advantages such as adaptation to new hosts, evasion of host immunity, or resistance to antiviral treatments. This process can occasionally result in the emergence of new strains or even entirely new viruses. Hence, it is imperative to further explore the mechanisms underlying genetic recombination [17]. In the case of SARS-CoV-2, nearly all circulating recombinant lineages of SARS-CoV-2 are derived from Omicron [13]. Since 2023, the recombinant lineage XBB emerged dominant in the epidemiological landscape, owing to its increased transmissibility [14]. The Spike (S) protein stands as a pivotal genomic region in viral evolution, with multiple genetic recombination events detected within its genome. Playing a fundamental role in the infection process, the S protein binds to the ACE2 receptor (Angiotensin-converting Enzyme 2) on human cell surfaces, facilitating viral entry [18].

In previous research, we identified a mathematical signature embedded in complete genomic sequences of HIV-1 that determined the recombinant feature [8]. Therefore, the existence of mathematical patterns related to the recombinant feature in SARS-CoV-2 is also plausible. Based on this hypothesis, we conducted a pilot study to explore the existence of the mathematical signature that characterizes a SARS-CoV-2 sequence as recombinant.

This article presents the obtained results, as well as an analysis of their biological significance.

2 Materials

All experiments were ran in this equipment: Processing Unit: Intel(R) Core(TM) i7-4770K CPU. 3.5 GHz. Installed RAM: 32 GB usable. Operative System: Windows 10 Education. Version: 22H2. GPU: NVIDIA GeForce RTX 3090. Total memory: 40 GB.

3 Methods

All analyses were developed in a Python environment, using (among others): Pandas for data manipulation in the form of DataFrames [10]. Numpy, for implementing numerical operations [2]. Math, for applying certain mathematical functions [4]. Os, for operations related to the operating system [5]. Re, for regular expression operations [6]. The Selenium WebDriver library (Python) for automating the web download of EMBL files using scripts [12].

In experiments from another field unrelated to the research objective of this article, we detected a relationship between the recombinant feature and arithmetic sequences with a span of 6 nucleotides in the S protein within specific recombinant sequences. Out of a total of 1,565 recombinant sequences, we identified a total of 39 sequences where this relationship seemed most evident, and we selected them as the pilot study group.

Subsequently, we selected the same number of non-recombinant sequences (39) from a total of 1,539,728 through an automated random subsampling process. This was done to approximate a search for differential elements in an environment where structural differences appeared to be more evident. In this manner, locating these differences between one study group and the other a priori could be more straightforward.

Subsequently, we extracted all arithmetic series with a common difference of 6 based on their initial position in the S, M, and N proteins in the recombinant sequences, aiming to detect the presence of any pattern exclusively inherent to S. From the selected non-recombinant sequences, we extracted such series in S to establish comparisons between the proteins of recombinant and non-recombinant sequences.

In each of the arithmetic series extracted in the previous step, we calculated the average occurrence of A, T, C, and G in each of the proteins analyzed, as well as the Standard Deviation (SD). The aim was to obtain information regarding the level of abundance of each nucleotide in each of these proteins, as well as the variability found in the sequences under analysis. These data may enable us to identify particularities among the arithmetic series in each analyzed protein. Furthermore, these data may provide clues about the mathematical signature embedded in the genome.

Then, we identified the common nucleotides within the S sequences among sequences belonging to the same group (recombinants and non-recombinants) and conducted a comparative analysis between the results of both groups. The differences between both nucleotide groups may provide information about the formulation of that mathematical signature.

Finally, we made an approach with existing literature in order to approximate the bio-centric discussion of the results.

4 Results

For each of the 39 selected recombinant sequences, we verified whether the position corresponding to the nucleotide periodicity of 6 aligns with the third letter of the second amino acid in S. Upon thorough examination, we confirmed that the sixth letter indeed matches in most cases. See Table 1. The "Position" column indicates the position of this sixth nucleotide from the start of S (not from the start of the entire sequence). *Position* = 6 means that the first sixth nucleotide of S (counting from the start of the sequence) aligns with the third nucleotide of the second amino acid in S protein.

Table 2 presents a statistical analysis of the occurrence of each nucleotide within the frames exhibiting a ratio of 6 in the S protein (recombinant sequences).

In all tables displaying similar outcomes, the columns labeled "No. Avg." denote the average occurrence of each nucleotide type in the corresponding protein within each frame. "Avg. ± SD (%)" indicates "No. Avg.", expressed as a percentage of the total number of nucleotides composing the S protein ± the standard deviation, also in %.

The amount of Thymine in multiples of 3 arithmetic series rises above 45%. The remaining 55% is distributed among the other three types of nucleotides, with a slight predominance of adenine. This phenomenon does not occur in sequences that are not multiples of 3. In non-multiples of 3 series, the distribution percentages among the 4 types of nucleotides are more balanced. In all cases, the standard deviation (SD) of each nucleotide was less than 2%. This means that in the 39 analyzed sequences, nucleotides at each position are generally similar with minor variations.

The results for the M proteins of these recombinant sequences are shown in Table 3.

Table 4 displays the results for the N protein.

In the comparisons made with the M and N proteins of these 39 recombinant sequences, we did not detect these patterns. The nucleotide quantities appeared more balanced than in the case of the S protein, especially regarding T, where the incidence levels were not reached in any of the arithmetic series in these proteins.

The next step was to compare the results of the S protein in the group of recombinant sequences with the results of the S protein in the non-recombinant sequences. See Table 5.

In the group of non-recombinant sequences, the presence of Thymine in the third codon nucleotide maintained the high percentages of occurrence detected in the recombinant sequences. Therefore, this detected pattern was common between both study groups. It was be necessary to determine the exact common nucleotides shared in both groups to establish a detailed comparison.

Table 1. Sixth Nucleotide Position

ID	Variant	Confidence Score	S		First 6th nt	Position
MZ558275	XB	99.99%	21,512	25,333	21,516	5
MZ280957	XB	69.42%	21,519	25,340	21,522	4
MZ817897	XC	68.77%	21,533	25,348	21,534	2
OK039706	XC	80.39%	21,532	25,353	21,534	3
OL791595	XC	99.99%	21,542	25,363	21,546	4
OL920359	XC	99.99%	21,533	25,354	21,534	2
OM059434	XC	99.99%	21,533	25,354	21,534	2
ON144454	XN	98.70%	21,529	25,341	21,534	6
ON330593	XAA	99.98%	21,530	25,342	21,534	5
ON594981	XAC	99.98%	21,529	25,341	21,534	6
ON650495	XAC	99.99%	21,529	25,341	21,534	6
ON800622	XAJ	65.51%	21,529	25,350	21,534	6
ON980049	XE	99.94%	21,526	25,338	21,528	3
OP129015	XAK	99.99%	21,529	25,341	21,534	6
OP294029	XAJ	99.88%	21,529	25,341	21,534	6
OP311263	XAG	74.12%	21,526	25,338	21,528	3
OP313193	XAJ	99.86%	21,529	25,341	21,534	6
OP313256	XAJ	99.99%	21,529	25,341	21,534	6
OP313383	XAJ	96.92%	21,526	25,338	21,528	3
OP359817	XAJ	99.84%	21,529	25,341	21,534	6
OP768851	XE	99.91%	21,526	25,338	21,528	3
OP934590	XBD	99.99%	21,529	25,341	21,534	6
OQ094825	XBB	99.97%	21,529	25,338	21,534	6
OQ111935	XBB	99.99%	21,529	25,338	21,534	6
OQ112611	XBB	99.99%	21,529	25,338	21,534	6
OQ112616	XBB	99.99%	21,542	25,351	21,546	4
OQ112619	XBB	99.99%	21,529	25,338	21,534	6
OQ112624	XBB	99.99%	21,529	25,338	21,534	6
OQ112639	XBB	99.99%	21,529	25,338	21,534	6
OQ112647	XBB	99.99%	21,529	25,338	21,534	6
OQ112649	XBB	99.99%	21,529	25,338	21,534	6
OQ112673	XBB	99.99%	21,529	25,338	21,534	6
OQ112686	XBB	99.99%	21,529	25,338	21,534	6
OQ112691	XBB	99.99%	21,529	25,338	21,534	6
OQ112730	XBB	99.99%	21,529	25,338	21,534	6
OQ112737	XBB	99.99%	21,529	25,338	21,534	6
OQ112740	XBB	99.99%	21,529	25,338	21,534	6
OQ112771	XBB	99.99%	21,529	25,338	21,534	6
OQ112893	XBB	99.99%	21,545	25,354	21,546	2

Table 2. SARS-CoV-2 Recombinant Sequences S Protein

	6, 12, ...		9, 15, ...	
	No. Avg.	Avg. ± SD (%)	No. Avg.	Avg. ± SD (%)
A	169.54	26.62 ± 1.75	170.92	26.87 ± 1.96
T	293.87	46.13± 1.69	288.90	45.42 ± 1.51
C	99.95	15.69 ± 0.71	99.46	15.64 ± 0.74
G	66.28	10.41 ± 1.21	70.13	11.03 ± 1.14
	7, 13, ...		**10, 16, ...**	
	No. Avg.	**Avg. ± SD (%)**	**No. Avg.**	**Avg. ± SD (%)**
A	188.59	29.65 ± 1.05	195.18	30.69 ± 0.63
T	155.72	24.48 ± 0.53	150.18	23.61 ± 1.02
C	106.54	16.75 ± 1.37	100.41	15.79 ± 1.51
G	178.15	28.01 ± 1.82	183.28	28.82 ± 1.24
	8, 14, ...		**11, 17, ...**	
	No. Avg.	**Avg. ± SD (%)**	**No. Avg.**	**Avg. ± SD (%)**
A	193.79	30.47 ± 0.69	196.21	30.85 ± 0.25
T	182.69	28.73 ± 1.75	183.79	28.90 ± 1.45
C	150.33	23.64 ± 0.99	155.03	24.38 ± 0.77
G	102.59	16.13 ± 1.05	93.62	14.72± 1.42

Table 3. SARS-CoV-2 Recombinant Sequences M Protein

	6, 12, ...		9, 15, ...	
	No. Avg.	Avg. ± SD (%)	No. Avg.	Avg. ± SD (%)
A	22.97	20.70 ± 0.14	31.00	27.93 ± 0.00
T	36.56	32.94± 0.45	46.03	41.46 ± 0.14
C	28.44	25.62± 0.45	21.97	19.80 ± 0.14
G	23.03	20.74 ± 0.14	12.00	10.81 ± 0.00
	7, 13, ...		**10, 16, ...**	
	No. Avg.	**Avg. ± SD (%)**	**No. Avg.**	**Avg. ± SD (%)**
A	31.67	28.53 ± 0.47	35.00	31.82 ± 0.00
T	28.00	25.23 ± 0.00	21.00	19.09 ± 0.00
C	21.33	19.22 ± 0.42	27.00	24.55 ± 0.00
G	30.00	27.03 ± 0.29	27.00	24.55 ± 0.00
	8, 14, ...		**11, 17, ...**	
	No. Avg.	**Avg. ± SD (%)**	**No. Avg.**	**Avg. ± SD (%)**
A	30.95	27.88 ± 0.20	19.00	17.27 ± 0.00
T	37.00	33.33 ± 0.00	43.92	39.93 ± 0.25
C	24.00	21.62 ± 0.00	21.08	19.16 ± 0.25
G	19.05	17.16 ± 0.20	26.00	23.64 ± 0.00

Table 4. SARS-CoV-2 Recombinant Sequences N Protein

	6, 12, ...		**9, 15, ...**	
	No. Avg.	Avg. ± SD (%)	No. Avg.	Avg. ± SD (%)
A	61.54	29.53 ± 0.45	65.51	31.47 ± 0.49
T	71.69	34.42 ± 2.55	61.33	29.46 ± 2.37
C	40.74	19.54 ± 3.83	53.41	25.66 ± 3.77
G	34.38	16.51 ± 1.73	27.92	13.41 ± 1.88
	7, 13, ...		**10, 16, ...**	
	No. Avg.	**Avg. ± SD (%)**	**No. Avg.**	**Avg. ± SD (%)**
A	60.46	29.04 ± 2.50	68.85	33.21 ± 2.36
T	33.62	16.15 ± 0.49	28.54	13.76 ± 0.51
C	49.82	23.93 ± 0.23	52.00	25.08 ± 0.09
G	64.28	30.88 ± 1.81	57.97	27.95 ± 1.95
	8, 14, ...		**11, 17, ...**	
	No. Avg.	**Avg. ± SD (%)**	**No. Avg.**	**Avg. ± SD (%)**
A	70.26	33.75 ± 0.23	69.64	33.59 ± 0.50
T	36.49	17.53 ± 0.57	32.46	15.65 ± 0.41
C	57.18	27.47 ± 0.14	59.92	28.90 ± 0.20
G	44.26	21.26 ± 0.27	45.33	21.86 ± 0.27

Table 5. SARS-CoV-2 Non-Recombinant Sequences S Protein

	6, 12, ...		**9, 15, ...**	
	No. Avg.	Avg. ± SD (%)	No. Avg.	Avg. ± SD (%)
A	167,05	26.59 ± 1.91	173.59	27.66 ± 1.96
T	290.74	46.29± 1.50	290.00	46.18 ± 1.69
C	99.15	15.78 ± 0.87	100.49	16.02 ± 0.88
G	71.21	11.35 ± 1.33	63.62	10.14 ± 1.17
	7, 13, ...		**10, 16, ...**	
	No. Avg.	**Avg. ± SD (%)**	**No. Avg.**	**Avg. ± SD (%)**
A	196.69	31.33 ± 1.03	185.74	29.62 ± 0.93
T	146.26	23.30 ± 0.91	157.11	25.05 ± 0.93
C	100.74	16.04 ± 1.30	105.85	16.89 ± 1.38
G	184.05	29.33 ± 1.37	178.38	28.44 ± 1.36
	8, 14, ...		**11, 17, ...**	
	No. Avg.	**Avg. ± SD (%)**	**No. Avg.**	**Avg. ± SD (%)**
A	196.67	31.32 ± 0.70	191.44	30.52 ± 0.70
T	182.00	29.00 ± 1.67	184.36	29.39 ± 1.49
C	151.97	24.20 ± 0.97	151.59	24.18 ± 0.80
G	97.21	15.48 ± 1.41	99.72	15.91 ± 1.29

5 Common Nucleotides

The common nucleotides in the case of the 39 recombinant sequences were those identified in Table 6. The "Position" column indicates the position of the common nucleotide in the 39 analyzed recombinant sequences, starting from the first nucleotide of S. The "Nucleotide" column specifies the type of nucleotide contained at that position, which is common in these 39 sequences.

Table 6. Common Nucleotides S Protein in Recombinant Sequences

Position	Nucleotide	Position	Nucleotide	Position	Nucleotide
3	G	48	T	123	A
6	T	51	T	165	C
9	T	54	T	177	T
12	T	57	A	189	T
15	T	63	A	198	T
18	T	66	T	318	T
21	A	69	A	363	T
24	G	72	A	369	T
27	A	78	T	399	T
30	A	93	T	405	T
36	T	102	T	582	T
39	T	108	T	1329	T
42	G	117	T	2382	T
45	T	120	C		

Surprisingly, all the common nucleotides in those 39 recombinant sequences were located at positions that were multiples of 3. That is, all the common elements were precisely the third nucleotide of the triplet. There was not a single common nucleotide at positions 1 and 2 of the triplet.

Table 7 compiles the common nucleotides in the 39 non-recombinant sequences under study.

Similar to the scenario observed in the 39 recombinant sequences, it is striking that once again, all the common elements in the S proteins of the 39 non-recombinant sequences analyzed were multiples of 3, the third nucleotides of the triplet.

The common nucleotides shared between the 39 recombinant and non-recombinant sequences were those displayed in Table 8.

The exclusive common elements of the recombinant sequences were positions 21 (A), 30 (A), 36 (T), 39 (T), 51 (T), 54 (T), 63 (A), 66 (T), 69 (A), 72 (A), 78 (T), 93 (T), 102 (T), 108 (T), 117 (T), 120 (C), 123 (A), 165 (C), 177 (T), 318 (T), 363 (T), 369 (T), 399 (T), 405 (T), 582 (T), 1329 (T), 2382 (T).

Table 7. Common Nucleotides S Protein in Non-Recombinant Sequences

Position	Nucleotide	Position	Nucleotide	Position	Nucleotide
3	G	18	T	48	T
6	T	24	G	57	A
9	T	27	A	189	T
12	T	42	G	198	T
15	T	45	T	2388	T

Table 8. Common Nucleotides in the S Protein Sequences, Shared between Recombinants and Non-Recombinants

Position	Nucleotide	Position	Nucleotide	Position	Nucleotide
3	G	18	T	48	T
6	T	24	G	57	A
9	T	27	A	189	T
12	T	42	G	198	T
15	T	45	T		

These exclusive common elements found within recombinant sequences could potentially bear relevance to a mathematically encrypted signature embedded within the third codon nucleotides of S. The pilot study offered valuable insights to guide future research endeavors focused on elucidating this mathematical signature.

6 Bio-Centric Discussion

In genetics and molecular biology, the third letter of a codon is frequently considered less crucial in determining the encoded amino acid compared to the first two letters. This concept was highlighted by Francis Crick in 1966 with his "wobble hypothesis" [3]. This fact provides some flexibility in the DNA sequence and allows mutations at this position to be more tolerated without affecting the final protein produced.

Therefore, we could infer that this third nucleotide is more prone to variability. However, in this pilot study, all the common nucleotides turned out to be precisely third nucleotides, not the first or second ones, which seemed to be more stable.

The limitation of the human ribosome to recognize the necessary information for generating transfer RNA can affect the synthesis of the corresponding amino acid. For instance, the CGC codon (arginine) is not efficiently recognized by the human ribosome, but the CGG, CGA, and CGU codons can encode this amino acid correctly. At times, the ribosome may opt for an alternative codon that fulfills the required function in mRNA translation [20]. The analysis of these factors in transcription must be studied thoroughly.

In arithmetic series multiples of 3, Thymine was significantly more abundant than the other three nucleotide types combined, accounting for nearly half of the entire set. However, this pattern was not observed in sequences not multiples of 3.

Hassanin (2022) discovered that genomes of coronaviruses related to SARS-CoV-2 contain fewer cytosines and more uracils at the third codon position compared to other sarbecoviruses [9], in alignment with findings by Rice et al. [15] and Tort et al. [19]. These studies indicate a bias in SARS-CoV-2 codon usage resulting from mutations that lead to an enrichment of $A \pm U$ or U, among other factors. Saldivar-Espinoza et al. [16] also documented that mutations where cytosine is replaced by uracil (C>U) are the most common in the SARS-CoV-2 genome. They proposed that host deaminases, enzymes that catalyze the deamination of unpaired nitrogenous bases, were accountable for a significant portion of these mutations.

In accordance with the human genetic code, as outlined in the Codon Usage Frequency Table [7], the third nucleotide of a codon can be either C or U without affecting the encoded amino acid. Hence, if the elevated quantity of U in the third codon position arises from a C>U transition, it would not modify the amino acid sequence of the resultant Spike protein.

However, it is noteworthy to emphasize that in our analysis, other structural proteins such as M and N exhibited distinct quantity distribution patterns compared to S. Consequently, we acknowledge that the elevated amount of U at a specific position may possess biological significance warranting further investigation for interpretation.

While these phenomena do not directly elucidate the connection between the identified mathematical pattern categorizing a SARS-CoV-2 sequence as recombinant and the frequencies of Uracil (Thymine) appearance in the S protein, we cannot dismiss the possibility of a correlation between them.

7 Conclusion

In this pilot study focusing on a group of recombinant SARS-CoV-2 sequences, we identified a pattern characterized by a high Thymine content in the third codon positions of the S protein, which was not observed in other structural proteins like M or N. Our research results, depicted in the genomic spectrogram, revealed this mathematical pattern associated with sequence recombination. By comparing the patterns detected in the recombinant group with equivalent patterns in a non-recombinant group of the same size, we observed a similar characteristic pattern specific to the S protein.

We extracted the common nucleotides in each group of sequences, recombinant and non-recombinant. All these common nucleotides were multiples of 3, that is, the third nucleotide of the triplet.

This search for common nucleotides was conducted without applying any type of multiple alignment; that is, in sequences of varying lengths in S, we found that precisely the common elements were third nucleotides of the codon without performing any prior "artificial" adjustment before the comparison.

Finally, we established which common elements were shared by both recombinants and non-recombinants to try to shed some light on that mathematical signature encrypted in the genome.

The evidence found suggests that this encrypted mathematical signature is located in the third nucleotide of the triplets in S (in the case of SARS-CoV-2).

This pilot study strengthens the hypothesis that the third nucleotide of the triplet, less relevant in terms of amino acid coding, may contain additional encrypted information that characterizes (in this study's case) a SARS-CoV-2 sequence as recombinant.

Using methodologies that do not require multiple alignments and very low-computation tools, we obtained sufficient evidence in this pilot study to firmly hypothesize the possibility that the third nucleotide of the triplet contains encrypted information related to viral characteristics.

Although much remains to be discovered about the intricate rules of the genome, this document may mark the beginning of a new perspective for understanding and analyzing the genome. The results obtained reveal the identification of mathematical signatures in the virus genome through genomic spectrogram analysis, opening up new possibilities for investigating potential functions associated with these mathematical patterns.

References

1. Atzrodt, C.L., et al.: A guide to COVID-19: a global pandemic caused by the novel coronavirus SARS-CoV-2. FEBS J. **287**(17), 3633–3650 (2020)
2. Council, N.S.: Numpy library (2024). https://numpy.org/. Accessed 30 Apr 2024
3. Crick, F.: Codon-anticodon pairing: the Wobble hypothesis. Mol. Biol. Sel. Papers **19**, 548–555 (1966)
4. Foundation, P.S.: Math Python library (2024). https://docs.python.org/3/library/math.html/. Accessed 30 Apr 2024
5. Foundation, P.S.: Os Python library (2024). https://docs.python.org/es/3.10/library/os.html/. Accessed 30 Apr 2024
6. Foundation, P.S.: Re Python library (2024). https://docs.python.org/es/3/library/re.html/. Accessed 30 Apr 2024
7. GenSscript: Genscript codon usage frequency Table (chart) Tool (Human Genetic Code). https://www.genscript.com/tools/codon-frequency-table/ (2024). Accessed 21 Mar 2024
8. Guerrero-Tamayo, A., Urquijo, B.S., Casado, C., Tosantos, M.D.M., Olivares, I., Pastor-López, I.: Discovering mathematical patterns behind HIV-1 genetic recombination: a new methodology to identify viral features. IEEE Access (2023)
9. Hassanin, A.: Variation in synonymous nucleotide composition among genomes of sarbecoviruses and consequences for the origin of COVID-19. Gene **835**, 146641 (2022)
10. Management, A.C., community of contributors: Pandas library (2024). https://pandas.pydata.org/. Accessed 30 Apr 2024
11. Marks, K.M., Gulick, R.M.: COVID-19. Annals of Internal Medicine **176**(10), ITC145–ITC160 (2023)

12. Muthukadan, B.: Selenium with Python. https://selenium-python.readthedocs.io/ (2024). Accessed 03 May 2024
13. Ou, J., et al.: Tracking SARS-CoV-2 Omicron diverse spike gene mutations identifies multiple inter-variant recombination events. Signal Transduct. Target. Ther. **7**(1), 138 (2022)
14. Parums, D.V.: The XBB. 1.5 (Kraken) subvariant of Omicron SARS-CoV-2 and its rapid global spread. Med. Sci. Monitor: Int. Med. J. Exper. Clin. Res. **29**, e939580–1 (2023)
15. Rice, A.M., et al.: Evidence for strong mutation bias toward, and selection against, U content in SARS-CoV-2: implications for vaccine design. Mol. Biol. Evol. **38**(1), 67–83 (2021)
16. Saldivar-Espinoza, B., et al.: The mutational landscape of SARS-CoV-2. Int. J. Mol. Sci. **24**(10), 9072 (2023)
17. Su, S., et al.: Epidemiology, genetic recombination, and pathogenesis of coronaviruses. Trends Microbiol. **24**(6), 490–502 (2016)
18. Tagliamonte, M.S., et al.: Multiple recombination events and strong purifying selection at the origin of SARS-CoV-2 spike glycoprotein increased correlated dynamic movements. Int. J. Mol. Sci. **22**(1), 80 (2020)
19. Tort, F.L., Castells, M., Cristina, J.: A comprehensive analysis of genome composition and codon usage patterns of emerging coronaviruses. Virus Res. **283**, 197976 (2020)
20. Zabolotskii, A.I., Kozlovskiy, S.V., Katrukha, A.G.: The influence of the nucleotide composition of genes and gene regulatory elements on the efficiency of protein expression in Escherichia coli. Biochem. Mosc. **88**(Suppl 1), S176–S191 (2023)

Machine Learning for the Identification of Biomarker and Risk Factors associated with Depression in Adult Population: Preliminary Results on a Small Cohort

Guillermo Cano-Escalera[1,2,3,4], Manuel Graa[1,2(✉)], Karina S. MacDowell[4,6], Juan C. Leza[4,6], Iaki Zorilla[3,4,5], and Ana Gonzlez-Pinto[3,4,5]

[1] Department of Computer Science and Artificial Intelligence, Faculty of Computer Science, University of the Basque Country (UPV/EHU), Paseo Manuel de Lardizabal, 1, 20018 Donostia-San Sebastian, Spain

[2] Computational Intelligence Group, University of the Basque Country (UPV/EHU), Bilbao, Spain

ccpgrrom@ei.ehu.eus

[3] Department of Psychiatry, Hospital Universitario de Araba, Vitoria, Spain

[4] Biomedical Research Centre in Mental Health Network (CIBERSAM) G10, Vitoria, Spain

[5] University of the Basque Country UPV/EHU, Vitoria-Gasteiz, Spain

[6] Department of Pharmacology and Toxicology, Faculty of Medicine, Universidad Complutense de Madrid (UCM), Madrid, Spain

Abstract. In this study we identify some risk factors for depression from the sociodemographic factors and inflammatory biomarkers from a sample of depressed subjects versus a matched group of healthy subjects. The multivariate logistic regression and random forest are used to identify the most significant factors associated with depression. We found significant differences demographic variables corresponding to education, higher levels of education seem to provide protection. Cognitive impairment (SCIP) positive results were also strongly associated with depression. The study also confirmed that married subjects suffer less of depression than separated or divorced subjects. Regarding inflammatory biomarkers, significant differences were obtained in IL6, TNFa, CAT, BDNF, and GSH Total, which indicate a strong association of depression and systemic inflamatory processes.

Keywords: Depression · Inflammatory biomarkers · Socio-demographic factors · Adult population · Machine learning · Random forest · Logistic Regression

1 Introduction

Depression is a highly prevalent mental condition in aging western societies that can be chronic and recurrent, causing high disease burden, functional impairment

H. Quintián et al. (Eds.): HAIS 2024, LNAI 14857, pp. 41–48, 2025.
https://doi.org/10.1007/978-3-031-74183-8_4

and high economic costs worldwide [21,25]. Accurate diagnosis and optimal disease management are of particular relevance to the development and severity of symptoms; however, correct disease management remains a challenge as it can be delayed by months or even years.

According to Chevance [4], of 137 areas of concern for patients with depression, the most common are improving access to a psychiatrist, raising awareness of the disorder, and stigma. To combat stigma, it is essential to provide clear messages based on scientific evidence, which can only be achieved with a better understanding of the mechanisms related to its pathophysiology and maintenance.

Depression is a complex phenomenon with a biopsychosocial aetiology, i.e. biological, psychological and environmental factors interact in this disorder. The risk of major depression in both adults and young people has been associated with stressful events [15], such as psychological trauma [11,16], cognitive impairment [24], personality traits [17], comorbidities with other mental disorders [8], genetic factors [6], neurobiological [20] and inflammatory alterationss [9].

In relation to the latter, there is growing evidence that inflammation and oxidative stress contribute to the pathophysiology of depression. An imbalance of pro- and anti-inflammatory cytokines [21,25] that modulate the synthesis and function of central nervous system (CNS) neurotransmitters causing changes in emotion, cognition and behaviour may be implicated in its onset and course [1,5,7].

Understanding the factors associated with depression is a needed step to its effective diagnosis, prevention and treatment. These factors, which encompass biological, psychological, social and environmental dimensions, interact in a complex and multifaceted manner, influencing the onset and severity of the disorder. Identifying these factors allows health professionals to propose personalised interventions and more effective management strategies, thereby improving the quality of life of those suffering from this condition [12]. The aim of this study is to compare which socio-demographic factors may significantly influence depressive versus healthy subjects, as well as to analyze the role of inflammation in depressed patients..

2 Materials and Methods

2.1 Study Design and Subjects

The design is an observational study of a cohort of 100 individuals, 50 patients presenting a major depressive episode and 50 healthy subjects matched by sex and age with the group of patients. For the patient group (n=50), those persons treated at the Araba University Hospital for a major depressive episode who meet the inclusion criteria and agree to participate in the study have been included. For the control group (n=50), volunteers have been recruited by placing advertisements in the hospital. Informed consent of all participants (n=100) has been obtained at the start of the study.

Inclusion criteria: age 18–65 years; current major depressive episode (DSM-5) and signature of informed consent.
Exclusion criteria: intellectual disability, severe cognitive impairment, organic disease of the central nervous system.

The study collected sociodemographic and neuropsychological (SCIP) variables, and inflammation biomarkers extracted from blood samples.

2.2 Statistical Methods

The Jasp package (https://jasp-stats.org) has been used for variable selection and machine learning algorithm application. Selection of statistically significant variables ($p < 0.05$) in this cohort regarding depression was carried out by multivariate Logistic Regression predicting the factors asocciated with depression and inflammatory biomarkers. Random Forest classification experiments predicting the factors associated with depression with greater importance with ten repetitions of hold-out validation were also performed. Variable relevance ranking was assessed from the out-of-bag accuracy estimation in each repettion. After the 10 repetitions of hould-out validation, variables are ranked by the number of times that a variable appears among the top ten relevant variables.

3 Results

Table 1 and 2 report the results obtained over the sociodemographic variables and the inflamation biomarkers, respectively. We selected significant variables ($p < 0.05$) in multivariate Logistic Regression discriminating depressed subjects versus healthy subjects.

Significant variables identified were Marital Status: Married ($p = 0.049$), Educational Level: Completed postgraduate studies ($p = 0.009$), Educational Level: Completed university studies ($p = 0.016$) and cognitive impairment (SCIP Test) ($p < 0.001$). And the significant inflammatory variables were: IL6 ($p = 0.010$), TNFa ($p = 0.032$), CAT ($p = 0.013$), BDNF ($p = 0.039$), GSH Total ($p = 0.016$).

Non linear multivariate discrimination was tested applying Random Forest as implemented in Jasp. Classification performance measures over ten repetitions of hold-out validation are presented in Tables 3 and 5 for the sociodemographic variables and inflamation biomarkers, respectively. The average accuracy was close to 0.9 for the RF classifier, therefore we attribute high confidence to the variable selection. Variable importance in these models was estimated by out-of-bag accuracy estimation. The repeated appearance of a variable in the subset of the ten most important variables accross the validation process was taken as the measure of variable importance, as well as Average Gini Importance Value in Tables 4 and 6. Relevant sociodemographic variables identified by Random Forest were Educational Level: Completed postgraduate studies, Marital Status: Lives with a partner, Work Status: Unemployed, Marital Status: Separated/Divorced, Educational Level: Completed bachelor or professional educationand Educational

Table 1. Multivariate Logistic Regression over Sociodemographic factors. Marital Status: MS. Educational Level: EL. WS: Work Status. The MLR achieved an AUC: 0.896

Variable	Estimate	Standard Error	Odds Ratio	z	Wald Statistic	df	p
Sex (Male)	0.777	1.157	2.174	0.672	0.451	1	0.502
Sex (Female)	0.823	0.862	2.277	0.947	0.897	1	0.344
MS (Never Married)	0.233	0.784	1.262	0.297	0.088	1	0.767
MS (Separated/Divorced)	19.555	20.432	31.100	0.010	0.0091	1	0.992
MS (Married)	-2.898	1.470	0.014	-1.972	3.889	1	0.049*
EL (Completed primary education)	17.678	46.075	47.570	0.004	0.00014	1	0.997
EL (Completed secundary education)	1.151	1.095	3.161	1.052	1.106	1	0.293
EL (Completed bachelor or professional education)	0.700	0.422	2.014	1.659	2.752	1	0.097
EL (Completed postgraduate studies)	-3.394	1.301	0.034	-2.608	6.804	1	0.009**
EL (Completed university studies)	-2.434	1.010	0.088	-2.411	5.812	1	0.016**
WS (Unemployed)	0.823	0.869	2.277	0.947	0.897	1	0.344
WS (Student)	-0.535	1.085	0.586	-0.493	0.243	1	0.622
WS (Incapacity for work)	-18.667	82.431	0.0078	-0.002	0.00051	1	0.998
WS (Retired)	-1.201	1.423	0.301	-0.844	0.712	1	0.399
WS (Working, but on sick leave)	0.142	0.633	1.153	0.225	0.051	1	0.822
SCIP Test	-0.121	0.036	0.886	-3.335	11.1213	1	<.001**

Table 2. Multivariate Logistic Regression: Inflammatory biomarkers. AUC: 0.839

Variable	Estimate	Standard Error	Odds Ratio	z	Wald Statistic	df	p
Interleukin 6 (IL6)	0.721	0.281	2.057	2.565	6.581	1	0.010**
IL1b	0.016	0.018	1.016	0.912	0.831	1	0.362
Tumor Necrosis Factor Alpha (TNFa)	0.119	0.056	1.127	2.145	4.602	1	0.032**
Catalase (CAT)	0.013	0.005	1.013	2.475	6.128	1	0.013**
Brain-Derived Neurotrophic Factor (BDNF)	-0.094	0.045	0.911	-2.064	4.259	1	0.039**
Total Glutathione (GSH total)	-3.215	1.334	0.040	-2.411	5.811	1	0.016**
Superoxide Dismutase (SOD)	0.102	0.756	1.108	0.135	0.018	1	0.892
Glutathione Peroxidase (GPx)	-0.010	0.008	0.990	-1.295	1.667	1	0.195
Oxidized Glutathione (GSSG)	1.607	2.464	4.988	0.652	0.425	1	0.514

Table 3. Classification performance results averaged over 10 repetitions of hold-out validation: average (standard deviation) on sociodemographic factors

	Test Accuracy	AUC	F1 Score
Random Forest	0.760 (0.105)	0.897 (0.087)	0.754 (0.111)

Level: Completed university studies. Relevant inflammatory biomarkers identified by Random Forest were BDNF, IL6, TNFa, GSH Total, CAT and SOD. However, the Random Forest variable importance does not provide information regarding the positive or negative influence on the outcome.

Table 4. Average Gini Importance of the Sociodemographic variables identified by Random Forest in the top 10 in the validation and test replicates. Average classification performance results over 10 validation folds.

Random Forest		
Variable	Average Gini Importance Value	Freq. on top 10
EL (Completed postgraduate studies)	3.45	10
MS (Married)	2.54	9
WS (Unemployed)	2.316	9
MS (Separated/Divorced)	2.233	9
EL (Completed bachelor or professional education)	1.71	10
EL (Completed university studies)	1.544	9
SCIP Test	1.357	9

Note: Marital Status: MS. Educational Level: EL. WS: Work Status

Table 5. Classification performance results averaged over 10 repetitions of hold-out validation: average (standard deviation) on inflammatory biomarkers

	Test Accuracy	AUC	F1 Score
Random Forest	0.794 (0.064)	0.901 (0.041)	0.800 (0.084)

Table 6. Average Gini Importance of the Inflammatory biomarkers identified by Random Forest in the top 10 in the validation and test replicates. Average classification performance results over 10 validation folds.

Random Forest		
Variable	Average Gini Importance Value	Freq. on top 10
BDNF	2.167	9
IL6	2.144	9
TNFa	1.975	8
GSH Total	1.086	8
CAT	1.063	8
SOD	1.043	8

4 Discussion

In a global context of quality of life, there is a growing interest in improving the quality of care for the depressed subjects and at the same time to have optimal management of healthcare resources. Therefore, the identification of risk factors for frail patients with depression is becoming increasingly important to prevent their increase in incidence. Gender, educational attainment, marital status and employment status are crucial socio-demographic determinants that can significantly influence mental health, including depression.

Gender differences are evident in the prevalence of depression, with women showing higher rates than men in numerous studies [14], however, our study does not reflect such significant differences. In terms of educational attainment, it is known that lower educational attainment is consistently associated with a higher incidence of depression, probably due to limitations in access to resources and stress management skills [10], as our studies also show, marital status also plays an important role, as single, divorced or widowed people are known to have higher rates of depression compared to those who are married or in stable relationships [22].

Cognitive impairment and depression are often interrelated, with research suggesting that each may influence the development and progression of the other. Depression can be both a risk factor and a consequence of cognitive impairment. For example, it has been observed that depression may precede cognitive decline in some individuals, suggesting that depressive symptoms may be an early manifestation of neurodegenerative disorders such as Alzheimer's disease [18]. In addition, cognitive impairment may exacerbate depressive symptoms, creating a negative feedback loop that exacerbates both problems [2]. The SCIP test confirms that depressive subjects greater cognitive impairment is statistically significant.

The study finds that a married status is a differential factor between healthy subjects and subjects with depression. Marriage seems to be a protecting factor against depression. Finally, risk differences were found in employment status, with unemployment and job instability showing a close relationship with depression, which can lead to chronic stress and a decrease in psychological well-being [19]. One variable that has not been considered in the study and may be some impact is the degree of isolation of the patients. The married status has a clear impact on the solitude of the persons, with divorced and widowed suffering stronger from social isolation. One suggested therapy is the use of pets as surrogares for social interaction [3]. Other kinds of non-pharmacological therapies that have proved some degree of success are gardening [13,23].

Regarding the influence of inflamation biomarkers, the IL-6, IL-1beta and the TNF -a have been previously associated with the regulation of the synaptic transmission, and neural plasticity. However, there is not a strong consensus around this issue. The preliminary results in this study confirm the association of IL-6 and TNF-a, and the absence of BDNF with depression in adults. However, standard treatments for depression do not include any therapy targeting systemic inflamation which may have some effect as far as they may reduce systemic stress.

5 Conclusions and Future Work

This study assessed which socio-demographic factors and inflammatory biomarkers were crucial in significantly influencing depressive versus healthy subjects. We found that there were significant differences in subjects who had higher levels of education, so that the more education they had (completed university and/or postgraduate studies) the more differences there were in depressed versus healthy subjects. The study also confirms that subjects who were married had less depression than subjects who were separated or divorced. In terms of inflammatory parameters, high IL6, TNFa and CAT are related to depression, while high levels of BDNF and GSH Total are protective for depression.

In conclusion, this study highlights the importance of variables that are related to higher education, accompanied lifestyle, a non-unemployed work status and some inflammatory biomarkers. For future studies it will be important to collect more related socio-demographic data that can provide more information, such as socio-economic status or lifestyle, and to expand the number of inflammatory biomarkers to analyse. A limitation of the study is its small sample size, which should be enlarged in future works built on top of this one.

References

1. Borsini, A., Zunszain, P.A., Thuret, S., Pariante, C.M.: The role of inflammatory cytokines as key modulators of neurogenesis. Trends Neurosci. **38**(3), 145–157 (2015)
2. Butters, M.A., et al.: Pathways linking late-life depression to persistent cognitive impairment and dementia. Dialogues Clin. Neurosci. **10**(3), 345–357 (2008)
3. Chakma, S.K., Islam, T.T., Shahjalal, Mitra, D.K.: Depression among pet owners and non-pet owners: a comparative cross-sectional study in Dhaka, Bangladesh. F1000Res, 10:574 (2021)
4. Chevance, A., et al.: Identifying outcomes for depression that matter to patients, informal caregivers, and health-care professionals: qualitative content analysis of a large international online survey. Lancet Psychiatry **7**(8), 692–702 (2020). https://doi.org/10.1016/S2215-0366(20)30191-7
5. Courtet, P., Giner, L., Seneque, M., Guillaume, S., Olie, E., Ducasse, D.: Neuroinflammation in suicide: toward a comprehensive model. World J. Biol. Psychiatry **17**(8), 564–586 (2015)
6. Ding, Y., Dai, J.: Advance in stress for depressive disorder. In: Fang, Y. (ed.) Depressive Disorders: Mechanisms, Measurement and Management, pp. 147–178. Springer, Singapore (2019). https://doi.org/10.1007/978-981-32-9271-0_8
7. Dunn, A.J.: Effects of cytokines and infections on brain neurochemistry. Clin. Neurosci. Res. **6**(1–2), 52–68 (2006)
8. Fusar-Poli, P., Nelson, B., Valmaggia, L., Yung, A.R., McGuire, P.K.: Comorbid depressive and anxiety disorders in 509 individuals with an at-risk mental state: impact on psychopathology and transition to psychosis. Schizophr. Bull. **40**(1), 120–131 (2012)
9. Hiles, S.A., Baker, A.L., de Malmanche, T., Attia, J.: Interleukin-6, c-reactive protein and interleukin-10 after antidepressant treatment in people with depression: a meta-analysis. Psychol. Med. **42**(10), 2015–2026 (2012)
10. Hudson, C.G.: Socioeconomic status and mental illness: tests of the social causation and selection hypotheses. Am. J. Orthopsychiatry **75**(1), 3–18 (2005)
11. Humphreys, K.L., LeMoult, J., Wear, J.G., Piersiak, H.A., Lee, A., Gotlib, I.H.: Child maltreatment and depression: a meta-analysis of studies using the childhood trauma questionnaire. Child Abuse Neglect **102**, 104361 (2020)
12. Kessler, R.C., Bromet, E.J.: The epidemiology of depression across cultures. Ann. Rev. Public Health **34**(1), 119–138 (2013)
13. Way Inn Koay and Denise Dillon. Community gardening: Stress, well-being, and resilience potentials. Int. J. Environ. Res. Public Health **17**(18) (2020)

14. Kuehner, C.: Why is depression more common among women than among men? Lancet Psychiatry **4**(2), 146–158 (2017)
15. Lewis, S.J., et al.: The epidemiology of trauma and post-traumatic stress disorder in a representative cohort of young people in England and wales. Lancet Psychiatry **6**(3), 247–256 (2019)
16. Mayer, S.E., et al.: The roles of comorbidity and trauma exposure and its timing in shaping HPA axis patterns in depression. Psychoneuroendocrinology **120**, 104776 (2020)
17. Nouri, F., Feizi, A., Keshteli, A.H., Roohafza, H., Afshar, H., Adibi, P.: Personality traits are differently associated with depression and anxiety: evidence from applying bivariate multiple binary logistic regression on a large sample of general adults. Psychiatria Danubina **31**(4), 448–456 (2019)
18. Ownby, R.L., Crocco, E., Acevedo, A., John, V., Loewenstein, D.: Depression and risk for Alzheimer disease: Systematic review, meta-analysis, and metaregression analysis. Arch. Gen. Psychiatry **63**(5), 530 (2006)
19. Paul, K.I., Moser, K.: Unemployment impairs mental health: meta-analyses. J. Vocat. Behav. **74**(3), 264–282 (2009)
20. Peng, S., Li, W., Lv, L., Zhang, Z., Zhan, X.: BDNF as a biomarker in diagnosis and evaluation of treatment for schizophrenia and depression. Discov. Med. **26**, 127–136 (2018)
21. Petralia, M.C., et al.: The cytokine network in the pathogenesis of major depressive disorder. close to translation? Autoimmunity Rev. **19**(5), 102504 (2020)
22. Simon, R.W.: Revisiting the relationships among gender, marital status, and mental health. Am. J. Sociol. **107**(4), 1065–1096 (2002)
23. Torres, E.R., Sampselle, C.M., Ronis, D.L., Neighbors, H.W., Gretebeck, K.A.: Gardening/yard work and depressive symptoms in African Americans. Arch. Psychiatr. Nurs., **30**(2), 155–161 (2016)
24. Wang, X., Ong, D., Auerbach, R.P., Yao, S.: Cognitive vulnerability to major depression: view from the intrinsic network and cross-network interactions. Harv. Rev. Psychiatry **24**(3), 188–201 (2016)
25. Zhao, G., Liu, X.: Neuroimmune advance in depressive disorder. In: Fang, Y. (ed.) Depressive Disorders: Mechanisms, Measurement and Management, pp. 85–98. Springer, Singapore (2019). https://doi.org/10.1007/978-981-32-9271-0_4

Unveiling HIV-1 U Sequences: Shedding Light Through Transfer Learning on Genomic Spectrograms

Ana Guerrero-Tamayo[1(✉)], Borja Sanz Urquijo[1], Isabel Olivares[2], María-Dolores Moragues Tosantos[3], Concepción Casado[2], and Iker Pastor-López[1]

[1] Faculty of Engineering - University of Deusto, Avenida de las Universidades, 24, Bilbao 48007, Biscay, Spain
ana.guerrero@deusto.es

[2] National Microbiology Center (NMC) - Instituto de Salud Carlos III (ISCIII), Ctra. de Pozuelo, 28, Majadahonda 28222, Madrid, Spain

[3] Faculty of Medicine and Nursing - University of the Basque Country UPV/EHU, Barrio Sarriena s/n, Leioa 48940, Biscay, Spain

Abstract. The human immunodeficiency virus type 1 (HIV-1) has caused one of the most pernicious pandemics in recent history. The current difficulty with effective treatments and vaccines is largely attributed to its high mutation rate and multiple complex genetic recombination events, resulting in various subtypes. Some fragments and complete sequences do not match any subtype (referred to as U, unclassified or unclassifiable). Further understanding of these sequences and fragments may provide insights into the phylogeny of HIV-1 and its viral evolution. By applying transfer learning to a pre-trained CNN (VGG-16) using all the genomic spectrograms of all complete HIV-1 genomic sequences, we achieved a total hit rate of 98.27%, with the CNN primarily focusing on detecting the recombinant features, mainly in the 5'LTR and 3'LTR regions. We also generated a phylogenetic tree of all complete HIV-1 sequences. Subsequently, we compared subtype U interpretability patterns with phylogenetic distance, yielding valuable information not only about subtype U but also about intersubtype parentage and their common and distinct genomic components. Interpretability patterns coincided with multiple microbiological evidences in 60.870% of the sequences, were inconclusive in 34.783%, and only one controversial sequence was detected (4.348%). Compared to multiple sequence alignment algorithms, our methodology is faster, requires low computing power, and does not necessitate manual adjustments.

Keywords: HIV-1 · Genetic Recombination · U Sequences · Deep Learning · Convolutional Neural Network · Interpretability Patterns · Mathematical Patterns

---

University of Deusto - Research Training Grants Program.

H. Quintián et al. (Eds.): HAIS 2024, LNAI 14857, pp. 49–60, 2025.
https://doi.org/10.1007/978-3-031-74183-8_5

1 Introduction

Human immunodeficiency virus type 1 (HIV-1) is responsible of one of the worst pandemics in recent story. Its strong variability due to its high rate of mutations and genetic recombination phenomena has a decisive influence on the lack of effective treatments and vaccines [24,26]. This changeability results in multiple subtypes and classifying a sequence in any of them can be complex and controversial [3,21].

HIV-1 is classified into four groups named M, N, O and P. Group M, the most globally widespread, is divided into nine pure subtypes (non-recombinant) designed as A, B, C, D, F, G, H, J and K. Circulating recombinant forms (CRFs) are those recombinant subtypes currently circulating [2], whose recombination points are common and perfectly described. These CRF sequences must be identified in at least three epidemiologically non-related individuals [20]. The nomenclature of each CRF subtype refers to the recombined subtypes involved. CRF02_AG means genetic recombination between subtypes A and G [12]. Complex recombination phenomena (cpx) is the designation of mosaic recombinants of multiple subtypes. CRF04_cpx is a mixture between A, G, H, K and U [18]. Non-CRF recombinant nomenclature refers to recombinated subtypes also. Non-CRF recombinant subtype A1GH, means a complex recombination phenomena between subtype A1, G and H [15].

This tricky HIV-1 subtype classification makes necessary to review nomenclatures regularly by expert committees. For instance, firstly named E subtype sequences, were finally renamed as CRF01_AE (recombinant between A and E subtypes) [4]. And formerly called F3 subtype was reissued as K subtype [8]. Some authors consider that CRF02_AG should be a non-recombinant subtype and G subtype as a recombinant of A, J and 02_AG [11].

Some fragments and complete sequences do not match with any subtype. These are U subtype (unclassified). If a recombinant contains unclassified (or unclassifiable) regions, U is included in the name. There are two general circumstances for the assignment of "U". One is when the sequence is so divergent from previously-classified sequences that a subtype cannot be assigned based on current reference sequences. The second situation is when the sequence is of such poor quality that the subtype cannot be determined with any reasonable certainty. There are 23 U subtype complete sequences. And about ten 10 CRFs subtypes contain U fragments. Further knowledge of these sequences and fragments may provide insight into the phylogeny of HIV-1 and its viral evolution.

This article presents the results of an in-depth analysis of the previous work conducted by Guerrero-Tamayo et al. [10], on the most mysterious HIV-1 U sequences, using a methodology based on genomic spectrograms, Deep Learning technologies, and interpretability with the aim not only of demonstrating the robustness and biological coherence of the obtained interpretability patterns, but also of contributing knowledge about the origin and phylogeny of these U sequences based on the interpretability results.

2 Materials and Methods

All experiments were ran in this equipment: Processing Unit: Intel(R) Xeon(R) Gold 5220R CPU @ 2.20 GHz. Installed RAM: 256 GB usable. Operative System: Windows 10 Education. Version: 21H1. GPU: NVIDIA RTX A6000. Total memory: 179451 MB. VRAM: 48571 MB.

Our methodology consisted of three phases described in Fig. 1.

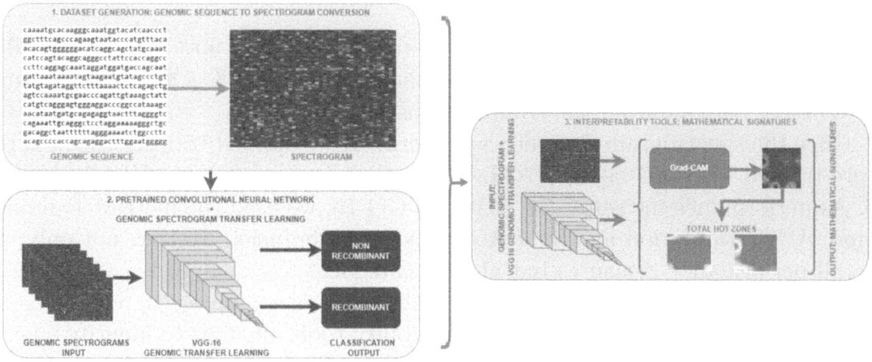

Fig. 1. Methodology

The first phase is a conversion of genomic sequences to biologically-coherent images, this is, genomic spectrograms. The x-axis corresponds to the concept of nucleotide position, so the total length of the x-axis is the length of the genomic sequence. A complete HIV-1 sequence contains approximately 10,000 nucleotides, making this the length of the x-axis. The y-axis represents the frequency range, in this case, from 0 to 0.5 Hz. The z-axis is the sum of the Fast Fourier Transform (FFT) values for each of the four types of nucleotides (A, C, G, and T). This means:

$$S = S_a + S_g + S_c + S_t \tag{1}$$

In order to work with two-dimensional spectrograms, the z-axis is assimilated to a "jet" color palette [16].

HIV-1 genome sequences were downloaded from Los Alamos National Laboratory HIV Database (all subtypes - complete genome) [15]. We generated the spectrogram dataset using Python, Scipy library, Spectrogram function [23]. In order to avoid biases and bad practices during the CNN training, we omitted axes, margins and any other elements that may distort the operation of the network. So, the image is limited to the spectrogram [5,6].

To build the dataset, we marked all CRF sequences as recombinant and non-CRF sequences as non-recombinant. We then randomly assigned these sequences to the training, validation, and test folders based on the guidelines specified in Table 1.

Table 1. Dataset Structure

Dataset	Recombinant	Non-Recombinant	TOTAL
Training	1,903 (16.89%)	9,364 (83.11%)	11,267
Validation	338 (17.01%)	1,649 (82.99%)	1,987
Test	150 (50.00%)	150 (50.00%)	300
TOTAL	**2,391**	**11,163**	**13,554**

As illustrated in Table 1, the test set distribution (50% / 50%) is intentionally different from that of the training and validation sets (17% / 83%) to identify underfitting biases during the training phases [9].

Once the spectrogram dataset was generated, we applied transfer learning to a pre-trained VGG-16 using MATLAB 2021b, which we named HIV-1_VGG-16. As performance measures for HIV-1_VGG-16, we used the metrics Training Time, AUC, Validation and Test Accuracy, and Confusion Matrix, not only as overall performance measures but also by category.

Then, we applied Grad-CAM to assess the most relevant areas in recombinant featuring of an HIV-1 sequence. Interpretability tools allow us to identify where the CNN looks to decide the recombinant feature of a sequence (hot zones). Grad-CAM is our tool of choice for visual comparison of interpretability patterns due to its easiest adaptation to human eye.

We calculated global interpretability patterns of non-recombinant and recombinant sequences as an arithmetic summation of the score maps (numerical vectors) using MATLAB 2021b.

To generate the phylogenetic tree, we downloaded the multiple alignment of all HIV-1 sequences up to 2020 from the Los Alamos Database. This multiple alignment includes a single sequence per patient and eliminates very similar sequences and problematic ones [15]. We generated the phylogenetic tree from this multiple alignment using MATLAB Bioinformatics Toolbox. On the basis of the phylogenetic position of all U subtype sequences in the HIV-1 complete sequences tree, we studied their closeness relationships and their interpretability patterns. This analysis was complemented with data from samples registered in the Los Alamos Sequence Database [15].

Our methodology enables deepen knowledge of HIV-1 genetic recombination phenomena. It also provides a way to characterize the virus through its interpretability patterns. By analyzing the results obtained within the U subtype, we were able to extract additional information from the perspective of recombinant featuring. Understanding HIV-1 genetic recombination can contribute to understanding HIV-1 viral evolution itself.

A better knowledge of both complete U sequences and U fragments detected in multiple CRFs will allow us to establish more precisely how the viral evolution of HIV-1 has been and how it is. The use of Deep Learning tools for this purpose may provide new approaches to elucidate knowledge.

3 Results and Discussion

3.1 Global Results of the Experiment

After testing multiple hyperparameter configurations on a pre-trained VGG-16, Table 2 shows the hyperparameters for the optimal configuration, as well as their results across all performance metrics. The top row in Confusion Matrix Results corresponds to the non-recombinant category (hit - error) and the bottom row to the recombinant category (error - hit).

Table 2. Performance Metrics Results

CNN	Hyperparameters	Validation Accuracy	Training Time	Training Time per Epoch	Test Accuracy	Confusion Matrix Results	AUC
VGG-16	Learning Rate: 0.0001 Batchsize: 52 Epochs: 10	92.90%	15 min 59 sec	1 min 35.90 sec	94.00%	143 - 7 11 - 139	0.9888

Multiple alignment techniques and algorithms are statistical approximations that require complex expert manual adjustments [7]. The execution time of these algorithms increases quadratically depending on the number of sequences and their average length.

For comparative purposes, we conducted multiple tests using traditional multiple sequence alignment methods, employing the most common algorithms (ClustalW and MUSCLE) on the same equipment. Due to computational limitations, it was not possible to complete any of the tests conducted, highlighting the effectiveness of our methodology in terms of computing efficiency and resource management for handling the 13,554 complete genomes of HIV-1 available.

HIV-1_VGG-16 hit rate detecting recombinant feature reached 98.27% on the total of the 13,554 complete HIV-1 sequences (Table 3).

This CNN successfully classified 10,993 HIV-1 complete sequences of the total of 11,163 non-recombinant sequences (hit rate of 98.48%). Of the total of 2,391 complete recombinant sequences, HIV-1_VGG-16 correctly identified 2,326 as recombinants (hit rate of 97.28%). We must take into account that it previously learned with sequences of training and validation sets, so these have higher hit rate than test set.

Table 3. HIV-1_VGG-16 Error Rates

	Non-recombinant		Recombinant	
	No.	%	No.	%
Errors	170	1.52	65	2.72%
Successes	10,993	98.48	2,326	97.28%
TOTAL	**11,163**	**100.00%**	**2,391**	**100.00%**

Figure 2 shows interpretability patterns for the two categories. Figure 2a is the result of the mathematical superposition of the 11,163 non-recombinant patterns and Fig. 2b is the recombinant global pattern of the 2,391 recombinant sequences. As shown in Fig. 2, the total hot zones are perfectly defined and distinguishable.

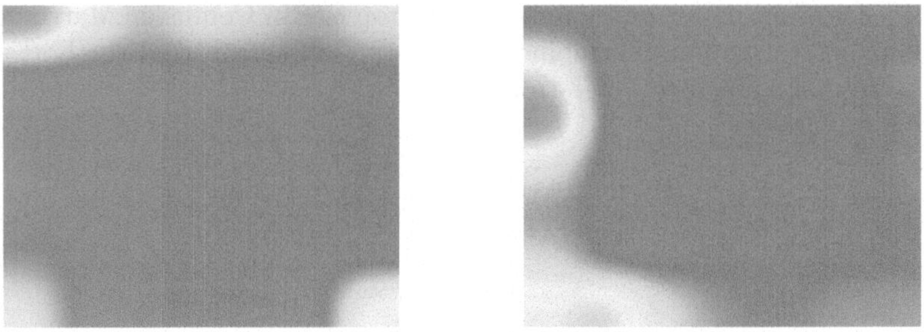

(a) Non-recombinant Total Hot Zones (b) Recombinant Total Hot Zones

Fig. 2. Total Interpretability Patterns by Category

Considering subtypes with over a 15% error rate and containing more than 15 complete sequences, we found that "U sequences" has the highest error rate (39.13%), compared to the second subtype with the highest error rate at 25.25%. The high error rate of U sequences suggests that there may be recombination phenomena that can help, not only to propose a review of this subtype sequences, but also to extract similarities through their interpretability patterns by low-computing algorithms. We analyzed in depth interpretability patterns related with recombinant feature of each U subtype sequence.

Our results were biologically consistent and robust. We obtained not only valuable information about U sequences, but we acquired knowledge of inter-subtype parentage and their common and distinct genomic components. All this with a fast, efficient and low computing methodology. Following subsections describe each level of homology between interpretability patterns and biological evidences.

3.2 Conclusive Biological Coherence

The cases of high homology among the classification results of HIV-1_VGG-16, the interpretability-driven hot zones, and the phylogeny, along with expert literature in the microbiological and virological field, correspond to EF029066, EF029067, EF029068, EF029069, FJ388921, HM215249, HM215251, JF683772, JX140679, KY392775, MN153489, MN153492, MN736701 and MN736702.

Below, we provide a more detailed presentation of the most representative cases.

- **HM215249 and HM215251**. HIV-1_VGG-16 classified these sequences as non-recombinant with confidence scores above 99%. Their scores were the maximum of all U sequences. Grad-CAM patterns were almost identical. These U sequences, HM215249 and HM215251, were the unique components of their clade. Quesnel-Vallières et al. considered that HIV-1 isolates infecting patients TV721 (HM215249) and TV749 (HM215251) cannot be considered CRFs. Our results confirmed this point [19]. Therefore, there is a clear logic in our results and the virological evidence.
- **JF683772**. Subtype 01G MN486045 was the only sister of U sequence JF683772 (Patient Code: CY223 - unique sequence). JF683772 was classified as recombinant by HIV-1_VGG-16 (trust level over 75%). JF683772 patterns were described similar to subtypes CRF02_AG and CRF63_02A6 (recombination between CRF02_AG and A6) [1]. This fact endorsed JF683772 recombinant feature. Some studies pointed the recombinant feature of this sequence [13], suggesting a recombination between A1, G, and H [22]. Interpretability patterns were consistent with this.
- **EF029066, EF029067, EF029068 and EF029069 and their related sequences FJ388921 and KY392775**. This case was particularly interesting because we detected a possible phenomenon of hidden recombination in the intrapatient sequences.

FJ388921 (Patient Code: CY090) [14], EF029066 (Patient Code: H10986) and KY392775 (patient code = NGSID12, intrapatient with partial sequences KY365200 and KY365214) [22] were three U direct relatives. Table 4 shows classification results. According to HIV-1_VGG-16, FJ388921 had a strong non-recombinant component, with standard interpretability patterns. EF029066 (classified as non-recombinant) had the lowest confidence score of all U subtype (under 52%). And HIV-1_VGG-16 classified its intrapatient sequences (EF029067, EF029068, EF029069) as recombinant, with medium confidence levels, around 70-75%. EF029066 interpretability patterns were coherent with global non - recombinant hot zones. EF029067, EF029068 and EF029069 had close determinant areas, fairly diffuse in EF029067 and EF029068. Their patterns did not particularly match global recombinant hot zones. KY392775 was classified as non-recombinant just under 90%. However, interpretability patterns were slightly controversial with non-recombinant ones.

FJ388921, EF029066 and KY392775 interpretability patterns were similar. This correlates with their phylogenetic positions. These three sequences shared clade with subtype FK MH705156. AJ249235 and AJ249239 are subtype K.

EF029066, EF029067, EF029068 and EF029069 are intrapatient sequences (Patient ID H10986). HIV-1_VGG-16 classified EF029066 as non-recombinant, but its reliability level was minimum (near 51.50%). EF029067, EF029068 and EF029069 were classified as recombinant. Their interpretability patterns were highly similar and divergent from EF029066. The intrapatient feature of these four sequences unabled to analyze deeply their phylogenetic relationship. But according to the results obtained, there was a clear recombination phenomenon. EF029067, EF029068 and EF029069 decision areas were

Table 4. U Sequences FJ388921, EF029066, EF029067, EF029068, EF029069 and KY392775 Results

Sequence ID	Classification	Confidence Score	Grad-CAM
FJ388921	Non-recombinant	91.853%	
EF029066	Non-recombinant	51.424%	
EF029067	Recombinant	76.708%	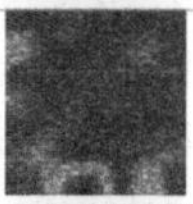
EF029068	Recombinant	69.344%	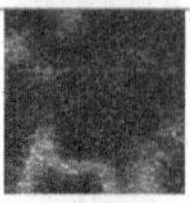
EF029069	Recombinant	73.163%	
KY392775	Non-recombinant	89.344%	

similar to several sequences of different recombinant subtypes. This is coherent with HIV-1_VGG-16 classification. Most similar hot areas corresponded to those of CRF26_A5U FM877782, and to a lesser extent to CRF02_AG AB286862, subtype CRF11_cpx AJ291718 and CRF13_cpx DQ845386. Their confidence scores were higher than 90%, except for CRF11_cpx AJ291718 (around 52%). The striking similarity level between these different subtypes suggests the existence of genomic components common to several different recombinant lineages, related with these three U subtype sequences.

Another point that requires further research is the possible relationship between low confidence scores and similarity between interpretability patterns (case of AJ291718).

Van Der Hoek et al. cataloged EF029066 and its intrapatient U sequences EF029067, EF029068 and EF029069 as a new subtype, or a new branch of subtype K [25]. This supports EF029066 classification as non-recombinant. EF029066 low reliability level and the similar recombinant hot zones of EF029067, EF029068 and EF029069 make it necessary to search for recombination events in these sequences.

A sister clade including subtype F2 sequences and the resemblance between EF029066 and these F2 sequences interpretability patterns suggest certain common features between them. Subtype F2 sequences KU749420, and especially AJ249237 and AY371158 had strongly similar hot zones to EF029066. This endorses the non-recombinant classification of EF029066 by HIV-1_VGG-16. However, its low confidence-score and recombinant sister sequences made us consider the presence of recombinant factors embedded.

3.3 Non-conclusive Biological Coherence

Analyzing the case of U sequences AB485664, AB485665, KP718920, KY392773, KY392774, KY392780, MH078559, and MK095236, homology among the classification results of HIV-1_VGG-16, the interpretability-driven hot zones, and the phylogeny, along with expert literature in the microbiological and virological fields, was rather inconclusive. Sequence AY046058 was the most controversial case.

Next, we provide a detailed analysis of the most significant cases.

- **AY046058, KY392780, MH078559, and MK095236**. MK095236 was classified as possibly recombinant with some uncertainty, while AY046058 and MH078559 were confidently non-recombinant. KY392780 showed similarity to both non - recombinant and recombinant sequences but with low confidence. These U sequences exhibited unique patterns, potentially indicating a shared element responsible for their non-recombinant status despite resemblances to recombinant sequences. Further research is needed to elucidate this common factor. Additionally, there are intriguing relationships between certain CRF sequences and U sequences, suggesting potential ancestral connections. The classification of AY046058 remains contentious due to its documented mixed classification [17].
- **KP718920**. Sequence KP718920 (patient code 469_66 - unique sequence) was labeled non-recombinant due to matching interpretability patterns with global non-recombinant sequences, particularly subtype F2 and A1. Most related sequences are subtype CRF11_cpx, except one (KR017778, subtype 11A1). KP718920's structure indicates a mix of CRF36_cpx, CRF11_cpx, CRF02_AG, and U. Its association with CRF11_cpx and CRF13_cpx suggests a potential for non-recombinant classification, as observed with similar sequences like CRF11_cpx KP718929, JF683802, and CRF13_cpx AY371154, hinting at hidden non-recombinant-like traits in their genomes. Further research is required to validate this hypothesis.

4 Conclusions

HIV-1_VGG-16 classifications as recombinant or non-recombinant and their corresponding patterns were phylogenetically coherent and consistent with sample data. And similarity level correlated with phylogenetic closeness.

Our results were coincident with multiple microbiological evidences, such is the case of EF029066, EF029067, EF029068, EF029069, FJ388921, HM215249, HM215251, JF683772, JX140679, KY392775, MN153489, MN153492, MN736701 and MN736702. Their interpretability patterns were consistent with phylogeny and multiple biological evidences (60.870% of the total U sequences). The 34.783% was rather inconclusive (AB485664, AB485665, KP718920, KY392773, KY392774, KY392780, MH078559 and MK095236). Sequence AY046058 was the most controversial case (4.348%).

We also were able to establish similarities between interpretability patterns of different subtypes whose sequences are phylogenetically close. This can help us to search for common genomic elements in the hot areas pointed by the CNN. Our results also reflected the leading role of genetic recombination in HIV-1 phylogeny.

Many of CRF cpx involved in this research contained subtype G sections. Engagement between subtypes U and G may denote some parentage level between them. And the possible recombinant origin of subtype G could influence U interpretability patterns.

Now we know where does the CNN look at to decide. Our next step is searching what exactly is seeing. MN736702 can significantly clarify this point. This sequence gave us the opportunity to make a direct comparison of both categories in a very specific genomic area (low frequencies of 5'LTR). Perhaps we can unravel those mathematical signatures that define a sequence as recombinant and better understand HIV-1 genetic recombination.

A deeper understanding of both U complete sequences and U fragments detected in multiple CRFs will allow to establish more precisely how HIV-1 viral evolution is. The use of Deep Learning tools for this purpose may provide new approaches to elucidate knowledge.

Our research is a demonstration of this point. Our methodology was alignment-free, much faster and low computing. And it did not need manual adjustments and multiple alignment.

We not only succeeded in demonstrating the robustness of our results in detecting the recombinant feature, but also in establishing homology between the CNN results and interpretability patterns with phylogeny and expert literature, even contributing interesting insights into the phylogenetic relationships of the U subtype, as well as potential hidden recombination events in these sequences.

By applying an alternative methodology, we deepen in the knowledge of U sequences, which are more problematic for classification. And more unknown.

Data Availability. The complete HIV-1 phylogenetic tree and the dataset are available at DOI: 10.21227/2917-1s55.

References

1. Baryshev, P.B., Bogachev, V.V., Gashnikova, N.M.: HIV-1 genetic diversity in Russia: CRF63_02A1, a new HIV Type 1 genetic variant spreading in Siberia. AIDS Res. Hum. Retroviruses **30**(6), 592–597 (2014)
2. Bbosa, N., Kaleebu, P., Ssemwanga, D.: HIV subtype diversity worldwide. Curr. Opin. HIV AIDS **14**(3), 153–160 (2019)
3. Camacho, R.: The significance of subtype-related genetic variability: controversies and unanswered questions. In: Antiretroviral Resistance in Clinical Practice (2006)

4. Carr, J.K., et al.: Full-length sequence and mosaic structure of a Human Immunodeficiency Virus Type 1 isolate from Thailand. J. Virol. **70**(9), 5935–5943 (1996)
5. Catalá, O.D.T., et al.: Bias analysis on public X-ray image datasets of pneumonia and COVID-19 patients. IEEE Access **9**, 42370–42383 (2021)
6. Chen, L., et al.: Hidden bias in the DUD-E dataset leads to misleading performance of deep learning in structure-based virtual screening. PLoS ONE **14**(8), e0220113 (2019)
7. Gaschen, B., et al.: Diversity considerations in HIV-1 vaccine selection. Science **296**(5577), 2354–2360 (2002)
8. Geretti, A.M.: HIV-1 subtypes: epidemiology and significance for HIV management. Curr. Opin. Infect. Dis. **19**(1), 1–7 (2006)
9. Goodfellow, I., Bengio, Y., Courville, A.: Deep Learning. MIT Press (2016)
10. Guerrero-Tamayo, A., Urquijo, B.S., Casado, C., Moragues-Tosantos, M.D., Olivares, I., Pastor-López, I.: Discovering mathematical patterns behind HIV-1 genetic recombination: a new methodology to identify viral features. IEEE Access (2023)
11. Hemelaar, J.: The origin and diversity of the HIV-1 pandemic. Trends Mol. Med. **18**(3), 182–192 (2012)
12. Howard, T.M., Rasheed, S.: Genomic structure and nucleotide sequence analysis of a new HIV Type 1 subtype A strain from Nigeria. AIDS Res. Hum. Retroviruses **12**(15), 1413–1425 (1996)
13. Kousiappa, I., et al.: Molecular characterization of HIV type 1 strains from newly diagnosed patients in Cyprus (2007–2009) recovers multiple clades including unique recombinant strains and lack of transmitted drug resistance. AIDS Res. Hum. Retroviruses **27**(11), 1183–1199 (2011)
14. Kousiappa, I., Van De Vijver, D.A., Kostrikis, L.G.: Near full-length genetic analysis of HIV sequences derived from Cyprus: evidence of a highly polyphyletic and evolving infection. AIDS Res. Hum. Retroviruses **25**(8), 727–740 (2009)
15. Laboratory, L.A.N.: The HIV database. https://www.hiv.lanl.gov/ (2023). Accessed 09 Jun 2023
16. MATLAB: MATLAB colormaps tutorial. https://matplotlib.org/stable/tutorials/colors/colormaps.html (2023). Accessed 09 Jun 2023
17. Paraskevis, D., et al.: Molecular characterization of a complex, recombinant Human Immunodeficiency Virus Type 1 (HIV-1) isolate (A/G/J/K/?): evidence to support the existence of a novel HIV-1 subtype. J. Gen. Virol. **82**(10), 2509–2514 (2001)
18. Paraskevis, D., Magiorkinis, M., Vandamme, A.M., Kostrikis, L.G., Hatzakis, A.: Re-analysis of Human Immunodeficiency Virus Type 1 isolates from Cyprus and Greece, initially designated subtype I, reveals a unique complex A/G/H/K/? Mosaic pattern. J. Gen. Virol. **82**(3), 575–580 (2001)
19. Quesnel-Vallières, M., et al.: Novel HIV-1 recombinant forms in antenatal cohort, Montreal, Quebec. Canada. Emerging Infectious Diseases **17**(2), 271 (2011)
20. Rivas, P., et al.: Tratamiento antirretroviral según tipos y subtipos del virus de la inmunodeficiencia humana. Enferm. Infecc. Microbiol. clín.(Ed. impr.), 29–33 (2006)
21. Robertson, D.L., et al.: HIV-1 nomenclature proposal. Science **288**(5463), 55–55 (2000)
22. Rodgers, M.A., Wilkinson, E., Vallari, A., McArthur, C., Sthreshley, L., Brennan, C.A., Cloherty, G., de Oliveira, T.: Sensitive next-generation sequencing method reveals deep genetic diversity of HIV-1 in the Democratic Republic of the Congo. J. Virol. **91**(6), e01841-16 (2017)
23. SciPy: Scipy v1.11.4 manual. https://docs.scipy.org/doc/scipy/reference/generated/scipy.signal.spectrogram.html (2023). Accessed 09 Jun 2023

24. Smyth, R.P., Davenport, M.P., Mak, J.: The origin of genetic diversity in HIV-1. Virus Res. **169**(2), 415–429 (2012)
25. Van Der Hoek, L., Pollakis, G., Lukashov, V.V., Jebbink, M.F., Jeeninga, R.E., Bakker, M., Dukers, N., Jurriaans, S., Paxton, W.A., Back, N.K., et al.: Characterization of an HIV-1 group M variant that is distinct from the known subtypes. AIDS Res. Hum. Retroviruses **23**(3), 466–470 (2007)
26. Williamson, C., Martin, D.P.: HIV-1 genetic diversity. HIV/AIDS in South Africa **2**, 117–126 (2010)

Model to Early Detection of Autism Spectrum Disorder Through Opinion Mining Approach

José Roberto Grande-Ramírez, Eduardo Roldán-Reyes(✉), Jesús Delgado-Maciel, Guillermo Cortes-Robles, and Ramiro Meza-Palacios

Tecnológico Nacional de México TecNM/Campus Orizaba, 94320 Veracruz, México
{roberto.gr,eduardo.rr,jesus.dm,guillermo.cr,
ramiro.mp}@orizaba.tecnm.mx

Abstract. Autism spectrum disorders (ASD) encompass a range of complex neurodevelopmental conditions characterized by challenges in communication, social interaction, and the presence of repetitive behaviors. The early and accurate diagnosis of ASD is crucial for optimizing outcomes and enhancing the quality of life for individuals and their families. The World health organization (WHO) reports that approximately 1 in 100 children are affected by ASD. Traditional diagnostic methods, such as the Autism diagnostic interview-revised (ADI-R) and the Autism diagnostic observation schedule (ADOS-2), provide structured and reliable evaluations. However, integrating advanced techniques such as Opinion mining (OM) from Machine learning (ML) framework offers promising enhancements to current diagnostic practices. OM leverages Natural language processing (NLP) to analyze textual data and discern human perceptions and emotions, potentially uncovering subtle indicators of ASD that standard methods may overlook. In this research, we propose an innovative diagnostic model combining OM with ML classifiers, including Support vector machines (SVM), K-nearest neighbors (KNN), and Naïve Bayes (NB). The results indicate that the KNN classifier exhibits superior accuracy with 88.78% in category 2, SVM showed the second-best performance with an accuracy of 86.75% in category 1, and NB had its best result in category 3 with an accuracy of 83.44%. This interdisciplinary approach underscores the value of integrating scientific advances with clinical experience, paving the way for more accurate and earlier detection of ASD.

Keywords: Autism spectrum disorder · Opinion mining · Diagnosis · Support vector machine · K-nearest neighbor · Naïve Bayes

1 Introduction

Autism spectrum disorders (ASD) are varied and complex conditions that are characterized by some degree of difficulty in communication and social interaction, and repetitive behaviors may also occur [1]. An efficient, comprehensive approach is required to address the issue and improve the quality of life of the person involved and their family. According to information from the World health organization (WHO), approximately 1 in 100 children has autism, and the characteristics can be detected in the first year and then show signs of autism between 18 and 24 months of age or even older late [2].

H. Quintián et al. (Eds.): HAIS 2024, LNAI 14857, pp. 61–72, 2025.
https://doi.org/10.1007/978-3-031-74183-8_6

Different approaches have been proposed to detect and diagnose ASD, and most of them depend on the experts and specialists who applied different instruments based on surveys to a prior diagnosis. However, these surveys usually take time to apply, and most included questions that can be ambiguous or difficult to respond. Opinion mining (OM) is a powerful technique based on specialized algorithms that attempt to decipher human perceptions and emotions through texts. Through advanced natural language processing (NLP) and machine learning (ML) techniques it allows organizations to extract potentially useful knowledge that can influence decision-making [3, 4]. OM has proven effective in the health sector, as shown in some works related to coronavirus (COVID-19) [5, 6], diabetes [7], vaccinations [8], and drugs [9].

In this research, a corroboration proposal is made through the OM process to obtain a more efficient diagnosis of ASD by the specialist. In current clinical practice, accurately diagnosing autism spectrum disorder remains a significant challenge [10]. This article is presented in four sections. Section two describes the works where models related to this approach are proposed: ASD-MO. Section three explains the proposed model and the results clearly and precisely. Finally, the conclusion, discussion, and open challenges are summarized in section four.

2 Related Works

The scientific community knows that the theoretical and methodological basis of the research guarantees that the contribution is helpful to the knowledge and development of the field of study. The connected papers tool was used to filter the related works, which generates a visual graph of articles related to the field of study. The key sentence "Autism spectrum disorder detection and classification" was entered, and the article by Loganathan et al. 2023 [11] was chosen as a reference due to the results highlighted in his writing (Fig. 1).

The search was refined, simplified, and updated with research work, as shown in Table 1. Nomenclature: Support vector machine (SVM), Decision tree (DT), K-nearest neighbor (KNN), Naïve Bayes (NB), Random forest (RF), Artificial neural network (ANN), Convolutional neural network (CNN), Deep neural network (DNN), Deep neuro fuzzy network (DNFN), Recurrent neural network (RNN), Deep learning (DL), Logistic regression (LR), Simple logistic (SL), Linear discriminant analysis (LDA), Bidirectional encoder representations from transformer (BERT), Modified grasshopper optimization algorithm - Random forest (MGOA-RF), Chaotic Henry gas solubility optimization (CHGSO), Autism brain imaging data exchange (ABIDE), Feedback-Henry gas optimization (FHGO), Box neighborhood search algorithm (BNSA), Iterative classifier optimizer (ICO), Random Tree (RT), Flexible discriminant analysis (FDA), Mixture discriminant analysis (MDA), Penalized discriminant analysis (PDA), Classification and regression trees (CART), Multi class classifier (MCC), Multilayer perceptron (MLP), Type 2 fuzzy and cuckoo search (T2FCS), Feature transformation methods (FTM), One Rule (OneR), Sequential minimal optimization (SMO), Matthews correlation coefficient (MCC), Logistic model tree (LMT), Long short-term memory (LSTM), Adam war strategy optimization (AWSO), War strategy optimization (WAO), Deep belief network (DBN), Region of interest (ROI), Gated recurrent units (GRUs), electroencephalogram (EGG), Stochastic gradient descent (SGD), Weighted average ensemble (WAE).

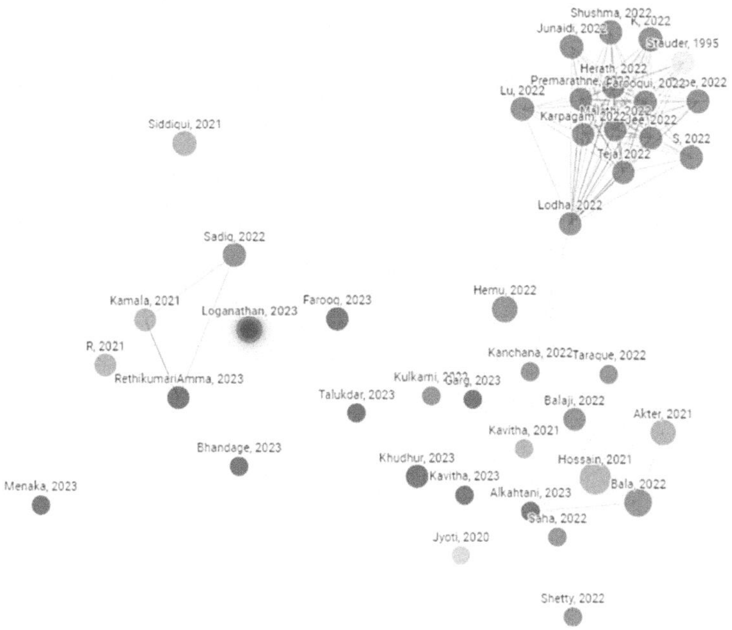

Fig. 1. Graph of similar articles in the study field of ASD detection and classification.

Table 1. Proposed models for ASD detection.

Autor/Year	Model/Approach	Classifiers/Methods	Accuracy/Best result
[12] 2019	The method includes several FTM, including log, Z-score, and sine functions	FTM: Log, Z-score, and Sine Classifiers: Adaboost, FDA, C5.0, LDA, MDA, PDA, SVM, and CART	The authors found 100% results in some cases
[13] 2020	Analysis and detection of ASD using ML techniques	NB, SVM, LR, KNN and CNN	CNN = 99.53%, adults
[14] 2020	A robust method for early diagnosis of autism of ASD from EGG signal	SVM and KNN	SVM = 90.57%

(continued)

Table 1. (*continued*)

Autor/Year	Model/Approach	Classifiers/Methods	Accuracy/Best result
[15] 2021	Detecting autism spectrum disorder using ML techniques	OneR, PART, JRip (RIPPER), Ridor, Nneg, NB, LibSVM, MLP, LR, SL, SMO, IBK, Kstar, LWL, Bagging, ICO, LB, MCC, RAB, J48 (C4.5), LMT, NBTree, RF, RT, Simple CART, SysFor	MLP = 100%
[16] 2021	Recommendation learning system model for children with autism	DNN_Clustering_SGD, SVM, CNN and ANN	DNN = 98.81%
[17] 2022	The suggested model uses an ML approach that identifies risk factors and impacts the prediction of ASD	RF and XGBoost	RF = 97.70% XGB = 97.70%
[18] 2022	This approach is to train and validate various models and conduct a comparative analysis based on various performance metrics	DT, RF, SVM, KNN and GRUs	RF = 100% GRUs = 100%
[19] 2023	Classification model that can predict the probability of ASD with the highest degree of accuracy using ML methods	DT, SVM, KNN, NB, LR and RF	DT = 100%
[20] 2023	Model detects ASD in children and adults using ML	SVM and LR	SVM = 99% and 81%
[21] 2023	ASD model with FHGO-based DNFN	ROI extraction, T2FCS filter, DNFN, and FHGO	93.3%
[22] 2023	The AWSO algorithm is modeled by assimilating the Adam optimizer with the WAO enabled DBN	ROI - Nisotropic diffusion, BNSA, ABIDE-I and ABIDE-II	92.4%

(*continued*)

Table 1. (*continued*)

Autor/Year	Model/Approach	Classifiers/Methods	Accuracy/Best result
[11] 2023	A hybrid model using ResNet101 and a Bidirectional Gated Recurrent Unit (Bi-GRU) with a WAE	CHGSO, SVM, KNN and MGOA-RF	Hybrid ensemble model = 98%
[23] 2024	Enhancing ASD detection accuracy: a combined approach of ML and DL models with NLP	DT, XGBoost, KNN, RNN, LSTM, Bi-LSTM, BERT-Base and BERTweet	BERTweet = 88%
[24] 2024	The model studies and highlights the distinctive nature of nonverbal behavior in ASD	SVM	79.5% and 68.8%
This article 2024	Model to early detection of ASD through OM approach	OM process, SVM, KNN and NB	KNN = 88.78%

Various models have been proposed to classify and diagnose autism using proven techniques with satisfactory results. The difference between the proposed model is its complete and easy-to-interpret architecture; it can also be considered a promising alternative when integrating OM.

3 Proposed Model

Figure 2 presents the model comprising three phases, representing the general panorama that begins from care in the specialized center until satisfactory results are achieved in the diagnosis of ASD.

3.1 Phase 1: ASD Care Center - Dataset

The initial phase of the model stands out as the first step to the specialized autism care center because it is considered important for families to go when detecting any symptom that may or may not be an ASD. Afterwards, standardized evaluation tests were applied, which, for this work, was Autism Diagnostic Interview-Revised (ADI-R) for children.

The ADI-R assessment has proven to be efficient because it allows a deep evaluation of people with suspected autism. The scope of application is recommended for a mental age greater than two years. This instrument focuses on three important domains of functioning: language-communication, level of reciprocal social interaction, and repetitive or stereotyped behaviors [25]. The procedure is standardized and rigorous to guarantee

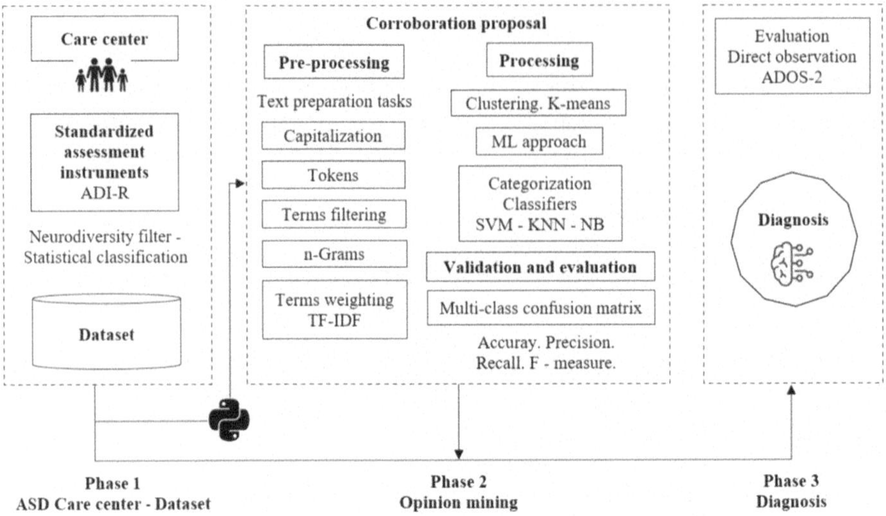

Fig. 2. ASD-OM model proposed for the early detection of ASD using the OM approach.

that the information provided contains detailed and systematic descriptions of the behavior of the evaluated subject. Some research works have adopted the ADI-R instrument because of its reliability [26–28].

The database to test the model consisted of the ADI-R application to the informants (primarily parents) of 62 children aged between two and eight years. In agreement with the Autismo Valle Azul A.C. association located in Veracruz, México, the informants accepted a signed consent form so that the information remains confidential and can be used for this research.

3.2 Phase 2: Opinion Mining

The corroboration proposal through OM is obtained from the questionnaires applied and patterns associated with the extended opinions of the responses. NLP Toolkit in Python 3.10.7 is used.

Pre-processing

Capitalization. This process converts all sentences to lowercase, making the textual analysis standardized and coherent.

Tokenization. The text is segmented into individual words; this is essential because the algorithms need the text to be broken down into smaller units to improve the effectiveness of the analysis.

Terms filtering. At this stage, rare words are excluded, known as stop words, which are usually auxiliary verbs, prepositions, conjunctions, or pronouns that do not contribute significantly to the clarity of the information.

Table 2 shows the results of the three processes described above in a real question with their respective answers.

Table 2. Example of capitalization, tokenization and terms filtering in a real question answered.

Process	Status	Item	Result
Capitalization	Before	Question	Does he prefer to play with small children or adults rather than children his age?
		Response	My child has null interaction with other children, in the neighborhood and at school
	After	Question	*{does he prefer to play with small children or adults rather than children his age?}*
		Response	*{my child has null interaction with other children, in the neighborhood and at school.}*
Tokenization	After	Response	*{"my", "child", "has", "null", "interaction", "with", "other", "children", "in", "the", "neighborhood", "and", "at", "school"}*
Terms filtering	After	Response	*{"child", "null", "interaction", "children", "neighborhood", "school"}*

n-Grams. It is a crucial step in text preprocessing to extract valuable features. An n-Gram is a series of consecutive tokens of length n that reduces ambiguity, provides features for ML models, and allows for more detailed and efficient text analysis.

Term weighting. In this step, a weight is assigned to each term. This weight reflects the relevance of each term within a document or in an entire corpus. For this work, we use Term Frequency - Inverse Document Frequency (TF-IDF):

$$IDF(t) = log\left(\frac{N}{df\,(t)}\right) \tag{1}$$

$$TD - IDF(t, d) = TF(t, d)xIDF(t) \tag{2}$$

In Eqs. 1 and 2, N represents the total number of documents, and $df\ (t)$ is the number of documents containing the term t. Likewise, TF $(t,\ d)$ is the frequency of term t in document d.

Processing

K-means clustering: Among all the clustering algorithms in the literature, K-means is one of the most popular and efficient [28]. This method divides a data set into k groups called clusters. The algorithm operates through an iterative process in which each data point is assigned to the centroid of its cluster, ensuring that it is closer to it than to the centroids of other clusters, minimizing the internal distance of the cluster at each step. Subsequently, considering that each group will be considered by language-communication (1), level of reciprocal social interaction (2), and repetitive or stereotyped behaviors (3), the initial value of k will be determined by the total number of functioning domains.

For the similarity metrics, the distance between the k-centroids of each instance present in the term matrix is calculated. The similarity calculation is based on the Euclidean distance shown in Eq. 3.

$$d(A, B) = \sqrt{\sum_{i=1}^{n} (X_{2i} - X_{1i})^2} \tag{3}$$

In this work, m = n is a two-dimensional space and refers to the dimensions of the space in which the points are being considered to calculate the Euclidean distance between them. The distance between the documents can be estimated by measuring the cosine similarity and represented as a vector, and each attribute is responsible for recording the frequency of the terms (Eq. 4).

$$\cos(d_1, d_2) = \frac{d_1 d_2}{\|d_1\| \cdot \|d_2\|} \tag{4}$$

where: The vector product is indicated by a dot and $\|d_1\|$ represents the length of the vector *d*.

ML approach - Categorization. We have chosen three classifiers due to the effectiveness of their results in this type of scientific context. SVMs are widely used supervised learning algorithms, especially suitable for classification problems involving large volumes of data and high dimensionality, but most importantly, they offer robust and reliable performance [29]. The KNN classifier is simple but effective during classification implementation [30]. Finally, we decided to use the NB classifier based on the common assumption that all features are independent. It is widely used in text and document categorizations due to its effectiveness with high-dimensional data [31].

Validation and evaluation. Specialists from the autism care center were consulted to classify the comments by language-communication, level of reciprocal social interaction, and repetitive or stereotyped behaviors. The test set labels all the comments in the primary dataset. The confusion matrix containing the classification results for the test data set was obtained. The dataset was partitioned into training and test sets with the 5-fold cross-validation operation. The GridSearchCV method was used to determine suitable parameters. GridSearchCV is useful in systematically evaluating and selecting the parameters of a Python-trained ML algorithm. The most popular metrics are used to evaluate the effectiveness of the model:

$$Accuracy = \frac{TP + TN}{TP + FP + FN + TN} \tag{5}$$

$$Precision = \frac{TP}{TP + FP} \tag{6}$$

$$Recall = \frac{TP}{TP + FN} \tag{7}$$

$$F - measure = \frac{2 * Precision * Recall}{Precision + Recall} \tag{8}$$

where, TN indicates the result of the true negative, TP specifies the true positive, FP denotes a false positive and also FN represents a false negative result.

Table 3 shows the performance comparison of the three classifiers used to test the model concerning the available dataset. KNN shows the best performance in all metrics and has the highest accuracy value in category 2 (88.78%). It can be seen that SVM showed the second-best performance with the highest accuracy value of 86.75% in category 1. Finally, NB showed the best result in category 3 (83.44%).

Table 3. Comparative analysis of the classifiers using different performance metrics.

Classifier	Categories	Accuracy (%)	Precision (%)	Recall (%)	F - measure (%)
	1	86.75	85.15	86.93	85.71
SVM	2	85.43	86.09	85.55	85.16
	3	84.1	85.32	86.98	85.6
	1	88.34	88.5	89.76	88.62
KNN	2	88.78	87.98	86.45	87.54
	3	87.03	86.18	86.72	87.1
	1	82.17	81.99	83.62	82.78
NB	2	83.15	82.92	82.78	82.61
	3	83.44	83.8	83.41	82.22

Figure 3 shows the KNN algorithm with the best results for the performance metrics.

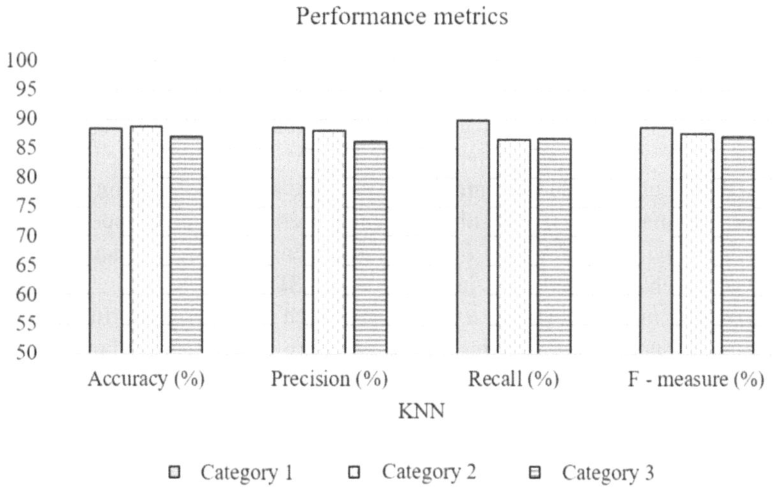

Fig. 3. KNN graph that highlights better accuracy compared to the other classifiers.

3.3 Phase 3: Diagnosis

The diagnostic phase of the proposed model suggests that, independently of the proposal of corroboration through OM, ADI-R complemented with other tests such as the ADOS-2 and M-CHAT contributes to more accurate and effective detection, especially in cases of mild or subtle autism. In most evaluations, especially those more subtle ones compatible with mild autism, both the ADI-R and the ADOS-2 are applied to collect as much information as possible to make a more precise diagnosis. The ADOS-2 is a semi-structured observational assessment that allows professionals to observe and interact with the person being evaluated in a controlled environment [32]. It is one of the most effective tests that has been demonstrated for detecting and diagnosing autism [33].

The results of the model show that the behaviors or main symptoms are language development, food selectivity, behavior (tantrums), sensory alteration (sleep disorder), tolerance to noise or clothing, and little social interaction (limited play). These symptoms allow the findings after observation to be validated and contribute to a better diagnosis by specialists to determine early if the child has mild, moderate, or severe autism.

4 Discussion

The scientific community continues to make significant efforts to improve the accuracy of ASD. In this paper, our model that uses OM is proposed to improve the diagnosis of ASD by specialists in the field. The initial phase emphasizes the importance of attending a specialized center when detecting ASD symptoms. The ADI-R is used to evaluate children, providing a thorough assessment in three important domains: language-communication, reciprocal social interaction, and repetitive or stereotyped behaviors. Text preprocessing and processing techniques are applied in the second phase, including capitalization, tokenization, term filtering, and term weighting using TF-IDF. Subsequently, the K-means clustering algorithm is used, and categorization is carried out using classifiers such as SVM, KNN, and NB. The comparative analysis of the classifiers used shows that KNN presents the best performance in all metrics, with an accuracy of 88.78% in category 2. SVM showed the second-best performance with an accuracy of 86.75% in category 1, and NB had its best result in category 3 with an accuracy of 83.44%. For the final stage of diagnosis, it is suggested that combining OM with standardized tests such as ADI-R, ADOS-2, and M-CHAT contributes to a more accurate detection of ASD. The ADOS-2 is particularly effective for observing and interacting with the person evaluated in a controlled environment, which facilitates the identification of affected social and communicative behaviors and skills in people with ASD.

The proposed model integrates a proven approach that uses powerful algorithmic tools to support specialists in having better certainty and an early diagnosis of this condition and, more importantly, improving the quality of life of patients and their families.

Open challenges remain, such as expanding and diversifying data sets, using more robust algorithms, improving accuracy in different clinical contexts, and ensuring practical implementation and accessibility of these technologies in healthcare settings.

Finally, the authors consider strengthening this wolrk to obtain better results and make more important and significant contributions.

Acknowledgment. This work is developing with the Autismo Valle Azul A.C. association, which has an official collaboration agreement with the TecNM-Campus Orizaba. Furthermore, this article is the result of the postdoctoral stay of the principal author with project application number 5905826, approved by TecNM-Campus Orizaba and the National Council of Humanities, Science and Technology (CONAHCYT).

References

1. Epalle, T.M., Song, Y., Liu, Z., Lu, H.: Multi-atlas classification of autism spectrum disorder with hinge loss trained deep architectures: ABIDE I results. Appl. Soft Comput. (2021). https://doi.org/10.1016/j.asoc.2021.107375
2. WHO: Autism. Data and numbers (2024). https://www.who.int/es/news-room/fact-sheets/detail/autism-spectrum-disorders
3. Liu, B.: Sentiment analysis and opinion mining. Morgan & Claypool (2012)
4. Grande-Ramírez, J.R., Roldán-Reyes, E., Aguilar-Lasserre, A.A., Juárez-Martínez, U.: Integration of sentiment analysis of social media in the strategic planning process to generate the balanced scorecard. Appl. Sci. (2022). https://doi.org/10.3390/app122312307
5. Wu, X., Wang, B., Li, W.: Comparing the accuracy of ANN with transformer models for sentiment analysis of tweets related to COVID-19 Pfizer vaccines. Chaos Solitons Fractals **185**, 115105 (2024)
6. Wang, T., Lu, K., Chow, K.P., Zhu, Q.: COVID-19 sensing: negative sentiment analysis on social media in China via BERT model. IEEE Access **8**, 1–8 (2020)
7. Gabarron, E., Dorronzoro, E., Rivera-Romero, O., Wynn, R.: Diabetes on Twitter: a sentiment analysis. J. Diabetes Sci. Technol. **13**, 439–444 (2019)
8. D'Andrea, E., Ducange, P., Bechini, A., Renda, A., Marcelloni, F.: Monitoring the public opinion about the vaccination topic from tweets analysis. Expert Syst. Appl. **116**, 209–226 (2019)
9. Gopalakrishnan, V., Ramaswamy, C.: Patient opinion mining to analyze drugs satisfaction using supervised learning. J. Appl. Res. Technol. **15**, 311–319 (2017)
10. Wang, Y., Liu, J., Xiang, Y., Wang, J., Chen, Q., Chong, J.: MAGE: automatic diagnosis of autism spectrum disorders using multi-atlas graph convolutional networks and ensemble learning. Neurocomputing **469**, 346–353 (2022)
11. Loganathan, S., Geetha, C., Nazaren, A.R., Harin Fernandez Fernandez, M.: Autism spectrum disorder detection and classification using chaotic optimization based Bi-GRU network: an weighted average ensemble model. Expert Syst. Appl. **230**, 120613 (2023)
12. Akter, T., et al.: Machine learning-based models for early stage detection of autism spectrum disorders. IEEE Access **7**, 166509–166527 (2019)
13. Raj, S., Masood, S.: Analysis and detection of autism spectrum disorder using machine learning techniques. Procedia Comput. Sci. **167**, 994–1004 (2020)
14. Abdolzadegan, D., Moattar, M.H., Ghoshuni, M.: A robust method for early diagnosis of autism spectrum disorder from EEG signals based on feature selection and DBSCAN method. Biocybern. Biomed. Eng. **40**, 482–493 (2020)
15. Hossain, M.D., Kabir, M.A., Anwar, A., Islam, M.Z.: Detecting autism spectrum disorder using machine learning techniques: an experimental analysis on toddler, child, adolescent and adult datasets. Heal Inf. Sci. Syst. (2021). https://doi.org/10.1007/s13755-021-00145-9
16. Balaji, V., Raja, S.K.S.: Recommendation learning system model for children with autism. Intell. Autom. Soft Comput. **31**, 1301–1315 (2022)

17. Hemu, A.A., Mim, R.B., Ali, M.M., Nayer, M., Ahmed, K., Bui, F.M.: Identification of significant risk factors and impact for ASD prediction among children using machine learning approach. In: 2022 2nd International Conference on Advances in Electrical, Computing, Communication and Sustainable Technologies ICAECT 2022, pp. 1–6 (2022)
18. Lodha, S., Lodha, N., Malani, H., Devashetti, P., Rajguru, A.: Early diagnosis of autism using machine learning techniques and gated recurrent units. In: 8th International Conference on Advanced Computing and Communication Systems ICACCS 2022, vol. 1, pp. 1152–1158 (2022)
19. Khudhur, D.D., Khudhur, S.D.: The classification of autism spectrum disorder by machine learning methods on multiple datasets for four age groups. Meas Sens. **27**, 100774 (2023)
20. Farooq, M.S., Tehseen, R., Sabir, M., Atal, Z.: Detection of autism spectrum disorder (ASD) in children and adults using machine learning. Sci. Rep. **13**, 1–13 (2023)
21. RethikumariAmma, K.N., Ranjana, P.: Pivotal region and optimized deep neuro fuzzy network for autism spectrum disorder detection. Biomed. Signal Process. Control **83**, 104634 (2023)
22. Bhandage, V., Mallikharjuna Rao, K., Muppidi, S.: Autism spectrum disorder classification using Adam war strategy optimization enabled deep belief network. Biomed. Signal Process. Control **86**, 104914 (2023)
23. Rubio-Martín, S., García-Ordás, M.T., Bayón-Gutiérrez, M., Prieto-Fernández, N., Benítez-Andrades, J.A.: Enhancing ASD detection accuracy: a combined approach of machine learning and deep learning models with natural language processing. Heal. Inf. Sci. Syst. (2024). https://doi.org/10.1007/s13755-024-00281-y
24. Koehler, J.C., et al.: Machine learning classification of autism spectrum disorder based on reciprocity in naturalistic social interactions. Transl. Psychiatry **14**, 1–9 (2024)
25. Rutter, M., Le couteur, A., Lord, C.: ADI-R. Entrevista para el diagnóstico del Autismo - Edición revisada (2024)
26. Lefort-Besnard, J., et al.: Patterns of autism symptoms: hidden structure in the ADOS and ADI-R instruments. Transl. Psychiatry (2020). https://doi.org/10.1038/s41398-020-00946-8
27. Hrdlicka, M., Urbanek, T., Rotreklova, A., Kultova, A., Valek, O., Dudova, I.: Predictors of age at diagnosis in autism spectrum disorders: the use of multiple regression analyses and a classification tree on a clinical sample. Eur. Child Adolesc. Psychiatry **33**, 1171–1177 (2024)
28. Vázquez-Rojas, C., Roldán-Reyes, E., Aguirre y Hernández, F., Guillermo, C-R.: Integration of a text mining approach in the strategic planning process of small and medium-sized enterprises. Ind. Manag. Data Syst. **118**, 745–764 (2018)
29. Goudjil, M., Koudil, M., Bedda, M., Ghoggali, N.: A novel active learning method using SVM for text classification. Int. J. Autom. Comput. **15**, 290–298 (2018)
30. Moldagulova, A., Sulaiman, R.B.: Using KNN algorithm for classification of textual documents. In: 2017 8th International Conference on Information Technology, pp. 665–671 (2017)
31. Xu, S.: Bayesian naïve Bayes classifiers to text classification. J. Inf. Sci., 1–12 (2016)
32. Saure, E., Laasonen, M., Kylliäinen, A., Hämäläinen, S., Lepistö-Paisley, T., Raevuori, A.: Social communication and restricted, repetitive behavior as assessed with a diagnostic tool for autism (ADOS-2) in women with anorexia nervosa. J. Clin. Psychol., 1–16 (2024)
33. Ji, S.I., Park, H., Yoon, S.A., Hong, S.B.: A validation study of the CARS-2 compared with the ADOS-2 in the diagnosis of autism spectrum disorder: a suggestion for Cutoff scores. J. Korean Acad. Child. Adolesc. Psychiatry **34**, 45–50 (2023)

A Short Analysis of Hybrid Approaches in COVID-19 for Detection and Diagnosing

Dragan Simić[1](✉), Zorana Banković[2], José R. Villar[3], José Luis Calvo-Rolle[4], Svetislav D. Simić[1], and Svetlana Simić[5]

[1] Faculty of Technical Sciences, University of Novi Sad, Trg Dositeja Obradovića 6, 21000 Novi Sad, Serbia
dsimic@eunet.rs, {dsimic,simicsvetislav}@uns.ac.rs
[2] Frontiers Media SA, Paseo de Castellana 77, Madrid, Spain
[3] University of Oviedo, Campus de Llamaquique, 33005 Oviedo, Spain
villarjose@uniovi.es
[4] Department of Industrial Engineering, University of A Coruña, 15405 Ferrol-A Coruña, Spain
jlcalvo@udc.es
[5] Faculty of Medicine, University of Novi Sad, Hajduk Veljkova 1–9, 21000 Novi Sad, Serbia
svetlana.simic@mf.uns.ac.rs

Abstract. The epidemic spread model of infectious diseases is a traditional epidemiological and mathematical problem with crucial practical value. The first transmission of coronavirus to humans started in Wuhan city of China and took the shape of a pandemic called Corona Virus Disease 2019 (COVID-19). Many papers and studies have been written from 2019 until today. The aim of this paper is to present and short-analyse hybrid AI techniques which have been applied: *k*-nearest neighbours algorithm, Support Vector Machine, Naive Bayes, Random Forest, *k*-means clustering, hierarchical clustering, fuzzy logic, Logistic Regression, Decision Tree, Artificial Neural Networks, Deep Learning, Convolutional Neural Network to extract significant features and classify various health conditions, detection and diagnoses of COVID-19 patients. The hybrid algorithm overcomes the lack of exploiting individual AI techniques and algorithms; and simultaneously, the obtained statistical results prove the efficiency and robustness compared over other state-of-the-art approaches.

Keywords: Artificial intelligence · infectious diseases · COVID-19 · machine learning · X-ray images · detection · diagnosing · severity level

1 Introduction

Infectious diseases are caused by pathogenic microorganisms, such as bacteria, viruses, parasites, or fungi. These microorganisms have the potential to cause infections in both humans and animals through a variety of means, such as exposure to bodily fluids, including blood, saliva, or mucus; contact with contaminated surfaces; proximity to infected individuals; consumption of contaminated food; and ingestion of contaminated water [1]. In the 20th century, infectious diseases were responsible for the largest number

H. Quintián et al. (Eds.): HAIS 2024, LNAI 14857, pp. 73–84, 2025.
https://doi.org/10.1007/978-3-031-74183-8_7

of premature death and disability worldwide. The Spanish flu occurred at the beginning of the previous century. It was estimated that one-third of the world's population was infected and had symptoms during the 1918–1919 pandemic. The disease was one of the deadliest of all influenza pandemics. It was estimated that at least 50 million individuals died following the infection.

Since the 1970s, newly emerging viruses of unknown origins have been continuously discovered. Since the first Ebola outbreak in 1976, Ebola outbreaks have continued to be reported. The fatality rate of Ebola fever is extremely high. Fortunately, Ebola outbreaks have been mainly restricted to Africa, in Zaire and Sudan. The potential for Ebola to become a widespread epidemic is low due to the high case-fatality rate and the rapid demise of patients. AIDS was first described as acquired immunodeficiency syndrome among homosexual males in 1981 and its culprit was soon identified in 1983 as HIV [2].

The 21st century has already seen emerging pandemic infections such as Severe Acute Respiratory Syndrome (SARS), Middle East Respiratory Syndrome (MERS), and Zika viruses. Recent Zika virus outbreak started in May 2015 in Brazil and reminded us of the importance of mosquito-borne flaviviruses. SARS, a respiratory disease caused by SARS-CoV, was first reported in Hong Kong in 2003. More recently, a novel coronavirus, Middle East Respiratory Syndrome-coronavirus (MERS-CoV), was discovered in 2012 in Saudi Arabia [2].

A virus is a protein-coated microscopic organism that hijacks the host cells for its development and in turn, makes the host sick. The best prevention is to detect early possible pandemics and stop the transmission, because one cannot always rely on medicine to develop vaccines or other treatments rapidly. By blocking transmission, this could eventually also reduce the mutation of the viruses and thus keep the virus in a stage that vaccines could help fighting.

The problem with infectious diseases, as introduced above, is their unpredictability as well as multiple factors that affect the process of infection and transmission. Artificial intelligence (AI) is the form of computing that allows mechanisms to act or react to input, similar to the way humans do, by performing cognitive functions. Opposite, traditional computing also reacts to data but the output has to be necessarily hand coded for the reaction, there is no cognitive function performed. AI platforms are constantly adapting their behaviour to change and modify their reactions accordingly.

The aim of this paper is to analyse some hybrid implementations of AI techniques and other metaheuristics-based algorithms to detect and diagnose in general infectious diseases, and particularly Coronavirus disease 2019 (COVID-19). This paper continues our previous research [3–6].

The rest of the paper is organised in the following way: Sect. 2 provides an overview of the infectious diseases, AI in general, and particularly machine learning (ML) techniques. Modelling and applications of the hybrid bio-inspired systems for detecting, diagnosing, and decision supporting for COVID-19 are presented in Sect. 3. Section 4 provides conclusions and some directions for future research.

2 Related Work in Infectious Diseases and Artificial Intelligence

Infectious diseases present a global challenge, requiring accurate diagnosis, effective treatments, and preventive measures. AI has emerged as a promising tool for analysing complex molecular data and improving the diagnosis, treatment, and prevention of infectious diseases. AI can track and trace infected individuals and identify potential hotspots, help reduce the spread of infectious diseases, and monitor patient symptoms, enabling healthcare professionals to provide effective treatment [7]. AI can be classified into three ways, as presented in Fig. 1 [8]. Any of the three approaches can be used to apply computational intelligence: (i) *Artificial neural network*; (ii) *Fuzzy logic*; and (iii) *Evolutionary computation.* Time line of newly emerging viruses in the 20th century and in the 21st century is displayed in Fig. 2 [9]. Time line of seven Public Health Emergencies of International Concern in the 21st century is displayed in Fig. 3 [10].

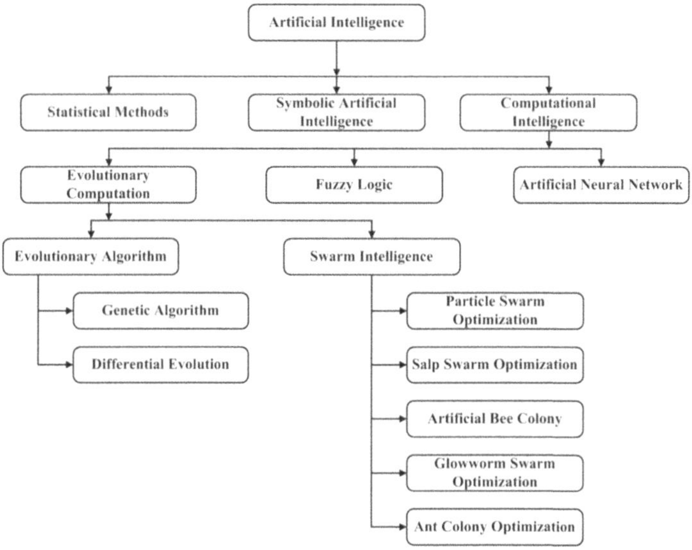

Fig. 1. Classification of artificial intelligence [8]

One of the earliest attempts at a computer-based clinical decision support system for infectious diseases was MYCIN, from 1972. The system's knowledge was encoded in the form of about 350 production rules which embodied the clinical decision criteria of infectious disease experts to determine the bacterial species responsible for an infection, provide a diagnosis, and recommend an antibody regimen [11]. However, it eventually became clear that the decision process clinicians made was far too complex to encode in explicitly defined rules. Furthermore, inputting a long series of answers to questions was not easily integrated into clinical practice for infectious diseases.

A neural network and fuzzy clustering method were used to successfully classify individuals at higher risk for influenza using respiration rate, heart rate, and facial temperature. It can be observed that *k*-nearest neighbours algorithm (KNN), support vector

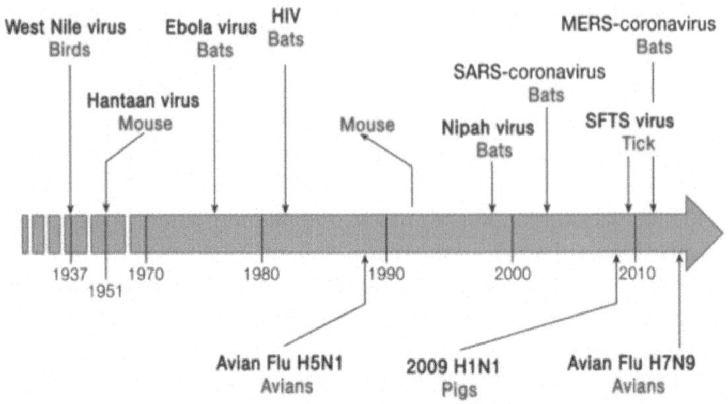

Fig. 2. Time line of newly emerging viruses [Adapted from 9]

machine (SVM), naive Bayes, Random forest (RF), *k*-means clustering, and hierarchical clustering have been widely employed in infectious disease research [12]. This infers that AI aids in detecting microorganisms and sub-subsequent infection surveillance.

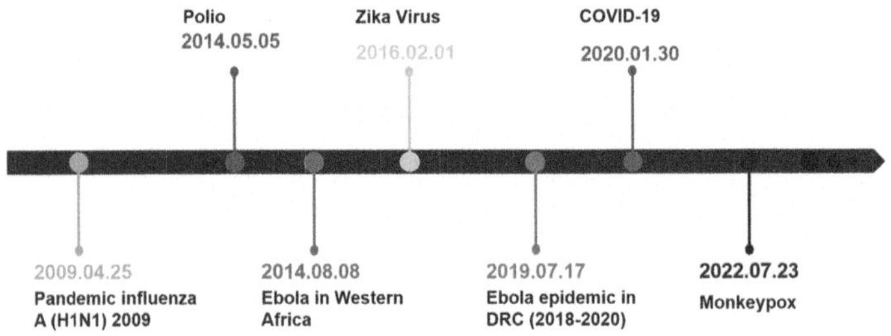

Fig. 3. Time line of seven Public Health Emergencies of International Concern in the 21st century [10]

Unstructured electronic medical records were classified using a deep learning (DL) model. Consequently, multiple classification models (MIDDM) were developed utilising DL to support the decision-making process of infectious disease diagnosis. Moreover, the Bayesian model, a decision tree, determined the model's accuracy and logistic regression used to evaluate the prediction accuracy of infectious diseases. The application of the MIDDM model in infectious disease diagnosis and prediction can improve the precision of disease detection [13].

DL employs deep neural networks to categorise data sets consisting of images, text, and sound and is instructed to label large data sets with manually retrieved relevant attributes. The features are then applied to build a model that classifies the objects using DL workflow. As the size of the data increases, the advantage of the deployment of DL networks enhances continuously. In addition, to assist clinicians with the diagnosis and severity of infectious diseases, this facilitates the selection of more effective treatments by analysing earlier electronic medical data, thereby accelerating the treatment process [14].

As mentioned before, a virus is a protein-coated microscopic organism that hijacks the host cells for its development and makes the host sick. Therefore, many studies have been based on the identification of different cell types [15]. The nearest neighbour approach is utilised to determine the optimal projection of a new query cell onto a reference data set. A tool for Single Cell Genomics - *Seurat* is a widely utilized toolkit for single-cell data analysis, and it adopts an approach based on canonical correlation analysis and mutual nearest neighbours [16]. Essentially, *Seurat* leverages these methodologies to pinpoint cells with shared properties across different data sets. The summary outlines the application of AI methods on single cell/spatial sequencing and single nuclei *Ribonucleic acid* (RNA) sequencing data for the recognition of cell types and subtypes based on different approaches. In a recent study, unsupervised language models were developed for influenza, HIV-1, and SARS-CoV-2 viral proteins, utilizing amino acid sequence information. These models accurately forecast escape patterns enabling these pathogens to elude the human immune response [16].

ML models that incorporate specific assumptions about biology, such as: (i) the relevance of syntax (grammar); and (ii) semantics (meaning) in biological sequences, or utilize structural information, hold the potential to inform the generation of biological hypotheses and enhance generalisability. Cellular immunity plays a pivotal role in defending the body against infectious diseases. Some AI-based algorithms can provide valuable insights into vaccine development by predicting information such as the T-cell epitope map of pathogens [17, 18].

In the era of antimicrobial resistance, the prevalence of multidrug-resistant microorganisms that defy conventional antibiotic treatment has steadily risen. It is now undeniable that infectious diseases present significant global challenges demanding innovative treatment strategies. Conventional drug discovery processes are daunting, involving the creation of novel molecules with multiple desirable properties [19]. This approach is not only costly and time-consuming but it also has a low success rate. To address these challenges, AI/ML-based models have revolutionised drug discovery. As the number of drug-like small molecules is essentially infinite as large as $\sim 10^{60}$, [20, 21] and possibly larger, given that typical antibiotics may not be traditionally drug-like, a major benefit of ML approaches is that they can virtually screen compound libraries at a scale, $> 10^9$ compounds, that would be impossible to screen empirically. They efficiently identify numerous plausible, diverse, and new candidate molecules within the vast molecular space [20, 22].

3 Modelling the Hybrid Approaches for COVID-19

The coronavirus disease 2019 (COVID-19) pandemic has affected more than 600 million individuals in more than 220 countries and regions, with more than 6.5 million deaths till 21 August, 2022 [23]. COVID-19 disease can manifest with a wide range of clinical features ranging from no symptoms to multi-organ failure [24]. COVID-19 infection causes systemic and respiratory disorders in the patient. Systemic disorders include fever, cough, fatigue, sputum production, headache, haemoptysis, acute cardiac injury, hypoxemia, dyspnoea, lymphopenia, and diarrhoea. Respiratory disorders consist of rhinorrhoea, sneezing, sore throat, pneumonia, ground-grass opacities, RNAemia, and acute respiratory distress syndrome. Fever, cough, and fatigue are the most common symptoms of COVID-19 at the early stages of the epidemic's advent. In contrast, later symptoms include sputum production, headache, haemoptysis, diarrhoea, dyspnoea, and lymphopenia [25].

Although Severe acute respiratory syndrome coronavirus 2 (SARS-CoV-2) mainly affects the lungs, cardiovascular, neurological, renal, and vascular complications can also contribute to mortality [26]. Accurate prognostication of clinical outcomes in this patient population can be challenging due to the high variability in disease severity; however, it is still essential considering the need for effective triage and efficient allocation of limited resources, for example, beds and ventilators.

Therefore, the identification of high-risk patients and the recognition of mortality predictors could possibly allow offering more targeted approaches and better allocated resources. The identification of contributing factors would allow for applying targeted strategies in patients with the highest mortality risk. Patients' accurate history, clinical signs, fever and oxygen saturation measurements, blood cell counts (CBCs), other laboratory findings, computed tomography (CT) scan imaging, and real-time reverse-transcription polymerase chain reaction (RT-PCR) test are included in prognostic and diagnostic criteria [7].

The accumulation of AI epidemic prevention knowledge in COVID-19, in general and with ML in particular, has become more scientific and reasonable in responding to the monkeypox epidemic; thus, accurate medical treatment, auxiliary diagnosis, pathogen analysis, scientific extension, and follow–up formulation have been significantly improved [27]. Not only that, AI is also doing well in the current seasonal flu response. In addition to the original online dynamic forecasting and precision medical guidance, other intelligent AI devices have also been applied, such as smart masks, for example, or temperature monitoring and respiratory detection [28]. All these demonstrate that ML epidemic prevention not only greatly enhances the ability of the medical system to cope with the epidemic, but also increases the way for people to prevent the epidemic independently.

3.1 Detection

AI often faces challenges in distinguishing between different infectious diseases that share similar symptoms during the detection phase. The disease's detection at the early stages was critical, because there were no specific therapeutic drugs for COVID-19. After detecting the infected patient's symptoms, he/she should be isolated immediately from the healthy population [29]. Until now, RT-PCR has been developed to assay COVID-19 in clinics. RT-PCR has become the reference standard to make a definitive diagnosis of COVID-19 infection. Still, the high false-negative rate and its unavailability in the early stage of the disease confine a quick diagnosis for infected patients [29]. Much research has been conducted to fight COVID-19 in various science domains in a limited time based on the provided information, including the use of AI/ML tools.

The research paper [30] proposes that using ML algorithms for identifying a person under investigation for the COVID-19 infection with a mobile phone-based web survey could identify the high-risk cases and quarantine them earlier, and subsequently decrease the chance of spread. Chest computed tomography (CT) can recognize the early phase of lung infection and prompt larger public health surveillance and response systems.

A convolutional neural network (CNN) can identify community-acquired pneumonia on chest CT exams and it can successfully distinguish COVID-19 cases from community-acquired pneumonia and other non-pneumonic lung diseases, as presented in [31]. In paper [32], a tool based on RF is modelled and trained to evaluate the severity of patients suffering from COVID-19 based on the chest CT images' quantitative features. In paper [33], they combine conventional statistics and ML to extract features from CT images and then classify extracted features by a hybrid classifier system based on Naive Bayes.

The effectiveness of ML, particularly DL models, in addressing infectious diseases is heavily dependent on the availability of data. *Deep neural networks* (DNN) thrive on large data sets. In the context of infectious disease surveillance, a recent analysis on COVID-19 mortality data highlighted a significant issue. The lack of properly encoded racial information led to the underreporting of deaths among Black and Hispanic individuals by up to 60% [34]. One potential solution to this problem lies in the development of transfer learning technology. The presence of abundant but low-quality or irrelevant data sources can adversely affect AI output results [35]. Furthermore, early detection of infectious diseases helps preventing future outbreaks.

Finally, it can be concluded that main classification of detection divides two types, binary and multiclass classification. In binary classification, the classification is performed between two classes (COVID + ve v/s COVID–ve), whereas in multi-class classification, the classification is performed among many classes (COVID v/s healthy, other viral/bacterial pneumonia, and other pulmonary diseases). The extracted features play an important role in this whole process as they are learned by different models during the training phase. The researchers have used a wide variety of ML and DL models during their implementation on the COVID-19 detection system. Some of these models are k-nearest neighbour (KNN), Logistic regression (LR), Decision tree, XGBoost, AdaBoost, Bagging classifier, and SVM. KNN classifies a particular object depending on the class of its k (an integer) nearest neighbouring object.

3.2 Diagnosing

X-ray scans propose computer-aided diagnosis (CAD) systems based on cascaded deep learning (DL) classifiers for COVID-19 in [36]. A similar study [37], analysing chest X-ray images, has been conducted for COVID-19 diagnosis and classification using a novel model hand-crafted with DL feature-based fusion. The research paper [38] based on the extracted features from the COVID-19 chest X-ray images, uses new fractional multichannel exponent moments (FrMEMs) to exploit a modified manta-ray foraging optimisation based on differential evolution (DE) to select the most significant features.

The development of speech processing framework based on the CNN architecture for COVID-19 patients' cough recordings is used to discriminate them accurately [39]. In the research paper [40], the authors utilize linear discriminant analysis (LDA) for investigating the characteristics and rules of haematology changes in COVID-19 patients. Moreover, clinical and laboratory patients' test results were analysed, and different haematological parameters fitted using LDA.

3.3 Decision Support Systems

Given the importance of the pandemic, the current study [41] attempts to propose an intelligent self-assessment decision support system (DSS) based on the combination of Bayesian network (BN) and fuzzy cognitive map (FCM) to utilise the key symptoms for distinguishing the severity of the disease between confirmed cases. In self-assessment systems, patients can obtain a general evaluation of their disease by reporting information about their symptoms. For designing an efficient self-assessment DSS, symptoms are analysed both entirely and in severity levels. First, BN is implemented to extract evidence-based paired (EBP) relationships and symptoms' impact probability for distinguishing severities for the whole data in various scenarios. To put it precisely, BN is applied to extract the EBP relationships between triple severity levels to develop FCM. BNs have various advantages: the ability to combine different knowledge sources, the capacity to handle small and defective datasets, and the availability of a wide range of validation methods besides data-driven validation methods.

The large study [42] proposes a DSS that integrates geographic information system (GIS), analytics, and simulation methods to help develop a priority-based distribution of COVID-19 vaccines in a large urban setting. The methodology applies novel hierarchical heuristic-simulation procedures to create a holistic algorithm for prioritising the process of demand allocation and optimizing vaccine distribution. Three vaccine supply scenarios, namely limited, excessive, and disruptive, were formulated to operationalise a two-dose vaccination programme. Vaccine distribution with hard constraints is simulated and then further validated with sensitivity analyses. The results display that vaccines can be prioritised to society's most vulnerable segments and distributed using the current logistics network with 10 vehicles. Compared with other vaccine distribution plans with no prioritisation, such as equal allocation of vaccines to local government areas based on population size or one on a first-come-first-serve basis, the plans generated by the proposed DSS ensure prioritised vaccination of the most needed and vulnerable population. The aim is to curb the spread of the infection and reduce mortality rate more effectively. They also achieve vaccination of the entire population with less logistical resources required.

Since AI approaches based on ML depend on large training data sets, currently neither easily accessible nor reliable, a COVID-19 pre-clinical diagnosis system using a *fuzzy inference system* (FIS) is constructed. With the use of this fuzzy inference system, complex decisions in the medical field could be able to be determined more effectively. The research paper [43] describes a methodology for the development of a tool that assists in the COVID-19 diagnosis process. This tool consists of a FIS based on the Mamdani model. The proposed system especially supports situations that can be compared to other respiratory conditions, especially allergies, common colds, influenza and flu.

3.4 A Short Clarification

It can be concluded that main AI and ML applications can be achieved in six areas: (i) epidemiology, (ii) diagnosis, (iii) progression, (iv) treatment, (v) psychological health impact, and (vi) data security. The ongoing development in AI has significantly improved prediction, contact tracing, screening, diagnosis, treatment, medication, and vaccine development for the COVID-19 Pandemic, as well as reduced human intervention in medical practice [44].

In general, ML and DL methods have been extensively employed in the health sector, and they can also be employed to quantify patient data as well as diagnose COVID-19. The following are the main contributions: (i) DL strategy empowers fast identification of COVID-19 on chest CT tests; (ii) it is fundamental to approve that the DL technique is a vast-scope data set; (iii) there is the innovation move that happened in the public arena during the COVID-19 epidemic with its impact; (iv) innovation-based systems can be used in controlling the pandemic and helping society; and (v) there is an impact of existing advances, as well as future effects on society [45].

4 Conclusion and Future Work

The utilisation of AI/ML techniques and algorithms is very promising, as shown with examples discussed in this paper. Nowadays, metaheuristic algorithms are widespread and studied, since they are used in various fields such as medicine, bioinformatics, and transportation. Therefore, this research paper presents an improved individual AI algorithm with some other hybrid metaheuristic algorithms used to create hybrid algorithms for the medical problem beyond the emergence of the COVID-19 pandemic.

On the other hand, some DSS are being developed and implemented. Self-report DSS can consider relationships between symptoms that cannot be inferred for humans. The experimental results demonstrate that common symptoms are not necessarily key factors for differentiating severity, and that relationships between symptoms should be considered for their analysis.

Regarding future work we are, already, collecting real-world data set from patients who were hospitalised during the corona pandemic in the Clinical Centre of Vojvodina. The future work will be focused on: (i) relationships between relevant symptoms; (ii) diagnosing; (iii) severity; and (iv) recovered patients from their illness.

References

1. Rabaan, A.A., Bakhrebah, M.A., Alotaibi, J., et al.: Unleashing the power of artificial intelligence for diagnosing and treating infectious diseases: a comprehensive review. J. Infect. Public Health **16**, 1837–1847 (2023). https://doi.org/10.1016/j.jiph.2023.08.021
2. Agrebi, S., Larbi, A.: Use of artificial intelligence in infectious diseases. In: Barh, D. (ed): Artificial Intelligence in Precision Health. Academic Press, Cambridge, Massachusetts, US (2020). https://doi.org/10.1016/B978-0-12-817133-2.00018-5
3. Villar, J.R., González, S., Sedano, J., Chira, C., Trejo-Gabriel-Galan, J.M.: Improving human activity recognition and its application in early stroke diagnosis. Int. J. Neural Syst. **25**(4), 1450036 (2015). https://doi.org/10.1142/S0129065714500361
4. Simić, S., Banković, Z., Villar, J,R., Simić, D., Simić, S.D.: A hybrid fuzzy clustering approach for diagnosing primary headache disorder. Logic J. IGPL **29**(2), pp. 220–235 (2021). https://doi.org/10.1093/jigpal/jzaa048
5. Simić, S., Simić, S.D., Banković, Z., Ivkov-Simić, M., Villar, J.R., Simić, D.: Deep convolutional neural networks on automatic classification for skin tumour images. Logic J. IGPL **30**(4), 649–663 (2022). https://doi.org/10.1093/jigpal/jzab009

6. Simić, S., et al.: A three-stage hybrid clustering system for diagnosing children with primary headache disorder. Logic J. IGPL **31**(2), 300–313 (2023). https://doi.org/10.1093/jigpal/jzac020
7. Brownstein, J.S., Rader, B., Astley, C.M., Tian, H.: Advances in artificial intelligence for infectious-disease surveillance. N. Engl. J. Med. **388**(17), 1597–1607 (2023). https://doi.org/10.1056/NEJMra2119215
8. Dhawan, S., Gupta, R., Rana, A., Sharma, S.: Various swarm optimization algorithms: review, challenges, and opportunities. In: Marriwala, N., Tripathi, C.C., Jain, S., Mathapathi, S.: Soft Computing for Intelligent Systems, Proceedings of ICSCIS 2020, pp. 291–301, Springer Nature, Singapore Pte Ltd. (2021). https://doi.org/10.1007/978-981-16-1048-6_22
9. Ryu, W.-S.: Molecular Virology of Human Pathogenic Viruses. Academic Press, Cambridge, Massachusetts, US (2017)
10. Li, C., Ye, G., Jiang, Y., Wang, Z., Yu, H., Yang, M.: Artificial intelligence in battling infectious diseases: a transformative role. J. Med. Virol. **96**(1), e29355 (2024). https://doi.org/10.1002/jmv.29355
11. van Melle, W.: MYCIN: a knowledge-based consultation program for infectious disease diagnosis. Int. J. Man Mach. Stud. **10**(3), 313–322 (1978). https://doi.org/10.1016/S0020-7373(78)80049-2
12. He, S., Leanse, L.G., Feng Y.: Artificial intelligence and machine learning assisted drug delivery for effective treatment of infectious diseases. Adv. Drug Deliv. Rev. **178**, 113922 (2021). https://doi.org/10.1016/j.addr.2021.113922
13. Wang, M., Wei, Z., Jia, M., et al.: Deep learning model for multi-classification of infectious diseases from unstructured electronic medical records. BMC Med. Inform. Decision Making **22**, 41 (2022). https://doi.org/10.1186/s12911-022-01776-y
14. Peiffer-Smadja, N., et al.: Machine learning for clinical decision support in infectious diseases: a narrative review of current applications. Clin. Microbiol. Infect. **26**(5), 584–595 (2020). https://doi.org/10.1016/j.cmi.2019.09.009
15. Yang, T., Yan, Q., Long, R., Liu, Z., Wang, X.: PreCanCell: an ensemble learning algorithm for predicting cancer and non-cancer cells from single-cell transcriptomes. Comput. Struct. Biotechnol. J. **21**, 3604–3614 (2023). https://doi.org/10.1016/j.csbj.2023.07.009
16. Hie, B., Zhong, E.D., Berger, B., Bryson, B.: Learning the language of viral evolution and escape. Science **371**, 6526, 284–288 (2021). https://doi.org/10.1126/science.abd7331
17. Gupta, A.K., Khan, M.S., Choudhurym S., et al.: CoronaVR: a computational resource and analysis of epitopes and therapeutics for severe acute respiratory syndrome coronavirus-2. Front. Microbiol. **11**, 1858 (2020). https://doi.org/10.3389/fmicb.2020.01858
18. Malone, B., Simovski, B., Molinèm C., et al.: Artificial intelligence predicts the immunogenic landscape of SARS-CoV-2 leading to universal blueprints for vaccine designs. Sci. Rep. 10, 22375 (2020). https://doi.org/10.1038/s41598-020-78758-5
19. Zhao, T., Hu, Y., Peng, J., Cheng, L.: DeepLGP: a novel deep learning method for prioritizing lncRNA target genes. Bioinformatics **36**(16), 4466–4472 (2020). https://doi.org/10.1093/bioinformatics/btaa428
20. Schneider, G.: Automating drug discovery. Nat. Rev. Drug Discov. **17**(2), 97–113 (2018). https://doi.org/10.1038/nrd.2017.232
21. Liang, P., Yang, W., Chen, X., et al.: Machine learning of single-cell transcriptome highly identifies mRNA signature by comparing F–score selection with DGE analysis. Molecular Therapy Nucleic Acids **20**, 155–163 (2020). https://doi.org/10.1016/j.omtn.2020.02.004
22. Wang, H., Liang, P., Zheng, L., Long, C., Li, H., Zuo, Y.: EHSCPr discriminating the cell identity involved in endothelial to hematopoietic transition. Bioinformatics **37**(15), 2157–2164 (2021). https://doi.org/10.1093/bioinformatics/btab071
23. Worldometer. https://www.worldometers.info/coronavirus/#countries. Accessed Aug 2022

24. Hassan, S., Sheikh, F.N., Jamal, S., Ezeh, J.K., Akhtar, A.: Coronavirus (COVID-19): a review of clinical features, diagnosis, and treatment. Cureus **12**(3), e7355 (2020). https://doi.org/10.7759/cureus.7355
25. Rothan, H.A., Byrareddy, S.N.: The epidemiology and pathogenesis of coronavirus disease (COVID-19) outbreak. J. Autoimmunity **109**, 102433 (2020). https://doi.org/10.1016/j.jaut.2020.102433
26. Guan, W., Ni, Z., Hu, Y., Liang, W., Ou, C., He, J., et al.: Clinical characteristics of coronavirus disease 2019 in China. N. Engl. J. Med. **382**, 1708–1720 (2020). https://doi.org/10.1056/NEJMoa2002032
27. Patel, M., Surti, M., Adnan, M.: Artificial intelligence (AI) in Monkeypox infection prevention. J. Biomol. Struct. Dyn. **41**(17), 8629–8633 (2023) https://doi.org/10.1080/07391102.2022.2134214
28. Zhao, T., Xiao, X., Wu, Y., et al.: Tracing the flu symptom progression via a smart face mask. Nano Lett. **23**(19), 8960–8969 (2023). https://doi.org/10.1021/acs.nanolett.3c02492
29. Ai, T., Yang, Z., Hou, H., Zhan, C., Chen, C., et al.: Correlation of chest CT and RT-PCR testing in Corona-virus Disease 2019 (COVID-19) in China: a report of 1014 cases. Radiology **296**(2), E32–E40 (2020). https://doi.org/10.1148/radiol.2020200642
30. Srinivasa Rao, A.S.R., Vazquez, J.A.: Identification of COVID-19 can be quicker through artificial intelligence framework using a mobile phone-based survey when cities and towns are under quarantine. Infect. Control Hospital Epidemiol. **41**(7), 826–830 (2020) https://doi.org/10.1017/ice.2020.61
31. Li, L., Qin, L., Xu, Z., et al.: Using artificial intelligence to detect COVID-19 and community-acquired pneumonia based on pulmonary CT: evaluation of the diagnostic accuracy. Radiology **296**(2), E65–E71 (2020). https://doi.org/10.1148/radiol.2020200905
32. Tang, Z., Zhao, W., Xie, X., et al.: Severity assessment of Coronavirus disease 2019 (COVID-19) using quantitative features from chest CT images. Phys. Med. Biol. **66**(3), 035015 (2020). https://doi.org/10.48550/arXiv.2003.11988
33. Farid, A.A., Selim, G.I., Awad, H., Khater, A.: A novel approach of CT images feature analysis and prediction to screen for corona virus disease (COVID-19). Int. J. Sci. Eng. Res. **11**(3) (2020) https://doi.org/10.20944/preprints202003.0284.v1
34. Labgold, K., Hamid, S., Shah, S., et al.: Estimating the unknown: greater racial and ethnic disparities in COVID-19 burden after accounting for missing race and ethnicity data. Epidemiology **32**(2), 157–161 (2021). https://doi.org/10.1097/EDE.0000000000001314
35. Maharaj, A.S., Parker, J., Hopkins, J.P., et al.: The effect of seasonal respiratory virus transmission on syndromic surveillance for COVID-19 in Ontario, Canada. Lancet Infect. Dis. **21**(5), 593–594 (2021). https://doi.org/10.1016/S1473-3099(21)00151-1
36. Karar, M.E., Hemdan, E.E.-D., Shouman, M.A.: Cascaded deep learning classifiers for computer-aided diagnosis of COVID-19 and pneumonia diseases in X-ray scans. Complex Intell. Syst. **7**(1), 235–247 (2020). https://doi.org/10.1007/s40747-020-00199-4
37. Shankar, K., Perumal, E.: A novel hand-crafted with deep learning features based fusion model for COVID-19 diagnosis and classification using chest X-ray images. Complex Intell. Syst. **7**(3), 1277–1293 (2021). https://doi.org/10.1007/s40747-020-00216-6
38. Elaziz, M.A., Hosny, K.M., Salah, A., Darwish, M.M., Lu, S., Sahlol, A.T.: New machine learning method for image based diagnosis of COVID-19. PLoS ONE **15**(6), e0235187 (2020). https://doi.org/10.1371/journal.pone.0235187
39. Laguarta, J., Hueto, F., Subirana, B.: COVID-19 artificial intelligence diagnosis using only cough recordings. IEEE Open J. Eng. Med. Biol. **1**, 275–281 (2020). https://doi.org/10.1109/OJEMB.2020.3026928
40. Wang, C.J., Ng, C.Y., Brook, R.H.: Response to COVID-19 in Taiwan: big data analytics, new technology, and proactive testing. JAMA **323**(14), 1341–1342 (2020). https://doi.org/10.1001/jama.2020.3151

41. Abbaspour Onari, M., Yousefi, S., Rabieepour, M., Alizadeh, A., Jahangoshai Rezaee, M.: A medical decision support system for predicting the severity level of COVID-19. Complex Intell. Syst. **7**(4), 2037–2051 (2021). https://doi.org/10.1007/s40747-021-00312-1
42. Orozco-del-Castillo, M.G., Novelo-Cruz, R.A., et al.: Fuzzy logic-based COVID-19 and other respiratory conditions pre-clinical diagnosis system. In: M. F. Mata-Rivera et al. (eds.): Telematics and Computing, Vol. 1280, pp. 402–419 (2020). https://doi.org/10.1007/978-3-030-62554-2_29
43. Shahparvari, S., et al.: A decision support system for prioritised COVID-19 two-dosage vaccination allocation and distribution. Transp. Res. Part E, **159**, 102598 (2022). https://doi.org/10.1016/j.tre.2021.102598
44. Chang, Z., et al.: Application of artificial intelligence in COVID-19 medical area: a systematic review. J. Thorac. Dis. **13**(12), 7034–7053 (2021). https://doi.org/10.21037/jtd-21-747
45. Vinod, D.N., Prabaharan, S.R.S.: COVID-19 – The role of artificial intelligence, machine learning, and deep learning: a newfangled. Arch. Comput. Methods Eng. **30**(4), 2667–2682 (2023). https://doi.org/10.1007/s11831-023-09882-4

A Graph Neural Network with Multi-head Attention for Universal Brain Disease Diagnosis from fMRI Images

Hyung-Jun Moon[1], Tae-Hoon Kang[2], and Sung-Bae Cho[2](✉)

[1] Department of Artificial Intelligence, Yonsei University, Seoul 03722, Republic of Korea
axtabio@yonsei.ac.kr

[2] Department of Computer Science, Yonsei University, Seoul 03722, Republic of Korea
{thkyang324,sbcho}@yonsei.ac.kr

Abstract. Developing an almighty model for brain disease diagnosis is challenging due to the biological brain changes that should be detected in the brain across a wide range of conditions. Most models for brain disease diagnosis depend on the unique characteristics of each disease, which limits their applicability to universal brain diseases. In this paper, we propose a method that extracts all brain activities with functional connectivity (FC) graphs based on medical evidence and classifies them via a graph neural network (GNN) with multi-head attention for diagnosis. We generate FC graphs that contain both local and global features of brain changes, as well as short- and long-term dependencies of each disease. The FC graphs are then gone through the GNN to recognize correlations among various brain regions. Experiments on four benchmark disease datasets of autism, Alzheimer's disease, ADHD, and schizophrenia show that the proposed method produces an average improvement of 1.6%p and up to 3%p in accuracy compared to the state-of-the-art methods. The results are verified with the medical knowledge on each disease, highlighting the effectiveness of the proposed method in advancing neurological research for brain disease diagnosis.

Keywords: Brain Disease Diagnosis · fMRI Images · Functional Connectivity · Graph Neural Network · Multi-head Attention

1 Introduction

The brain is the most vital organ in the human body, consisting of 100 billion neurons and over 100 trillion connections, representing complex spatiotemporal correlations [1, 2]. With the advent of neural networks, recent advancements in fMRI neuroimaging technology have successfully progressed in diagnosing various brain diseases [3]. However, the conventional methods are designed to diagnose based on a single specific disease [4–7], aiming to differentiate images between normal and disease. These methods have difficulty to be applied to other diseases. For example, as certain neurodegenerative diseases triggered by stimuli cause transient brain activity changes [1, 8], a method for one disease does not work to model features for other diseases that affect the brain broadly.

H. Quintián et al. (Eds.): HAIS 2024, LNAI 14857, pp. 85–97, 2025.
https://doi.org/10.1007/978-3-031-74183-8_8

As seen in Fig. 1, the brain exhibits different characteristics in fMRI images depending on the type of disease.

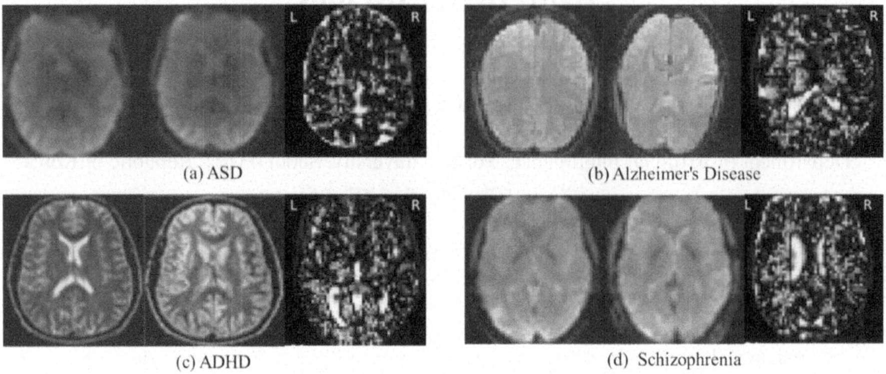

Fig. 1. Four types of brain diseases and the differences in brain region images between normal and disease states are depicted. From left to right, the images show the normal brain, the disease brain, and the differences after scaling.

According to various medical studies [1, 8–10], in cases of ASD or Alzheimer's disease [9, 10], there is generally a difference in the overall brain activity response compared to other diseases. In the case of ADHD or schizophrenia [7, 11], the differences between normal and disease states are more pronounced in specific regions. This indicates that these differing characteristics among diseases suggest that traditional methods, which capture only simple differences in images, make it challenging to construct an almighty model.

This paper proposes a method that, based on medical evidence, converts and diagnoses the general characteristics of brain diseases into functional connectivity (FC) by considering the long- and short-term dependencies of diseases and their global and local effects. The proposed method is based on a graph neural network with multi-head attention to capture the characteristics of all diseases and automatically learn the appropriate FC configurations. It focuses on detecting subtle changes based on global spatiotemporal brain images; extracts the correlations for each region based on the actual local brain functions and converts them into graphs. The converted FC graphs encompass regional correlations, allowing for effective disease diagnosis with a graph neural network (GNN) with edge labels to classify the correlations. This method seeks to model brain activities, the regional and global characteristics across different areas, and the short- and long-term temporal dependencies, creating a universal map of the brain for disease diagnosis. To evaluate the proposed method, we perform several experiments on four types of brain diseases collected from fMRI images. Also, we conduct a performance analysis based on the medical knowledge of each disease, further demonstrating the advantages of the proposed method.

2 Related Works

Table 1 summarizes recent methods and descriptions related to fMRI brain disease research. An ensemble of convolutional neural networks (CNNs) has shown proficiency in extracting spatial features from brain images, critical for analyzing spatial conditions. These models have achieved high accuracy and facilitated the analysis of both structural

Table 1. The methods related to fMRI brain disease benchmark datasets.

Task (dataset)		Method	Description
Autism		Self-supervised ensemble [18]	Spatial CNN based ensemble
		ResNet-LSTM with self-attention [3]	Spatio-temporal CNN-LSTM with attention
		CNN ensemble [13]	Spatial CNN based ensemble
		R-walk [4]	Algorithm-based feature selection
		ASD-SAEnet [11]	Spare autoencoder-based feature extraction
		Multi-view ensemble learning [15]	FC-based ensemble
		ASD-DiagNet [16]	FC-based feature extraction
		Bootstrapping ensemble of GCNNs [19]	GNN-based ensemble
ADHD		Distributed 3D-CNNs [12]	Spatial CNN-based data generation
		Triplet-Attention CNN [20]	Attention autoencoder-based feature extraction
		Seed-based CNN [17]	Seed-based FC with CNN
		4D-CNN [21]	Spatio-temporal CNN-LSTM
		STAAE [5]	Attention autoencoder-based FC
Alzheimer	**Binary**	3D-CNN-LSTM [14]	Spatio-temporal CNN-LSTM
		3D-CNN [22]	Spatial CNN
	Multi	3D-CNN-LSTM [14]	Spatio-temporal CNN-LSTM
		3D-CNN [22]	Spatial CNN
		3D-CNN-LSTM [6]	Spatio-temporal CNN-LSTM
Schizophrenia		SURF/FAST [23]	Feature selection with SVM
		Capsule Network [24]	Multi-view image-based capsule network
		DFCN [7]	Spatio-temporal FC

and functional brain aspects [12, 13]. However, their focus on specific disease characteristics limits their applicability for creating a universal model. Combining CNNs for spatial features and recurrent neural networks (RNNs), such as LSTMs, for temporal features has been validated for capturing intricate spatiotemporal characteristics of the brain, leading to superior performance in specific disease diagnosis. CNNs excel in identifying patterns within fMRI images, while LSTMs analyze temporal dynamics, crucial for understanding brain activity over time [3, 6, 14]. Despite this synergy, these models are typically designed for single-disease scenarios, making it challenging to generalize across multiple diseases.

FC analysis is fundamental in brain research, crucial for uncovering biomarkers for various neurological and mental diseases [15, 16]. Traditional FC-based methods map the brain's neural network by creating graphs where nodes represent regions of interest (ROIs), and edges symbolize functional connections [17].

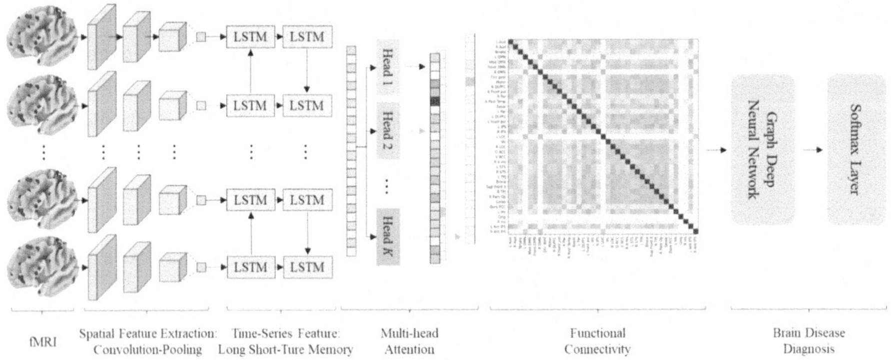

Fig. 2. Overview of the proposed method.

Graph-based methods for fMRI analysis have advanced the understanding of brain structure and functionality by providing a comprehensive view of the interconnectedness of brain regions. These methods uncover patterns and associations not immediately apparent through standard imaging analysis [19]. However, as they often target specific diseases, graphs created tend to be heavily weighted or overfitted in special areas.

3 Proposed Method

Figure 2 illustrates the proposed model, which uses a residual convolutional bidirectional LSTM with a multi-head attention mechanism to model spatial and temporal features. In the preprocessing phase, 4D fMRI images are segmented into 3D blocks at each time interval, creating overlapping k-slice windows.

3.1 Universal Brain Map

The key idea is to diagnose diseases by recognizing common patterns in disease and normal brain images based on spatiotemporal features across brain regions. Unlike previous methods that focus on differences between normal and disease brains to predict a single disease, we prioritize creating a comprehensive map of overall brain activity across different regions. Firstly, to model the brain's spatial features, we use a residual convolutional network to capture overall spatial characteristics. This network is highly effective in image-related deep learning tasks. Concurrently, we employ a bidirectional LSTM to model temporal features, as it captures long- and short-term dependencies in 4D fMRI images. To ensure the model focuses on relevant information, we utilize the attention mechanism.

Using the intermediate layer information, we segregate brain activity images by specific regions to construct a correlation matrix. The primary contribution lies in creating a correlation map that considers the brain's overall, regional, and long-term temporal dependencies. This method allows us to develop a generalized process that forms a common matrix for the brain rather than focusing on specific disease characteristics. We then convert the matrix into a graph and use a GNN to predict diseases by understanding and diagnosing the graph. By leveraging this comprehensive method, we aim to move beyond single-disease prediction to a more holistic understanding of brain activity patterns, potentially enhancing the accuracy and reliability of brain disease diagnoses.

3.2 Model Architecture and Learning Process

Capturing Universal Disease Pattern with Multi-head Attention
The proposed model uses a residual convolutional neural network (ResNet) to model spatial features from 4D fMRI images. During preprocessing, these images are segmented into 3D blocks at each time interval, creating overlapping k-slice windows. The ResNet, designed with a more extensive and deeper architecture compared to traditional CNNs, processes these blocks to capture spatial characteristics effectively. The network employs a specific residual operation $H(x) = F(x) + x$, where:

$$F(x) = \Sigma_{a=0}^{m-1} \Sigma_{b=0}^{m-1} w_{ab}^{l} x_{(i+a)(j+b)}^{l-1} \tag{1}$$

This residual connection helps maintain the gradient $F'(x) + 1$ across layers, addressing gradient vanishing issues and enhancing the extraction of spatial features.

The spatial features modeled by the ResNet are fed into a bidirectional LSTM (BiLSTM) network to model temporal dependencies. BiLSTM is chosen for its ability to capture both long-term and short-term dependencies in time-series data, making it well-suited for analyzing the dynamic nature of fMRI data. The BiLSTM processes the features, producing a series of hidden states $h_1, h_2, \ldots, h_N$ which serve as the basis for temporal feature. To enhance the modeling of meaningful temporal features and prevent the model from being overwhelmed by the overall features, a multi-head attention mechanism is incorporated. The attention mechanism assigns weights to significant temporal attributes, allowing the model to focus on specific time frames. The attention weights a_{ij} are computed as:

$$a_{ij} = softmax_j\left(h_{ij}\right) = \frac{\exp\left(score\left(h_i, h_j \cdot W_v h_i\right)\right)}{\Sigma_{n=1}^{N} \exp(h_i, h_n \cdot W_v h_i)} \tag{2}$$

where $score(h_i, h_j) = f(W_q h_i, W_k h_j)$. The output representation r_i for each hidden state h_i is then computed as a weighted sum of all hidden states:

$$r_i = \Sigma_{n=1}^{N} a_{in} \cdot h_n \tag{3}$$

This process is repeated independently K times, and the results are concatenated to form a single vector.

Region Correlation FC and Classification with GNN

Using the intermediate layer information from the spatiotemporal model, the brain activity images are segregated by specific brain regions to construct an interrelationship matrix. This matrix delineates the relationships between 39 distinct brain regions, considering overall, regional, and long-term temporal dependencies. The connectivity matrix C is derived from feature representations $r_1, r_2, \ldots, r_T$ as:

$$C_{ij} = ConnectivityMeasure(r_i, r_j) \tag{4}$$

Various metrics such as correlation, partial correlation, tangent, or covariance can be applied, resulting in different forms of the matrix C, each capturing unique aspects of inter-regional brain dynamics.

The connectivity matrix C is interpreted as the adjacency matrix A of a graph, where each element C_{ij} represents the strength of the connection between brain regions i and j. This matrix is crucial for understanding the complex interconnections within the brain. Continuous correlation values in matrix C are categorized into discrete edge labels based on quartiles, making it suitable for GNN analysis. To facilitate graph-based analysis, we categorize the continuous correlation values in matrix C into discrete edge labels based on quartiles, as follows:

$$\begin{cases} 1 if C_{ij} \in Q_1 \\ 2 if C_{ij} \in Q_2 \\ 3 if C_{ij} \in Q_3 \\ 4 if C_{ij} \in Q_4 \end{cases}, \text{ where} Q_n \text{ is the} n - th \text{quartile} \tag{5}$$

This labeling method allows us to transform the continuous brain connectivity data into a format suitable for GNN analysis.

The edge-conditioned convolution (ECC) layer embeds the graph by computing a signal X_l at each node v, considering the node's features and neighborhood structure:

$$X^l(v) = \sigma\left(\Sigma_{u \in \mathcal{N}(v)} \Theta^l_{uv} \cdot X^{l-1}(u)\right) \tag{6}$$

where $\Theta^l_{uv} = f^l(L(u, v))$ is the edge-conditioned weight matrix. Through successive ECC layers, the graph is embedded into a high-dimensional space, capturing intricate connectivity patterns. The final classification is performed by feeding the embedded graph representation through a series of fully connected layers, culminating in a softmax layer for disease categorization:

$$Y = \text{softmax}(\text{FC}(X^L)) \tag{7}$$

4 Experiments

Experimental setup is conducted using a Nvidia DGX station equipped with 2560 Nvidia tensor cores, running on a Ubuntu desktop Linux OS. The hardware includes 4X Tesla V100 GPUs (64 GB each) and 256 GB of LRDIMM DDR4 memory. For the software environment, we utilize Ubuntu with Python 3.x and TensorFlow version 2.3. Additionally, various Python libraries such as Scikit-learn, Nilearn, and Networkx are utilized for the experiments.

4.1 Data Preprocessing and Implementation

We use the datasets for four major brain disorders (autism, Alzheimer's disease, ADHD, schizophrenia) for the experiments. The datasets are split into training (90%) and validation (10%) sets based on individual patients. Table 2 provides a comprehensive summary of the datasets and preprocessing steps used in the study. The proposed model receives 4D images, outputting a softmax probability for classification. It comprises 5 conv3D layers, 2 BiLSTM layers with multi-head attention, and 2 MLP layers. The GNN includes 3 layers ECC with skip connections and 2 MLP layers. We use the Adam optimizer to reduce training time and optimize the loss function effectively.

4.2 Experimental Results

ADHD: ADHD is characterized by changes in brain activity in response to specific tasks or stimuli, confined to particular time periods [8]. These temporal patterns are crucial for accurate diagnosis, reflecting how ADHD affects brain function. The proposed method achieves an accuracy of $99.41 \pm 0.25\%$ for ADHD, as shown in Table 3. This improvement over other techniques, such as distributed 3D-CNNs and triplet-attention CNN, is due to the attention mechanism, which isolates and analyzes crucial time-specific changes in brain activity, capturing the transient features associated with ADHD accurately. This focus enhances the diagnostic process, making it more precise and reliable.

Schizophrenia: Schizophrenia manifests through disrupted thought processes and cognitive function, with unique patterns in brain activity response to stimuli [1]. These changes can be more pronounced at certain moments, reflecting the disorder's episodic nature. The proposed method achieves an accuracy of $90.61 \pm 0.94\%$ for schizophrenia, outperforming methods like SURF/FAST and 3D-CNN-LSTM, as detailed in Table 3. The superior performance is due to the multi-head attention mechanism, which captures complex, time-specific characteristics of schizophrenia. This focus on significant temporal variations leads to more accurate and early diagnosis.

Alzheimer's Disease: Alzheimer's disease involves progressive structural and functional brain changes, with consistent characteristic information over time [9]. It shows a gradual decline in cognitive function and memory, with widespread changes in brain connectivity. The proposed method achieves an accuracy of 98.11% in binary-class and 96.57% in multi-class Alzheimer's, as presented in Table 4. This performance is due to the graph-based method, capturing distributed changes and patterns over time. This

Table 2. Description of datasets and preprocessing for brain disorder experiments.

Disease	Task	Subjects	Preprocessing
Autism	ABIDE I	800 (389 with ASD, 411 controls)	Standardizing fMRI images to 24 × 24 × 24, sliding window technique
Alzheimer's disease	ADNI	120 across 4 classes (AD, LMCI, EMCI, CN)	Motion correction, intensity normalization, co-registration to MNI space, noise and signal drifts removal
ADHD	ADHD-200	Balanced between typically developing and ADHD patients	Using 'The Athena' pipeline for consistent data quality across five sites
Schizophrenia	COBRE	121 (57 with schizophrenia, 64 controls)	Slice timing correction, realignment, spatial normalization, spatial smoothing, parcellation into 120 ROIs

extensive analysis enables high accuracy in predicting Alzheimer's disease, addressing its progressive nature effectively.

Autism: Autism spectrum disorder (ASD) is characterized by persistent deficits in social communication and interaction, alongside repetitive behaviors and restricted interests [10]. These functional differences in various brain regions display consistent patterns over time. The proposed method achieves an accuracy of 97.88% for autism, as shown in Table 4, surpassing other competitive methods. The graph-based representation allows effective analysis of continuous brain activity patterns associated with autism. This detailed and comprehensive view enhances the accuracy and reliability of autism diagnosis, offering significant improvements over traditional techniques.

4.3 Ablation Study

The experimental results with and without each component of the proposed method for each disease are summarized in Table 5. The results show that for ADHD and schizophrenia, where disease characteristics are observed in specific regions or at specific times, there is a significant difference in performance depending on the presence of the attention mechanism. For autism and Alzheimer's, where the brain diseases exhibit general characteristics across brain regions, there is a significant difference depending on the presence of universal FC, which captures these features and supports universal mapping. Additionally, the Edge GNN is found to contribute to overall performance improvement.

Figure 3 illustrates the performance variations in terms of the *ConnectivityMeasure* used to construct FC and the number of layers in the GNN used for classification.

Notably, FC constructed using covariance outperforms other metrics overall. Besides, the performance comparison in terms of the number of GNN layers reveals that using three layers yields the best results across all metrics, while further increasing the number of layers leads to a decrease in performance. This decline is attributed to the oversmoothing problem inherent in spatial GNNs, where increasing the number of GNN layers causes specific and local information to be diluted. Based on these experimental results, we use the covariance and three layers for all other experiments.

4.4 Discussion

The proposed method's ability to adapt to the unique characteristics of each disease, whether they manifest as time-specific or overall temporal patterns, results in highly accurate and reliable brain disease diagnoses. The integration of attention mechanism and graph neural network provides a robust method for understanding and predicting the complex dynamics of brain activity associated with different neurological conditions. In summary, the proposed attention mechanism, universal FC, and GNN each play complementary roles in creating a universal diagnostic model, effectively detecting disease characteristics across various conditions. Their functional roles align with the specific features of each disease, demonstrating their effectiveness in disease diagnosis.

Table 3. Accuracy comparison for diseases (ADHD and schizophrenia).

Disease	Method	Accuracy
ADHD	STAAE [5]	65.71 ± 1.34
	3D-CNN [22]	70.12 ±1. 21
	4D-CNN [21]	71.33 ± 0.80
	Seed-based CNN [17]	84.15 ± 0.61
	Covariance FC with GCN	86.32 ±3.44
	3D-CNN-LSTM [14]	90.51 ±0.33
	Triplet-Attention CNN [20]	99.38 ± 0.21
	Distributed 3D-CNNs [12]	99.22 ± 0.23
	Ours	**99.41 ± 0.25**
Schizophrenia	DFCN [7]	81.82 ± 1.43
	Capsuled network [24]	82.83 ± 0.85
	3D-CNN [22]	85.49 ± 2.15
	Covariance FC with GCN	87.35 ± 1.23
	SURF/FAST [23]	87.51 ± 0.23
	3D-CNN-LSTM [14]	88.49 ± 3.48
	Ours	91.61 ± 0.94

Table 4. Accuracy comparison for diseases (autism and Alzheimer).

Disease		Method	Accuracy
Autism		Self-supervised ensemble [18]	94.13 ± 3.12
		ResNet-LSTM with self-attention [3]	86.74 ± 1.34
		CNN ensemble [13]	83.67 ± 3.24
		R-walk [4]	73.45 ± 2.81
		ASD-SAEnet [11]	77.13 ± 5.44
		Multi-view ensemble learning [15]	74.16 ± 1.31
		ASD-DiagNet [16]	76.22 ± 2.29
		Bootstrapping ensemble of GCNNs [19]	68.46 ± 7.94
		Ours	**97.88** ± **1.64**
Alzheimer	Binary	3D-CNN-LSTM [14]	97.46 ± 0.85
		3D-CNN [22]	93.52 ± 0.96
		Ours	**98.11** ± **0.71**
	Multi	3D -CNN-LSTM [6]	95.58 ± 1.99
		3D-CNN [22]	94.83 ± 2.85
		3D-CNN-LSTM [14]	90.48 ± 2.46
		Ours	96.57 ± 1.52

Table 5. Ablation study for each disease on the proposed method.

Task (dataset)	Attention	Universal FC	GNN	Accuracy
ADHD	X	X	X	90.45 ±0.14
	V	X	X	98.24 ± 0.77
	X	V	X	91.53 ± 0.55
	X	X	V	94.43 ± 0.15
	V	V	X	98.91 ± 0.45
	V	V	V	**99.41** ± **0.25**
Schizophrenia	X	X	X	79.42 ±1.15
	V	X	X	85.94 ± 2.34
	X	V	X	86.44 ± 0.72
	X	X	V	83.82 ± 0.55
	V	V	X	89.88 ± 1.45

(*continued*)

Table 5. (*continued*)

Task (dataset)	Attention	Universal FC	GNN	Accuracy
	V	V	V	**91.61** ±0. **94**
Autism	X	X	X	90.16 ±1. 15
	V	X	X	92.11 ± 2.11
	X	V	X	95.88 ± 1.84
	X	X	V	93.55 ± 1.56
	V	V	X	96.41 ±1. 88
	V	V	V	**97.88** ±1. **64**
Alzheimer (multi)	X	X	X	90.17 ±1. 20
	V	X	X	90.85 ±1. 66
	X	V	X	94.84 ±1. 47
	X	X	V	91.25 ±1.11
	V	V	X	95.94 ±1.39
	V	V	V	**96.57** ±1.52

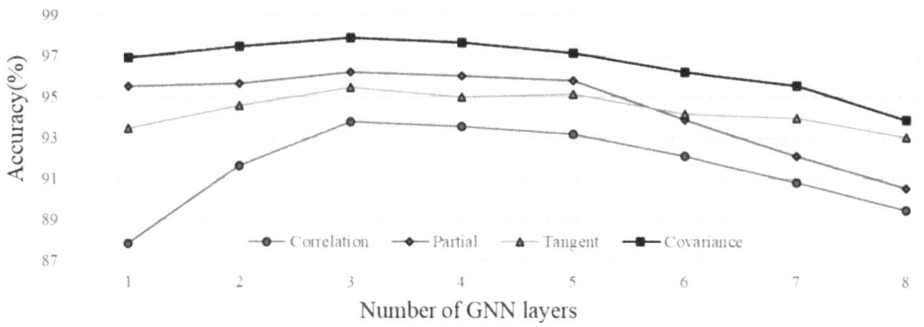

Fig. 3. Performance on ABIDE I for connectivity measures and number of GNN layers.

5 Concluding Remarks

The proposed method, incorporating attention-based brain map generation, graph transformation, and graph neural networks, demonstrates superior accuracy in identifying brain diseases and differentiating them from normal brain patterns. The proposed method captures global and local features, considering short- and long-term dependencies for a comprehensive analysis of brain activity. Experimental results across various datasets archive the method's ability to model disease-specific features and enhance diagnostic accuracy, highlighting its potential to transition into a universal model for brain disease diagnosis.

Future research will focus on improving the feature modeling process, particularly for identifying patterns in continuous images [25]. We aim to integrate contrastive learning with the proposed method to enhance the refinement and accuracy of neural network models in brain disease diagnostics, advance the field and improve the precision of brain disease diagnosis [26].

Acknowledgements. This work was supported by the Yonsei Fellow Program funded by Lee Youn Jae, IITP grant funded by the Korea government (MSIT) (No. RS-2020-II201361, Artificial Intelligence Graduate School Program (Yonsei University)) and ETRI grant funded by the Korean government (24ZB1100, Core Technology Research for Self-Improving Integrated Artificial Intelligence System).

References

1. Dabiri, M., Dehghani Firouzabadi, F., Yang, K., Barker, P.B., Lee, R.R., Yousem, D.M.: Neuroimaging in schizophrenia: a review article. Front. Neurosci. **16**, 1042814 (2022)
2. Gur, R.E., Gur, R.C.: Functional magnetic resonance imaging in schizophrenia. Dialogues Clin. Neurosci. **12**, 333–343 (2010)
3. Park, K.-W., Cho, S.-B.: A residual graph convolutional network with spatio-temporal features for autism classification from fMRI brain images. Appl. Soft Comput. **142**, 110363 (2023)
4. Sotero, R.C., Sanchez-Bornot, J.M., Iturria-Medina, Y.: Improving fMRI-based autism spectrum disorder classification with random walks-informed feature extraction and selection. bioRxiv, pp. 41–47 (2023)
5. Dong, Q., Qiang, N., Lv, J., Li, X., Liu, T., Li, Q.: Spatiotemporal attention autoencoder (STAAE) for ADHD classification. Med. Image Comput. Comput. Assist. Interv. **23**, 508–517 (2020)
6. Noh, J.-H., Kim, J.-H., Yang, H.-D.: Classification of Alzheimer's progression using fMRI data. Sensors **23**(14), 6330 (2023)
7. Pan, C., Yu, H., Fei, X., Zheng, X., Yu, R.: Temporal-spatial dynamic functional connectivity analysis in schizophrenia classification. Front. Neurosci. **16**, 965937 (2022)
8. Pereira-Sanchez, V., Castellanos, F.X.: Neuroimaging in attention-deficit/hyperactivity disorder. Curr. Opin. Psychiatry **34**(2), 105 (2021)
9. Amini, M., Pedram, M., Moradi, A., Ouchani, M.: Diagnosis of Alzheimer's disease severity with fMRI images using robust multitask feature extraction method and convolutional neural network (CNN). Comput. Math. Methods Med. **2021**, 1–15 (2021)
10. Liu, M., Li, B., Hu, D.: Autism spectrum disorder studies using fMRI data and machine learning: a review. Front. Neurosci. **15**, 697870 (2021)
11. Almuqhim, F., Saeed, F.: ASD-SAENet: a sparse autoencoder, and deep-neural network model for detecting autism spectrum disorder (ASD) using fMRI data. Front. Comput. Neurosci. **15**, 654315 (2021)
12. Sims, C.: Highly accurate FMRI ADHD classification using time distributed multi modal 3D CNNs. arXiv preprint arXiv:2205.11993 (2022)
13. Ahmed, M.R., Zhang, Y., Liu, Y., Liao, H.: Single volume image generator and deep learning-based ASD classification. IEEE J. Biomed. Health Inform. **24**(11), 3044–3054 (2020)
14. Li, W., Lin, X., Chen, X.: Detecting Alzheimer's disease Based on 4D fMRI: an exploration under deep learning framework. Neurocomputing **388**, 280–287 (2020)
15. Kang, L., Chen, J., Huang, J., Jiang, J.: Autism spectrum disorder recognition based on multi-view ensemble learning with multi-site fMRI. Cogn. Neurodyn. **17**(2), 345–355 (2023)
16. Eslami, T., Mirjalili, V., Fong, A., Laird, A.R., Saeed, F.: ASD-DiagNet: a hybrid learning approach for detection of autism spectrum disorder using fMRI data. Front. Neuroinform. **13**, 70 (2019)

17. Ariyarathne, G., De Silva, S., Dayarathna, S., Meedeniya, D., Jayarathne, S.: ADHD identification using convolutional neural network with seed-based approach for fMRI data. In: proceedings of the 2020 9th international conference on software and computer applications, vol. 9, pp. 31–35 (2020)
18. Gaur, M., Chaturvedi, K., Vishwakarma, D.K., Ramasamy, S., Prasad, M.: Self-supervised ensembled learning for autism spectrum classification. Res. Autism Spectr. Disord. **107**, 102223 (2023)
19. Chen, Z., Ji, J., Liang, Y.: Convolutional neural network with an element-wise filter to classify dynamic functional connectivity. In: 2019 IEEE International Conference on Bioinformatics and Biomedicine (BIBM), pp. 643–646 (2019)
20. Tang, Y., Chen, Y., Gao, Y., Jiang, A., Zhou, L.: ADHD classification with biomarker identification using a triplet loss attention auto-encoding network. In: ICASSP 2023-2023 IEEE International Conference on Acoustics, Speech and Signal Processing (ICASSP), pp. 1–5 (2023)
21. Mao, Z., et al.: Spatio-temporal deep learning method for ADHD FMRI classification. Inf. Sci. **499**, 1–11 (2019)
22. Parmar, H.S., Nutter, B., Long, R., Antani, S., Mitra, S.: Deep learning of volumetric 3D CNN for fMRI in Alzheimer's disease classification. Med. Imaging Biomed. Appl. Mol. Struct. Funct. Imaging **11317**, 66–71 (2020)
23. Jiji, G.W., Rajesh, A., Kanagaraj, A.: Analysis of schizophrenia using support vector machine classifier. Multimedia Tools Appl. **82**, 32505–32517 (2023). https://doi.org/10.1007/s11042-023-14513-y
24. Yang, B., et al.: Schizophrenia classification using fMRI data based on a multiple feature image capsule network ensemble. IEEE Access **7**, 109956–109968 (2019)
25. Moon, H.-J., Cho, S.-B.: A subgraph embedded GIN with attention for graph classification. In: International Conference on Intelligent Data Engineering and Automated Learning, pp. 356–367 (2023)
26. Moon, H.-J., Cho, S.-B.: Contrastive learning of multivariate Gaussian distributions of incremental classes for continual learning. In: International Work-Conference on Interplay between Natural and Artificial Computation, pp. 518–527 (2024). https://doi.org/10.1007/978-3-031-61140-7_49

A Computer Vision Approach to Detect Facial Characteristics Related to Encephalopathy in Term Infants

Nuria Velasco-Pérez[1(✉)], Samuel Lozano-Juárez[1], Lucía Núñez-Calvo[1], Nuño Basurto[1], Juan Arnaez[2,3,4], and Daniel Urda[1]

[1] Grupo de Inteligencia Computacional Aplicada (GICAP), Departamento de Digitalización, Escuela Politécnica Superior, Universidad de Burgos, Avda Cantabria s/n, 09006 Burgos, Spain
{nuriavp,sljuarez,lncalvof,durda}@ubu.es

[2] Unidad Neonatal, Hospital Universitario de Burgos, Avda Islas Baleares 3, 09006 Burgos, Spain

[3] Neurología Neonatal, Fundación NeNe, Calle Eloy Gonzalo, 3, 28010 Madrid, Spain
juan.arnaez@neurologianeonatal.org

[4] Profesor Sociedad Iberoamericana de Neonatología (SIBEN), Jersey City, NJ, USA

Abstract. Neonatal encephalopathy is one of the most common problems in newborns leading to severe complications and even death. Although current diagnosis is mainly performed by clinicians, artificial intelligence-based systems could potentially aid them in the diagnose. To this end, this work employs 73 videos of affected newborns from the 'Hospital Universitario de Burgos' to develop several convolutional neural network models capable of detecting one of the main signs of neonatal encephalopathy: lethargy. The detection of this sign has been divided into 3 items: Eye opening, Mouth contraction and Eye frowning. For each item, several models were trained and evaluated using the frames of these videos. The results obtained were positive especially for the Mouth contraction detection, with a balanced accuracy value of 0.822 and a recall of 0.85. Further improvements need to be carried out in order to make these models available as an aid-diagnostic tool in clinical practice.

Keywords: Neonatal encephalopathy · Early diagnose · Convolutional Neural Networks · Deep Learning · Transfer Learning

1 Introduction

Neonatal encephalopathy (NE) is a clinical syndrome affecting newborns at or beyond 35 weeks of gestation, characterized by impaired neurological function during their first week of life. It manifests as decreased consciousness, seizures, difficulty breathing, and reduced muscle tone and reflexes. While less common in high-income countries (under 2 per 1000 live births), it affects over 8 per

H. Quintián et al. (Eds.): HAIS 2024, LNAI 14857, pp. 98–109, 2025.
https://doi.org/10.1007/978-3-031-74183-8_9

1000 live births in low- and middle-income countries [9]. NE is the second most significant neonatal issue after prematurity, representing a leading cause of death, severe neurological complications, and seizures in term newborns. It accounts for roughly 20% of childhood cerebral palsy cases. The burden of NE, measured in years lived with disability, has surged in recent decades, underscoring the need for enhanced diagnostic and management support [2,20].

Initiating therapeutic hypothermia within 6 h of birth significantly reduces mortality and major neurodevelopmental disability in moderate-to-severe NE [27]. This makes early NE identification a perinatal emergency. Given the dynamic nature of NE, and the reliance of diagnosis and severity grading on clinical assessment, repeated neurological exams within the first 6 h of life are recommended [3]. These examinations are usually performed by a clinician, monitoring the response to various nociceptive stimuli. However, expertise levels vary across and within centers [22]. To prevent misdiagnosis, telemedicine enables community providers to consult with specialists at referral centers about potential NE cases [15]. A study by our group showed that video recordings can facilitate NE identification and severity grading, with expert review further improving diagnosis [4].

The rapid growth of Artificial Intelligence (AI) in medicine has opened exciting possibilities. Applying Machine Learning (ML) algorithms to identify patterns in clinical data could greatly enhance diagnostic accuracy [18]. A clear sign of these possibilities is the increase in the number of publications about AI applications in medicine, which has increased by 84.6% between 2008 and 2018 [31]. There are several examples where ML is being successfully applied in medicine, such as the use of Support Vector Machines for the diagnosis of cardiovascular diseases [1], the application of Deep Neural Networks for the prediction of the response to cancer treatments [24], or the usage of Convolutional Neural Networks (CNNs) for the interpretation of images in the diagnosis of neurodegenerative diseases [19].

Among all ML models, CNNs stand out for their efficiency in the recognition of elements in images, positioning themselves as one of the most common strategies for the analysis of medical images. These models have demonstrated good performance in the detection of discomfort features in newborns [16] and in neonatal facial recognition [26]. Thus, they are a promising tool when analysing facial expression and features in newborns. In this sense, this paper presents different CNN models trained with videos of newborns provided by the "Hospital Universitario de Burgos", with the aim of detecting the response of neonates to nociceptive stimuli. Specifically, individual models have been developed for the identification of 3 facial characteristics within the reaction of neonates: Eye Opening, Mouth Contraction and Eye Frowning. By analyzing these 3 characteristics, it is possible to know the alertness of the newborn, which acts as a proxy to determine the degree of encephalopathy.

The rest of the paper is organized as follows. Section 2 describes the set of videos used in the training of the models and the processes for image acquisition. The methods and experimental design are described in Sect. 3 and 4 respectively.

Next, Sect. 5 includes the results obtained, and Sect. 6 presents the conclusions of the project, as well as future lines of work.

2 Dataset

This research study recruited newborn babies born at the "Hospital Universitario de Burgos" maternity ward in Spain. The newborns had a hypoxic-ischemic event at birth and were examined on several occasions in the first 6 h of life to determine the presence and severity of NE. These examinations were recorded with parents' permission who voluntarily signed the informed consent form.

Neonatologists filmed routine checkups of each baby to assess their health status. These checkups involve sight, sound, and touch tests to see how well the babies respond to stimulation and stay awake. Doctors looked for specific signs of awareness, like turning the head towards sounds or focusing on things they see. The babies might have also been checked for movements, stretches, or strong reflexes like the Moro reflex (startle reflex) and the plantar reflex (foot curl) [5].

The study collected 73 videos of varying lengths (around 30 s to 5 min). Some videos only captured a single test during the checkup, while others documented the entire examination. Most videos were filmed vertically to show the baby's whole body for a complete assessment. However, doctors sometimes zoomed in on the baby's face for a closer look at specific features, or briefly adjusted the camera angle as needed during the examination.

The videos were captured using two different smartphones, each with distinct image properties. Firstly, a set of videos (stored as .mov files) was obtained at a frame rate of 29.89 frames per second (FPS), with each frame having a resolution of 1920×1080 pixels. Secondly, another set of videos (stored as .mp4 files) was recorded using a different smartphone at a frame rate of 30 FPS and a resolution of 848×480 pixels.

2.1 Problems Addressed

According to the GarcíÂŋa-AlíÂŋx scoring scale [8], there are multiple aspects that must be taken into account to determine the presence neonatal encephalopathy in a newborn. However, GarcíÂŋa-AlíÂŋx and other authors agree that the state of alertness is one of the most important of them all [14,25]. To assess this item, the following 3 main characteristics were considered on each of the videos to determine the newborn's response to a stimulus: eye opening, mouth contraction and eye frowning, which are next described:

- Eye opening. Assesses eye opening in response to various visual stimuli presented by neonatologists. Two possible labels have been assigned: *Closed eyes* as negative event or *Open eyes* as positive event [6].
- Mouth contraction. It determines if the mouth contracts after a stimulus or if it remains relaxed. Two possible labels were assigned to this item: *Relaxed mouth* as negative event and *Contracted mouth* as positive event [6].

- Eye frowning. This task involves identifying whether the newborn is frowning. This is a common response to discomfort caused by certain stimuli, such as a pinch, and is an indicator of sensory capacity. Two labels have been used for this item: *Relaxed eyes* as negative event and *Pucked eyes* as positive event [23].

In addition, it should be mentioned that labeling was required and carried out as a preprocessing step since prior information about the presence of these features in the entire video was not available.

2.2 Frame Acquisition and Labelling

Out of the 73 videos available, 62 of them (85%) were dedicated to fine-tune the models, while the remaining 11 videos (15%) were left apart for evaluation purposes.

Training Images Acquisition. In order to generate images for the training of the models, the frames of the 62 videos were processed by collecting one random frame for every second of video. As a result of this processing, a total of 2524 images were obtained. This set of images was then manually examined and curated for each of the problems addressed, eliminating those images in which the desired feature to be detected by the model could not be seen. Manual labelling of the images was also performed. Using the labelImg tool [30], the area box and the label of the feature to be detected were indicated, generating for each image an XML file in which the assigned label and the coordinates of the area box are stored. The image-XML pair constitutes the necessary input for the fine-tuning of our models. The distribution of the images labelled for each item among the possible labels can be seen in Table 1.

Table 1. Distribution of training frames for each item in its possible labels. The number of frames varies between items as a consequence of the manual elimination of those images in which the feature to be detected is not visible

Item	Label	No. of images	Total
Eye opening	Closed eyes	1504	2420
	Open eyes	916	
Mouth contraction	Relaxed mouth	1600	2201
	Contracted mouth	601	
	Relaxed eyes	1761	2424
Eye frowning	Pucked eyes	663	

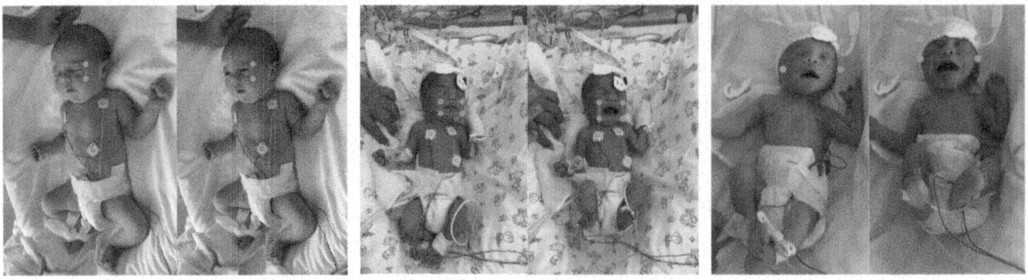

Fig. 1. Overview of the labelled frames for the different items and their field of view. From left to right can be seen frames corresponding to: Closed eyes/Open eyes, Relaxed mouth/Contracted mouth and Relaxed eyes/Pucked eyes.

Evaluation Images Acquisition. The 11 videos for the evaluation of the models were also manually annotated. Each second of each video was recorded as a positive or negative event for each of the features to be studied. The area of each label was not recorded as this information will not be used for model evaluation. Once the videos were annotated, they were cut into their different frames, generating for each frame an XML with the corresponding label. All generated labels were then grouped in batches of 30 in order to obtain a single consensus label for each second of video. These consensus labels constitute the ground truth values to be used in the evaluation.

3 Methods

This section delves into the Deep Learning (DL) methods and techniques employed in this study to develop a precise model to identify newborn alertness based on the characterization of three key features.

Recently, DL has introduced a significant change in neonatal assessment, offering an objective and automated method rooted in data analysis. Through the examination of extensive datasets, pretrained DL models can detect hidden patterns that traditional techniques might overlook. This advancement could transform neonatal care, potentially resulting in better outcomes [21]. In this sense, DL capabilities are largely powered by CNNs [10], which excel at analyzing images, making them particularly effective at extracting meaningful information from videos or photographs of newborns. By examining facial expressions, eye movements, and body movements, CNNs could potentially assess a babyÃćâĆňâĎćs level of alertness. Additionally, this study leverages the power of object detection, a subfield of DL focused on identifying and locating objects within images or videos, to provide a better clasification of the labels of interest.

The use of pretrained models offer the advantage of transfer learning, where these networks are trained on vast datasets and can be fine-tuned for specific tasks. This approach accelerates the training process, reduces the need for large labeled datasets, and leads to more accurate models for solving this problem. Additionally, unifying the three object detection models' results enables a more precise and robust assessment of neonate alertness due to the emergent insights gained from combining facial feature information [13]. In this work, pre-trained CNNs specifically designed for object detection were considered. In concrete, three separate CNN models, which are next described, were trained specializing in identifying each of the three key facial features [7].

3.1 Image Analysis Models

The object detection models employed in this work can be found in the official TensorFlow 2 Detection Model Zoo repository[1] https://github.com/tensorflow/models/blob/master/research/object_detection/g3doc/tf2_detection_zoo.md They use 3-channel images with 640×640 pixel dimensions as input. Therefore, frames obtained from the videos will be automatically resized to fit these dimensions.

SSD MobileNet V2 FPNLite. This model combines the Single Shot Multi-Box Detector (SSD) method with the MobileNet architecture. SSD is specifically designed for object detection. It enables highly reliable and fast item recognition by integrating a single deep neural network instead of multiple layers like other methods [17]. The MobileNet architecture is a type of lightweight CNN for mobile devices. It is composed of multiple convolutional layers, a pooling layer and finally a softmax classifier [12]. It has been pre-trained using large datasets such as ImageNet, which gives it the ability to capture general features. Only fine tuning is needed to specialise the network on the set of images we are concerned with. Finally, it uses Feature Pyramid Network Lite (FPN) as a feature extractor, as it allows to improve the model's capability but in a lightweight way. This combination of method and architecture has proven to be suitable for object detection tasks applied to face recognition, making it suitable for our purpose [29].

SSD ResNet50 V1 FPN. Like the previous model, the object detection method on which this model is based is SSD. However, in this case the network used is ResNet50. It is a more complex architecture than MobileNet, consisting of 50 layers. Thanks to this higher number of layers, it has a greater ability to detect patterns in images, allowing for better performance in image analysis requiring fine-grained discrimination [11]. Like MobileNet, ResNet50 has also been trained on large datasets such as ImageNet, so only the fine tuning is necessary. Unlike the previous model, this one uses FPN, without being a Lite version. This increases the capacity to extract features but also requires more computational power.

[1] https://github.com/tensorflow/models/blob/master/research/object_detection/g3doc/tf2_detection_zoo.md.

EfficientDet D1. This model is based on the single-stage method, which furthermore uses an EfficientNet architecture combined with a bi-directional feature pyramid network (BiFPN) feature extractor. Thanks to its design following the single-stage paradigm, this model is able to perform with high efficiency but in a simple and lightweight way. The EfficientNet network on which it is based is composed of more than 7 layers, and has been trained using a large image set such as ImageNet [28]. The tag D1 refers to the complexity of the network and the size of the input image data, with D0 being the simplest variant with the smallest image size and D7 the most complex network with the largest image size.

4 Experimental Design

Some important aspects of the training configuration are described below.

- **Validation Strategy**. This study employs hold-out, a common validation strategy used in DL to assess model performance. Here, the dataset generated from the frames of the 73 videos is split into two subsets: 85% for training and 15% for testing. That 85% of videos used for training was again divided into two subsets: 80% for training and 20% for validation.
- **Early Stopping**. To prevent overfitting, a custom early stopping mechanism was implemented within the training process of the object detection model, monitoring validation loss. This approach prevented the model from memorizing the training data and improved its ability to generalize to new data.

4.1 Evaluation of the Models

To measure the performance of the models, a per second video evaluation has been chosen, instead of a more classical approach such as a frame-by-frame evaluation. To obtain the prediction per second for each model, frames from the different test videos were fed into the models and the outputs provided by the models were grouped in batches of 30 to generate a consensus prediction label, using the majority label as a criterion (in case of a tie, the positive event of the element was considered consensus). Similarly, the ground truth values for the evaluation was generated by grouping the test frames into batches of 30 to generate consensus labels, also following the majority criterion.

The performance of each proposed model is assessed using a set of evaluation metrics. These metrics are derived from the values in the confusion matrix, and they reflect the models' ability to accurately classify both positive and negative items. The metrics also help identify cases of misclassification, which should be evaluated based on the clinical consequences of incorrectly classifying a stimulus.

- Balanced accuracy (BA). It is a metric for evaluating the performance of classification models, particularly in imbalanced datasets. Unlike overall accuracy, which only considers the overall proportion of correct predictions, BA takes

into account the model's individual performance for each class, avoiding biases towards the majority class. Mathematically, BA is the average of sensitivity (the ability to identify true positives) and specificity (the ability to avoid false positives).
- Recall. Also known as sensitivity, is a metric that measures the proportion of actual positives that are correctly identified by a model. In simpler terms, it represents the model's ability to catch all the true positives.
- Specificity. Also called the true negative ratio, this is a measure of the negative cases that have been identified as negative by the model. It gives us information about the ability of our model to detect the absence of response to the stimulus.

5 Results

This section presents the results obtained after the evaluation of the different DL models considered in this research. Table 2 shows a comparison between the 3 models considered for each of the items assessed: SSD MobileNet V2 FPNLite as SSD MobNet, SSD ResNet50 V1 FPN as SSD ResNet and EfficientDet D1 as EfficientDet.

Table 2. Balanced Accuracy, Recall and Specificity values for each of the models and for each item

Item	Model	Bal. Acc.	Recall	Specificity
Eye opening	SSD MobNet	0.5494	0.2085	0.8904
	SSD ResNet	0.6656	0.8344	0.4968
	Efficiendet	0.6484	0.4183	0.8784
	SSD MobNet	0.587	0.2356	0.9384
	SSD ResNet	0.7101	0.885	0.5352
Mouth contraction	Efficiendet	0.8222	0.8506	0.7939
	SSD MobNet	0.5715	0.221	0.922
	SSD ResNet	0.6455	0.5364	0.7546
Eye frowning	Efficiendet	0.6857	0.6866	0.6848

Overall, the highest metrics obtained are for specificity metric which measures the true negative rate of the trained models. As seen in Table 2, SSD MobNet achieves a specificity of 0.93 for *Mouth Contraction*. These values indicate that in the confusion matrices shown in Fig. 3, the presence of false positives is minimal.

Since balanced accuracy is an equitable measure across classes, Fig. 2 shows the best values achieved for this metric for problem addressed. For Eyes Frowning and Mouth Contraction, EfficientDet was the most effective model, while for

Eyes Opening, SSD ResNet was slightly better by a few tenths. Additionally, the vertices of the graph reflect that the highest result corresponds to the Mouth Contraction item.

Figure 3 shows the confusion matrices of the best model for each item. The rows represent the actual classes, while the columns correspond to the predictions made by each model. The highest values are found on the main diagonal, indicating good performance. The intensity of the colors shows that the controls are generally well classified. The number of false negatives (lower left corner) is relatively low. However, the overall metrics are still significantly affected by the high number of false positives.

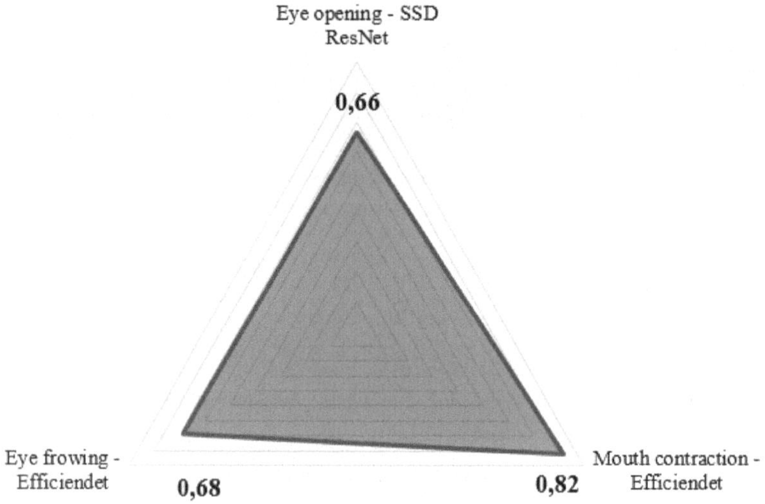

Fig. 2. Network plot containing the values of the balanced accuracy obtained for the best trained model for each item.

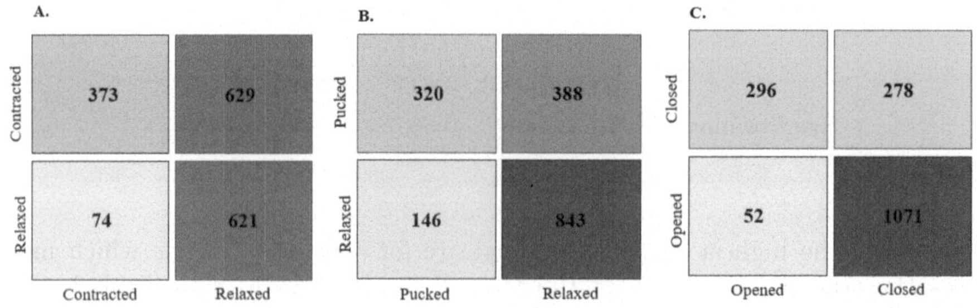

Fig. 3. Confusion matrices for the most efficient models for each item using balanced accuracy as a selection criterion. From left to right: Efficiendet for *Eye opening* (A), Effiendet for *Eye frowing* (B) and SSD ResNet for *Mouth contraction* (C)).

6 Conclusions

This study has evaluated the performance of various DL models in assessing newborn alertness by detecting specific facial features from video recordings. Three different pretrained object detection models were considered and trained on a local cohort of 73 nociceptive stimuli videos provided by the "Hospital Universitario de Burgos". Individual frames were extracted and labelled from this videos, and a common hold-out evaluation strategy (ratio 85%-15%) was used to train and evaluate the performance of the models. For the evaluation process, frames within a second of time were grouped in the same batch to compare the majority prediction and ground truths, since facial expression in newborns contain minor changes within frames in this short period of time.

Our analysis revealed that models exhibit high specificity, indicating a strong ability to correctly identify negative instances, but struggle somewhat with positive instance classification. Besides, the use of balanced accuracy as a metric has been particularly valuable, providing a more equitable evaluation across classes and highlighting the models' strengths in correctly identifying both positive and negative instances despite the imbalanced nature of the dataset. Our findings underscore the potential of Deep Learning models in neonatal care, particularly in reducing the subjectivity and variability inherent in manual assessments.

One of the limitations of the work done here is the small size of the dataset we have used in training the models. This is why increasing the size of the dataset has been considered as one of the lines of improvement in future work. Besides, advanced data augmentation techniques and cross-validation strategies will provide a more comprehensive understanding of model performance, ensuring they can handle a wider range of clinical scenarios.

Additionally, expanding the diagnostic capabilities of these models is crucial. This involves extending the detection framework to identify additional signs of neonatal encephalopathy, such as seizures and respiratory irregularities. Moreover, incorporating temporal analysis of video sequences and integrating multimodal data (e.g., physiological signals and clinical records) may enhance model precision and accuracy, providing a more detailed understanding of the infant's overall health condition.

Acknowledgments. This research is part of the SITAD-NPCN project funded in 2022 in the "Desafío Universidad-Empresa" call by the "Plan de Transferencia de Conocimiento Universidad - Empresa (Plan TCUE) 2021-2023'.

References

1. Ahsan, M.M., Siddique, Z.: Machine learning-based heart disease diagnosis: a systematic literature review. Artif. Intell. Med. **128**, 102289 (2022)
2. Arnaez, J., et al.: Population-based study of the national implementation of therapeutic hypothermia in infants with hypoxic-ischemic encephalopathy. Therapeutic Hypothermia Temp. Manage. **8**(1), 24–29 (2018)

3. Arnaez, J., et al.: Care of the newborn with perinatal asphyxia candidate for therapeutic hypothermia during the first six hours of life in Spain. Anales de Pediatría (English Edition) **89**(4), 211–221 (2018)
4. Arnaez, J., et al.: Usefulness of video recordings for validating neonatal encephalopathy exams: a population-based cohort study. Arch. Dis. Child. Fetal Neonatal Ed. **106**(5), 522–528 (2021)
5. Baston, H., Durward, H.: Examination of the Newborn: a Practical Guide. Routledge, London (2016)
6. Brown, J.L.: States in newborn infants. Merrill-Palmer Quart. Behav. Dev. **10**(4), 313–327 (1964)
7. Dosso, Y.S., Kyrollos, D., Greenwood, K.J., Harrold, J., Green, J.R.: NICUface: robust neonatal face detection in complex NICU scenes. IEEE Access **10**, 62893–62909 (2022)
8. Garcia-Alix, A., et al.: Development, reliability, and testing of a new rating scale for neonatal encephalopathy. J. Pediatr. **235**, 83–91 (2021)
9. Garcia-Alix, A., Arnaez, J., Arca, G., Martinez-Biarge, M.: Hypoxic-ischaemic encephalopathy code: a systematic review for resource-limited settings. Anales de Pediatría (English Edition) (2024)
10. Gu, J., et al.: Recent advances in convolutional neural networks. Pattern Recogn. **77**, 354–377 (2018)
11. He, K., Zhang, X., Ren, S., Sun, J.: Deep residual learning for image recognition. In: Proceedings of the IEEE Conference on Computer Vision and Pattern Recognition, pp. 770–778 (2016)
12. Howard, A.G., et al.: Mobilenets: efficient convolutional neural networks for mobile vision applications. arXiv preprint arXiv:1704.04861 (2017)
13. Krishna, S.T., Kalluri, H.K.: Deep learning and transfer learning approaches for image classification. Int. J. Recent Technol. Eng. (IJRTE) **7**(5S4), 427–432 (2019)
14. Kurinczuk, J.J., White-Koning, M., Badawi, N.: Epidemiology of neonatal encephalopathy and hypoxic-ischaemic encephalopathy. Early Human Dev. **86**(6), 329–338 (2010)
15. Laptook, A.: Initiating therapeutic hypothermia during transport for encephalopathy: current state and future direction. J. Perinatol. **33**(3), 169–170 (2013)
16. Li, C., Pourtaherian, A., Van Onzenoort, L., a Ten, W.E.T., de With, P.H.: Infant monitoring system for real-time and remote discomfort detection. IEEE Trans. Consum. Electron. **66**(4), 336–345 (2020)
17. Liu, W., Anguelov, D., Erhan, D., Szegedy, C., Reed, S., Fu, C.-Y., Berg, A.C.: SSD: single shot multibox detector. In: Leibe, B., Matas, J., Sebe, N., Welling, M. (eds.) ECCV 2016. LNCS, vol. 9905, pp. 21–37. Springer, Cham (2016). https://doi.org/10.1007/978-3-319-46448-0_2
18. Mooney, C., et al.: Predictive modelling of hypoxic ischaemic encephalopathy risk following perinatal asphyxia. Heliyon **7**(7) (2021)
19. Myszczynska, M.A., et al.: Applications of machine learning to diagnosis and treatment of neurodegenerative diseases. Nat. Rev. Neurol. **16**(8), 440–456 (2020)
20. Newton, C.R.: Global burden of pediatric neurological disorders. In: Seminars in Pediatric Neurology, vol. 27, pp. 10–15. Elsevier (2018)
21. Obermeyer, Z., Emanuel, E.J.: Predicting the future-big data, machine learning, and clinical medicine. N. Engl. J. Med. **375**(13), 1216 (2016)
22. Olsen, S.L., et al.: Optimizing therapeutic hypothermia for neonatal encephalopathy. Pediatrics **131**(2), e591–e603 (2013)
23. Quintero Ramirez, N., Sanchez Garcia, Y., Toncel, Y., Reales Hernandez, L.: Estimulacion tactil kinestesica: abordaje desde enfermeria (2021)

24. Rafique, R., Islam, S.R., Kazi, J.U.: Machine learning in the prediction of cancer therapy. Comput. Struct. Biotechnol. J. **19**, 4003–4017 (2021)
25. Sarnat, H.B., Sarnat, M.S.: Neonatal encephalopathy following fetal distress: a clinical and electroencephalographic study. Arch. Neurol. **33**(10), 696–705 (1976)
26. Singh, R., Om, H.: Newborn face recognition using deep convolutional neural network. Multimedia Tools Appl **76**(18), 19005–19015 (2017)
27. Tagin, M.A., Woolcott, C.G., Vincer, M.J., Whyte, R.K., Stinson, D.A.: Hypothermia for neonatal hypoxic ischemic encephalopathy: an updated systematic review and meta-analysis. Arch. Pediatrics Adolescent Med. **166**(6), 558–566 (2012)
28. Tan, M., Pang, R., Le, Q.V.: Efficientdet: scalable and efficient object detection. In: Proceedings of the IEEE/CVF Conference on Computer Vision and Pattern Recognition, pp. 10781–10790 (2020)
29. Tang, J., Peng, X., Chen, X., Luo, B.: An improved Mobilenet-SSD approach for face detection. In: 2021 40th Chinese Control Conference (CCC), pp. 8072–8076. IEEE (2021)
30. Tkachenko, M., Malyuk, M., Holmanyuk, A., Liubimov, N.: Label studio: data labeling software (2020-2022). https://github.com/heartexlabs/label-studio, open source software available from https://github.com/heartexlabs/label-studio
31. Tran, B.X., et al.: Global evolution of research in artificial intelligence in health and medicine: a bibliometric study. J. Clin. Med. **8**, 360 (2019)

Data Mining and Decision Support Systems

SPADE Norms: a Distributed General Framework for Normative Multi-agent Systems

Miguel García-Bohigues[1(✉)], Joaquin Taverner[1], Javier Palanca[1], and Vicente Botti[1,2]

[1] Valencian Research Institute for Artificial Intelligence (VRAIN), Universitat Politècnica De València, Valencia, Spain
migarbo1@vrain.upv.es

[2] Valencian Graduate School and Research Network of Artificial Intelligence (valgrAI), Valencia, Spain

Abstract. In this paper, we present SPADE Norms, an extension of the SPADE platform designed specifically for the design of normative multi-agent systems. SPADE Norms facilitates the integral management of norms, covering life-cycle monitoring, definition of activation conditions, verification of compliance with norms, application of sanctions and rewards, and offers tools to develop normative reasoning processes adapted to the agent that allow it to decide on compliance with the norms according to its objectives. The overall norms management process is decoupled from the agent and is performed internally in the platform itself. This makes SPADE Norms a versatile platform capable of adapting to different agent types and application domains. Our approach also supports the definition of roles and domains, which increases performance and enables a variety of agent behaviours and organisational simulations.

Keywords: Normative reasoning · multi-agent platforms · SPADE · agent reasoning

1 Introduction

The study of the effect of incorporating both norms and normative reasoning in agent models is crucial both for simulating the behaviour of human social organisations as well as for improving coordination and decision-making processes in autonomous systems. In this sense, different models incorporating norms in multi-agent systems (MAS) have been developed [11,12,17,23]. Most of these models are based on the use of deontic logic (that defines norms using concepts such as obligations, permissions, or prohibitions [14]) for the definition of norms [16,22]. On the other hand, it is important to highlight that in the design of MAS, a crucial factor relies on the platforms on which these systems are developed [2,3,6,10]. MAS platforms generally provide tools for the implementation,

H. Quintián et al. (Eds.): HAIS 2024, LNAI 14857, pp. 113–125, 2025.
https://doi.org/10.1007/978-3-031-74183-8_10

execution, and communication of the agents. Among the most prominent platforms in this area is SPADE [18], which integrates different agent architectures and provides a modular design capable of adapting to a variety of contexts and agent types, providing scalability and adaptability to different scenarios, domains, and requirements.

There are currently different platforms that support the development of normative agents [5,7,13]. However, many of them tend to be focused on a single type (e.g., FSM or BDI) of agent and /or are difficult to generalise to other contexts or application domains. Some also require the use of an agent that monitors compliance with norms and, generally, the normative processes are developed and executed by the agent itself.

In this paper, we present SPADE Norms, an extension for SPADE to develop normative MAS (NMAS). SPADE Norms provides management of the life-cycle of norms, allows the definition of activation conditions, performs compliance verification, performs the application of sanctions and rewards, and provide tools for defining agent's normative reasoning. To do so, our approach includes two main components: the *Normative Evaluation Engine*, responsible for the integrated management of norms; and the *Normative Reasoning Engine*, which allows agents to make decisions considering the norms. All SPADE Norms processes operate decoupled from the agent, ensuring adaptability to different agent type and application domains. Another key aspect of this approach is the possibility of defining roles and domains for the application of norms. This improves the performance of normative processes and makes it possible to simulate a variety of behaviours and organisational structures of agents.

2 Related Work

The integration of norms in the MAS is a step forward in the development of socially conscious autonomous agents as well as facilitates the coordination and cooperation between agents. In this sense, in recent years different platforms have been developed that allow the development of NMAS. One of the most relevant works on the use of norms in MAS is *IOVIS* [16]. *IOVIS* is a framework for BDI [19] agents (implemented in AgentSpeak [6]) that manages the representation, perception and processing of obligations and prohibitions. The framework allows the definition of an activation condition for norms. When a norm is activated, the agent can decide whether to accept it or not. Similarly, in [5], *JaCaMo*, a platform for MAS also based on BDI and AgentSpeak, is proposed. *JaCaMo* combines *Jason* [6], *CArtAgO* [20], and *MOISE* [9], and allows the representation of norms through the use of obligation predicates, i.e., the agent must achieve some states for certain predicates to be *True*. The control of compliance with the norms and the application of sanctions and rewards is done through special agents who act as supervisors.

Another interesting example can be found in [7], which describes *MaNEA*, an architecture for normative agents on the *Magentix2* platform [21]. This architecture manages obligations and prohibitions from a closed-world approach, where everything is allowed unless otherwise specified. Compliance with the norms is controlled by a global component that performs an asynchronous review, i.e., after the agent has violated the norm.

Similarly, in [13], *NorJADE*, an extension to JADE [4] that provides support for normative reasoning, is presented. *NorJADE* defines an ontology in which norms are expressed using deontic logic. The use of this ontology allows the platform to determine whether an action is regulated or not, as well as the normative evaluation of the action. Norms can be internal to the agent or central to the entire organisation and can be defined as prohibitions, obligations, and recommendations. Rewards and sanctions can be self-imposed or reinforced by third parties.

The majority of methods suggested in the literature to tackle the NMAS paradigm are typically tied to particular problem definitions or are inflexible regarding norm definitions, hindering their generalization and adaptability. To overcome these challenges, we introduce SPADE Norms. SPADE [18] is a highly versatile, distributed, and scalable platform for developing MAS that aims to facilitate the integration of various agent architectures and communication protocols. The main advantage of SPADE is its ability to bridge different agent technologies and protocols, providing a cohesive framework for MAS development. Furthermore, SPADE's architecture is designed to be lightweight, modular, and easy to extend, which makes it suitable for a wide range of applications from IoT to complex decision-making systems.

SPADE has several advantages that make it a suitable platform for the development of generalisable NMAS. First, SPADE supports a variety of agent architectures and communication standards. It is therefore easily adaptable to a diverse range of applications, from IoT environments to complex decision-making systems. This interoperability ensures that it functions as a unifying platform for different agent-based models and protocols. Second, this platform is scalable, supporting a large number of agents without significant performance degradation. Third, SPADE distinguishes itself for its modular approach, which facilitates the addition and modification of functionalities, ensuring its adaptability to changes in requirements and technological advances. In addition, SPADE focuses on providing an easy and simplified development experience, with intuitive interfaces and clear documentation, to facilitate the creation, deployment, and management of agents. Finally, it is an open-source platform and is strengthened by an active community of developers and researchers who collaborate in its constant improvement, offering solutions and sharing best practices.

3 SPADE Norms

In general, platforms developed in the literature that support normative agents focus on including the normative reasoning processes in the agent model itself [1,7,13] or are highly dependent on the domain, or agent type or language [5,16]. This limits the flexibility of the normative model and the capability to be generalised for different application domains. To address this limitation, we propose SPADE Norms[1] a novel framework for NMAS that enables the development of normative-aware agents using deontic logic. As a component based on the SPADE platform, our model is completely independent of the domain, the type of the agent (e.g., BDI or FSM) and the language in which the agent is implemented (e.g., AgentSpeak, Java, or Python). Our approach focuses on the design of a generic and common framework for the definition of norms within a MAS, as well as on the proposal of a normative system decoupled from the agent's internal reasoning processes. To this end, we propose the use of two main components. On the one hand, the *Normative Evaluation Engine*, a decoupled component (i.e. it runs in parallel on the SPADE platform itself) that is responsible for the integrated management of norms. On the other hand, the *Normative Reasoning Engine*, that is specified in the SPADE Norm agent definition and allows the agent to reason about norms.

When an agent, either external (i.e., coming from another platform such as Jason) or internal (i.e., generated in the SPADE platform itself), joins the SPADE Norms platform, the agent is automatically associated with an instance of the Normative Evaluation Engine. The agent uses the protocol defined in SPADE to communicate by exchanging messages with the normative processes. In addition, the agent is associated with a Normative Reasoning Engine that provides the agent with tools to develop a normative reasoning process allowing it to decide on its actions based on the active norms in the environment. This process is also in charge of communicating sanctions or rewards to the agent.

The inclusion of this normative component in SPADE has several advantages. On the one hand, SPADE is focused on open systems in which agents developed by different parties must coexist and cooperate. Here, the incorporation of norms provides a mechanism for defining acceptable behaviours, ensures that agents act consistently with system objectives, reduces conflicts, and facilitates coordination among agents. On the other hand, our normative framework promotes the dynamic adaptation of norms, allowing the system to evolve over time in response to new information or changes in the context of the environment. Furthermore, the integration of norms allows the development of agents capable of reasoning about the norms and deciding whether to adhere to them based on their objectives and context, making them suitable to operate in dynamic and complex environments.

Our proposal also includes two new concepts to facilitate the management of the norms' life cycle: the role and the domain of the norm. On the one hand, the role (or roles) makes it possible to specify the set of agents that are affected by a given norm. For example, in the domain of traffic norms, the norm to brake at a STOP sign affects drivers but not pedestrians. We can also find norms that affect more than one role, such as the norm to stop at a red traffic light, which affects both drivers and pedestrians. Roles can be assigned dynamically, i.e., a driver agent can become a pedestrian when getting out of the vehicle.

On the other hand, the domain (or domains) allows for establishing the context of applicability of the norms. Using the previous example, there are traffic

[1] Full code available at: https://github.com/javipalanca/spade_norms.git,.

norms that may differ from others depending on the type of road, i.e. maximum allowed speed in city streets is much smaller than on highways. Both roles and domains simplify and strengthen the definition of agent behaviour and lighten the normative processes by excluding those norms that are not relevant to the domains or roles at hand.

3.1 Normative Agent Formalisation

Considering the aforementioned, an agent in SPADE Norms is defined by the tuple $\langle ag, Rl, Ne, Nr, C, A\rangle$ where:

- *ag*: represents the formalisation of an agent defined in terms of the reasoning system used. For example, in a BDI-based model, formalisation would involve both the agent's knowledge (i.e., beliefs, desires, and intentions) and the reasoning processes inherent to the model.
- *Rl*: is a set of roles $\{r_0, r_1, \cdots\}$ to which the agent belongs. The role or roles of an agent can be changed dynamically but all agents must belong to at least one role.
- *Ne*: corresponds to the normative engine (see Sect. 3.3), which is a logical process responsible for the evaluation of the normative context, measuring its impact on the current action decision.
- *Nr*: is the normative reasoning engine (see Sect. 3.3), which is a custom decision-making process that determines the norm compliance.
- *C*: is a set of internal (private) norms $\{c_0, c_1, \cdots\}$, that may or may not be shared by other agents in the environment, representing the agent's "concerns".
- *A*: corresponds to a catalogue of actions $\{a_0, a_1, \cdots\}$ that agents can execute to achieve their objectives. Each action a_i is composed of a tuple $\langle id, Fn, D\rangle$, where:

- *id*: represents the identifier of the action.
- *Fn*: is the function representing the action to perform. Usually, it is defined in terms of the agent's observation (S) received from the environment at instant t: $Fn(S_t) : S_t \rightarrow S_{t+1}$.
- *D*: corresponds to a non-empty ($D \neq \emptyset$) set of domains $\{d_0, d_1, \cdots\}$ in which the action can be performed.

As can be seen from this representation, the formalisation of the agent is completely decoupled from the specification of the normative system. This allows for flexibility and generalisation of the normative model, making it applicable to various agent models and types.

3.2 Norm Formalisation

In our proposal, norms are considered as logical indicators of states in which certain actions that the agent can perform may not be allowed. Therefore, we define a norm n as a tuple $\langle id, Dn, Nc, Ac, R, S, Rl, D, I, Sc\rangle$ where:

- *id*: represents the unique identifier of the norm.
- *Dn*: corresponds to the deontic type of the norm (e.g., permission or prohibition).
- *Nc*: is the condition of fulfilment or violation of the norm. It is a function $Nc(S) : S \rightarrow \{True, False\}$ defined in terms of the state space that outputs when the condition of the norm is matched.
- *Ac*: is a function $Ac(S) : S \rightarrow \{True, False\}$ that establishes when the norm is active or not.
- *R*: corresponds to the reward received by the agent for complying with a norm.
- *S*: is the sanction for violating the norm.
- *Rl*: is the set of roles $\{r_0, r_1, \cdots\}$ that are affected by the norm.
- *D*: represents a set of domains $\{d_0, d_1, \cdots\}$ in which the norm is applied.
- *I*: is a condition that allows specifying the inviolability status of the norm (e.g., a physical norm like crossing a wall or an organisational norm that all agents must follow undoubtedly).
- *Sc*: is an identifier that permits to specify the source of the norm (e.g., social, individual, or organisational).

This formal definition of norms in SPADE Norms entails a number of implicit advantages. First, in our proposal, the conditions associated with the norms (i.e., Nc and Ac) are defined by using second-order logical expressions. In this way, our model offers greater flexibility and expressiveness than previously proposed models in the literature, which generally represent these conditions by using propositional logic [7,16].

Second, the use of domains makes it possible to handle contradictions (or normative conflicts) that may arise during the life cycle of norms. Two active norms n_1 and n_2 contradict each other for an action a when $Dn_{n_1} \neq prohibition \wedge Dn_{n_2} = prohibition$, where Dn_{n_i} is the deontic operator of the norm n_i. Following the previous example, knowing that the maximum speed at highways is $120km/h$ (n_1) and at city streets is $50km/h$ (n_2), the same action a: driving at $90km/h$ can be allowed or forbidden depending on the domain where it is performed (i.e. $D_{n_1} = \{Highway\}$, $D_{n_2} = \{City\_Street\}$).

Finally, roles handle contradictions at the agent level. Including them in both the agent and the norms allows for specifying the set of agents affected by a given norm. This enables the definition of different responsibilities within an organisation or allows for different responses to the same input. For instance, a red traffic light for cars has different normative repercussions depending on the agent's role(i.e. $Rl_1 = \{Driver\}$ and $Rl_2 = \{Pedestrian\}$). Both role definition and Domain granularity allow the management of norm contradiction by setting more precise contexts of application.

3.3 Normative Agent Life-Cycle

In traditional architectures, agents typically perceive the environment, perform the reasoning process taking into account the normative implications, and finally commit an action. While these solutions are effective, they are limited to an agent model or type (FSM, BDI, ...) and at the same time are less flexible in formalising norms and states, due to the relationship between the norms and the agent's internal representation of the environment. Therefore, these solutions may not be suitable for its use in open NMAS where agents of different types and origins interact with each other.

To overcome these limitations, in SPADE Norms we decouple the normative processes from the internal logic of the agent. This way, the processes that manage the life cycle of norms and normative reasoning are independent from the agent's reasoning. Moreover, SPADE Norms can be adapted to any agent type, based only on a single choice of action and an observation of the environment. Furthermore, this decoupled architecture allows norms to be dynamically added to the system, also supporting the inclusion of emergent norms (i.e., an agent sharing its concern with other agents and adopted as a shared norm).

Figure 1 shows the reasoning cycle of an agent in SPADE Norms. As can be seen, in SPADE Norms, (i) the agent decides, using its reasoning engine (e.g., BDI, FSM, or RL), which action is the best one to take given a particular state. Then, (ii) the normative system automatically evaluates the normative implications of that action in the normative evaluation phase (i.e., whether the action is regulated and whether it violates a norm or not). Finally, (iii) in the normative decision phase, the agent decides, using its separate normative reasoning engine, whether to perform the action or not.

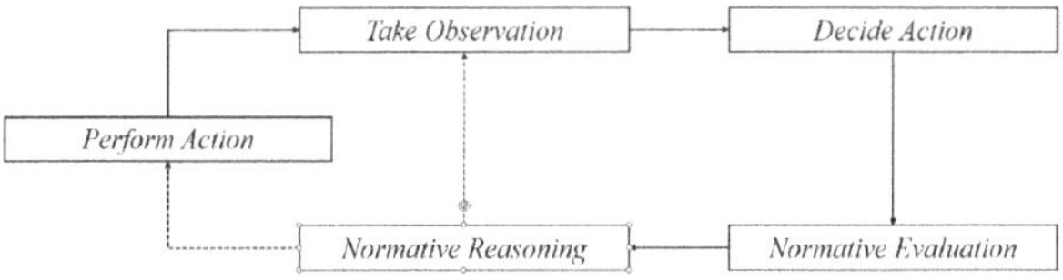

Fig. 1. SPADE Norms Agent life-cycle

Normative Evaluation Engine. Once the agent has performed the analysis of the environment and has decided which action a is most suitable to achieve its objectives, the agent communicates this decision to the normative evaluation process. This process assesses the implications of performing action a taking into account the active norms. Algorithm 1 shows the normative evaluation process. As can be seen, the process is performed in two phases. In the first phase, the set of relevant norms δ is obtained. For this, the set α is created by joining the norms defined in the environment N and the agent's particular concerns ag_C. Then, for each norm $n \in \alpha$ it is verified: (4) its activation condition n_{Ac}; (5) the existence of a common domain between the set of domains of the norm n_D and the set of domains of the action a_D; and (6) the existence of a common role between the set of roles of the norm n_{Rl} and the set of roles of the agent ag_{Rl}. If all

Algorithm 1. Normative Evaluation Engine

Require: $Org.Norms : N, Agent : ag, State : S, Action : a$ ▷ Phase 1: Norm retrieval

1: $\alpha \leftarrow N \cup ag_C$
2: **for** $n \in \alpha$ **do**
3:     **if** $n_{Ac} =$ `True` **then**
4:         **if** $n_D \cap a_D \neq \emptyset$ **then**
5:             **if** $n_{Rl} \cap ag_{Rl} \neq \emptyset$ **then**
6:                 $\delta \leftarrow \delta \cup n$
7:             **end if**
8:         **end if**
9:     **end if**
10: **end for** ▷ Phase 2: Norm evaluation
11: **if** $\delta = \emptyset$ **then**
12:     **return** *Unregulated*, $\emptyset, \emptyset$
13: **else**
14:     *Status* $\leftarrow$ *Allowed*
15:     **for** $n \in \delta$ **do**
16:         **if** $n_{Nc}(S) =$ `True` **then**
17:             $\theta^F \leftarrow \theta^F \cup n$
18:             **if** $n_I =$ `True` **then**
19:                 *Status* $\leftarrow$ *Inviolable*
20:             **else**
21:                 *Status* $\leftarrow$ *Forbidden*
22:             **end if**
23:         **else**
24:             $\theta^A \leftarrow \theta^A \cup n$
25:         **end if**
26:     **end for**
27:     **return** *Status*, θ^A, θ^F
28: **end if**

conditions are met the norm is added to δ. With this procedure we avoid the evaluation of norms that are not relevant to the agent and the action in question, thus avoiding possible conflicts with norms concerning other domains or roles. This also increases the performance of the system, since fewer conditions are evaluated per action.

In the second phase, the conditions of the relevant norms are evaluated to estimate whether the action a is allowed or forbidden given the current state S. The state S contains all the relevant information that has led the agent to decide to perform action a. If the set of relevant norms is empty, (14) then the process finalises by indicating that the action a is not regulated by any norm. Otherwise, the process estimates and returns the sets of norms that prohibit θ^F and permit θ^A the action, along with the resulting status: allowed, forbidden or inviolable. If the norm condition evaluates to true, (19) then it is added to the set of norms that prohibit θ^F, otherwise, (26) it is added to the set of norms that allow θ^A. If there is a single norm that forbids the action, then the result will be *Forbidden* (23). Moreover, if there is a single inviolable norm that finds its

Algorithm 2. Normative Reasoning Engine

Require: $Ne : \langle Status, \theta^A, \theta^F \rangle$, $Action : a$, $Agent : Ag$
1: $do\_action \leftarrow n\_decision(a, Status, \theta^A, \theta^F)$
2: **if** do_action **then**
3: $\quad result \leftarrow commit\_action(a)$
4: **end if**
5: **for** $n \in \theta^F$ **do**
6: $\quad$ **if** do_action **then**
7: $\quad\quad apply\_sanction(Ag, n_S)$
8: $\quad$ **else**
9: $\quad\quad apply\_reward(Ag, n_R)$
10: $\quad$ **end if**
11: **end for**
12: **return** $result$

condition matched, the result will be then *Inviolable* (21). The separation of the norms into two independent sets allows the agent to be the one who ultimately decides whether or not to perform the action taking into account the norms it fulfils and violates.

To estimate the compliance condition of the norm, the normative evaluation process assumes a restrictive definition of the norms, so that, by default, all actions are "allowed" unless specified on the contrary[2].

Normative Reasoning Engine. The normative reasoning engine (*Nr*) is a process that can be specified in the agent's definition and is responsible for determining the decision to perform or not a certain action a based on the normative context obtained through the process performed by the normative evaluation engine. As previously explained this context is: *Status*, the general status of the action (Allowed, Forbidden, ...); θ^A, the set of norms that allow action a; θ^F, the set of norms that prohibit action a. Additionally, the process manages the assessment and consequences of taking or not taking action a, including the application of sanctions or rewards if necessary.

Algorithm 2 shows the proposed normative reasoning process. Initially, the agent employs the normative decision process to determine whether to execute action a based on the information obtained from the normative reasoning engine (1). By default, this function is defined as:

$$n\_decision(a, Status, \theta^A, \theta^F) = \begin{cases} \texttt{True}, & \text{if } Status = Allowed \\ \texttt{False}, & \text{otherwise} \end{cases}$$

[2] The decision to use deontic operators in defining norms allows for equivalence between different types of norms [15]. This means that, in a restrictive society where everything is allowed unless specified otherwise, deontic operators such as prohibition, obligation, and permission can be simplified to prohibition alone.

This implies that the agent performs the action a whenever it is allowed. However, this decision function can be adapted to different domains and requirements to simulate different behaviours, even allowing to implement agents capable of violating certain norms as discussed in [8]. Subsequently, after the agent has made the decision, if this decision involves the execution of the action a, the *commit_action* process will notify the agent of the decision and wait for the agent to perform the action to evaluate the consequences (3). This *commit_action* process must be adapted to the domain taking into account the agent's requirements and the behaviour to be modelled in the simulation. Finally, the consequences are evaluated through an iterative process by applying the corresponding sanctions or rewards for each norm (5–11). The evaluation considers whether the agent has decided to perform action a. Only the norms that the agent has potentially violated are considered. For each norm in θ^F, the process applies a sanction or reward depending on whether the agent decided to perform the action or not.

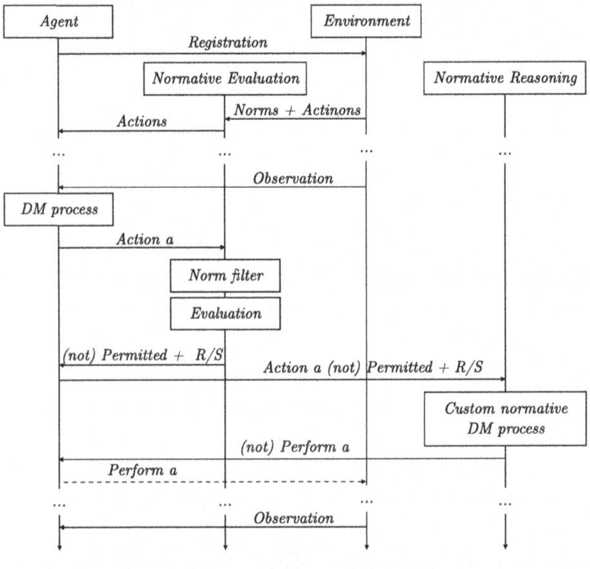

Fig. 2. Functionality of the framework

Figure 2 illustrates the functionality of the framework, showing how the different components interact with each other in the event of a decision to be taken by the agent. As it can be observed, once the agent is registered in the environment, it receives both the normative Evaluation and Reasoning components. Along with the collection of norms ruling the environment and the actions that the agent can perform. In the event of an observation, the agent decides on the next action to take with its own internal decision making process. Then it communicates the result to the normative evaluation component, which will asses the implications of performing that action given the current context (i.e. whether the action is allowed or forbidden along with the possible rewards and sanctions that could be applied). After the process in completed, the agent receives the response. At this point, the agent queries the normative reasoning component with the normative information, to proceed with the final decision on whether to perform the action or not. In either case, the agent begins again its loop with an observation.

4 Conclusions

Most of the approaches proposed in the literature to address the NMAS paradigm are closely related to specific problem definitions or lack flexibility in terms of norm definition, which makes their generalisation and adaptability difficult. To address these limitations, in this paper, we have presented SPADE Norms, a new component of SPADE that facilitates the development of generalisable NMAS centred on open systems. In these systems, agents developed by different parties must coexist and cooperate, independently of the domain and type of these agents. For this purpose, our approach is based on two main processes. On the one hand, the Normative Evaluation Engine process works in a decoupled way with the agents and is in charge of performing the integral management of the norms, evaluating their applicability, and generating the corresponding sanctions and rewards. On the other hand, the Normative Reasoning Engine is defined in the agent itself, providing it with the ability to reason about the norms and the context to make its decisions. SPADE Norms also addresses the problems of norm representation by using second-order logic instead of the propositional logic widely used in current platforms. Moreover, the definition of domains and roles allows us to reduce system inconsistencies and contradictions by relating norms, actions, and agents while improving the efficiency of the system.

In future work, we plan to explore integrating a societys moral values into the normative reasoning process more concretely. This will involve developing algorithms that allow agents to prioritise actions not only based on prescribed norms but also on specific underlying values such as justice, fairness, and social responsibility. For instance, we will create case studies and simulations where agents face ethical dilemmas, analysing their decision-making processes and outcomes.

Acknowledgements. Work partially supported by Generalitat Valenciana CI-PROM/2021/077, Spanish Government projects PID2020-113416RB-I00 and TED-2021-131295B-C32 and TAILOR funded by EU Horizon 2020 under GA No 952215.

References

1. Argente, E., Del Val, E., Perez-Garcia, D., Botti, V.: Normative emotional agents: a viewpoint paper. IEEE Trans. Affect. Comput. **13**(3), 1254–1273 (2020)
2. Artikis, A., Pitt, J.: A formal model of open agent societies. In: Proceedings of the Fifth International Conference on Autonomous Agents, pp. 192–193 (2001)

3. Bellifemine, F., Bergenti, F., Caire, G., Poggi, A.: Jade–a java agent development framework. In: Multi-agent Programming: Languages, Platforms and Applications, pp. 125–147 (2005)
4. Bellifemine, F., Poggi, A., Rimassa, G.: Jade–a Fipa-compliant agent framework. In: Proceedings of PAAM, vol. 99, p. 33. London (1999)
5. Boissier, O., Hübner, J.F., Ricci, A.: The JaCaMo framework. In: Aldewereld, H., Boissier, O., Dignum, V., Noriega, P., Padget, J. (eds.) Social Coordination Frameworks for Social Technical Systems. LGTS, vol. 30, pp. 125–151. Springer, Cham (2016). https://doi.org/10.1007/978-3-319-33570-4_7
6. Bordini, R.H., Hubner, J.F., Wooldridge, M.: Programming Multi-agent Systems in AgentSpeak using Jason. Wiley, Hoboken (2007)
7. Criado, N., Argente, E., Noriega, P., Botti, V.: MaNEA: a distributed architecture for enforcing norms in open mas. Eng. Appl. Artif. Intell. **26**(1), 76–95 (2013)
8. Derakhshan, F., Bench-Capon, T., McBurney, P.: Dynamic assignment of roles, rights and responsibilities in normative multi-agent systems. J. Log. Comput. **23**(2), 355–372 (2013)
9. Hubner, J.F., Sichman, J.S., Boissier, O.: Developing organised multiagent systems using the moise+ model: programming issues at the system and agent levels. Int. J. Agent-Oriented Softw. Eng. **1**(3–4), 370–395 (2007)
10. Khayyat, M., Awasthi, A.: An intelligent multi-agent based model for collaborative logistics systems. Transp. Res. Procedia **12**, 325–338 (2016)
11. Kollmann, S., Siafara, L.C., Schaat, S., Wendt, A.: Towards a cognitive multi-agent system for building control. Procedia Comput. Sci. **88**, 191–197 (2016)
12. López, F.L.y., Luck, M., dInverno, M.: A normative framework for agent-based systems. Comput. Math. Organ. Theor. **12**, 227–250 (2006)
13. Marir, T., Mokhati, F., Gherbi, A., Bali, A., et al.: Norjade: an open source jade-based framework for programming normative multi-agent systems. Int. J. Open Source Softw. Process. (IJOSSP) **10**(2), 1–20 (2019)
14. McNamara, P.: Deontic logic. In: Handbook of the History of Logic, vol. 7, pp. 197–288. Elsevier (2006)
15. McNamara, P.: Deontic logic. In: Gabbay, D.M., Woods, J. (eds.) Logic and the Modalities in the Twentieth Century, vol. 7, pp. 197–288. North-Holland (2006)
16. Meneguzzi, F.R., Luck, M.: Norm-based behaviour modification in BDI agents. In: AAMAS, no. 1, pp. 177–184 (2009)
17. Oren, N., Panagiotidi, S., Vázquez-Salceda, J., Modgil, S., Luck, M., Miles, S.: Towards a formalisation of electronic contracting environments. In: Hübner, J.F., Matson, E., Boissier, O., Dignum, V. (eds.) COIN -2008. LNCS (LNAI), vol. 5428, pp. 156–171. Springer, Heidelberg (2009). https://doi.org/10.1007/978-3-642-00443-8_11
18. Palanca, J., Terrasa, A., Julian, V., Carrascosa, C.: Spade 3: supporting the new generation of multi-agent systems. IEEE Access **8**, 182537–182549 (2020)
19. Rao, A.S., Georgeff, M.P., et al.: BDI agents: from theory to practice. In: Icmas, vol. 95, pp. 312–319 (1995)
20. Ricci, A., Piunti, M., Viroli, M., Omicini, A.: Environment programming in CArtAgO. In: El Fallah Seghrouchni, A., Dix, J., Dastani, M., Bordini, R.H. (eds.) Multi-Agent Programming, pp. 259–288. Springer, Boston, MA (2009). https://doi.org/10.1007/978-0-387-89299-3_8
21. Such, J.M., García-Fornes, A., Espinosa, A., Bellver, J.: Magentix2: a privacy-enhancing agent platform. Eng. Appl. Artif. Intell. **26**(1), 96–109 (2013)

22. Taverner, J., Cordova, C., Val, E., Valero, S., Argente, E.: Exploring the relationship between emotions and norms in decision-making processes of intelligent agents. In: Proceedings of the 16th International Conference on Agents and Artificial Intelligence - Volume 1: EAA, pp. 471–479. INSTICC, SciTePress (2024)
23. Tzeng, S.T.: Engineering normative and cognitive agents with emotions and values. In: Proceedings of the 21st International Conference on Autonomous Agents and Multiagent Systems, pp. 1878–1880 (2022)

Finding Optimal Classroom Arrangements to Minimize Cheating in Exams Using a Hybrid AI System

Pablo León Alazraki Salas(✉) and Andrés Gómez de Silva Garza

Instituto Tecnológico Autónomo de México, 01080 Mexico City, Mexico
{pablo.alazraki,agomez}@itam.mx

Abstract. In this work, we propose a hybrid AI system consisting of a multi-agent system simulating students during an exam and a teacher monitoring them, as well as an evolutionary algorithm that finds classroom arrangements which minimize cheating incentives. The students will answer the exam based on how much knowledge they have about the topic of the exam. In our simulation, then they enter a decision phase in which, for those questions they don't know the answer to, they will either cheat or answer by guessing. If a student gets caught cheating, his/her exam will be cancelled. The purpose of this study is to examine the question of how different monitoring behaviors on the part of the teacher affect the cheating behaviors of students. The results of this study show that an unbiased teacher, that is, a teacher that monitors every student with the same probability, produces minimal cheating incentives for students.

Keywords: Intelligent agent-based systems · Evolutionary Computation · Simulation of educational assessment environments

1 Introduction

Cheating in academic environments has been extensively studied from multiple perspectives and is regarded as a problem with numerous detrimental consequences for society, as it is considered a serious issue that has negative educational, social, and psychological effects [4]. Therefore, the act of cheating has been analyzed through the lenses of many disciplines, such as behavioral economics, sociology, and psychology. Furthermore, numerous field studies have been conducted to identify the social or psychological factors that influence the decision to cheat [3, 4, 8], as well as the most common methods of cheating [3, 14]. Additionally, technological advancements have enabled the development of new monitoring methods, such as suspicious activity recognition using video processing techniques [5].

In previous computational studies of cheating, intelligent agent-based systems have been developed to try to simulate students in academic environments [9, 10, 13], but they have focused on the interactions between students and how those interactions affect students' learning processes rather than their behavior in exam environments. In addition,

H. Quintián et al. (Eds.): HAIS 2024, LNAI 14857, pp. 126–138, 2025.
https://doi.org/10.1007/978-3-031-74183-8_11

project [7] presents a multi-agent system which intends to simulate students engaging in academic dishonesty.

That project defines cheating as direct communication between two students (for example, sending notes or whispering to each other) and implements penalties if their exam answers are significantly similar beyond a certain threshold. In their model, the decision to cheat is influenced primarily by the physical distance between students (agents), the frequency of their interactions and the penalties imposed if cheating is detected. Additionally, within the framework presented in [7], each student must decide on a question-by-question basis whether to cheat, depending on whether the student has knowledge om how the question or not.

We consider that their type of cheating may not be that common in a typical exam because direct interactions in a typical exam may be rather an exception when a teacher is monitoring the whole class during the examination. To recreate a more typical classroom examination, we decided to model cheating in a different way (see Sect. 3), aiming to complement this work and seek to simulate more realistic scenarios of students cheating on exams.

The rest of the article is organized as follows: Sect. 2 briefly discusses our methodology in exploring cheating using computers. Section 3 delves into the model implementation and describes each of its systems and subsystems. Section 4 proposes two types of experiments dealing with the teacher's behavior and how it affects each student's behavior. In Sect. 5, we present the results of both experiments and determine how many generations of the evolutionary algorithm are required to achieve a significant result. Lastly, Sect. 6 presents an analysis of the obtained results, our conclusions, and possible model extensions.

2 Methodology

We propose a hybrid artificial intelligence system that simulates students during an exam and finds how to arrange them within a classroom to significantly reduce cheating. This system could be employed in academic environments to prevent academic dishonesty. The hybrid AI system is composed of a multi-agent system [11], which simulates both students taking, and a teacher monitoring, the exam, and an evolutionary algorithm [6] which, given a set of students and the characteristics of the exam, identifies the locally minimal cheating arrangement for that set of students. Each generation of the evolutionary algorithm gives a different classroom arrangement in which the exam simulation will take place. Each simulation consists of running the multi-agent system for a fixed number of time-steps. This will be explained in more detail in Sect. 3.

In our simulation, we will consider a multiple-choice exam with four answer options per question, with only one correct answer. We will assume that the teacher and the students all know each other by the time the simulated exam takes place. The exam is designed so that every student who knows the correct answer can respond correctly within a specified time limit. The duration of the exam is fixed, and the number of questions is determined by dividing the exam's total duration by the maximum time allotted for answering each question (assuming the time limit applies to all questions).

We will consider a scenario with a set of n students and one teacher arranged in a classroom so that each student can see the other students and the teacher. Each student has a knowledge factor that determines how many correct answers they know, and the remainder of the exam will be answered either by guessing randomly or by cheating. We assume that students will first attempt to answer questions based on their knowledge before deciding whether to cheat or guess, and the only way a student can cheat is by copying the answer from a neighbor in the classroom, i.e., other students seated next to and in front of them, because those are the students whose answers we assume could be clearly seen by the cheater. This means that, in contrast with [7], our simulation involves indirect, less blatant cheating, unlike cheating as direct communication assumed in that project.

For each question whose answer a student doesn't know, s/he will decide to cheat if the expected grade from cheating is greater than the grade expected from answering randomly. Given that the teacher and the students all know each other, we will assume that each student has perfect information about the teacher's monitoring behavior and knows the probability that other students will know how the answer the different exam questions. Thus, the expected grade from cheating is determined by two factors: the probability that the teacher catches the student cheating and the probability that the neighbor has the correct answer. Given said behavior for students, we will examine how different monitoring behaviors affect the cheating behaviors of students.

During the exam, the teacher will monitor the students and will cancel the exam of any student s/he directly observes cheating. The teacher will only consider a student to be cheating if s/he observes the student engaging in dishonest behavior.

3 Model Implementation

In this section, we explain in greater depth how the agents in the multi-agent system behave in each step of the simulation, as well as how the evolutionary algorithm works.

3.1 Exam Simulation

As mentioned in Sect. 1, we will consider a teacher and a set of n students, each with a knowledge factor that determines how many questions the student answers without needing to cheat or guess. For this work, we will consider that such a knowledge factor is equivalent to a student's overall average grade and will be modeled as a normally distributed random variable with mean μ and standard deviation σ. The idea behind this interpretation is that a student's knowledge is proportional to his/her academic performance, but the model does not rely on this interpretation, and other alternatives to calculating the knowledge factor could be proposed, such as one that includes how much a student studied for an exam.

After each student agent is given its own personality, we will randomly assign students to seats in a classroom. The classroom will be represented by a grid. A blank space can be left between grid cells representing corridors, which is intended to simulate more accurately the physical space of a traditional classroom. After each student is given an individual grid cell, the teacher is added to the classroom, and the exam simulation will begin. Figure 1 shows a representation of how such a simulated classroom could look like.

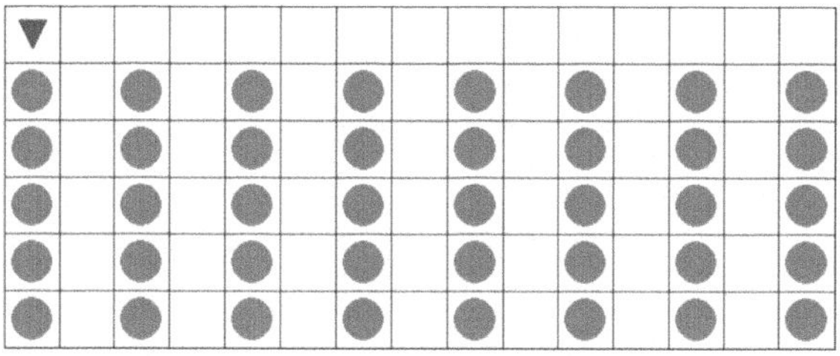

Fig. 1. Diagram of the simulated classroom using a grid. Each circle represents a student allocated in a classroom seat, and the triangle represents the teacher who will be monitoring the exam.

The duration of the exam is modeled with a tick system, in which every tick represents a second. Correct answers to the exam will be stored in an array with a length equal to the total number of questions and will be filled randomly with values between one and four in our simulation.

The teacher will randomly select a student from the grid to monitor and will do so for a random duration within a certain time interval. This duration can be adjusted to model a specific teacher's behavior more appropriately if further studies provide a better understanding of the monitoring tendencies of a teacher. If the teacher finds that a student is cheating, s/he will immediately cancel the student's exam and will enter a monitoring cooldown, which represents the time that the teacher sends the student to the school office or any equivalent. In the following subsection, we will detail the student's behavior and how the cheating decision is made.

3.2 Student Behavior

Student Initialization. Given the knowledge factor, each student will have a certainty array, which represents the exam questions whose answers s/he knows. Let us assume that a student has a knowledge factor k, which, in our model, ranges between zero and ten. Consequently, the number of answers the student will know, denoted in our work by r, which depends on the total number of questions in the exam, denoted by t, is determined by the following expression:

$$r = \left\lfloor \frac{k}{10} \times t \right\rfloor \tag{1}$$

where the floor brackets denote the floor function, which will round down the decimals in the expression to the next smallest integer. As the knowledge factor is a number between zero and ten, dividing the knowledge factor by ten represents the percentage of the exam s/he will know the answers to. Multiplying that percentage by the number of total questions and rounding that number to the next lowest integer gives the number of known answers. Once the number of known answers is determined, a Boolean array with a length equal to the total number of questions in the exam is filled with as many *True* values as there are known answers and the rest of the array items are initialized with *False*. Then, the certainty array is shuffled to determine which answers the simulated student will know. For example, let's say that there are 30 questions in the exam, and a student 'A' has a knowledge factor of 6.23 out of ten. Then, using (1), we assume that student 'A' will know the answer to 18 questions. After the certainty array has been initialized, each student is given an array initially filled with zeros, which represents an empty answer sheet.

Each student also generates a list of neighbors, which are students seated next to and in front of him/her from whom s/he could potentially copy. We will consider that, given a student, a neighbor is *cheatable* if the neighbor's knowledge factor is greater than the student's. Such a list will be sorted in descendent order so that the first object in the list is the cheatable neighbor with the highest knowledge factor. This is intended to simulate students wanting to copy from the student with the highest grades, for it gives them the highest chance of getting a better grade.

After the list of cheatable neighbors, the certainty array, and the answer sheet are generated, the exam simulation begins. For the students, the exam consists of two phases: the knowledge-based phase and the cheating decision phase.

Knowledge-Based Phase. During the initial part of the exam, each student will answer all the questions s/he knows. As outlined in Sect. 1, each student will respond to each question within a predetermined time limit. The duration allocated for each question is determined by a random number within the given time interval. Upon completing a question, a student will update his/her answer sheet by marking the correct option, then proceed to the next question, generating a new time duration for answering it.

This phase ends when the student has finished answering what s/he knows. This could mean that either the student has finished the exam (if his/her knowledge factor was equal to ten) or that there are still unanswered questions, but s/he doesn't know their answers. At this point, each student will have a base expected grade, equal to the number of answers s/he knows divided by the number of questions in the exam multiplied by ten. Continuing from the example in the previous subsection, the base expected grade for student 'A', who knows the answer to 18 questions, will be 6.0. After computing this base expected grade, the cheating decision phase starts.

Cheating Decision Phase. During this stage, each student is faced with the decision of how to answer the questions whose answers s/he is not aware of, and s/he must choose between attempting to cheat or guessing randomly. To make this decision, the student looks at all the cheatable neighbors' answer sheets and sees if any have already answered the question s/he is currently considering. If there is such a neighbor, the student will decide to cheat if the expected grade from cheating is greater than the grade expected from answering randomly (as detailed below). If none of the cheatable neighbors have answered the current question, then s/he guesses by answering randomly.

Expected Grade from Cheating. This calculation must consider both the probability of being caught by the teacher and the probability that the neighbor's answer is the correct one. Let us suppose the event A represents the scenario where the student is caught cheating by the teacher, and event B represents the scenario where the neighbor has the correct answer for the current question. To formalize this, let $P(A)$ be the probability of being caught cheating (see Sects. 4.1 and 4.2 for details on how this probability is obtained), and $P(B)$ be the probability that the neighbor has the correct answer. $P(B)$ can be obtained by dividing the number of known answers, obtained with expression

(1), by the total number of questions in the exam. That is:

$$P(B) = \frac{r}{t} \tag{2}$$

Furthermore, let g represent the current expected grade to be obtained by the student in the exam. Then, g^* represents the potential improvement if the question is answered correctly by either guessing or cheating. Thus, we can calculate g^* as follows:

$$g^* = g + \frac{1}{t} \times 10 \tag{3}$$

In expression (3), dividing 1 by the number of questions and then multiplying the result by 10 represents the potential improvement in the grade, expressed as a decimal in a 10-point grading system. To calculate the expected grade from cheating, we will take the sum of multiplying the value of each possible outcome by the probability of that outcome occurring, just like an expected profit in decision theory [12]. Considering the events A and B defined previously, the complements of both events, denoted as A^c and B^c, and expressions (1), (2) and (3), we obtain that the expected grade from cheating will be given by the following expression:

$$E(C) = P\left(A^C\right) \times P(B) \times g^* + P\left(A^c\right) \times P\left(B^c\right) \times g \tag{4}$$

Note that, in expression (3), if the student gets caught cheating (event A), his/her grade will be zero. Thus, the events related to being caught cheating end up summing zero.

Expected Grade from Answering Randomly. Unlike the previous calculation, the expected grade from answering randomly is given by a very straight-forward expression. As every question has four answering options, and thus the probability of answering that question correctly is ¼, the calculation will be given by:

$$E(G) = g^*\left(\frac{1}{4}\right) + g\left(\frac{3}{4}\right) \tag{5}$$

Final Decision. If the value calculated from expression (4) is greater than that of expression (5), then the student decides to cheat. Upon making that decision, the duration of the cheating activity is randomly determined within a specified interval. If the student cheats successfully and is not caught by the teacher, the current expected grade is updated to match the value from expression (4). Then, the student will enter a cheating cooldown, which is designated to simulate a student in real life who does not want to raise suspicions. However, if the student decides not to cheat, then s/he will guess the answer and update his/her current expected grade to match the value given by expression (5).

After making whichever of the two possible decisions, the student will go onto the next question, and the decision will have to be made again following the steps described in the cheating decision phase. It is crucial to note that if a student does not complete all questions by the time the exam ends, s/he will have unanswered questions and must turn in the exam that way. This situation may occur if a student cheats too much and the designated time to answer each question is not enough to compensate for the cheating cooldowns.

3.3 Numerical example

Let's resume the example provided in Sect. 3.2 which considers an exam with 30 questions and let's consider that the probability of being caught cheating is 0.35. Let's say that student 'A' has one cheatable neighbor (student 'B') with a knowledge factor of 9.2. At the end of the knowledge-based phase, student 'A' has a base expected grade (g) of 6.0 (as shown above) and the probability of student 'B' having the correct answer to the current question will be 0.9, as calculated using expressions (1) and (2). Using expression (3) we can also determine that the potential improvement obtained from cheating successfully (g^*) will be 6.33. Thus, for student 'A', the expected grade from cheating will be:

$$E(C) = (.65)(0.9)(6.33) + (.65)(0.1)(6.0) \approx 4$$

However, the expected grade from answering randomly will be:

$$E(G) = (6.33)\left(\frac{1}{4}\right) + (6.0)\left(\frac{3}{4}\right) \approx 6.1$$

This suggests that student 'A' will not decide to cheat, as the expected grade from guessing is greater than the expected grade from cheating. However, if the student had a much lower knowledge factor and had the same cheatable neighbor 'B', student 'A' would indeed decide to cheat.

3.4 Finding a Minimal-Cheating Classroom Arrangement

Given the initial conditions, which are n students with their knowledge factor, the duration of the exam, the planned time limit for every question in the exam, and the physical classroom in which the students will take the test, an evolutionary algorithm will be employed. In this evolutionary algorithm, the population consists of one individual, which contains an array of size n, where each array position contains the knowledge factor of each student. In each generation, the multi-agent simulation is initialized and performed, where the distribution of students in the classroom is determined by the individual from the evolutionary algorithm. After the multi-agent simulation ends, a new individual is generated by shuffling the elements in the array, and we end up with one new individual for the next evolutionary generation. In our model, randomly shuffling the array is considered as an implementation of the mutation operator. The description provided falls into the category of an evolution strategy [1]. After a specified number of generations, the proposed model will return the classroom arrangement that minimizes the incidence of cheating in the simulation runs.

We propose the use of an evolution strategy given that the total number of possible classroom arrangements for n students is $n!$. For a small classroom, it would be feasible to explore all potential scenarios by permuting the classroom arrangements with a more traditional evolutionary algorithm that would have a larger population. However, for larger classrooms, exploring all possible combinations becomes computationally impractical, if not impossible, which is why an evolution strategy, with just one individual in its population, makes more sense.

In Sect. 5, we will show the results of how many evolutionary generations are necessary to find significantly relevant results, and in the next section we will propose some experiments to test our model.

4 Experimental Design

In this section, we present two possible monitoring behaviors on the part of the teacher, and then explain how each student would calculate the probability of being caught cheating depending on his/her teacher's monitoring behavior. Furthermore, we propose the initial conditions of the experiments that will take place.

4.1 Fair Teacher

We say that the teacher is fair if the probability that s/he monitors a student is the same for every student in the classroom. So, if one of n students decides to cheat, the probability of being caught by the teacher would be:

$$P(A) = \frac{1}{n} \tag{6}$$

Thus, the expected grade from cheating, as proposed in expression (4), would be:

$$E(C) = \left(\frac{n-1}{n}\right)\left(\frac{r}{t}\right)g^* + \left(\frac{n-1}{n}\right)\left(\frac{t-r}{t}\right)g \tag{7}$$

4.2 Biased Teacher

On the other hand, we say that a teacher is biased if s/he monitors a set of students more frequently than the rest of the class. These students could be either specifically introduced to the model or could be the ones in certain zones of the classroom (e.g., the front and back rows). To model this behavior, we will first have to divide the students into two groups. Let S be a set that represent the group of students that the teacher monitors more frequently. The complement of this set, denoted as S^c, refers to the rest of the classroom. The teacher monitors students in set S with a probability p and those in set S^c with probability $1 - p$. Upon selecting a group, s/he will choose any student within that group to monitor, each having an equal opportunity of being selected. As noted in Sect. 1, students are fully aware of the teacher's monitoring behavior and know his/her position, as well as their own position, in the classroom. Consequently, each student knows to which group s/he belongs.

For a Student in Group S. If the student decided to cheat, the probability of being caught cheating would be:

$$P(A) = p * \frac{1}{|S|} \tag{8}$$

where the vertical bars denote the cardinality of said set. Therefore, the expected grade from cheating would be:

$$E(C) = \left(\frac{|S| - p}{|S|}\right)\left(\frac{r}{t}\right)g^{*} + \left(\frac{|S| - p}{|S|}\right)\left(\frac{t - r}{t}\right)g \tag{9}$$

For a Student in Group S^c. If the student decided to cheat, the probability of being caught cheating would be:

$$P(A) = (1 - p) * \frac{1}{|S^c|} \tag{10}$$

Therefore, the expected grade from cheating would be:

$$E(C) = \left(\frac{|S^c| - (1 - p)}{|S^c|}\right)\left(\frac{r}{t}\right)g^{*} + \left(\frac{|S^c| - (1 - p)}{|S^c|}\right)\left(\frac{t - r}{t}\right)g \tag{11}$$

4.3 Initial Conditions of the Experiments

For our experiments, we will consider a group of 40 students, each assigned a knowledge factor that is randomly generated based on a normal distribution with a mean of 6 and a standard deviation of 2.5, and only knowledge factors between zero and ten are considered. This intends to simulate a more realistic classroom, but the acceptable range or the distribution could be modified. The exam is set for a duration of one hour, designed so that every student who knows the answer to a question can accurately answer it within a maximum timeframe of 1.25 minutes. Thus, the number of questions in the exam will be 48, which intends to simulate a typical high school-like exam.

Students will take between 60 and 75 seconds to answer each question to add variability and to simulate more realistically the behavior of the students. If a student opts to cheat, a cheating cooldown period of 120 seconds will be imposed, emulating a student who doesn't want to raise suspicions. As for the teacher, monitoring periods will last between 25 and 45 seconds. If cheating is detected during monitoring, the student's exam will be cancelled, and the teacher will then undergo a monitoring cooldown of 120 seconds, which tries to emulate the time the teacher takes to send students to the principal's office.

We will conduct experiments with both a fair teacher and a biased teacher. In the biased scenario, the teacher has a 70% likelihood of choosing to monitor students situated in the front and back rows, leaving a 30% chance for monitoring the remaining students.

5 Results

A preliminary experiment allowed us to identify, after executing it 30 times, that 500 generations of the evolution strategy are sufficient to obtain good results in the search for an optimal classroom arrangement for both the biased and nonbiased teacher scenarios, as can be seen in Fig. 2. Having determined that 500 generations are enough and adding another 500 just in case, considering the computational resources needed versus benefits obtained in our setup, we will now conduct the fair and biased teacher experiments for 1000 generations to find the classroom arrangements that minimized cheating without worrying that we might be missing out on finding better configurations.

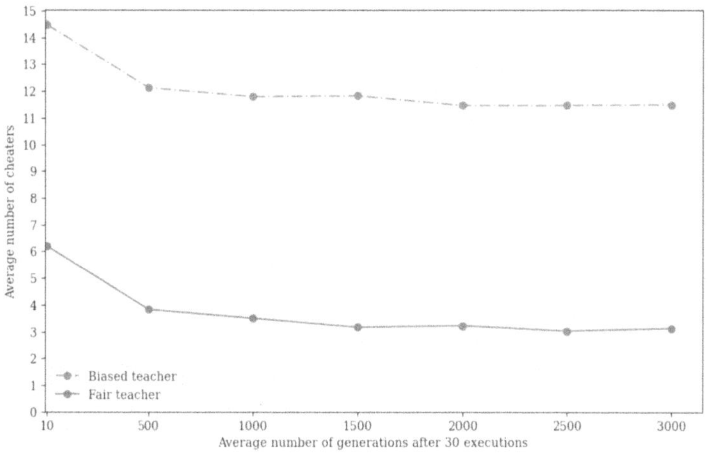

Fig. 2. Average number of cheaters versus average number of generations after executing the experiment 30 times. After 500 evolutionary generations, the number of cheaters stabilizes.

5.1 Fair Teacher Results after 1000 Generations

Figure 3 shows the resulting arrangement of the classroom after 1000 evolutionary generations during the fair teacher experiment. This arrangement caused three students to incur in academic dishonesty (see Fig. 4).

Fig. 3. Resulting arrangement of students during the fair teacher experiment for 1000 generations. Each circle represents a student, and each number represents his/her knowledge factor.

5.2 Biased Teacher Results after 1000 Generations

Figure 5 shows the resulting arrangement of the classroom after 1000 evolutionary generations during the biased teacher experiment. This arrangement caused 12 students to incur in academic dishonesty (see Fig. 6). It is important to note that none of the students in group S decided to cheat, while 50% of the students in S^c decided to cheat. In comparison, only 7.5% of students overall during the fair teacher experiment decided to cheat, as the previous section shows.

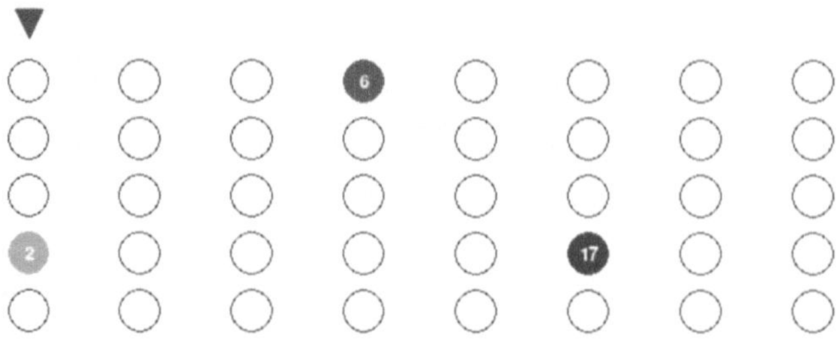

Fig. 4. Cheating count for every student in the classroom during the fair teacher experiment after 1000 generations. White circles represent students who didn't cheat.

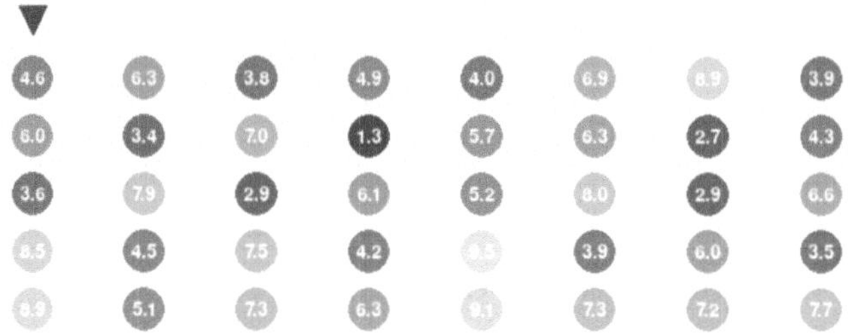

Fig. 5. Resulting arrangement of students during the biased teacher experiment for 1000 generations with 70% chance of choosing a student in group *S*. Each circle represents a student, and each number represents his/her knowledge factor.

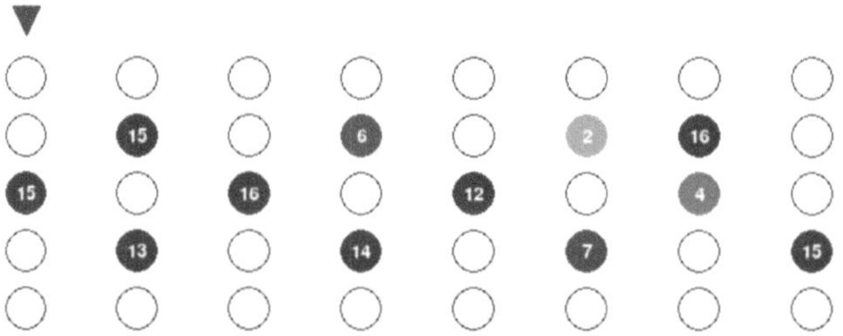

Fig. 6. Cheating count for every student in the classroom during the biased teacher experiment after 1000 generations. White circles represent students who didn't cheat.

6 Discussion

Results show that bias in the monitoring behavior of the teacher leads to a significant increase in cheating amongst the students who are less likely to be observed. This is because, for these students, the expected grade from cheating will most of the time be greater than the expected grade from guessing the correct answer, thus deciding to cheat more frequently. As the students decide to cheat more often, more students are not able to finish the exam due to the cheating cooldown.

On the other hand, in an unbiased setting cheating cases are more evenly distributed throughout the classroom, with the number of cheating cases quickly stabilizing at around

10% of the total number of students. As the probability that the teacher catches the student is evenly distributed, the only students who are willing to risk their grade are the ones with very low knowledge factors. These results demonstrate that an unbiased monitoring approach effectively reduces the opportunities for cheating because of how the monitoring tendencies of the teacher changes the student's behavior.

Even though our model is simple, in future work several of this model's assumptions could be modified to cover much more complex scenarios. Some potential changes could be either adding more monitoring observers (such as teachers and teaching assistants) or implementing moving monitoring observers, in which case the probability of being caught would change over time. Other proposed model extensions include changing the penalties if a student gets caught cheating, considering more cheating mechanisms, changing the configuration of the physical classroom that is to be simulated in which the exam takes place, or extending the types of simulated exam questions beyond multiple choice. These changes would help refine the model to better mimic real-world scenarios and potentially offer more robust solutions to minimize cheating in educational settings. Other potential future work could be comparing the optimal classroom arrangement obtained with our model with student behavior in real examinations operating under the model's assumptions.

Acknowledgments. This work has been supported by Asociación Mexicana de Cultura, A.C.

Disclosure of Interests. The authors have no competing interests to declare that are relevant to the content of this article.

References

1. Bäck, T.: Evolutionary Algorithms in Theory and Practice: Evolution Strategies, Evolutionary Programming. Genetic Algorithms. Oxford University Press, New York (1996)
2. Bucciol, A., Cicognani, S., Montinari, N.: Cheating in university exams: the relevance of social factors. International Review of Economics **67**(3), 319–338 (2020). https://doi.org/10.1007/s12232-019-00343-8
3. Cagala, T., Glogowsky, U., Rincke, J.: Detecting and preventing cheating in exams: evidence from a field experiment. J. Hum. Resour. **59**(1), 210–241 (2024)
4. Dodeen, H.M.: Undergraduate student cheating in exams. Damascus Univ. J. **28**(1), 37–55 (2012)
5. Genemo, M.D.: Suspicious activity recognition for monitoring cheating in exams. Proc. Indian Natl. Sci. Acad. **88**, 1–10 (2022). https://doi.org/10.1007/s43538-022-00069-2
6. Mitchell, M.: An Introduction to Genetic Algorithms (Complex Adaptive Systems Series), 1st edn. MIT Press, Cambridge, Massachusetts (1998)
7. Ramezanian, R., Emdadi, A.: Simulation of Skulduggery in a Multi-Agent System. Int. J. Agent Technol. Syst. **7**(1), 17–31 (2015)
8. Siev, S., Kliger, D.: Cheating in academic exams: a field study. In: Buccicol, A., Montinari, N. (eds.) Dishonesty in Behavioral Economics. 1st edn., pp. 111–140. Academic Press (2019)
9. Sklar, E., Davies, M., Co, M.S.T.: SimEd: simulating education as a multi agent system. In: Proceedings of the Third International Joint Conference on Autonomous Agents and Multiagent Systems, vol. 4, pp. 998–1005 (2004)

10. Sklar, E., Davies, M.: Multiagent simulation of learning environments. In: Proceedings of the Fourth International Joint Conference on Autonomous Agents and Multiagent Systems (AAMAS '05), pp. 953–959 (2005)
11. Sun, R.: Cognition and Multi-Agent Interaction: From Cognitive Modeling to Social Simulation. Cambridge University Press (2006)
12. Tryfos, P.: Business Statistics, 1st edn. McGraw-Hill, Ryerson (1989)
13. Wang, Y., Niu, L., Ren, F.: A multi-agent-based approach for the study of student behavior dynamics in peer learning environments. In: 2021 IEEE International Conference on Engineering, Technology and Education (TALE), pp. 689–694 (2021)
14. Yee, K., MacKown, P.: Detecting and Preventing Cheating During Exams. In: Pedagogy, not Policing, vol. 141, pp. 141–147 (2009)

Resilience to the Flowing Unknown: An Open Set Recognition Framework for Data Streams

Marcos Barcina-Blanco[1,2](✉), Jesus L. Lobo[1], Pablo Garcia-Bringas[2], and Javier Del Ser[1,3]

[1] TECNALIA, Basque Research and Technology Alliance (BRTA), 48160 Derio, Spain
marcos.barcina@tecnalia.com
[2] Faculty of Engineering, University of Deusto, 48007 Bilbao, Spain
[3] University of the Basque Country (UPV/EHU), 48013 Bilbao, Spain

Abstract. Modern digital applications extensively integrate Artificial Intelligence models for automated decision-making. However, these AI-based systems encounter reliability and safety challenges when handling continuous data streams in dynamic scenarios. This work explores the concept of resilient AI systems that must operate in the face of unexpected events and unseen patterns. This is a common issue that regular closed-set classifiers encounter in streaming scenarios, as they are designed to compulsory classify any new observation into one of the training patterns (i.e., the so-called *over-occupied space* problem). In batch learning, the Open Set Recognition field addresses this issue by requiring models to maintain classification performance when processing unknown patterns. This work investigates the application of an Open Set Recognition framework that combines classification and clustering to address the *over-occupied space* problem in streaming scenarios. We devise a benchmark comprising different classification datasets with varying ratios of known to unknown classes, and experiments compare the performance of the proposed framework with that of individual incremental classifiers. Discussions held over the obtained results highlight situations where the framework performs best and the limitations of incremental classifiers in open-world streaming environments.

Keywords: Open set recognition · Unknown classes · Data streams · Open-world learning · Incremental learning

1 Introduction

The rapid expansion of Artificial Intelligence (AI) systems over the last decade has raised major concerns about their resilience and safety [3]. In real-world scenarios AI-based systems are challenged by unforeseen operational conditions and novel inputs [13]. One promising field for making AI systems resilient against

H. Quintián et al. (Eds.): HAIS 2024, LNAI 14857, pp. 139–152, 2025.
https://doi.org/10.1007/978-3-031-74183-8_12

Unknown Classes (UC) is the field of Open Set Recognition (OSR) [10]. Closed-set classification assumes that all query instances of the model in inference belong to one of the classes present in the training data. OSR goes beyond this assumption by confronting a case where UC may emerge during the inference phase of the model. Such an open-set scenario is common in applications that ingest streams of data [8], in which UC are more likely to occur at any point in time. In their simplest formulation, OSR models must detect instances belonging to UC, while correctly classifying those belonging to Known Classes (KC). This is essential for developing further strategies to characterize UC and to incorporate them to the knowledge base of the model. The OSR field is not to be confused with other fields such as semi-supervised learning. While both fields address situations where training information is incomplete, they differ significantly in nature. In semi-supervised learning, the incompleteness is caused by a lack of labels for most of the training data, with labels available only for a small subset. In OSR, the challenge lies in the absence of representation for all possible classes during training.

Together with the formal definition of OSR, the seminal work in [27] also introduced the problem of *over-occupied space*. It refers to the extra feature space that closed-set classifiers assign across all KC in order to create meaningful boundaries. Although the *over-occupied space* is purposed to increase the generalization capabilities of the model, it also implies that any instance belonging to an UC will inevitably fall in this space and be incorrectly classified as a KC. Hence, traditional classification models require adaptation for open-set environments [12,21,27]. Figure 1 shows an example of OSR classification, where the model limits the open space assigned to the KC, and also detects samples from UC. The recent work [10] suggests that the combination of clustering and classification can effectively address this issue. However, scarce attempts have been made hybridizing clustering and classification techniques [6,30]. Although promising experiments in this area are confined to static batch environments, OSR scenarios are more prevalent in data streaming setups, where additional challenges exist. Models must not only deal with the appearance of UC, but also continuously adapt and learn from novel data distributions [1].

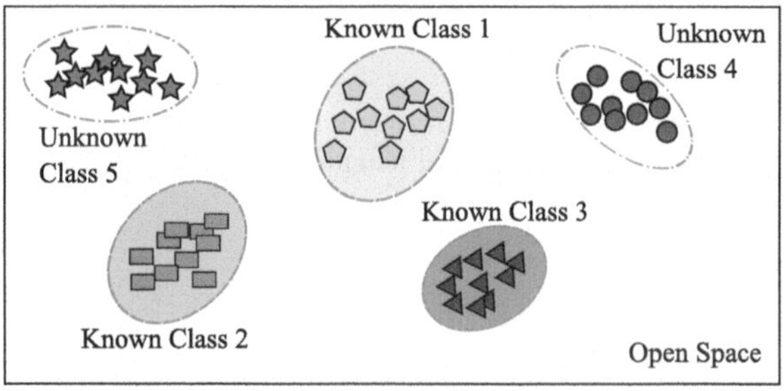

Fig. 1. Example of OSR classification.

This work aims to showcase how a hybrid clustering and classification framework can overcome the *over-occupied space* issue, evaluating its efficacy in streaming contexts with varying known-to-unknown class ratios. The main contributions are summarized as follows:

- A framework that blends together incremental clustering and classification to reduce the *over-occupied space* and to yield a resilient OSR model.
- An evaluation of the proposed hybrid framework under streaming conditions, and a performance comparison with a regular and an incremental classifier, exposing the limitations of these single classifiers when dealing with UC.
- A discussion on the limitations of UC detection methods in streaming settings, and an outline of possible research directions by which clustering and classification methods can be used together to tackle OSR in non-stationary environments.

The rest of this work is structured as follows: Sect. 2 briefly revisits relevant literature on OSR, whereas Sect. 3 formally states the *over-occupied space* problem in OSR. Next, Sect. 4 provides an explanation of the proposed hybrid framework. Section 5 describes the datasets, methods, and metrics used in our experiments. Section 6 presents and discusses on the results from the experiments. Finally, Sect. 7 draws concluding remarks and sketches future research paths basedon our findings.

2 Related Work

Before delving into the work done in OSR, it is important to mention that the appearance of UC has been tackled from other research areas in Machine Learning, such as Novelty Detection (ND) and Out-of-Distribution (OoD) detection [31]. Although these two research areas focus on detecting and dealing with novel instances, they possess some key differences with OSR. ND is mainly considered to be an unsupervised task and does not require the classification of instances from KC. On the other hand, OoD differs in the training and benchmarking procedure. Unlike OoD, OSR avoids training with real outliers to control the positively labeled open space. While adding a "background" class is effective, it does not restrict the *over-occupied space*. OSR benchmarks split a dataset into KC (*in-distribution*) and UC (*out-of-distribution*) instances. In contrast, OoD typically regards one dataset as in-distribution and other datasets as OoD. Contributions done so far in the field agree on the division of OSR approaches into two main categories [2,10,20]: discriminative and generative. We now revisit contributions in these two categories (Subsect. 2.1), followed by a justification of the contribution of this work (Subsect. 2.2).

2.1 OSR Approaches

This first category of OSR approaches (discriminative) focuses on modeling the data into smaller areas in the feature space to distinguish between KC and UC. Early approaches adapted traditional classification models to the open-world

[12,21,27]. Other approaches employ methods better suited for predicting UC, such as Gaussian Processes [5], which assign an uncertainty measure to predictions. Deep neural networks have also been extensively used in OSR due to their strong representation capabilities [4,15]. Alternatively, the authors in [18] argue that representing data in the frequency domain instead of the usual spatial domain is more suited for OSR. Prototype learning tightens feature representations, enhancing boundary clarity between KC and UC [7].

The second class of OSR approaches (generative) seeks to generate artificial instances that represent the UC and train the model with them. Most works done in this line rely on Generative Adversarial Networks (GAN) [16]. Recent activity has placed greater emphasis on the quality of the synthesized instances [25] and on learning extra synthesized classes to make the model reserve space suitable for future UC [19].

2.2 Contribution

In discriminative approaches, clustering and classification models can be combined to address the *over-occupied space* problem. Clustering models adjust KC to a smaller area, while classification models are used to discriminate between them. Approaches in the field employ sequential [30] or simultaneous [6,33] strategies. Finally, the research in streaming conditions tackles challenges like identifying new classes from unknown instances and updating models with new knowledge, which still remain untackled [9,17]. Few works explicitly address OSR in streaming setups [24]. However, the literature lacks a detailed exploration of the *over-occupied space* problem and the connection of OSR to ND and concept evolution in stream learning [1].

3 Problem Statement

Traditional streaming classification tasks assume that there is an infinite sequence of pairs $(\mathbf{x}_t, y_t)$, where $\mathbf{x}_t \in \boldsymbol{\mathcal{X}}$ and $y_t \in \mathcal{C}_{KC} = \{y_1, y_2, \ldots, y_N\}$ (KC). In the absence of unexpected classes and non-stationarities, classifiers are either trained offline with instances from $\mathcal{C}_{KC}$ or, alternatively, learn incrementally from the stream if no extreme verification latency is held. Classifiers compute a probability distribution over the training classes $p(y|\mathbf{x})$ with $y \in \mathcal{C}_{KC}$. Since this conditional distribution is defined for any $\mathbf{x} \in \boldsymbol{\mathcal{X}}$, feature space is over-occupied by the classifier as it characterizes regions in $\boldsymbol{\mathcal{X}}$ that may eventually belong to UC. Since any predicted label $\hat{y}_t$ belongs to $\mathcal{C}_{KC}$, whenever a new query instance $\mathbf{x}_t$ whose true label does not belong to $\mathcal{C}_{KC}$ appears in the stream, a classification error occurs.

By contrast, streaming OSR classification models are designed to work in an environment similar to the above, but where y_t does not necessarily belong to $\mathcal{C}_{KC}$ $\forall t$. They are trained to correctly classify instances $\mathbf{x}_t$ from $\mathcal{C}_{KC}$, but instances may also belong to $\mathcal{C}_{UC}$, with $\mathcal{C}_{KC} \cap \mathcal{C}_{UC} = \emptyset$. A streaming OSR model should be able to determine whether any new instance $\mathbf{x}_t$ belongs to $\mathcal{C}_{KC}$

or $\mathcal{C}_{UC}$. Additionally, if $\mathbf{x}_t$ is determined to be from $\mathcal{C}_{KC}$, the model should also predict its class label $\hat{y}_t \in \mathcal{C}_{KC}$.

4 Proposed Streaming OSR Framework

As explained in the previous section, the predictions of a single closed-set classifier are limited to C_{KC}. The addition of a clustering model can help circumvent this flaw by capturing the structure of arriving data, whereas a closed-set classification model can be deployed and updated incrementally with instances arriving from the stream verified to belong to $\mathcal{C}_{KC}$.

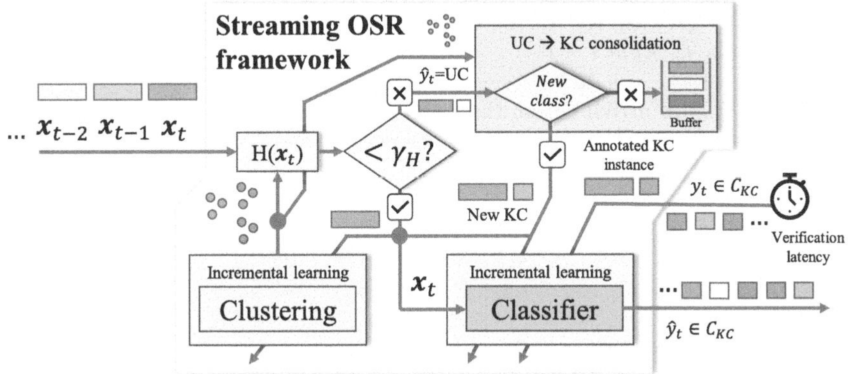

Fig. 2. Block diagram of the proposed streaming OSR framework.

This rationale guides the design of the proposed OSR framework for data streams depicted in Fig. 2. Stream instances $\{\mathbf{x}_t\}$ are received over time, each first processed in order to estimate the degree to which stream instance $\mathbf{x}_t$ is unknown. This estimation exploits an incremental clustering algorithm to characterize the feature space, continuously updating cluster arrangements upon each arrival of instances. Let M_t denote the number of clusters discovered by the cluster algorithm at time t, and $\mathbf{c}_t^m \in \mathcal{X}$ the centroid corresponding to the m-th cluster. A measure of novelty of $\mathbf{x}_t$ can be produced through the use of entropy [22,28]. Based on the assumption that instances closer to each other are more similar than those further apart, we can compute a pseudo-probability $\tilde{p}(m|\mathbf{x}_t)$ of every arriving instance $\mathbf{x}_t$ to every cluster $m \in \{1, \ldots, M_t\}$:

$$\tilde{p}(m|\mathbf{x}_t) = \frac{1/d(\mathbf{x}_t, \mathbf{c}_t^m)^2}{\sum_{m'=1}^{M_t} 1/d(\mathbf{x}_t, \mathbf{c}_t^{m'})^2} \tag{1}$$

where $d(\cdot, \cdot)$ stands for the Euclidean distance. The $1/d(\mathbf{x}_t, \mathbf{c}_t^m)^2$ is adopted as the weight representation function because it quickly diminishes with distance, granting that those elements nearer to the clusters show much higher weights than those farther away. Based on the pseudo-probability vector $\{\tilde{p}(m|\mathbf{x}_t)\}_{m=1}^{M_t}$, the framework computes the entropy associated to $\mathbf{x}_t$ as:

$$H(\mathbf{x}_t) = \sum_{m=1}^{M_t} -\tilde{p}(m|\mathbf{x}_t)\log_{M_t}\tilde{p}(m|\mathbf{x}_t) \tag{2}$$

in which instances with lower $H(\mathbf{x}_t)$ belong to $\mathcal{C}_{KC}$, while instances with higher entropy are declared to be unknown.

Algorithm 1. Proposed streaming OSR framework

Require: $\mathcal{C}_{KC}$, incremental clustering algorithm $f_{\odot}(\mathbf{x})$, incremental classifier $f_C(\mathbf{x})$, threshold γ_H

Ensure: Warm-up with KC instances providing a classifier $f_C(\mathbf{x})$ and centroids $\{\mathbf{c}_1^m\}_{m=1}^{M_1}$ via $f_{\odot}(\mathbf{x})$ at $t = 1$

for all $t \in \{1, \ldots, \infty\}$ **do**
  Collect $\mathbf{x}_t \in \boldsymbol{\mathcal{X}}$ arriving from the stream
  Compute $\tilde{p}(m|\mathbf{x}_t)$ $\forall m \in \{1, \ldots, M_t\}$ as per Eq. (1)
  Compute $H(\mathbf{x}_t)$ as per Eq. (2)
  if $H(\mathbf{x}_t) < \gamma_H$ **then**
    Predict $\hat{y}_t = f_C(\mathbf{x}_t) = \arg\max_{y \in \mathcal{C}_{KC}} p(y|\mathbf{x}_t)$
    Update $f_C(\mathbf{x}_t)$ with $(\mathbf{x}_t, y_t)$ (s.t. verification latency)
    Update $\{\mathbf{c}_t^m\}_{m=1}^{M_t}$ to $\{\mathbf{c}_{t+1}^m\}_{m=1}^{M_{t+1}}$ via $f_{\odot}(\mathbf{x}_t)$
  else
    Analyze $\mathbf{x}_t$ and other buffered UC instances
    if criterion to consolidate a new class y^* is met **then**
      Predict $\hat{y}_t = y^*$
      Update $f_C(\mathbf{x}_t)$ with $(\mathbf{x}_t, y^*)$
      Update $\{\mathbf{c}_t^m\}_{m=1}^{M_t}$ to $\{\mathbf{c}_{t+1}^m\}_{m=1}^{M_{t+1}}$ via $f_{\odot}(\mathbf{x}_t)$
    else
      Predict $\hat{y}_t$ = UC (*unknown*)

The workflow is summarized in Algorithm 1. New instances first arrive to the clustering model, where their entropy is measured against a predefined threshold $\gamma_H \in \mathbb{R}(0, 1]$. Instances with $H(\mathbf{x}_t) \geq \gamma_H$ are considered *unknown*, so they are predicted as UC and then, fed to a UC→KC consolidation module. Based on the current UC instance and the current cluster space, this module decides whether a new KC should be incrementally learned by the classifier. Diverse criteria can be followed for this purpose based on a buffer of recently detected UC instances. If the presence of a new KC is determined, the instance $\mathbf{x}_t$ annotated with a new class identifier y^* is fed and incrementally learned by the classifier and the clustering algorithm. By contrast, instances with $H(\mathbf{x}_t) < \gamma_H$ are passed to the clustering algorithm and the classifier for normal closed-set classification, yielding prediction $\hat{y}_t \in \mathcal{C}_{KC}$. KC samples are retained until their true label is known, whose feasibility depends on the buffer size requirements imposed by the verification latency of the stream. If feasible, the classifier can be updated incrementally with each stored $\mathbf{x}_t$ and its annotation y_t.

5 Experimental Setup

Before delving into the limitations of the proposed framework and forthcoming challenges, we review the results of an experimental benchmark. We aim to empirically assess the performance of the framework over several streaming datasets under different ratios of known-to-unknown classes. Furthermore, we consider three baselines:

1. A regular, non-incremental classifier that does not update its knowledge nor is it helped by a clustering algorithm to determine whether stream instances are known (`static`).
2. An incremental classifier updated with the verified labels of the incoming stream instance, but without any functionality to detect unknown instances (`incremental`).
3. The proposed stream OSR framework (`sOSR`).

As will be later discussed, the UC→KC consolidation module can be affected by the presence of non-stationarities in the classification task (*concept drift* [26]). To avoid a comparison biased by the design of this module, we follow a common practice in the literature and assume a *test-then-train* scheme, by which the true label y_t of $\mathbf{x}_t$ is made known to `incremental` and `sOSR` immediately after predicting $\hat{y}_t$. Given the immediate verification of every test instance, the consolidation module in the `sOSR` framework is not needed. All UC instances will be grouped into one UC to focus on the detection ability of this unified UC by the proposed framework. Works that address this problem usually apply clustering algorithms on the UC samples in the data buffer to extract new classes [7].

We evaluate the above baselines over 40 synthetic datasets and two real datasets (`insects` [29], `covertype` [14]) at different values of missing classes $\beta = |\mathcal{C}_{UC}|/(|\mathcal{C}_{KC}| + |\mathcal{C}_{UC}|)$. For example, a dataset with 10 classes are evaluated at $\beta = 0.2$ and are composed of $|\mathcal{C}_{KC}| = 8$ KC during training, while $|\mathcal{C}_{KC}| + |\mathcal{C}_{UC}| = 10$ classes may appear during inference, with $|\mathcal{C}_{UC}| = 2$ UC. Selecting a wide range β values is crucial as it enables the evaluation of model robustness across diverse scenarios, reflecting the dynamic and unpredictable nature of real-world settings. KC data instances are split into training (80%) and testing (20%) partitions. We then interleave at random test data instances of the KC with a 10% of the total instances from each UC. Synthetic datasets

Table 1. Parameters from the synthetic datasets

Parameters	D1-D4	D5-D8	D9-11	D12-D14	D15-17	D18-D20
Number of instances	1000	2000	3000	5000	7500	10000
Number of classes	5	8	10	12	15	20
Number of features	3	4	6	8	10	12
StdDev (`isoGauss`)	0.75	1	1.25	1.5	1.75	2
Class Sep. (`hyperCube`)	1.4	1.2	1	0.8	0.6	0.4

StdDev: intra-cluster standard deviation. Class Sep.: factor multiplying the hypercube size consist of 20 isotropic Gaussian point clouds (`isoGauss`) and 20 classification datasets generated by an multidimensional adaptation of the hypercube-based Medelon dataset generation procedure in [11] (`hyperCube`). Table 1 describes the different parameters of each synthetic dataset, from the simplest (D_1-D_4) to the most challenging ones (D_{18}-D_{20}). These datasets vary not only in the number of classes and features but also in StdDev and ClassSep parameters. Higher StdDev increases instance spread around class centers and the likelihood of overlap between classes. Conversely, lower Class Separation implies closer class centers, increased class overlap, and reduced feature discriminative power. These parameters aim to simulate increasingly complex class structures, challenging the ability of the approach to delineate the *over-occupied space*. The `insects` dataset also poses a multi-class classification problem with 52, 848 instances across 6 types of insects, each described by 33 features. The `covertype` dataset poses a challenging and more imbalanced multi-class classification problem with 581012 instances and 7 types of forests described by 53 features. A subset of 50000 instances from this dataset is randomly drawn for the experiments.

We employ the Softmax and HoeffdingTree classification implementations for the classification models, both of which suffer from the *over-occupied space* problem. For the clustering model, we choose STREAMKmeans, an adaptation of K-means that is simple, efficient, and relies on distance to group similar data points together, which helps in distinguishing between known and unknown instances. Both are provided by the River framework [23] which is widely used by the scientific community focused on stream learning. The STREAMKmeans algorithm requires to set beforehand the number of clusters to run. Since a warm-up period is assumed (Algorithm 1), we use the number of KC for this purpose. For a fair comparison, we do not perform hyperparameter tuning on any model. Models are configured with their default values from the River framework as the search of the best individual performance is not the focus of this work.

We evaluate the implemented models based on KC (KC-Acc) and UC (UC-Acc) accuracy. We adopt the open macro F1 metric (F1) defined in [21] which is similar to the conventional macro F1-measure, but true positives from UC are not considered. We also use the Area Under the ROC Curve (AUROC) to evaluate the baselines on the reduction of *over-occupied space*. Unlike other metrics, AUROC does not need threshold a selection. However, it is not applicable to single classifier models as they cannot explicitly predict UC. As such, we do not report the AUROC associated to `static` and `incremental` baselines. The true positive rates and the false positive rates used to calculate the AUROC are sorted by their Youden Index [32]. The threshold with the highest Youden Index is selected for evaluating the proposed `sOSR`. We report on average results of each baseline across all datasets for every value of β. To assess the significance of performance gaps, a non-parametric Wilcoxon signed-rank test with significance level $\alpha = 0.05$ is performed over the scores of the `static` and `incremental` baselines with the scores of the `sOSR` baseline for every β. For the sake of transparency and to support follow-up studies, all scripts, datasets and results have been made publicly available in a GitHub repository[1].

[1] https://github.com/Unknownhedgehog/CCH_overoccupied_space_OSR.

6 Results and Discussion

The results of the experiments are shown in Tables 2 (synthetic datasets) and 3 (real datasets) as average ± standard deviation for the three baselines: `static` (top position in each cell), `incremental` (middle) and `sOSR` (bottom). Best results for every (β, dataset, score) combination considering the statistical significance as per the Wilcoxon test are highlighted in gray. As expected, the regular `static` classifier lacks the ability to detect any instances from the UC. The UC-Acc of the `incremental` classifier grows with higher levels of missing classes and higher number of instances from the UC. The KC-Acc and F1 are generally higher for the single classifier methods. Overall, the UC-Acc is the highest for the proposed `sOSR` approach, as it is able to better detect instances from UC, and to manage the *over-occupied space* than the other classifiers. Furthermore, the gaps between baselines in terms of the KC-Acc and UC-Acc scores are statistically significant. The results of F1 are an exception for higher levels of missing classes due to a more balanced amount of instances from KC and UC. The higher F1

Table 2. Results[a] (average±std) over synthetic datasets

		isoGauss				hyperCube			
	β	KC-Acc	UC-Acc	F1	AUC	KC-Acc	UC-Acc	F1	AUC
Softmax Classification	0.1	0.98 ± 0.05	0.00 ± 0.00	0.84 ± 0.08	-	0.55 ± 0.25	0.00 ± 0.00	0.46 ± 0.18	-
		0.98 ± 0.04	0.04 ± 0.09	0.84 ± 0.08	-	0.55 ± 0.25	0.00 ± 0.00	0.46 ± 0.18	-
		0.59 ± 0.15	0.92 ± 0.05	0.55 ± 0.11	0.73 ± 0.11	0.28 ± 0.2	0.75 ± 0.08	0.28 ± 0.17	0.59 ± 0.10
	0.25	0.98 ± 0.04	0.00 ± 0.00	0.83 ± 0.08	-	0.57 ± 0.24	0.00 ± 0.00	0.47 ± 0.18	-
		0.98 ± 0.03	0.03 ± 0.09	0.84 ± 0.07	-	0.57 ± 0.24	0.00 ± 0.01	0.47 ± 0.18	-
		0.66 ± 0.13	0.90 ± 0.07	0.61 ± 0.08	0.80 ± 0.09	0.29 ± 0.18	0.74 ± 0.08	0.29 ± 0.16	0.58 ± 0.07
	0.4	0.99 ± 0.02	0.00 ± 0.00	0.81 ± 0.07	-	0.62 ± 0.24	0.00 ± 0.00	0.49 ± 0.16	-
		0.99 ± 0.02	0.05 ± 0.10	0.81 ± 0.07	-	0.62 ± 0.24	0.03 ± 0.11	0.49 ± 0.16	-
		0.75 ± 0.13	0.91 ± 0.05	0.66 ± 0.07	0.86 ± 0.08	0.33 ± 0.20	0.74 ± 0.08	0.32 ± 0.16	0.61 ± 0.11
	0.6	1.00 ± 0.01	0.00 ± 0.00	0.74 ± 0.09	-	0.70 ± 0.24	0.00 ± 0.00	0.50 ± 0.13	-
		1.00 ± 0.01	0.24 ± 0.24	0.75 ± 0.08	-	0.69 ± 0.24	0.11 ± 0.19	0.50 ± 0.13	-
		0.84 ± 0.11	0.93 ± 0.05	0.68 ± 0.05	0.92 ± 0.06	0.37 ± 0.17	0.74 ± 0.10	0.33 ± 0.13	0.61 ± 0.08
	0.75	1.00 ± 0.00	0.00 ± 0.00	0.66 ± 0.08	-	0.79 ± 0.21	0.00 ± 0.00	0.51 ± 0.09	-
		1.00 ± 0.01	0.39 ± 0.23	0.69 ± 0.07	-	0.78 ± 0.20	0.16 ± 0.17	0.51 ± 0.01	-
		0.90 ± 0.07	0.95 ± 0.04	0.67 ± 0.04	0.96 ± 0.03	0.39 ± 0.19	0.81 ± 0.07	0.33 ± 0.12	0.63 ± 0.01
HoeffdingTree Classification	0.1	1.00 ± 0.01	0.00 ± 0.00	0.86 ± 0.06	-	0.58 ± 0.24	0.00 ± 0.00	0.49 ± 0.18	-
		1.00 ± 0.01	0.95 ± 0.02	0.88 ± 0.05	-	0.57 ± 0.24	0.14 ± 0.16	0.49 ± 0.18	-
		0.68 ± 0.15	0.98 ± 0.01	0.64 ± 0.10	0.81 ± 0.10	0.25 ± 0.17	0.78 ± 0.09	0.26 ± 0.15	0.57 ± 0.07
	0.25	1.00 ± 0.01	0.00 ± 0.00	0.85 ± 0.06	-	0.60 ± 0.22	0.00 ± 0.00	0.49 ± 0.16	-
		1.00 ± 0.00	0.93 ± 0.03	0.87 ± 0.05	-	0.59 ± 0.23	0.11 ± 0.17	0.50 ± 0.17	-
		0.67 ± 0.15	0.97 ± 0.01	0.62 ± 0.10	0.80 ± 0.11	0.27 ± 0.18	0.79 ± 0.06	0.28 ± 0.16	0.58 ± 0.08
	0.4	1.00 ± 0.00	0.00 ± 0.00	0.82 ± 0.07	-	0.64 ± 0.22	0.00 ± 0.00	0.50 ± 0.15	-
		1.00 ± 0.00	0.89 ± 0.09	0.84 ± 0.06	-	0.63 ± 0.22	0.09 ± 0.11	0.50 ± 0.15	-
		0.72 ± 0.14	0.96 ± 0.03	0.64 ± 0.07	0.83 ± 0.08	0.31 ± 0.18	0.75 ± 0.08	0.30 ± 0.15	0.59 ± 0.08
	0.6	0.98 ± 0.07	0.00 ± 0.00	0.73 ± 0.09	-	0.70 ± 0.21	0.00 ± 0.00	0.50 ± 0.11	-
		0.98 ± 0.05	0.88 ± 0.19	0.77 ± 0.08	-	0.69 ± 0.21	0.10 ± 0.13	0.50 ± 0.11	-
		0.81 ± 0.15	0.97 ± 0.03	0.66 ± 0.07	0.91 ± 0.07	0.37 ± 0.19	0.76 ± 0.09	0.33 ± 0.13	0.63 ± 0.11
	0.75	1.00 ± 0.00	0.00 ± 0.00	0.66 ± 0.08	-	0.79 ± 0.19	0.00 ± 0.00	0.51 ± 0.08	-
		1.00 ± 0.00	0.93 ± 0.05	0.72 ± 0.07	-	0.78 ± 0.19	0.15 ± 0.15	0.51 ± 0.08	-
		0.90 ± 0.09	0.98 ± 0.01	0.67 ± 0.04	0.96 ± 0.04	0.38 ± 0.17	0.81 ± 0.07	0.32 ± 0.11	0.63 ± 0.09

[a]The upper result in each cell corresponds to the `static` classifier, the middle result corresponds to the `incremental` classifier, and the bottom result stands for the scores of the proposed `sOSR` framework.

Table 3. Results[a] (average±std) over the `insects` and `covertype` datasets

		insects				covertype			
	β	KC-Acc	UC-Acc	F1	AUC	KC-Acc	UC-Acc	F1	AUC
Softmax Classification	0.1	0.67 ± 0.01	0.00 ± 0.00	0.52 ± 0.01	-	0.71 ± 0.01	0.00 ± 0.00	0.33 ± 0.02	-
		0.65 ± 0.00	0.14 ± 0.02	0.52 ± 0.00	-	0.69 ± 0.01	0.66 ± 0.01	0.41 ± 0.01	-
		0.35 ± 0.15	0.62 ± 0.20	0.34 ± 0.11	0.57 ± 0.04	0.64 ± 0.02	0.93 ± 0.01	0.35 ± 0.02	0.93 ± 0.01
	0.25	0.64 ± 0.01	0.00 ± 0.00	0.47 ± 0.01	-	0.92 ± 0.00	0.00 ± 0.00	0.30 ± 0.03	-
		0.62 ± 0.01	0.31 ± 0.02	0.47 ± 0.00	-	0.90 ± 0.00	0.08 ± 0.02	0.33 ± 0.01	-
		0.41 ± 0.15	0.54 ± 0.17	0.36 ± 0.12	0.55 ± 0.05	0.59 ± 0.13	0.47 ± 0.13	0.07 ± 0.03	0.54 ± 0.02
	0.5	0.73 ± 0.01	0.00 ± 0.00	0.51 ± 0.01	-	0.79 ± 0.01	0.00 ± 0.00	0.41 ± 0.03	-
		0.70 ± 0.00	0.51 ± 0.02	0.51 ± 0.00	-	0.72 ± 0.01	0.83 ± 0.01	0.46 ± 0.01	-
		0.49 ± 0.05	0.69 ± 0.04	0.42 ± 0.03	0.64 ± 0.04	0.64 ± 0.03	0.89 ± 0.01	0.42 ± 0.02	0.87 ± 0.02
	0.7	0.96 ± 0.00	0.00 ± 0.00	0.57 ± 0.00	-	0.95 ± 0.00	0.00 ± 0.00	0.44 ± 0.01	-
		0.93 ± 0.00	0.14 ± 0.02	0.57 ± 0.00	-	0.92 ± 0.00	0.18 ± 0.01	0.44 ± 0.01	-
		0.59 ± 0.21	0.47 ± 0.17	0.43 ± 0.14	0.52 ± 0.02	0.68 ± 0.07	0.51 ± 0.06	0.21 ± 0.02	0.60 ± 0.03
HoeffdingTree Classification	0.1	0.57 ± 0.04	0.00 ± 0.00	0.44 ± 0.04	-	0.53 ± 0.03	0.00 ± 0.00	0.21 ± 0.03	-
		0.53 ± 0.03	0.41 ± 0.12	0.44 ± 0.02	-	0.53 ± 0.03	0.01 ± 0.02	0.22 ± 0.03	-
		0.17 ± 0.16	0.87 ± 0.14	0.14 ± 0.13	0.50 ± 0.06	0.31 ± 0.04	0.61 ± 0.11	0.12 ± 0.02	0.59 ± 0.04
	0.25	0.70 ± 0.02	0.00 ± 0.00	0.52 ± 0.01	-	0.62 ± 0.02	0.00 ± 0.00	0.21 ± 0.03	-
		0.68 ± 0.02	0.06 ± 0.03	0.52 ± 0.01	-	0.62 ± 0.01	0.00 ± 0.00	0.22 ± 0.03	-
		0.13 ± 0.16	0.85 ± 0.22	0.14 ± 0.13	0.50 ± 0.04	0.43 ± 0.07	0.86 ± 0.10	0.16 ± 0.02	0.81 ± 0.04
	0.5	0.80 ± 0.02	0.00 ± 0.00	0.55 ± 0.02	-	0.94 ± 0.00	0.00 ± 0.00	0.33 ± 0.01	-
		0.78 ± 0.02	0.23 ± 0.07	0.56 ± 0.01	-	0.93 ± 0.02	0.08 ± 0.08	0.34 ± 0.03	-
		0.39 ± 0.17	0.71 ± 0.17	0.36 ± 0.12	0.60 ± 0.05	0.64 ± 0.11	0.54 ± 0.13	0.09 ± 0.03	0.59 ± 0.02
	0.7	0.81 ± 0.02	0.00 ± 0.00	0.48 ± 0.01	-	0.91 ± 0.01	0.00 ± 0.00	0.46 ± 0.05	-
		0.78 ± 0.02	0.46 ± 0.08	0.50 ± 0.01	-	0.91 ± 0.00	0.06 ± 0.02	0.44 ± 0.01	-
		0.35 ± 0.09	0.84 ± 0.07	0.30 ± 0.05	0.63 ± 0.05	0.83 ± 0.29	0.29 ± 0.03	0.40 ± 0.01	0.54 ± 0.02

[a]Same interpretation of scores in each cell as in Table 2.

scores of single classifier approaches (`static` and `incremental`) compared to the proposed `sOSR` arise from the majority of arriving instances being KC. This trend is partially replicated by the `incremental` classifier. Notably, the performance of the `incremental` classifier when detecting UC instances varies greatly with levels of missing classes. Initially, with few UC instances, it struggles to learn a new space for the UC, reflected in extremely low UC-Acc scores at lower β that gradually improve with higher β. Additionally, as UC detection improves, KC accuracy tends to decrease. This can be clearly seen in the `incremental` classifier KC-Acc and UC-Acc values of the `covertype` dataset. Moreover, the standard deviation of UC-Acc at $\beta \in \{0.6, 0.75\}$ also becomes higher due to the unpredictability of the position of the UC in the feature space. Although the `incremental` classifier is learning a new space for the new instances, it may be at the expense of the space occupied by the KC, which does not solve the *over-occupied space* problem robustly.

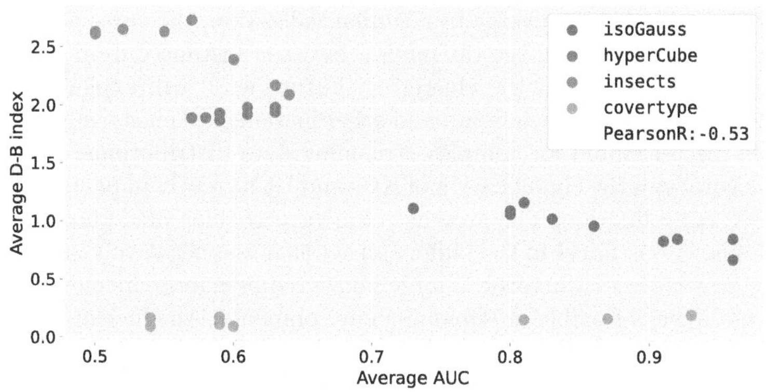

Fig. 3. Average AUC vs D-B index for the sOSR approach and the datasets from the benchmark at different values of β.

7 Conclusions, Limitations and Future Work

This work has elaborated on the *over-occupied space* issue of OSR, focusing on its complexity in streaming environments. We have proposed a streaming OSR framework, that combines an incremental classifier with incremental clustering, to yield a generic processing workflow to perform classification modeling tasks over open-world data streams. We have compared three approaches: a regular classifier, an incremental classifier, and the streaming OSR framework configured with an incremental version of the K-Means clustering. Our results have exposed that the proposed framework can help a classifier overcome the *over-occupied space* problem by virtue of a simple entropy-based detection based on the incrementally updated distribution of clusters.

Although our proposal effectively learns to detect UC, it still undergoes similar issues to a regular classifier and is not enough to solve the issue. As discussed in Sect. 4, the reliability of the *entropy* measure depends on the ability of the clustering model to find representative centers. This statement is buttressed by Fig. 3, which depicts the Davies-Bouldin (D-B) index of the sOSR approach for all datasets at each level of β. The higher the D-B index is, the lower the quality of the clustering will be. The core limitation of the STREAMKmeans algorithm, together with the fixed value of γ_H used in the experiments, make the overall framework not to be suitable to properly characterize all data streams in the benchmark, as evinced by the correlation between the D-B indices and the AUC scores of the sOSR framework in Tables 2 and 3. An incorrect threshold also damages the performance of the closed-set classifier due to many KC instances being identified as UC. Furthermore, some experiments (from the covertype dataset) show a low AUC score while having high quality clusters. We believe that this is caused by the large number of features of the covertype dataset. Since the entropy method is based on the distance to the cluster centers, it does not scale well into high-dimensional feature spaces. In such spaces, the distance between any two points tends to converge to a similar value (i.e., the curse of dimensionality), greatly complicating the distinction between instances from KC and UC regardless of the quality of the clustering. Future work will explore the use of automated configuration techniques and other incremental clustering algorithms, potentially better suited for complex streaming data distributions.

The accuracy of the classification of KCs and UCs greatly impacts the process of UC→KC consolidation. The presence of incorrectly classified known instances among unknown instances in the buffer can act as noise, negatively impacting the search for new classes. Moreover, a large buffer requires more memory resources, which is not always feasible in streaming environments. An efficient buffer needs to automatically adapt to the dynamic nature of the UC by learning the optimal time to start the consolidation process. Another aspect demanding further thought is between the different types of concept drift and OSR. Unlike virtual ($p_{\mathbf{X}}(\mathbf{x})$ changes) and real drift ($p_{Y|\mathbf{X}}(y|\mathbf{x})$ changes), in OSR what changes is the discrete support $\mathcal{Y}$ of the statistical variable Y, which represents the different classes in the stream. It can be challenging for the UC→KC consolidation module to decide whether a set of UC instances detected over time corresponds to a sharp distributional change of $\mathbf{X}$ (i.e. a virtual drift) or, alternatively, should be consolidated as a new class and incorporated as such to the classifier. Additionally, when these drifts are recurring, re-learning old concepts can result in a waste of model resources and can result in the degradation of closed-set classification accuracy. These limitations and other points of improvement will guide our research efforts in the near future, with the overarching goal of discovering hybrid streaming OSR approaches that operate resiliently with evolving data in open-world environments.

Acknowledgements. All authors approved the version of the manuscript to be published. This research has received funding from the Basque Government (BEREZ-IA project with grant number KK-2023/00012), and the research groups MATHMODE (IT1456-22) and D4K-Deusto for Knowledge (IT1528-22).

References

1. Agrahari, S., Srivastava, S., Singh, A.K.: Review on novelty detection in the non-stationary environment. Knowl. Inf. Syst. **66**(3), 1549–1574 (2024)
2. Barcina-Blanco, M., Lobo, J.L., Garcia-Bringas, P., Del Ser, J.: Managing the unknown in machine learning: definitions, related areas, recent advances, and prospects. Neurocomputing **599**, 128073 (2024)
3. Bengio, Y., et al.: Managing extreme AI risks amid rapid progress. Science **384**(6698), 842–845 (2024)
4. Cevikalp, H., et al.: From anomaly detection to open set recognition: bridging the gap. Pattern Recogn. **138**, 109385 (2023)
5. Chen, T., Feng, G., Djurić, P.M.: Improving open-set recognition with bayesian metric learning. In: ICASSP 2024-2024 IEEE International Conference on Acoustics, Speech and Signal Processing (ICASSP), pp. 6185–6189. IEEE (2024)
6. Coletta, L.F., et al.: Combining clustering and active learning for the detection and learning of new image classes. Neurocomputing **358**, 150–165 (2019)

7. Din, S.U., Ullah, A., Mawuli, C.B., Yang, Q., Shao, J.: A reliable adaptive prototype-based learning for evolving data streams with limited labels. Inf. Process. Manage. **61**(1), 103532 (2024)
8. Fahy, C., Yang, S., Gongora, M.: Scarcity of labels in non-stationary data streams: a survey. ACM Comput. Surv. **55**(2), 1–39 (2022)
9. Gao, Y., et al.: SIM: open-world multi-task stream classifier with integral similarity metrics. In: IEEE International Conference on Big Data, pp. 751–760 (2019)
10. Geng, C., Huang, S.J., Chen, S.: Recent advances in open set recognition: a survey. IEEE Trans. Pattern Anal. Mach. Intell. **43**(10), 3614–3631 (2020)
11. Guyon, I.M.: Design of experiments for the NIPS 2003 variable selection benchmark. In: NIPS 2003 Workshop on Feature Extraction and Feature Selection, vol. 253 (2003)
12. Hui, X.M., Liu, Z.G.: A new k-NN based open-set recognition method. In: IEEE International Conference on Control, Automation, Robotics and Vision (ICARCV), pp. 481–486 (2022)
13. Kejriwal, M., Kildebeck, E., Steininger, R., Shrivastava, A.: Challenges, evaluation and opportunities for open-world learning. Nat. Mach. Intell. **6**, 580–588 (2024)
14. Kempka, M., Kotlowski, W., Warmuth, M.K.: Adaptive scale-invariant online algorithms for learning linear models. In: International Conference on Machine Learning, pp. 3321–3330. PMLR (2019)
15. Komorniczak, J., Ksieniewicz, P.: Distance profile layer for binary classification and density estimation. Neurocomputing **579**, 127436 (2024)
16. Kong, S., Ramanan, D.: OpenGAN: open-set recognition via open data generation. In: IEEE/CVF International Conference on Computer Vision, pp. 813–822 (2021)
17. Leo, J., Kalita, J.: Moving towards open set incremental learning: readily discovering new authors. In: Future of Information and Communication Conference (FICC), pp. 739–751 (2020)
18. Liu, L., Wang, R., Wang, Y., Jing, L., Wang, C.: Frequency shuffling and enhancement for open set recognition. In: Proceedings of the AAAI Conference on Artificial Intelligence, vol. 38, pp. 3675–3683 (2024)
19. Ma, B., Cong, Y., Ren, Y.: IOSL: incremental open set learning. IEEE Trans. Circ. Syst. Video Technol. **34**, 2235–2248 (2024)
20. Mahdavi, A., Carvalho, M.: A survey on open set recognition. In: IEEE International Conference on Artificial Intelligence and Knowledge Engineering (AIKE), pp. 37–44 (2021)
21. Mendes Júnior, P.R., et al.: Nearest neighbors distance ratio open-set classifier. Mach. Learn. **106**(3), 359–386 (2017)
22. Meyer, B.J., Drummond, T.: The importance of metric learning for robotic vision: open set recognition and active learning. In: IEEE International Conference on Robotics and Automation (ICRA), pp. 2924–2931 (2019)
23. Montiel, J., et al.: River: machine learning for streaming data in python. J. Mach. Learn. Res. **22**(110), 1–8 (2021)
24. Mundt, M., et al.: Unified probabilistic deep continual learning through generative replay and open set recognition. J. Imaging **8**(4), 93 (2022)
25. Pal, D., Bose, S., Banerjee, B., Jeppu, Y.: MORGAN: meta-learning-based few-shot open-set recognition via generative adversarial network. In: IEEE/CVF Winter Conference on Applications of Computer Vision, pp. 6295–6304 (2023)
26. Sato, D.M.V., De Freitas, S.C., Barddal, J.P., Scalabrin, E.E.: A survey on concept drift in process mining. ACM Comput. Surv. (CSUR) **54**(9), 1–38 (2021)
27. Scheirer, W.J., de Rezende Rocha, A., Sapkota, A., Boult, T.E.: Toward open set recognition. IEEE Trans. Pattern Anal. Mach. Intell. **35**(7), 1757–1772 (2012)

28. Shannon, C.E.: A mathematical theory of communication. Bell Syst. Tech. J. **27**(3), 379–423 (1948)
29. Souza, V.M., et al.: Challenges in benchmarking stream learning algorithms with real-world data. Data Min. Knowl. Disc. **34**, 1805–1858 (2020)
30. Wang, B., et al.: Open-set source camera identification based on envelope of data clustering optimization (EDCO). Comput. Secur. **113**, 102571 (2022)
31. Yang, J., Zhou, K., Li, Y., Liu, Z.: Generalized out-of-distribution detection: a survey. arXiv preprint arXiv:2110.11334 (2021)
32. Youden, W.J.: Index for rating diagnostic tests. Cancer **3**(1), 32–35 (1950)
33. Zhang, H., Li, A., Guo, J., Guo, Y.: Hybrid models for open set recognition. In: European Conference on Computer Vision (ECCV), pp. 102–117 (2020)

A Comparison Procedure for the Evaluation of Metaheuristics

Enol García González[1(✉)], José R. Villar[1], and Javier Sedano[2]

[1] Computer Science Department, University of Oviedo, Oviedo, Spain
{garciaenol,villarjose}@uniovi.es

[2] Instituto Tecnológico de Castilla y León, Burgos, Spain
javier.sedano@itcl.es

Abstract. Metaheuristics are one of the most widespread solutions in the literature to address optimization problems. This application of metaheuristics makes them suitable for many problems in different fields of knowledge. However, the constant increase of new metaheuristics proposals has a problem; the comparison between different metaheuristics to determine which one to use is a very complex task for which it does not help that each author uses his way of evaluating his metaheuristics. In this work, we analyze and study different techniques used by authors of metaheuristics and evaluate their problems to propose a testing methodology that is objective, neutral, and fair for all metaheuristics evaluated. This methodology will also consider how to set the parameter optimization so that it is the same for all metaheuristics and problem instances to get as close as possible to an actual application of the metaheuristics. This new methodology will be tested in the experimentation by evaluating five metaheuristics widely known and extended in the literature.

Keywords: Metaheuristics · Benchmark · Comparison

1 Introduction

Optimization problems represent one of the most challenging tasks in a wide variety of domains, such as economics [4,5], medicine [9,10], robotics [11,22], and education [16]. Metaheuristics have proven useful in solving these tasks [3,24]; the reasons for their success include their generalization capabilities that can be adapted to different problems and their constrained computational cost.

This research has been funded by the Spanish Ministry of Economics and Industry –grant PID2020-112726RB-I00–, the Spanish Research Agency –grant PID2023-146257OB-I00–, and Missions Science and Innovation project MIG-20211008 (INMERBOT). Also, by Principado de Asturias, grant SV-PA-21-AYUD/2021/50994, and by the Council of Gijón through the University Institute of Industrial Technology of Asturias grants SV-21-GIJON-1-19, SV-22-GIJON-1-19, SV-22-GIJON-1-22, SV-23-GIJON-1-09, and SV-23-GIJON-1-17. Finally, this research has also been funded by Fundación Universidad de Oviedo grants FUO-23-008 and FUO-22-450.

H. Quintián et al. (Eds.): HAIS 2024, LNAI 14857, pp. 153–164, 2025.
https://doi.org/10.1007/978-3-031-74183-8_13

Thus, solving optimization problems using a metaheuristic comprises the selection of the most promising metaheuristic technique and the hyperparameter tuning. Choosing the most promising one becomes a hard task considering the hundreds of different metaheuristic proposals [18]. Not only the wide number of techniques represents a problem itself, but the selection of the most suitable one turns into an ordeal due to the lack of valid comparisons among the different metaheuristics. This is because there is neither common ground nor standard experimentation procedure in the comparisons published.

This research proposes a procedure to address this problem by, first, selecting a set of standard optimization problems; second, promoting a fair comparison by normalizing the hyperparameter tuning stage; and finally, defining the performance measurements that would assist in selecting the final candidate.

The structure of this research is as follows. Section 2 describes how the most cited metaheuristic techniques solved the comparison experimentation, focusing on the main pros and cons from each case. The comparison procedure is completely detailed in Sect. 3, while Sect. 4 shows an example of how to develop the procedure for the most cited metaheuristics. Finally, the last Section draws the main conclusions from this study.

2 Related Work

As mentioned before, comparing metaheuristics is tough due to the differences between experimentation settings among the studies in the literature. A revision of these diverting strategies is performed in the next paragraphs, extracting the best practices together with the pros and cons of each of the studies. These remarks would help in establishing a common framework for comparison that is as fair as possible with all the candidates, easing the metaheuristic selection process.

On the one hand, the experimental strategy followed in Differential Evolution (DE) [25] proposes a set of mathematical functions to minimize, setting the desired minimum value for each case, and comparing the number of evaluations needed to reach this goal. This comparison is an excellent method to analyze the voracity of the studied metaheuristics; however, they have a big problem: those metaheuristics that fail to find the goal appear as "Not available" in the comparison.

Moth Flame Optimization (MFO) [19], Grey Wolf Optimizer (GWO) [21], and Whale Optimization Algorithm (WOA) [20] are three metaheuristics proposed by Mirjalili et al. In these studies, the authors minimized mathematical problems in the comparisons using the criteria that the smaller the found minimum, the better the metaheuristic's performance. The advantage of this comparison approach is that the variety of the mathematical problems posed makes it possible to analyze different aspects of the metaheuristic, such as its ability to explore the entire search space or escape from local minima. However, this form presents two main problems: the lack of use of standard functions and the lack of repetitiveness analysis. Indeed, each study employed a different set of functions, making it hard to compare metaheuristics from one to another. Furthermore, the metaheuristics are only compared with their best function value found, without setting specific requirements on the number of iterations or evaluations, and without comparing aspects such as convergence speed or execution time of the metaheuristics. This experimental approach is also suitable for comparison with other metaheuristics, such as Black Hole (BH) [12].

An intermediate point between the two previous proposals is Big Bang-Big Crunch (BB-BC) [7], also minimizing mathematical optimization problems. As opposed to the studies of Mirjalili et al., a maximum number of iterations is set, so all the metaheuristics in the comparison are somehow restricted with similar limits. Moreover, using performance metrics measuring the difference between the minimum obtained value and the goal solved the problem mentioned with DE. Besides, the results of the BB-BC experimentation are presented using a graph representing each iteration's fitness value, a significant improvement in depicting the comparison's results that allow us to analyze the convergence speed of the metaheuristics, check if they can converge with the indicated number of iterations, and study the distance to the optimal solution in case it is not reached.

This form proposed in BB-BC is quite popular and has been adopted by other authors to compare, such as Artificial Chemical Reaction Optimization Algorithm (ACROA) [2] or Ray Optimization (RO) [13]. RO points out in the experimentation that fixing the number of iterations is not enough since, with the same number of iterations, there can be a big difference if the number of search agents is varied, so it also proposes to fix the number of search agents to make the comparison fairer. This need to fix the number of agents to make a more fair comparison extends to other metaheuristics such as Charged System Search (CSS) [14] or Small World Optimization Algorithm (SWOA) [6]. However, this approach has a problem: it is only valid in population-based metaheuristics, where the number of agents represents the number of fitness function evaluations in each iteration.

Metaheuristics such as Electromagnetic Field Optimization (EFO) [1] or Coyote Optimization Algorithm (COA) [23] propose in their experimentation that this limitation should be set as a maximum number of evaluations rather than as a maximum number of iterations since setting a maximum number of evaluations would be analogous to setting a fixed population size and a maximum number of iterations. However, it allows extending the comparison to include metaheuristics in which the number of evaluations does not depend on the number of search agents.

3 Comparison Procedure

The proposed comparison procedure aims to establish a fair and neutral method following the best practices described in the literature while solving some of the mentioned drawbacks. For this purpose, this procedure defines three main elements to determine: the benchmark definition, a standard parameter tuning process, and the performance criterion. Furthermore, the procedure itself must be defined.

Benchmark Definition. The metaheuristics must compete on the same collection of problems. This collection must include different contexts and settings, allowing the researcher to record the performance of each metaheuristic in several dissimilar situations. For this reason, this comparison procedure defines the 23 mathematical optimization problems shown below, each function belonging to one of the three following categories [8]:

- ***i***) Unimodal functions (F_1 to F_7) with a single minimum in the domain space.
- ***ii***) Multimodal functions (F_8 to F_{13}), which are those functions that have multiple minimum values in the domain space. We propose having one global minimum and several local minima.
- ***iii***) Fixed-dimensional multimodal functions (F_{14} to F_{23}), like the previous category, but introducing restrictions and constraints.

Standard Parameter Tuning Process. A fair comparison not only needs a common testbed but also a standard method to determine the hyperparameters' values. This study proposes to find the best hyperparameter set that works well for the main percentage of the problems. Iterated Race technique (irace) [17] drives this hyperparameter tuning process for each metaheuristic over all the benchmark problems; irace proposes a strategy to guide the search for the hyperparameters of an algorithm by executing multiple instances of the problem.

Performance Criterion. A unique criterion for stopping the optimization processes, together with a unified set of performance metrics, yields comparable results. In this experimentation phase, the number of fitness function evaluations determines the stopping criterion for the metaheuristics. To study the evolution of the fitness over time and the voracity of the algorithms, the maximum number of evaluations was set at 300,000, representing a sufficiently large number of evaluations to analyze the stagnation of any metaheuristic. During this part of the experimentation, two metrics are collected to measure the performance of the methods: i) the fitness function score at each evaluation, and ii) the total execution time. Each optimization is repeated a predefined number of times N –in this study, $N = 10$–.

Procedure. The following algorithm defines the procedure to follow.

```
for each metaheuristic M do
  Determine the best hyperparameter set for M using irace
  for n from 1 to N do
    for each function f do
      Obtain, record, and aggregate the performance of M on f
    end for
  end for
end for
```

The standard set of functions that are included in this procedure are the following ones:

- $F_1 = \sum_{i=1}^{n} x_i^2, \quad x_i \in [-100, 100] \quad \forall i : 1, \ldots, n = 30.$
- $F_2 = \sum_{i=1}^{n} |x_i| + \prod_{i=1}^{n} |x_i|$, $x_i \in [-10, 10]$ $\forall i : 1, \ldots, n$, $n = 30$.
- $F_3 = \sum_{i=1}^{n} (\sum_{j=1}^{i} x_j)^2$, $x_i \in [-100, 100]$ $\forall i : 1, \ldots, n$, $n = 30$.
- $F_4 = \max_i \{x_i, 1 \leq i \leq n\}, \quad x_i \in [-100, 100] \quad \forall i : 1, \ldots, n = 30.$
- $F_5 = \sum_{i=1}^{n-1} [100(x_{x+1} - x_i^2)^2 + (x_i - 1)^2]$, $x_i \in [-30, 30]$ $\forall i : 1, \ldots, n$, $n = 30$.
- $F_6 = \sum_{i=1}^{n} (x_i + 0.5)^2$, $x_i \in [-100, 100]$ $\forall i : 1, \ldots, n$, $n = 30$.
- $F_7 = \sum_{i=1}^{n} i x_i^4 + random[0, 1)$, $x_i \in [-1.28, 1.28]$ $\forall i : 1, \ldots, n$, $n = 30$.
- $F_8 = \sum_{i=1}^{n} (-x_i \sin \sqrt{|x_i|}), \quad x_i \in [-500, 500] \quad \forall i : 1, \ldots, n = 30.$
- $F_9 = \sum_{i=1}^{n} [x_i^2 - 10 \cos 2\pi x_i + 10]$, $x_i \in [-5.12, 5.12]$ $\forall i : 1, \ldots, n$, $n = 30$.
- $F_{10} = -20 \exp -0.2\sqrt{\frac{1}{n} \sum_{i=0}^{n} x_i^2} - \exp \frac{1}{n} \sum_{i=0}^{n} \cos 2\pi x_i + 20 - e$, $x_i \in [-32, 32]$ $\forall i : 1, \ldots, n$, $n = 30$.
- $F_{11} = \frac{1}{4000} \sum_{i=0}^{n} x_i^2 - \prod_{i=1}^{n} \frac{x_i}{\sqrt{i}} + 1, \quad x_i \in [-600, 600] \quad \forall i : 1, \ldots, n = 30.$
- $F_{12} = \frac{\pi}{n}\{10 \sin \pi y_1 + \sum_{i=1}^{n} [(y_i)^2 [1 + 10 \sin \pi {y_{i+1}}^2]] + (y_n - 1)^2\} + \sum_{i=1}^{n} u(x_i, 10, 100, 4)$, $x_i \in [-50, 50]$ $\forall i : 1, \ldots, n$, $n = 30$.

  Where $y_i = 1 + \frac{x_i + 1}{4}$, and $u(x_i, a, k, m) = \begin{cases} k(x_i - a)^m & x_i \geq a \\ 0 & -a \leq x_i \leq a \\ k(-x_i - a)^m & x \leq -a \end{cases}$
- $F_{13} = 0.1\{\sin 3\pi {x_1}^2 + \sum_{i=1}^{n} [(x_i - 1)^2 [1 + \sin 3\pi x_i + 1^2]] +$, $x_i \in [-50, 50]$ $\forall i : 1, \ldots, n$, $n = 30$.

  Where u is defined in the same way like F_{12}
- $F_{14} = (\frac{1}{500} + \sum_{j=1}^{25} \frac{1}{j + \sum_{i=1}^{2} (x_i - a_{ij})^6})^{-1}, \quad x_i \in [-65, 65] \quad \forall i : 1, \ldots, n = 2.$
- $F_{15} = \sum_{i=1}^{11} [a_i - \frac{x_1(b_i^2 + b_i x_2)}{b_i^2 + b_i x_3 + x_4}]^2$, $x_i \in [-5, 5]$ $\forall i : 1, \ldots, n$, $n = 4$.

  Where:

  $a = [.1957, .1947, .1735, .16, .0844, .0627, .0456, .0342, .0323, .0235, .0246]$ and $b = [4, 2, 1, .5, .25, \frac{1}{6}, .125, -1, \frac{1}{12}, \frac{1}{14}, .0625]$
- $F_{16} = 4x_1^2 - 2.1x_1^4 + \frac{1}{3}x_1^6 + x_1 x_2 - 4x_2^2 + 4x_2^4$, $x_i \in [-5, 5]$ $\forall i : 1, \ldots, n$, $n = 2$.
- $F_{17} = (x_2 - \frac{5.1}{4\pi^2} x_1^2 + \frac{5}{\pi} x_1 - 6)^2 + 10(1 - -\frac{1}{8\pi}) \cos x_1 + 10, \quad x_i \in [-5, 5]$ $\forall i : 1, \ldots, n = 2$.
- $F_{18} = [1 + (x_1 + x_2 + 1)^2 (19 - 14x_1 + 3x_1^2 - 14x_2 + 6x_1 x_2 + 3x_2^2)] \cdot [30 + (2x_1 - 3x_2)^2 (18 - 32x_1 + 12x_1^2 + 48x_2 - 36x_1 x_2 + 27x_2^2)]$, $x_i \in [-2, 2]$ $\forall i : 1, \ldots, n$, $n = 2$.
- $F_{19} = \sum_{i=1}^{4} c_i \exp - \sum_{j=1}^{3} a_{ij}(x_j - p_{ij})^2$, $x_i \in [1, 3]$ $\forall i : 1, \ldots, n$, $n = 3$.

  Where: $a = \begin{bmatrix} 10 & .05 & 3 & 17 \\ 3 & 10 & 3.5 & 8 \\ 17 & 17 & 1.7 & .05 \\ 3.5 & .1 & 10 & 10 \\ 1.7 & 8 & 17 & .1 \\ 8 & 14 & 8 & 14 \end{bmatrix}$, $c = [1 \; 1.2 \; 3 \; 3.2]$, and

  $$p = \begin{bmatrix} .1312 & .2329 & .2348 & .4047 \\ .1696 & .4135 & .1415 & .8828 \\ .5569 & .8307 & .3522 & .8732 \\ .0124 & .3736 & .2883 & .5743 \\ .8283 & .1004 & .3047 & .1091 \\ .5886 & .9991 & .6650 & .0381 \end{bmatrix}$$

- $F_{20} = \sum_{i=1}^{4} c_i \exp - \sum_{j=1}^{6} a_{ij}(x_j - p_{ij})^2$, $x_i \in [0,1]$ $\forall i : 1, \ldots, n$, $n = 6$.
  Where a, c and p, are the defined identical as F_{19}
- $F_{21} = -\sum_{i=0}^{5} [(X - a_i)(X - a_i)^T + c_i]^{-1}$, $x_i \in [0,10]$ $\forall i : 1, \ldots, n = 4$.

  Where: $a = \begin{bmatrix} 4 & 1 & 8 & 6 & 3 & 2 & 5 & 8 & 6 & 7 \\ 4 & 1 & 8 & 6 & 7 & 9 & 5 & 1 & 2 & 3.6 \\ 4 & 1 & 8 & 6 & 3 & 2 & 3 & 8 & 6 & 7 \\ 4 & 1 & 8 & 6 & 7 & 9 & 3 & 1 & 2 & 3.6 \end{bmatrix}$, and $c = \begin{bmatrix} .1 & .2 & .2 & .4 & .4 & .6 & .3 & .7 & .5 & .5 \end{bmatrix}$
- $F_{22} = -\sum_{i=0}^{7} [(X - a_i)(X - a_i)^T + c_i]^{-1}$, $x_i \in [0,10]$ $\forall i : 1, \ldots, n$, $n = 4$.
  Where a, c and p, are the defined identical as F_{21}
- $F_{23} = -\sum_{i=0}^{10} [(X - a_i)(X - a_i)^T + c_i]^{-1}$, $x_i \in [0,10]$ $\forall i : 1, \ldots, n$, $n = 4$.
  Where a, c and p, are the defined identical as F_{21}

4 Results and Discussion

To test this proposed methodology, 5 widely known and cited metaheuristics will be compared: Differential Evolution (DE) [25], Grey Wolf Optimizer (GWO) [21], Particle Swarm Optimization (PSO) [15], Moth Flame Optimization (MFO) [19], Whale Optimization Algorithm (WOA) [20].

According to the procedure, the first part is to optimize the parameters. The best ones found for each metaheuristic are:

- DE. 210 individuals in the population and 0.78 and 0.21 for the crossover and mutation probabilities.
- GWO. 180 individuals in the population.
- PSO. 180 individuals in the population, and 1.86 and 2.18 for c1 and c2.
- MFO. 190 individuals in the population, and 1.86 for b.
- WOA. 190 individuals in the population, and 1.72 for b.

Table 1 contains the mean and deviation of the best solution found by each metaheuristic to each problem. From this table, it can be seen how WOA is the metaheuristic that performs better in almost all the problems, being the one that finds the best solution in 17 of the 23 proposed problems.

However, a comparison considering the final values only provides very little information about the voracity and the metaheuristic's convergence speed. Figure 1 visualizes this issue. This figure depicts the fitness evolution along the evaluations, allowing us to observe the needed number of calls to the evaluation function to reach the suboptimal solution. It also helps to determine whether a method converges to the suboptimal solution.

It can be observed that WOA, despite being the metaheuristic that reaches the best solution for the majority of the problems, also takes a higher number of evaluations to converge to that solution. On the other hand, DE represents the fastest method for most problems, converging to a suboptimal solution with a relatively small number of evaluations.

The last metric collected on execution is the execution time of the metaheuristics. Figure 2 displays the execution time of each metaheuristic participating in the iteration. Its analysis is similar to that of the convergence speed. In

Table 1. Comparison results: Mean and standard deviation –just under the mean value and delimited with parenthesis– of the best fitness value achieved by each metaheuristic. In bold the best values of each function

	DE	GWO	PSO	MFO	WOA
F1	8,9788E-58 (5,6E-58)	1,7808E-175 (0,0E+00)	6,6240E-24 (1,8E-23)	1,0000E+03 (3,1E+03)	**0,0000E+00** (0,0E+00)
F2	1,2385E-33 (2,5E-34)	1,4025E-99 (1,6E-99)	1,0000E+00 (3,1E+00)	2,9000E+01 (1,8E+01)	**2,7070E-186** (0,0E+00)
F3	4,2378E+00 (9,2E+00)	**2,2005E-60** (6,1E-60)	1,2583E-01 (5,6E-02)	1,6167E+04 (1,1E+04)	1,7565E+02 (2,2E+02)
F4	6,1912E-01 (6,8E-01)	**2,8705E-43** (5,8E-43)	4,9054E-02 (2,3E-02)	4,8742E+00 (3,1E+00)	8,6626E+00 (1,8E+01)
F5	2,8511E+01 (4,7E+00)	2,5341E+01 (8,8E-01)	4,8678E+01 (3,5E+01)	1,8077E+04 (3,7E+04)	**1,9263E+01** (1,0E+01)
F6	**0,0000E+00** (0,0E+00)	1,0012E-01 (1,2E-01)	5,1912E-25 (7,6E-25)	2,0001E+03 (4,2E+03)	1,4594E-06 (6,1E-07)
F7	2,1339E-07 (6,7E-07)	1,6311E-297 (0,0E+00)	1,3422E+00 (1,4E+00)	2,6844E-01 (8,4E-01)	**0,0000E+00** (0,0E+00)
F8	−1,1096E+04 (1,7E+03)	−6,6669E+03 (6,9E+02)	−7,0575E+03 (7,0E+02)	−8,4930E+03 (6,7E+02)	**−1,2421E+04** (4,2E+02)
F9	6,7204E+01 (6,7E+00)	1,2037E+00 (3,8E+00)	5,5980E+01 (2,8E+01)	1,0932E+02 (3,9E+01)	**0,0000E+00** (0,0E+00)
F10	4,3521E-15 (1,1E-15)	7,5495E-15 (1,6E-30)	2,6477E-13 (1,9E-13)	1,5960E+01 (8,4E+00)	**3,2863E-15** (2,2E-15)
F11	**0,0000E+00** (0,0E+00)	2,7756E-20 (6,3E-36)	2,7756E-20 (6,3E-36)	1,8000E+01 (3,7E+01)	5,5511E-21 (1,1E-20)
F12	**−1,0472E+00** (2,3E-16)	−1,0407E+00 (7,5E-03)	**−1,0472E+00** (2,3E-16)	**−1,0472E+00** (6,2E-14)	**−1,0472E+00** (1,2E-07)
F13	**1,3498E-32** (2,8E-48)	1,5626E-01 (1,7E-01)	9,6305E-25 (2,8E-24)	1,1305E-01 (3,3E-01)	7,2768E-06 (3,7E-06)
F14	**9,9800E-01** (0,0E+00)	**9,9800E-01** (1,5E-13)	**9,9800E-01** (0,0E+00)	**9,9800E-01** (0,0E+00)	**9,9800E-01** (1,0E-15)
F15	1,9926E-02 (1,3E-03)	**1,7811E-02** (1,0E-10)	2,0012E-02 (3,5E-03)	**1,7811E-02** (0,0E+00)	**1,7811E-02** (2,3E-12)
F16	**0,0000E+00** (0,0E+00)	**0,0000E+00** (0,0E+00)	1,0192E-205 (0,0E+00)	**0,0000E+00** (0,0E+00)	**0,0000E+00** (0,0E+00)
F17	**3,9789E-01** (5,8E-17)	**3,9789E-01** (1,5E-08)	**3,9789E-01** (5,8E-17)	**3,9789E-01** (5,8E-17)	**3,9789E-01** (1,5E-11)
F18	**3,0000E+00** (4,9E-15)	**3,0000E+00** (8,7E-08)	**3,0000E+00** (4,3E-15)	**3,0000E+00** (4,6E-16)	**3,0000E+00** (4,7E-10)
F19	**−3,0048E-01** (5,8E-17)	**−3,0048E-01** (5,8E-17)	**−3,0048E-01** (5,8E-17)	**−3,0048E-01** (5,8E-17)	**−3,0048E-01** (5,8E-17)
F20	**−3,4085E-05** (7,1E-21)	**−3,4085E-05** (7,1E-21)	**−3,4085E-05** (7,1E-21)	**−3,4085E-05** (7,1E-21)	**−3,4085E-05** (7,1E-21)
F21	−9,6019E+00 (1,5E+00)	−9,0995E+00 (2,1E+00)	−7,5890E+00 (2,6E+00)	−7,5774E+00 (2,6E+00)	**−1,0104E+01** (4,8E-08)
F22	−9,6019E+00 (1,5E+00)	−8,5973E+00 (2,4E+00)	−8,5896E+00 (2,4E+00)	−8,0835E+00 (2,6E+00)	**−1,0104E+01** (7,6E-08)
F23	−1,0028E+01 (2,3E-01)	−8,5973E+00 (2,4E+00)	−7,0829E+00 (2,6E+00)	−7,3365E+00 (3,0E+00)	**−1,0104E+01** (3,3E-08)

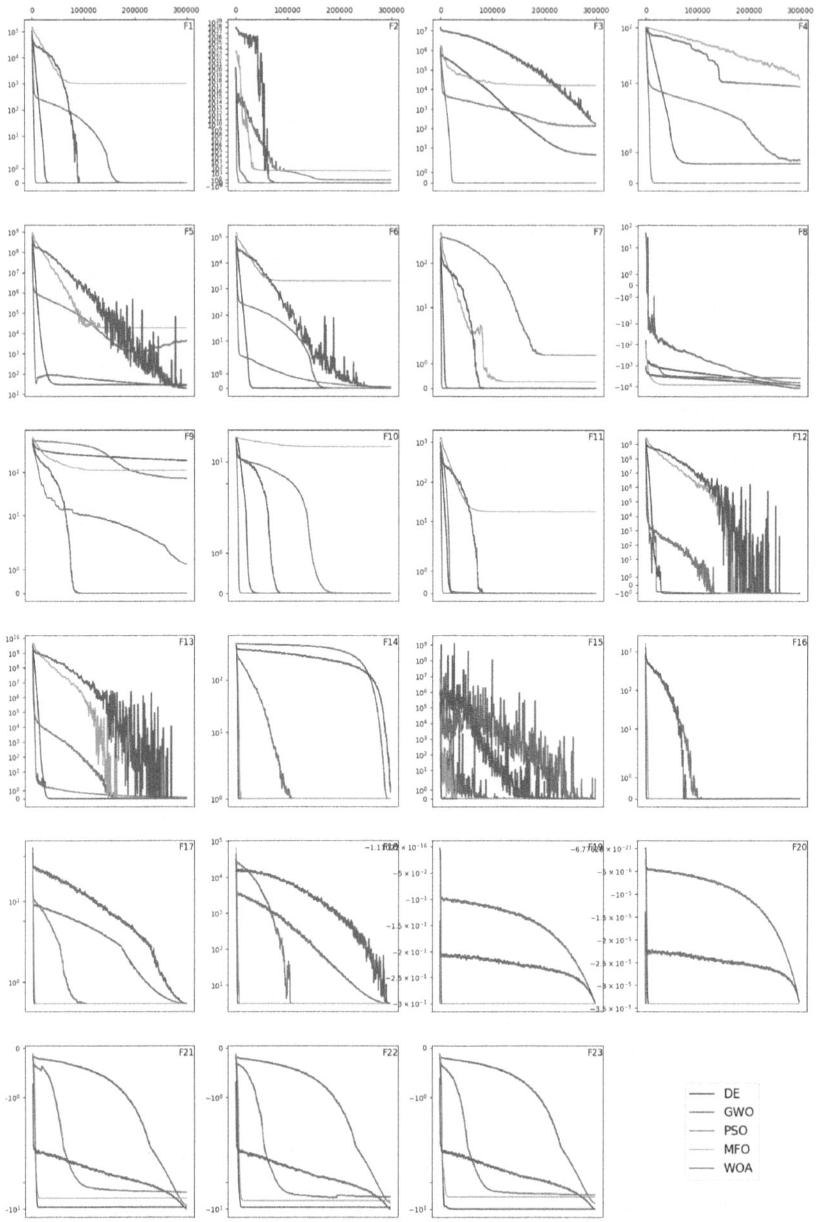

Fig. 1. Evolution of the fitness for the number of individual evaluations. The plots show the mean of the recorded fitness along the different evaluations for all methods and functions in the comparison

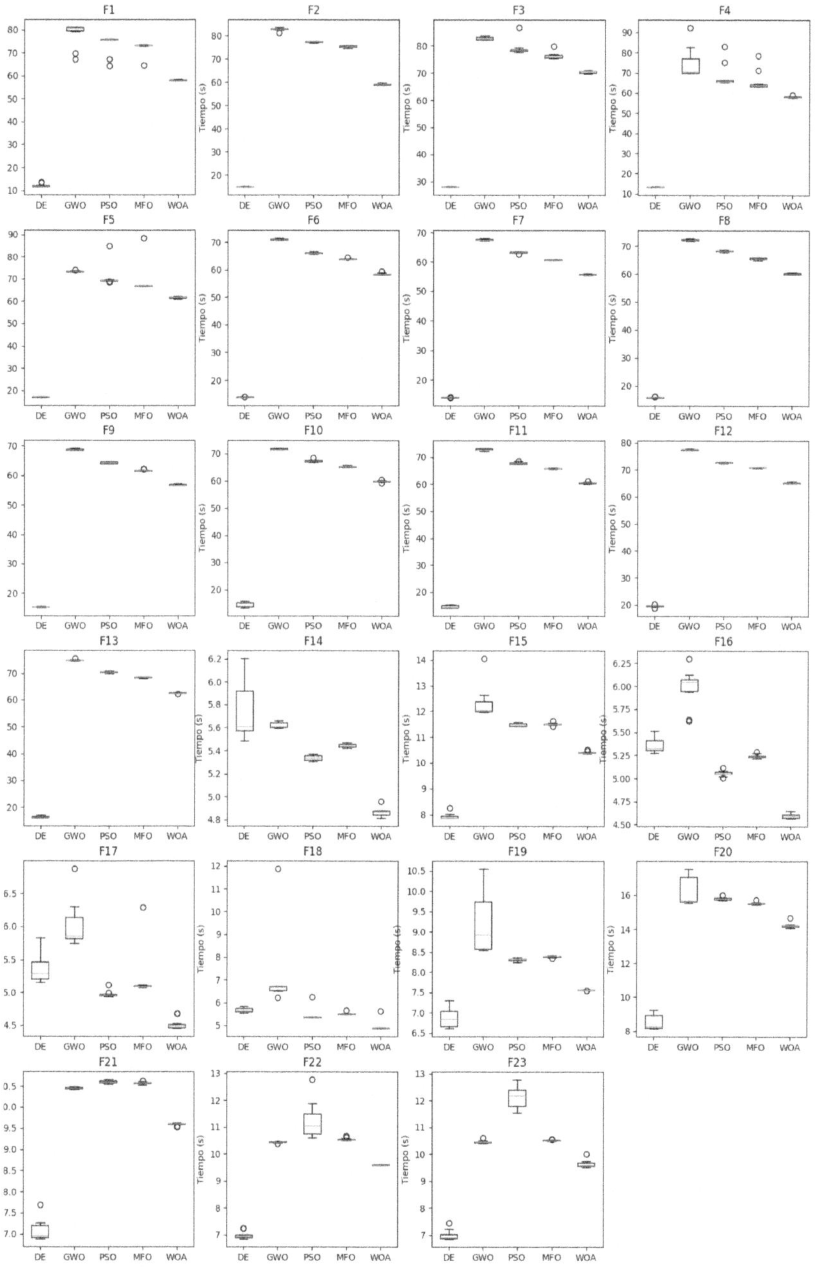

Fig. 2. Execution cost, in seconds, for all the methods (DE, GWO, PSO, MFO and WOA, respectively) and functions in the comparison

this metric, DE also proves to be the fastest method in the comparison, while the other methods have a similar time cost. Interestingly, WOA is the second fastest method after DE: the low time complexity of the function evaluations is responsible for this fact.

5 Conclusion

In this work, we have made an exhaustive study of the methods used in the literature to compare the metaheuristics. From the analysis of the strengths and weaknesses of the existing proposals, a new fair and neutral metaheuristic comparison procedure was proposed, aiming to measure the versatility of a method facing different problems. In the experimentation, our procedure evaluated some of the most popular metaheuristics in the literature, showing that DE and WOA are the two with the best quality among all those studied. These two metaheuristics compete on two different objectives. WOA is the metaheuristic that offers better solutions to a more significant number of problems. At the same time, DE is the metaheuristic that proves to obtain acceptable solutions more efficiently using a smaller number of evaluations and with a lower computational cost.

Future work includes the possibility of extending this study to perform a systematic analysis of a significant number of metaheuristics, and to complete the metaheuristic evaluation methodology with more recent studies published in the literature.

References

1. Abedinpourshotorban, H., Mariyam Shamsuddin, S., Beheshti, Z., Jawawi, D.N.: Electromagnetic field optimization: a physics-inspired metaheuristic optimization algorithm. Swarm Evol. Comput. **26**, 8–22 (2016). https://doi.org/10.1016/j.swevo.2015.07.002
2. Alatas, B.: ACROA: artificial chemical reaction optimization algorithm for global optimization. Expert Syst. Appl. **38**(10), 13170–13180 (2011). https://doi.org/10.1016/j.eswa.2011.04.126
3. Camacho-Vallejo, J.F., Corpus, C., Villegas, J.G.: Metaheuristics for bilevel optimization: a comprehensive review. Comput. Oper. Res. **161**, 106410 (2024). https://doi.org/10.1016/j.cor.2023.106410
4. Chen, N., Ribeiro, B., Vieira, A.S., Duarte, J., Neves, J.C.: A genetic algorithm-based approach to cost-sensitive bankruptcy prediction. Expert Syst. Appl. **38**(10), 12939–12945 (2011). https://doi.org/10.1016/j.eswa.2011.04.090
5. Deng, S., Yoshiyama, K., Mitsubuchi, T., Sakurai, A.: Hybrid method of multiple kernel learning and genetic algorithm for forecasting short-term Foreign exchange rates. Comput. Econ. **45**(1), 49–89 (2015). https://doi.org/10.1007/s10614-013-9407-6
6. Du, H., Wu, X., Zhuang, J.: Small-world optimization algorithm for function optimization. In: Advances in Natural Computation, pp. 264–273 (2006). https://doi.org/10.1007/11881223_33
7. Erol, O.K., Eksin, I.: A new optimization method: big bang-big crunch. Adv. Eng. Softw. **37**(2), 106–111 (2006). https://doi.org/10.1016/j.advengsoft.2005.04.005

8. González, E.G., Villar, J.R., Sedano, J., Chira, C.: Benchmarking analysis for biological-based metaheuristics. Dyna (2024). https://doi.org/10.6036/11070
9. Goodarzian, F., Hosseini-Nasab, H., Fakhrzad, M.B.: A multi-objective sustainable medicine supply chain network design using a novel hybrid multi-objective metaheuristic algorithm. Int. J. Eng. **33**(10), 1986–1995 (2020). https://doi.org/10.5829/ije.2020.33.10a.17
10. Goodarzian, F., Wamba, S.F., Mathiyazhagan, K., Taghipour, A.: A new bi-objective green medicine supply chain network design under fuzzy environment: hybrid metaheuristic algorithms. Comput. Ind. Eng. **160**, 107535 (2021). https://doi.org/10.1016/j.cie.2021.107535
11. Gul, F., Rahiman, W., Alhady, S.S.N., Ali, A., Mir, I., Jalil, A.: Meta-heuristic approach for solving multi-objective path planning for autonomous guided robot using PSO-GWO optimization algorithm with evolutionary programming. J. Ambient. Intell. Humaniz. Comput. **12**(7), 7873–7890 (2021). https://doi.org/10.1007/s12652-020-02514-w
12. Hatamlou, A.: Black hole: a new heuristic optimization approach for data clustering. Inf. Sci. **222**, 175–184 (2013). https://doi.org/10.1016/j.ins.2012.08.023
13. Kaveh, A., Khayatazad, M.: rA new meta-heuristic method: ay optimization. Comput. Struct. **112–113**, 283–294 (2012). https://doi.org/10.1016/j.compstruc.2012.09.003
14. Kaveh, A., Talatahari, S.: A novel heuristic optimization method: charged system search. Acta Mech. **213**(3), 267–289 (2010). https://doi.org/10.1007/s00707-009-0270-4
15. Kennedy, J., Eberhart, R.: Particle swarm optimization. In: Proceedings of ICNN 1995 - International Conference on Neural Networks, vol. 4, pp. 1942–1948 (1995). https://doi.org/10.1109/ICNN.1995.488968
16. Lambi, D., Lazovi, B., Djeni, A., Mari, M.: A novel metaheuristic approach for collaborative learning group formation. J. Comput. Assist. Learn. **34**(6), 907–916 (2018). https://doi.org/10.1111/jcal.12299
17. López-Ibáñez, M., Dubois-Lacoste, J., Pérez Cáceres, L., Stützle, T., Birattari, M.: The irace package: iterated racing for automatic algorithm configuration. Oper. Res. Perspect. **3**, 43–58 (2016). https://doi.org/10.1016/j.orp.2016.09.002
18. Ma, Z., Wu, G., Suganthan, P.N., Song, A., Luo, Q.: Performance assessment and exhaustive listing of 500+ nature-inspired metaheuristic algorithms. Swarm Evol. Comput. **77**, 101248 (2023). https://doi.org/10.1016/j.swevo.2023.101248
19. Mirjalili, S.: Moth-flame optimization algorithm: a novel nature-inspired heuristic paradigm. Knowl.-Based Syst. **89**, 228–249 (2015). https://doi.org/10.1016/j.knosys.2015.07.006
20. Mirjalili, S., Lewis, A.: The whale optimization algorithm. Adv. Eng. Softw. **95**, 51–67 (2016). https://doi.org/10.1016/j.advengsoft.2016.01.008
21. Mirjalili, S., Mirjalili, S.M., Lewis, A.: Grey wolf optimizer. Adv. Eng. Softw. **69**, 46–61 (2014). https://doi.org/10.1016/j.advengsoft.2013.12.007
22. Serrano-Pérez, O., Villarreal-Cervantes, M.G., González-Robles, J.C., Rodríguez-Molina, A.: Meta-heuristic algorithms for the control tuning of omnidirectional mobile robots. Eng. Optim. **52**(2), 325–342 (2020). https://doi.org/10.1080/0305215X.2019.1585834
23. Pierezan, J., Dos Santos Coelho, L.: Coyote optimization algorithm: a new metaheuristic for global optimization problems. In: 2018 IEEE Congress on Evolutionary Computation (CEC), pp. 1–8 (2018). https://doi.org/10.1109/CEC.2018.8477769

24. Sotoudeh-Anvari, A., Hafezalkotob, A.: A bibliography of metaheuristics-review from 2009 to 2015. Int. J. Knowl.-Based Intell. Eng. Syst. **22**, 83–95 (2018). https://doi.org/10.3233/KES-180376
25. Storn, R., Price, K.: Differential evolution - a simple and efficient heuristic for global optimization over continuous spaces. J. Global Optim. **11**(4), 341–359 (1997). https://doi.org/10.1023/A:1008202821328

Nyström and RFF Ensembles for Large-Scale Kernel Predictions

Blanca Cano(✉), Ángela Fernández, and José R. Dorronsoro

Universidad Autónoma de Madrid, Madrid, Spain
{blanca.cano,a.fernandez,jose.dorronsoro}@uam.es

Abstract. Kernel Support Vector Machines (KSVMs) are known for their robust performance in supervised learning tasks. However, their computational costs often make them impractical for large datasets. In this study, we investigate two alternatives: the Nyström and Random Fourier Features (RFF) methods, which offer significantly lower computational cost but in their basic form might yield inferior results compared to KSVMs. In this article, we experimentally explore the differences in performance and training time between KSVMs and approximation methods on classification datasets, and the potential of Nyström and RFF ensembles to mitigate the performance gap while maintaining computational efficiency.

Keywords: Kernel Methods · Nyström Method · Random Fourier Features · Ensembles

1 Introduction

Kernel methods are a powerful paradigm for developing non-parametric modeling techniques for a wide range of problems in machine learning. A relevant example are *Kernel Support Vector Machines* (KSVM) [25], which have shown outstanding results in supervised learning. However, due to their high computational cost, they are only applicable to small to medium size datasets. To extend their application to larger datasets, other methods such as Nyström [27] or Random Fourier Features (RFF) [17,18] have emerged.

Counting with these two options, there are some studies about the nature of both methods with the aim of understanding the differences between them. Of particular interest here is [21], which explores the use of randomized features as a computationally efficient approximation method for kernel machines. However, the study is limited to a single classification dataset and uses logistic regression, which usually performs worse than SVM [13,20]. Other articles such as [12,22,26,28], while introducing modifications and new bounds, lack a detailed hyperparameter selection, statistical analysis, or a comparison against the Nyström method.

Given the state of the art mentioned above, our main contributions here are:

H. Quintián et al. (Eds.): HAIS 2024, LNAI 14857, pp. 165–176, 2025.
https://doi.org/10.1007/978-3-031-74183-8_14

- First, we will present a comparison of balanced accuracy and training time, within the same framework for RFF, the Nyström method, and KSVM. From now on, we will refer to balanced accuracy simply as accuracy.
- Second, we will exploit the randomness inherent in these methods to build ensembles, which will lead to a robust accuracy improvement.
- In addition, we will show that this accuracy improvement can potentially outperform kernel SVM while reducing training time.

This paper is organized as follows: in Sect. 2 we will briefly describe KSVM, Nyström and RFF methods. In Sect. 3 we will present and comment on our proposed ensemble methods. In Sect. 4 we will show the different experiments that we have carried out and, finally, in Sect. 5 we will offer some conclusions and point out to lines of further work.

2 SVM, Nyström's Method and Random Fourier Features

2.1 SVM

One of the most important models for supervised learning are the Kernel Support Vector Machines (KSVM) [3]. Given the training data $(x_1, y_1), \ldots, (x_n, y_n) \in X \times Y$, where $X \subseteq \mathbb{R}^{n \times d}$ is the input domain, each corresponding output $y \in Y$ belongs to the set $\{-1, 1\}$ and represents the target labels for a binary classification task. Given a positive definitive kernel function $k : X \times X \longrightarrow \mathbb{R}$, the response for a given input x is given by:

$$f(x) = \text{sign}(w^T \phi(x) + b) = \text{sign}\left(\sum_{i=1}^{n} y_i \alpha_i k(x_i, x) + b\right), \tag{1}$$

where sign denotes the sign function and $\phi(x)$ a lifting which maps x into a higher-dimensional space, verifying that $k(x_i, x_j) = \phi(x_i)^T \phi(x_j)$. The values of w and b are the solutions of the following primal optimization problem

$$\min_{w,b,\xi} \left\{\frac{1}{2} w^T w + C \sum_{i=1}^{n} \xi_i \right\} \quad \text{s.t.} \quad \begin{cases} y_i(w^T \phi(x_i) + b) \geq 1 - \xi_i, \\ \xi_i \geq 0, i \in \{1, \ldots n\}. \end{cases} \tag{2}$$

However, often the primal problem cannot be solved for kernels because $\phi(x)$ may remain unknown, so the following dual problem is usually approached:

$$\min_{\alpha} \left\{\alpha^T Q \alpha - \sum_{i} \alpha_i \right\} \quad \text{s.t.} \quad \begin{cases} y^T \alpha = 0, \\ 0 \leq \alpha_i \leq C, \ \ i \in \{1, \ldots n\}, \end{cases} \tag{3}$$

where $Q_{i,j} = y_i y_j k(x_i, x_j)$. After solving the dual problem (3), the optimal w satisfies $w^* = \sum_{i \in SV} y_i \alpha_j^* \phi(x_i)$ and we would say that x_i with i in the index subset SV of size s, is a support vector if α_i^* is not null. The optimal b is computed as follows

$$b^* = \frac{1}{s} \sum_{j \in SV} y_j - (w^*)^t \phi(x_j) = \frac{1}{s} \sum_{j \in SV} y_j \sum_{i \in SV} \alpha_i^* y_i k(x_i, x_j). \tag{4}$$

The dual problem (3) is usually solved with the Sequential Minimum Optimization (SMO) algorithm [16]. As [23] pointed out, SMO requires at least n iterations, each of which costs $\mathcal{O}(n)$. As a consequence, the training cost is at least $\Omega(n^2)$ (and usually higher), even without counting kernel operations. Therefore, computing SMO may be prohibitively expensive for large datasets.

2.2 Nyström's Method

As just mentioned, a major problem with KSVM is its high computational cost, so we will show how Nyström's method [27] is used to approximate the kernel of a KSVM by the dot product of an approximated lifting $\tilde{\phi} : \mathbb{R}^d \longrightarrow \mathbb{R}^q$ and solve the primal problem (7), reducing the computational complexity to $\mathcal{O}(qn)$ [14].

It is mathematically justified by Mercer's theorem [8], which states that

$$k(x, y) = \sum_i \lambda_i \phi_i(x) \phi_i(y), \tag{5}$$

where $\lambda_1 \geq \lambda_2 \geq \cdots \geq 0$ denote the eigenvalues and $\phi_1, \phi_2, \ldots,$ the orthonormal eigenfunctions of the operator whose kernel is k.

The Nyström's method is described as follows:

1. Pick q samples $X^{(q)} = \{x_1, \ldots, x_q\}$ from the training dataset.
2. Compute its kernel matrix $\tilde{K} \in \mathbb{R}^{q \times q}$ from the previous samples.
3. Solve the associated eigenproblem: $\frac{1}{q} \tilde{K} \tilde{U} \approx \tilde{U} \tilde{\Lambda}$ where $\tilde{U}$ is orthonormal.

   By (5), we have for each eigenvector $\tilde{U}_{i,j} \approx \phi_j(x_i)$, and therefore

$$\phi_j(x) \approx \frac{\sqrt{q}}{\tilde{\lambda}_j} \sum_{i=1}^{q} k(x, x_i) \tilde{U}_{ij}. \tag{6}$$

4. For a new vector x, a matricial formula for the randomized feature map $\tilde{\phi}(x) : \mathbb{R}^d \longrightarrow \mathbb{R}^q$ so that $\tilde{\phi}(x)^T \tilde{\phi}(y) \approx k(x, y)$ is:

$$\tilde{\phi}(x) = \sqrt{q} \tilde{\Lambda}^{-1} K(x, X^{(q)}) \tilde{U}^T, \tag{7}$$

   where $K(x, X^{(q)})$ is a vector with components $k(x, x_i)$ where $x_i \in X^{(q)}$.

The computational cost of computing $\tilde{\phi}$ is determined by the cost of the eigendecomposition, resulting in $\mathcal{O}(q^3 + nq)$ time and $\mathcal{O}(q^2 + nq)$ memory [9].

2.3 Random Fourier Features

Another approach to build an approximation of k through $\tilde{\phi}$ is to use RFF [17]. Its mathematical foundation is based in Bochner's Theorem [19]:

Theorem 1 (Bochner's Theorem). *A continuous and shift-invariant kernel* $k(x, y) = \hat{k}(x - y)$ *on* $\mathbb{R}^d$ *is positive definite if and only if* $\hat{k}(s)$ *is the Fourier transform of a non-negative measure.*

To build the RFF approximation map $\tilde{\phi}(x) : \mathbb{R}^d \longrightarrow \mathbb{R}^q$ so that $\tilde{\phi}(x)^T\tilde{\phi}(y) \approx k(x, y)$ we follow these steps:

1. Compute the Fourier transform p of the shift-invariant kernel k: $p(w) = \frac{1}{2\pi}\int e^{-jw^T s}\hat{k}(s)ds$ and normalize it to be a probability if necessary.
2. Draw q iid samples $\{w_1, \ldots, w_q\} \subset \mathbb{R}^d$ from the distribution of p, and q iid samples $\{b_1, \ldots, b_q\} \in \mathbb{R}$ from the uniform distribution on $[0, 2\pi]$.
3. Define $\tilde{\phi}$ in one of the following ways

$$\tilde{\phi}(x) = \sqrt{\frac{2}{q}}\left[\cos(w_1^T x + b_1), \ldots, \cos(w_q^T x + b_q)\right]^T \tag{8}$$

or

$$\tilde{\phi}(x) = \sqrt{\frac{2}{q}}\left[\cos\left(w_1^T x\right), \sin\left(w_1^T x\right), \ldots, \cos\left(w_{q/2}^T x\right), \sin\left(w_{q/2}^T x\right)\right]^T. \tag{9}$$

Notice that the estimators defined by (8) and (9) are unbiased estimator of the kernel k, since it can be expressed as:

$$k(x, y) = \hat{k}(x - y) = \int_{\mathbb{R}^d} p(w)e^{iw^\top(x-y)}dw = E\left[\tilde{\phi}(x)^T\tilde{\phi}(y)\right]. \tag{10}$$

The computational cost of constructing $\tilde{\phi}$ is $\mathcal{O}(q)$ in time and $\mathcal{O}(qn)$ to transform the training data; while in memory is $\mathcal{O}(q(d + n + 1))$, since we only need to draw samples up to q for a known distribution.

2.4 Nyström and RFF for Approximate SVM Learning

For using the Nyström and RFF methods to solve nonlinear supervised problems the following steps are needed:

1. Compute $\tilde{\phi}$, which, as we have seen, depends only on the chosen kernel in RFF and also on a data subsample in the case of Nyström.
2. Transform the training data from X to $\tilde{\phi}(X)$.
3. Train a linear SVM by solving the primal problem (2). It can be solved using a coordinate descent method whose computational cost is $\mathcal{O}(nq)$ per iteration, see [6].

The prediction for a new vector x is obtained by:

1. Computing $\tilde{\phi}(x)$ using the previous expression for $\tilde{\phi}$.
2. Predicting the class label of $\tilde{\phi}(x)$ using the previously trained linear SVM and the formula in (1).

3 Parallel Ensembles

As we have seen, the Nyström and RFF methods introduce randomness into the samples used to approximate the kernel, either by randomly selecting them or directly generating them according to a probability distribution. Therefore, it seems reasonable to apply ensembles to these techniques, which may improve the results obtained and contribute to the robustness of the generated models [29].

The simplest ensemble method is voting [29] and it will be the approximation followed in this article. If there are T independent binary classification estimators $h_1, \ldots, h_T$ with accuracy greater than 50%, a voting estimator H defined as

$$H(x) = \arg\max_{c} \left\{ \sum_{i=1}^{T} \mathcal{I}[h_i(x) = c] \right\}, \tag{11}$$

can lead to an improvement of these results. In (11) $\mathcal{I}$ is the indicator function, that is, it returns one if the input is true and zero otherwise.

However, as [24] pointed out, ensemble diversity is important since the error of the estimator H depends on

$$Err(H) = \frac{1 + \theta(T-1)}{T} Err(h), \tag{12}$$

where $Err(h)$ is the mean expected error of the individual learners and θ is the overall correlation between the predictions of the individual learners.

Although the Nyström method might implicitly resemble a form of bootstrapping, it is fundamentally different. Indeed, note that the Nyström and RFF methods discussed are not related to bootstrap sampling [5], which is the most common strategy for generating diversity in an ensemble. Nevertheless, these methods could be used in conjunction with it.

Despite the prospective advantages mentioned, with the exception of a few articles such as [7], it appears that Nyström and RFF ensembles have generally not been considered in the literature. A few studies, such as [11], have explored Nyström ensembles theoretically and experimentally, providing error bounds that ensure better convergence rates than those of the single Nyström method. However, to the best of the authors' knowledge, there is a lack of comparisons between Nyström and RFF ensembles, which we will tackle in Sect. 4.

4 Experiments

4.1 Data and Methods

The experimental section focuses on balanced accuracy and training time. We will focus our efforts on datasets containing binary classification problems. First, we have chosen some that have already been studied in relevant articles such as [17,28], which are: svmguide1, a5a, a9a and w3a. Additionally, we have incorporated supplementary datasets to ensure diversity in terms of scale and dimensionality; namely madelon, gisette, mushrooms and phishing. All datasets and

Table 1. Datasets shape and class balance.

Dataset	Size	Dimension	Smaller Class Size
madelon	2600	500	50%
gisette	7000	5000	50%
svmguide1 [10]	7089	4	43%
mushrooms	8124	112	48%
phishing	11055	68	44%
a5a	32561	123	24%
a9a	48842	123	24%
w3a	49749	300	3%

Table 2. Values of L and U for γ grid.

	L	U
madelon	−4	4
gisette	−4	4
svmguide	−2	4
mushroom	−4	4
phishing	−3	4
a5a	−7	1
a9a	−7	1
w3a	−6	3

their information can be accessed via the LIBSVM website (https://www.csie.ntu.edu.tw/~cjlin/libsvmtools/datasets/). In cases where this source provides training and testing data in different files, we have combined both of them into a single dataset. This decision was made to unify experiments and to ensure robust scores, as they will be obtained through nested cross-validation. Nested cross-validation involves two levels of cross-validation: an outer loop for assessing the model's test performance and an inner loop for tuning hyperparameters. The outer loop splits the data into k folds, and for each fold, the inner loop further splits the training data into m folds. Hyperparameters are optimized within the inner loop, and the best model is then evaluated on the outer loop's test fold; in our case $m = k = 5$. These subset splits are done using the same fixed seed for all the models considered. The resultant size, dimensionality and class distribution of each dataset are outlined in Table 1.

We are going to compare KSVM, Nyström, RFF, and Nyström and RFF ensembles. All the methods except ensembles are provided by the Python library *scikit-learn* [15]. For KSVM, the faster and more widely used approach is taken from the LIBSVM library [2], while for approximation methods, we must first compute the Nyström or RFF lifting approximation $\tilde{\phi}$ and then solve the primal problem of a linear SVM using LIBLINEAR [6]. For the ensemble models introduced in Sect. 3, we have created our own custom class based on (11), which uses individual random seed for each ensemble estimator.

Regarding the configuration of the SVM and the approximation-kernel methods, the kernel chosen is the Gaussian (RBF) and the tolerance for both KSVM and linear SVM is set to 10^{-4}. As for the hyperparameters to be tuned, C and γ are selected through the inner 5-fold of the stratified nested cross-validation using the grid search values specified in Table 3. As γ depends on the dataset, the grid has been chosen carefully for each one, setting different lower L and upper U bounds, as specified in Table 2, where d is the dataset dimension.

Before building $\tilde{\phi}$, the number of components q must be chosen. To observe the relationship between the size of q, balanced accuracy, and training time, we choose q over the configurations in Table 4. It has two size options: the smaller one corresponds to $\mathcal{B}$, which, depending on the dataset size, will be around 1%

Table 3. KSVM hyperparameters selected and the grid used to find them.

Hyperparameters	Range
C	$\{10^k : k \in \{-2, 0, 2, 4\}\}$
γ	$\{4^k/d : L \leq k \leq U\}$

Table 4. Number of components for each dataset.

Configuration	madelon	gisette	svmguide1	mushrooms	phishing	a5a	a9a	w3a
$\mathcal{A}$	260	700	710	813	1110	3260	3700	815
$\mathcal{B}$	26	70	71	82	111	326	370	370

if it has less than 30000 samples or 0.1% otherwise. Size $\mathcal{A}$ will be larger and will generally be around 10%. In addition, for ensemble methods, we fixed 11 estimators.

When showing training times, for both Nyström and RFF, they include the construction of $\tilde{\phi}$ and the training of the linear SVM. Furthermore, since ensembles can be parallelized, the reported training time for them reflects that of a single estimator. Finally, note that the accuracies and training times presented here present the average values obtained by repeating each experiment through stratified nested cross-validation of five outer and inner folds.

4.2 Results

One of the main objectives of this article was to verify the performance of the approximation methods and how much their training times improved. To this end, we first present Table 5, which shows the balanced accuracy of the KSVM, Nyström, RFF, ensemble Nyström, and ensemble RFF methods, setting the number of components of the approximation methods as shown in Table 4. For clarification, the best accuracy in approximation methods for each dataset is shown in bold.

Note that the datasets are sorted from left to right by their size. For simplicity, we will refer to a method and its number of components as its name and the configuration. For example, Nyström $\mathcal{A}$ would express the Nyström approximation model with a number of components equal to $\mathcal{A}$ in the configuration in Table 4.

In addition, in order to find differences between models, we performed a significance test. For that, within each dataset, we took the test predictions of the models and compare if they have the same distribution by using the Wilcoxon rank test and applied Bonferroni's correction [1,4]. For the Wilcoxon rank test, we reject the null hypothesis, that the predictions of the models have the same distributions if $p \leq 0.01$ for $\alpha = 0.05$. In Table 6 we show the p-value from comparing the KSVM predictions with those of the best approximation model; as we can see, there are no significant differences between them. However, by

Table 5. Balanced accuracy for KSVM, Nyström, RFF, and Nyström and RFF ensembles with a certain number of components.

	madelon	gisette	svmguide1	mushrooms	phishing	a5a	a9a	w3a
KSVM	59.68	97.57	96.97	100.00	97.04	81.89	81.84	89.22
Nyström $\mathcal{A}$	59.26	**97.52**	96.84	**100.00**	**96.40**	**82.16**	80.47	89.15
Nyström $\mathcal{B}$	56.15	95.26	96.82	99.99	94.16	81.92	80.14	88.94
RFF $\mathcal{A}$	57.50	93.74	96.86	**100.00**	96.14	81.91	80.45	**89.29**
RFF $\mathcal{B}$	51.65	82.71	96.95	99.95	94.34	82.06	80.16	88.68
Ens. Nys. $\mathcal{A}$	60.11	96.96	97.01	**100.00**	95.29	82.09	82.03	88.40
Ens. Nys. $\mathcal{B}$	60.92	97.25	97.04	**100.00**	94.83	82.14	**82.13**	88.37
Ens. RFF $\mathcal{A}$	63.92	93.22	97.05	**100.00**	94.62	81.76	82.05	87.98
Ens. RFF $\mathcal{B}$	**64.38**	93.60	**97.11**	**100.00**	94.70	82.12	82.06	88.34

Table 6. $p-$values of the Wilcoxon test over the predictions of KSVM and the best approximation model for each dataset.

madelon	gisette	svmguide1	mushrooms	phishing	a5a	a9a	w3a
0.212	0.037	0.792	1	0.039	0.676	0.801	0.857

relaxing the significance level to $\alpha = 0.15$, the gissete and phishing models would reject the hypothesis of having equal distributions with KSVM. In the case of gissete, although the predictions are different, the accuracy is practically the same. In the case of phishing, the accuracy gap is greater, indicating the need to increase the number of components.

Moreover, we have computed all the $p-$value model combinations for each dataset. To economize space and since in most cases there are no significant differences, we will not show them but will instead comment on the special cases in the following analysis.

As we can see in Table 5, for the madelon dataset, among the single Nyström and RFF approximation models, only Nyström $\mathcal{A}$ has managed to come close to KSVM, being within less than 1%. However, for the ensemble methods, all variants are above KSVM in accuracy. It is interesting to realize that although the performance of RFF models for madelon is lower than that of the the Nyström models, the RFF ensembles perform better than the Nyström ensembles. This could be explained by the Eq. (12): the predictions of each RFF model are less correlated than those of Nyström ones, because RFF components are generated from a random distribution, while Nyström's are generated by subsampling the training dataset. The trade-off appears again in the Nyström and RFF ensembles, with the best performance for $\mathcal{B}$ components.

In the case of gisette, Nyström $\mathcal{A}$ and its ensembles $\mathcal{A}$ and $\mathcal{B}$ have managed to come within less than 1% of the KSVM accuracy. It is interesting to note that with regard to the Wilcoxon signed-rank test between the predictions of Nyström

Table 7. Differences between ensemble methods and their respective base methods (ensemble - method) for balanced accuracy

Difference	madelon	gisette	svmguide1	mushrooms	phishing	a5a	a9a	w3a	Mean
Ens. Nys. $\mathcal{A}$ - Nys. $\mathcal{A}$	0.85	-0.56	0.17	0.00	-1.11	-0.07	1.56	-0.75	0.01
Ens. Nys. $\mathcal{B}$ - Nys. $\mathcal{B}$	4.77	1.99	0.22	0.01	0.67	0.22	1.99	-0.57	1.41
Ens. RFF $\mathcal{A}$ - RFF $\mathcal{A}$	6.42	-0.52	0.19	0.00	-1.52	-0.15	1.60	-1.31	0.59
Ens. RFF $\mathcal{B}$ - RFF $\mathcal{B}$	12.73	10.89	0.16	0.05	0.36	0.06	1.90	-0.34	3.97

$\mathcal{A}$ and Nyström ensemble $\mathcal{B}$ a $p-$value of 0.425 was obtained, so we cannot reject the null hypothesis that the distributions are the same. Considering the number of components in the $\mathcal{B}$ model and the accuracy difference, this situation makes the ensemble model interesting compared to the individual model. For Nyström ensemble $\mathcal{A}$, its accuracy is worse than that of Nyström $\mathcal{A}$. However, in the remaining percentages of Nyström and RFF, we see that the ensemble models have indeed improved the accuracy of the individual estimators with the same number of components. Additionally, as in madelon, due to the dataset's high dimensionality, Nyström and RFF $\tilde{\phi}$ transformations have reduced data dimensionality.

For the svmguide1 dataset, all the methods are within less than 1% of the accuracy of KSVM. It is noteworthy that $\mathcal{A}$ and $\mathcal{B}$ ensemble methods improve Nyström and RFF methods and KSVM. The mushrooms dataset is interesting because it can be solved perfectly with KSVM. It clearly shows that the more components there are, the better the approximations become, and there is also an improvement of the Nyström and RFF methods when they are used in ensembles. Phishing is a dataset similar to gisette, only Nyström $\mathcal{A}$ and RFF $\mathcal{A}$ manage to approximate KSVM.

For the a5a dataset, all the approximation methods perform better than KSVM. For the a9a dataset, all methods except Nyström $\mathcal{B}$ and RFF $\mathcal{B}$ have better accuracy than KSVM. For the w3a dataset, every $\mathcal{A}$ and $\mathcal{B}$ method are within less than 1% of KSVM.

In terms of ensembles, fixing the same number of components we have not found any indication of whether Nyström or RFF ensembles are better; it depends on the dataset. However, we have computed the difference between an ensemble model and a single model for each dataset, see Table 7 and we summarize the average differences over all datasets in the right column. As we can see, the RFF ensembles have shown better mean improvement than the Nyström ensembles, but $\mathcal{B}$ components are preferable because as we increase the number of components, their ensembles become less valuable.

The training times for the results in Table 5, are given in seconds in Table 8. Since ensemble methods can be run in parallel, we assume that their average times are the same as that of a single estimator method. In this context, for KSVM we can observe a trend of increasing time with the number of data points, slightly modified by the dimension of the dataset (recall that the dimen-

Table 8. Training times in the best hyperparameters for KSVM, Nyström, RFF, and Nyström and RFF ensembles with a specified number of components.

	madelon	gisette	svmguide1	mushrooms	phishing	a5a	a9a	w3a
KSVM	3.55	10.03	1.02	21.32	5.57	158.93	535.58	177.86
Nyström $\mathcal{A}$	0.10	2.65	1.57	1.21	10.95	68.98	100.38	12.37
Nyström $\mathcal{B}$	0.01	0.77	0.18	0.10	0.46	16.07	16.74	16.10
RFF $\mathcal{A}$	0.05	2.18	0.98	0.63	8.38	53.42	53.43	20.51
RFF $\mathcal{B}$	0.01	0.27	0.19	0.09	0.65	5.37	47.87	12.85

sions were shown in Table 1). In order to better appreciate the gain, we have condensed in Table 9 the ratio between the training time of KSVM and the approximation model, i.e., *KSVM-training-times/approximation-methods-times*. If the coefficient is greater than one, it indicates that the approximation method is that many times faster; otherwise, it would be slower. Additionally, we have highlighted in bold when the approximation methods are slower than KSVM.

Table 9. Speed comparison between KSVM and the approximation models. The ratio shows how many times faster each model is compared to KSVM.

	madelon	gisette	svmguide1	mushrooms	phishing	a5a	a9a	w3a
Nyström $\mathcal{A}$	35.50	3.82	**0.65**	17.62	**0.51**	2.30	5.34	14.38
Nyström $\mathcal{B}$	355.00	13.15	5.67	213.20	12.11	9.89	31.99	6.94
RFF $\mathcal{A}$	71.00	4.64	1.04	33.84	**0.66**	2.97	10.02	8.67
RFF $\mathcal{B}$	355.00	37.51	5.37	236.89	8.57	29.61	11.19	8.04

Table 10. Mean number of support vectors for each dataset.

	madelon	gisette	svmguide1	mushrooms	phishing	a5a	a9a	w3a
Total	2037	1252	458	5522	2530	10722	15978	63368
Relative size %	78.35	17.89	6.46	68.00	22.89	32.92	32.72	127.39

Looking at the Table 9, we can see that only in three cases the approximation methods were slower than KSVM, and these occurred on datasets where KSVM was faster than theoretically expected. This can be explained by the significantly lower number of support vectors in relation with the dataset size as Table 10 shows. Moreover, in the case of svmguide1, Nyström $\mathcal{A}$ was found to be slower than KSVM. However, the other methods, as can be seen in the Table 5, it is possible to achieve the accuracy of KSVM in svmguide1.

5 Conclusion

Throughout this paper, our goal has been to study and compare the Nyström and RFF methods for approximating KSVM, taking advantage of the random nature of the approximated components to define ensemble models. To achieve this, we selected medium and large datasets of binary classification tasks and, within a unified framework, measured their error and training time for different numbers of components.

The results obtained indicate that the Nyström and RFF methods are potentially good alternatives to KSVM for achieving similar accuracies and significantly reducing training times. In general, with a number of components of 10% of the number of samples we obtained similar results to KSVM. In addition, within the same number of components, the usage of ensembles generally improve the accuracy of the Nyström and RFF methods.

Overall, our results highlight the importance of considering both accuracy and computational efficiency when selecting approximation methods for large-scale classification tasks. Regarding future work, larger datasets and the number of components required in relation to the value of the eigenvectors could be studied. Additionally, the use of other models, such as neural networks, could be explored for constructing the lifting approximation.

Acknowledgments. The authors acknowledge financial support from project PID2022-139856NB-I00 funded by MCIN/ AEI / 10.13039/501100011033 / FEDER, UE, from the Autonomous Community of Madrid (ELLIS Unit Madrid), Cátedra UAM-IIC de Ciencia de Datos y Aprendizaje Automático, FPI-UAM and gratefully acknowledge the use of the facilities of Centro de Computación Científica (CCC) at UAM.

References

1. Benavoli, A., Corani, G., Mangili, F.: Should we really use post-hoc tests based on mean-ranks? J. Mach. Learn. Res. **17**(1), 152–161 (2016)
2. Chang, C.C., Lin, C.J.: LIBSVM: a library for support vector machines. ACM Trans. Intell. Syst. Technol. (TIST) **2**(3), 1–27 (2011)
3. Cortes, C., Vapnik, V.: Support-vector networks. Mach. Learn. **20**, 273–297 (1995)
4. Demšar, J.: Statistical comparisons of classifiers over multiple data sets. J. Mach. Learn. Res. **7**, 1–30 (2006)
5. Efron, B., Tibshirani, R.J.: An Introduction to the Bootstrap. Chapman and Hall/CRC (1994)
6. Fan, R.E., Chang, K.W., Hsieh, C.J., Wang, X.R., Lin, C.J.: LIBLINEAR: a library for large linear classification. J. Mach. Learn. Res. **9**, 1871–1874 (2008)
7. Gautheron, L., et al.: Landmark-based ensemble learning with random Fourier features and gradient boosting. In: Hutter, F., Kersting, K., Lijffijt, J., Valera, I. (eds.) ECML PKDD 2020. LNCS (LNAI), vol. 12459, pp. 141–157. Springer, Cham (2021). https://doi.org/10.1007/978-3-030-67664-3_9
8. Ghojogh, B., Ghodsi, A., Karray, F., Crowley, M.: Reproducing Kernel Hilbert Space, Mercer's Theorem, eigenfunctions, Nyström on method, and use of kernels in machine learning: tutorial and survey. arXiv preprint arXiv:2106.08443 (2021)

9. Golub, G.H., Van Loan, C.F.: Matrix Computations. JHU Press (2013)
10. Hsu, C.W., Chang, C.C., Lin, C.J., et al.: A practical guide to support vector classification (2003)
11. Kumar, S., Mohri, M., Talwalkar, A.: Ensemble Nyström method. In: Advances in Neural Information Processing Systems, vol. 22 (2009)
12. Liu, F., Huang, X., Chen, Y., Suykens, J.A.: Random features for kernel approximation: a survey on algorithms, theory, and beyond. IEEE Trans. Pattern Anal. Mach. Intell. **44**(10), 7128–7148 (2021)
13. Musa, A.B.: Comparative study on classification performance between support vector machine and logistic regression. Int. J. Mach. Learn. Cybern. **4**(1), 13–24 (2013)
14. Nie, F., Huang, Y., Wang, X., Huang, H.: New primal SVM solver with linear computational cost for big data classifications. In: Proceedings of the 31st International Conference on International Conference on Machine Learning-Volume 32, pp. II–505 (2014)
15. Pedregosa, F., et al.: Scikit-learn: machine learning in Python. J. Mach. Learn. Res. **12**, 2825–2830 (2011)
16. Platt, J.: Sequential minimal optimization: a fast algorithm for training support vector machines. In: Advances in Kernel Methods-Support Vector Learning 208 (1998)
17. Rahimi, A., Recht, B.: Random features for large-scale kernel machines. In: Platt, J., Koller, D., Singer, Y., Roweis, S. (eds.) Advances in Neural Information Processing Systems, vol. 20 (2007)
18. Rahimi, A., Recht, B.: Weighted sums of random kitchen sinks: replacing minimization with randomization in learning. In: Advances in Neural Information Processing Systems, vol. 21 (2008)
19. Rudin, W.: Fourier Analysis on Groups. Courier Dover Publications (2017)
20. Salazar, D.A., Vélez, J.I., Salazar, J.C.: Comparison between SVM and logistic regression: which one is better to discriminate? Revista Colombiana de Estadística **35**(2), 223–237 (2012)
21. Sinha, A., Duchi, J.C.: Learning kernels with random features. In: Advances in Neural Information Processing Systems, vol. 29 (2016)
22. Sutherland, D.J., Schneider, J.: On the error of random Fourier features. arXiv preprint arXiv:1506.02785 (2015)
23. Torres-Barrán, A., Alaíz, C.M., Dorronsoro, J.R.: Faster SVM training via conjugate SMO. Pattern Recogn. **111**, 107644 (2021)
24. Tumer, K., Ghosh, J.: Theoretical foundations of linear and order statistics combiners for neural pattern classifiers. IEEE Trans. Neural Networks (1995)
25. Vapnik, V.N.: The Nature of Statistical Learning Theory. Springer, New York (1995). https://doi.org/10.1007/978-1-4757-3264-1
26. Wang, M., Fu, W., He, X., Hao, S., Wu, X.: A survey on large-scale machine learning. IEEE Trans. Knowl. Data Eng. **34**(6), 2574–2594 (2020)
27. Williams, C.K., Seeger, M.: Using the Nyström method to speed up kernel machines. In: Dietterich, T.G., Becker, S., Ghahramani, Z. (eds.) Neural Information Processing Systems, vol. 14, pp. 585–591. MIT Press, Cambridge, MA (2001)
28. Yang, T., Li, Y.F., Mahdavi, M., Jin, R., Zhou, Z.H.: Nyström method vs random Fourier features: a theoretical and empirical comparison. In: Advances in Neural Information Processing Systems, vol. 25 (2012)
29. Zhou, Z.H.: Ensemble Methods: Foundations and Algorithms. CRC Press (2012)

Application of Transfer Learning to Online Models in Malware Detection

David Escudero García[1(✉)] and Noemí DeCastro-García[2]

[1] Research Institute of Applied science in Cybersecurity, Universidad de León, Campus de Vegazana s/n, 24071 León, Spain
descg@unileon.es

[2] Department of Mathematics, Universidad de León, Campus de Vegazana s/n, 24071 León, Spain
ncasg@unileon.es

Abstract. Machine learning is one of the main strategies applied to malware detection in the literature, since machine learning models are more adaptive than signature based solutions. One of the main challenges in the application of machine learning to malware detection is the presence of concept drift, which is a change in the data distribution over time caused by the evolving nature of malware; for example, the development of new malware families. To tackle drift, online models that can be dynamically updated are applied. However, labelled data is needed to keep the model up to date and reliable labels are expensive to obtain. In this paper, we study the effectiveness of the application of transfer learning to improve model performance in malware detection. Transfer learning is based on exploiting knowledge of related datasets to improve predictions in a target dataset, and requires no labels in the target. Therefore, it may help to improve predictions on new malware families by making use of past data. The results show that transfer learning algorithms provide inconsistent performance that, despite significant improvements in some cases, does not extend to different models or algorithms.

Keywords: Machine learning · Malware detection · Concept drift · Cybersecurity · Transfer Learning

1 Introduction

The increased use of digital systems in both enterprises and administrations has led to an interest in developing new methods of dealing with threats such as malware. Manual analysis is costly and relatively slow, so machine learning (ML) is commonly proposed as a solution in the literature [4]. The application of ML can help automate the process of detection and is expected to be able to generalise to new threats more easily than traditional signature-based solutions. However,

Supported by EU Next Generation funds.

H. Quintián et al. (Eds.): HAIS 2024, LNAI 14857, pp. 177–189, 2025.
https://doi.org/10.1007/978-3-031-74183-8_15

some hurdles must be overcome in order to effectively apply ML solutions to the problem of malware detection.

One of the main challenges in the application of machine learning to malware detection is the change in the data distribution of both malicious and benign samples. This change in data distribution, known as concept drift, decreases the performance of the models. Concept drift mainly affects malware samples and has a smaller magnitude in benign ones [7] mainly because of the development of new malware families [4] and the emergence of new approaches to exploiting vulnerabilities.

The application of transfer learning (TL) may be useful to deal with drift in this setting. TL is a branch of ML whose goal is to make use of data from a source domain, which would correspond to past data, in order to improve model predictions on a different but related dataset named target domain, which would correspond to recent data [16]. TL techniques assume that source and target domains may have different distributions and try to reduce these differences, usually by transforming the source and target domains. Therefore, TL can be helpful to deal with the changes in data distribution associated with concept drift. The knowledge extracted from known types of malware could be used to improve model predictions for the new families that are developed over time.

In this work, we assess the usefulness of TL algorithms to detect malware in the presence of concept drift. We will compare the performance of different TL algorithms when applied along with online ML models. We will take into account common challenges such as data imbalance and the limited availability of labelled instances for model updating. All experiments are carried out using the KronoDroid dataset [6], which spans both benign and malicious apps from 2008 to 2020. Our hypothesis is that TL algorithms may provide better predictive performance by decreasing the differences in distribution between past and recent data and, indirectly, reducing the need for labelled instances to update the model.

This work is organised as follows: in Sect. 2, we introduce the concepts of TL and concept drift, along with a review of relevant works. In Sect. 3, we detail the experimental protocol and give an overview of the ML models and TL algorithms applied. In Sect. 4, we present and comment on the results of the experiments. Finally, in Sect. 5, we provide a conclusion.

2 Related Work

First, we provide a brief description of concept drift and transfer learning and then we introduce other works that deal with those concepts in malware detection.

2.1 Concept Drift and Transfer Learning

One of the main assumptions in the field of machine learning is that the distribution of the data does not change over time. This is an unrealistic assumption in the field of malware detection [4], since new malware families may appear with new ways of exploiting system vulnerabilities. Malware authors also implement evasion techniques [4] in order to make detection more difficult. The result is that the samples modify both their dynamic and static features. These changes in data distribution over time are known as concept drift [13] and compromise the predictive performance of the models because the knowledge they acquired from training on past samples may not generalise well to new samples.

Concept drift is a change in the distribution of data over time [13]. A machine learning model seeks to assign a label $y_i \in Y$ to an observation $x_i \in \mathcal{R}^d$ that contains a numerical representation of certain features of interest to the problem. For example, in malware detection, the vector x_i may contain information such as API calls from the sample. Each instance will be assigned a label in $\{malicious, not\ malicious\}$. A concept is a joint distribution $Concept = P(X,Y) = P(Y \mid X)P(X)$ over the set of features of the data and the space of labels.

$P_t(X)$ denotes the marginal distribution of the data at an instant of time t and $P_t(Y \mid X)$ the conditional distribution of the data at that same instant. Concept drift appears when at a later instant u any of the two previous distributions changes: $P_t(y \mid X) \neq P_u(y \mid X)$ and/or $P_t(X) \neq P_u(X)$ [13].

In machine learning problems, it is common to assume that the concept is the same at any pair of time instants t and u: $P_t(X,Y) = P_u(X,Y)$. If this condition is not met, and it is not commonly met in real problems [13], the performance of the models will tend to decrease over time.

The goal of concept drift detection and adaptation techniques is to limit the impact of distribution changes through different mechanisms.

The main formal characterization of TL is given in [16]. A domain $\mathcal{D} = \{\mathcal{X}, P(X)\}$ is defined by two components: a feature space $\mathcal{X}$ which is the set of features of the data, and a marginal probability distribution $P(X)$ over $\mathcal{X}$. Two data sets referring to the same problem are considered to belong to different domains if they differ in their feature space $\mathcal{X}$ or in their distribution $P(X)$. On the other hand, a task $\mathcal{T} = \{\mathcal{Y}, P(y \mid X)\}$ consists of a label space $\mathcal{Y}$ that are the different classes to which the instances can belong (malicious and non-malicious, for example) and a predictive function $f(.)$ that assigns to an event x_i a label y from $\mathcal{Y}$. This function is interpreted as $P(y \mid X = x_i)$. The goal of TL techniques is to improve the predictive function of the target domain, $f(.)_T$, using the information obtained from the source domain and task D_S and $\mathcal{T}_S$. The main obstacle is that the domains and/or tasks of both domains may be different ($D_S \neq D_T$ or $\mathcal{T}_S \neq \mathcal{T}_T$).

Given the definition of concept drift, it is easy to consider that the data from instant t makes up a source domain from which knowledge can be extracted, and the data at present instant u constitutes a target domain with a different distribution in which to make predictions. Unlike in this work, other works that apply TL in cybersecurity are not particularly interested in preserving model performance over time, but in using data from certain types of attacks to detect others in a bi-class task. We hypothesise that the application of the TL to this problem can give good results, as in other works focused on malware detection [7].

2.2 Concept Drift and Transfer Learning in Malware Detection

In the literature, different approaches have been proposed to address changes in the data distribution [2,7]. Much of this work focuses on the application of online models, which can be updated dynamically without the need to retrain from scratch. Most works use a prequential methodology, where it is assumed that new instances are labelled and can be used to update models, which is unlikely to be the case in realistic environments: manual labelling is costly and time-consuming, so only a limited set of labelled instances could be expected to be available.

Some works use a passive adaptation strategy through batch processing, maintaining a set of constantly updated models. This is the case of [7]. Each new batch of data is used to test the models and substitute the worst performers. This technique improves accuracy by an average of 0.3 compared to static models. Other works apply an active adaptation strategy against concept drift, including drift detection algorithms that signal when the distribution has shifted and it is necessary to update or retrain the model. These algorithms usually detect drift by a decrease in model performance; therefore, data are assumed to be labelled. In [2] improvements of 0.15 are achieved with this approach. Other approaches make use of pseudolabels to reduce the dependence on manually labelled instances. In [9], an ensemble of linear models is kept updated by using the predictions of the total ensemble. Individual models are aged out when they make errors on a set of representative instances. This method improves the accuracy rate by 0.1 compared to traditional models. The main problem is that there is no mechanism to determine the reliability of the pseudo-labels. If the pseudo-label assignment is unfavourable, the effectiveness of the model is compromised and the presence of an imbalance in the data may contribute to a decrease in pseudo-label quality. In certain cases, the accuracy can be worse than that of a static model, showing a decreasing trend when new instances are processed due to the accumulation of errors.

A great number of applications of TL techniques to the problem of malware detection are usually based on deep neural networks and the transformation of the sample into an image, usually using its raw bytes. The idea is to apply neural networks pretrained on image classification problems and fine-tune them to tackle the specific problem of malware classification by applying another cycle of model training to the deeper layers (that create problem-specific representations [20]) while "freezing" the external layers. In this way, the network acts as a feature extractor that creates new data representations adapted to the target domain. The work in [10] is an example of this approach. The application of TL improves accuracy by 0.1 in comparison to base models with no TL. The problem with this approach is the high computational cost and the necessity of transforming the feature space to be compatible with the pretrained models, which may not be simple. A different approach is the application of model-agnostic TL algorithms, such as in [11]. In this case, the problem is a bi-class one: using samples from certain known malicious samples, the TL algorithm transforms the data so that different types of malicious samples may be easier to classify in the transformed feature space. The application of TL almost halves the false positive rate in comparison to an existing method with no TL.

The approach in this work is based on the application of model-agnostic TL algorithms. Given that a significant component of drift is the presence of new malware families [4] and that TL, as in [11] exploits the knowledge from known malicious samples to improve the detection of different ones, we believe that the application of TL may be useful to improve model performance in problems of malware detection with concept drift.

3 Materials and Methods

The goal of this work is to determine whether TL algorithms can improve the performance of online models in the problem of malware detection with data imbalance and label scarcity.

In this section, we describe the dataset used in the experiments, the applied models and the evaluation protocol. Code is available[1].

3.1 Dataset

We use the KronoDroid dataset [6], which contains malicious and benign Android applications obtained from other datasets and public repositories. We have selected it because it contains dated samples from 2008 to 2020, which is a wide interval of time. In addition, it contains 240 different malware families. Therefore, it provides a reasonably good approximation of a real sample of apps. Since the apps are dated, it is easy to simulate a data stream by processing samples ordered by date. The collected apps are dynamically and statically analysed using both an emulator and a real device. In this work, we use the real device dataset, which contains a total of 78137 samples, 41382 malware and 36755 benign.

The dataset contains 489 features, obtained from dynamic (frequency of API calls) and static analysis (permissions and intents). These two feature sets are commonly used in the literature on Android malware [12]. For simplicity, we will discard list-like features, such as the list of intent filters and services defined by the application. We also discard non-informative features such as the SHA-256 of the sample or its associated timestamps. We will make use of a total of 477 features, summarised in Table 1.

[1] https://github.com/amunc/Application-of-transfer-learning-to-online-models-in-malware-detection.

Table 1. Summary of features in the KronoDroid dataset

Description	Count
Frequency of system calls during execution	288
Binary feature that indicates whether a standard permission was requested	166
Number of activities, actions, services declared in intent filters	7
Compressed and uncompressed file size	2
Total number of files	1
Number of normal, dangerous, signature, custom and standard permissions requested	5
Total number of services, activities, intent filters, and others	8

3.2 Models and Algorithms

We have tried to select commonly used algorithms for online learning. Since we use the Python language, we make use of existing libraries. From River [15], we obtain all the supervised learning models used in the experiments: Adaptive Hoeffding Tree (AHT) [1], Logistic Regression (LR) [3] and Adaptive Random Forest (ARF) [5].

Since we are dealing with concept drift, it is difficult to extrapolate performance from a reserved test set to future data. Therefore, we apply a random search to select hyperparameter configurations for all models and report the average results. In Table 2, we list the models and search spaces for their hyperparameters. All other parameters are left at the default values used by each library.

Table 2. Models and their hyperparameters.

Model	Hyperparameter	Search space
AHT	split criterion	$[gini, hellinger, information\ gain]$
	max depth	$[8, 10, 12, 14]$
ARF	split criterion	$[gini, hellinger, information\ gain]$
	number of models	$[10, 25, 50, 100]$
	max depth	$[8, 10, 12, 14]$
LR	l2 regularization	$[0, 0.001, 0.025, 0.05, 0.1, 0.125]$

We have applied four different TL algorithms that have been implemented in Python in the experiments.

- **CORAL** [17]. This method is based on equating the covariance of the features of the source domain to those of the target domain. This is accomplished by

whitening the data and then inducing the covariance of the target domain. The original feature space is not modified.
- **SDA** [18]. This method implements modifications to principal component analysis (PCA) to align the components of the source and target domains.
- **DTFC, SRARA** [8,19]. These methods are based on autoencoders but use a formulation based on probabilistically adding noise to the input data in order to increase generalization.

All of these algorithms have their own hyperparameters that are also optimized. These are shown in Table 3. The ranges of the hyperparameters have been fixed based on the results of some preliminary experiments.

Table 3. Hyperparameters of TL algorithms.

Algorithm	Hyperparameters	Value range
MSLDA	noise	$[multinomial, bernouilli]$
DTFC	p	$[0.1, 0.9]$
SRARA	number of layers	$[1, 4]$
	α	$[0.5, 10]$
	λ	$[0.1, 10]$
SDA, VSA	number of features	$[1, 20]$
CORAL	λ	$[0, 5]$

3.3 Experimental Protocol

In the experiments, different proportions of malicious samples and available labels for model updating are tested. To set the proportion of malicious samples, we apply a random downsample to adjust their number. The number of instances of the dataset is reduced as a side effect. The proportion of available labels for model updating is also controlled with a random sample that determines which instances will have a label available. For fairness, the sample will be the same for all models. Finally, to simulate that instance labels may not be immediately available, we introduce a delay of 2000 instances before they are used to update the models.

The process is as follows:

- First, we use the corresponding downsampled dataset according to the selected malware proportion.
- The first 10% of instances, sorted by date as mentioned in Sect. 3.1 is assumed to be fully labelled and used to train the models / TL algorithms. This corresponds roughly to applications in the interval from 2008 to 2010.

- The model makes predictions on instances one by one and updates itself with each instance after the set delay if its label is available.

This process is repeated for each model, proportion of malware and labels. As commented in the previous section, we randomly select hyperparameter configurations and report the average results.

The Matthews correlation coefficient (MCC) [14] is used as a metric. It is chosen because it is a more informative metric than the accuracy or F1-score in unbalanced data sets, such as the one used in this work (see Sect. 3.1). It is defined in Eq. 1. TP, TN, FP, and FN denote true positives, true negatives, false positives, and false negatives.

$$MCC = \frac{TP \cdot TN - FP \cdot FN}{\sqrt{(TP + FP)(TP + FN)(TN + FP)(TN + FN)}} \tag{1}$$

4 Results and Discussion

The performance of tested models with different proportions of malware and availability of labels is shown in Table 4.

In general, the TL algorithms appear to not be particularly effective at solving the problem. There are some cases in which significant improvements are achieved, such as with a malware proportion of 0.5336 and no labelled instances for ARF and AHT, with an increase of 0.1 in MCC. However, there are several cases in which no algorithm provides a performance improvement, mostly with AHT, but even when some algorithm offers better performance, the others do not, and they may even significantly decrease the accuracy of the predictions. For example, with a malware proportion of 0.05 and no labelled examples, SRARA improves the performance of LR, but the other TL methods offer significantly worse performance. The fact that no algorithm is able to provide consistent improvements in performance may be an indicator of their dependence on a favourable hyperparameter configuration. This sensitivity would be particularly disadvantageous in an online setting since the changes in data distribution would make it difficult to extrapolate the fitness of a configuration based on the results in a reserved test set.

To show more clearly the performance of the TL algorithms, in Fig. 1 we show their percentages of improvement in MCC for each model, averaged over the proportion of labelled instances available to update the model and the proportion of malware in the dataset.

In Figs. 1a and 1b, we show the percentage of improvement for ARF. It can be seen that there are no significant increases or decreases in model performance across the number of available labels, except for CORAL and SDA when no labels are available, in which case there is a significant decrease (23% for CORAL and 32% for SDA). The biggest improvement is provided by SRARA, with a 6% when no labels are available, although when labels are available there is a decrease in performance of around 4%. This reinforces the lack of consistency in the performance of the TL algorithms. When considering the proportion of malware

Table 4. MCC of models with different proportions of malware and available labels. The best result in each row is bolded.

malware proportion	label proportion	model	NoTL	CORAL	DTFC	SDA	SRARA	Increase
0.05	0.0	ARF	**0.000**	**0.000**	**0.000**	**0.000**	**0.000**	0.000
		AHT	0.334	0.334	0.334	0.000	**0.341**	0.007
		LR	0.224	0.136	0.183	0.000	**0.257**	0.033
	0.05	ARF	0.347	**0.350**	0.302	0.349	0.295	0.004
		AHT	**0.345**	0.325	0.314	0.232	0.313	−0.020
		LR	0.285	**0.302**	0.237	0.048	0.230	0.017
	0.1	ARF	0.369	0.369	0.345	**0.371**	0.337	0.002
		AHT	**0.421**	0.359	0.404	0.331	0.326	−0.017
		LR	0.298	**0.317**	0.248	0.049	0.250	0.019
	1.0	ARF	0.384	0.377	**0.386**	0.382	0.346	0.002
		AHT	0.362	**0.395**	0.328	0.367	0.385	0.033
		LR	0.318	**0.350**	0.266	0.065	0.276	0.032
0.1	0.0	ARF	**0.000**	**0.000**	**0.000**	**0.000**	**0.000**	0.000
		AHT	0.381	0.355	0.381	0.000	**0.387**	0.006
		LR	0.354	0.251	**0.358**	0.000	0.342	0.004
	0.05	ARF	0.420	0.440	**0.446**	0.425	0.413	0.025
		AHT	**0.449**	0.418	0.442	0.304	0.412	−0.007
		LR	0.435	**0.441**	0.390	0.126	0.360	0.007
	0.1	ARF	**0.506**	0.491	0.491	0.502	0.477	−0.004
		AHT	**0.502**	0.461	0.473	0.406	0.476	−0.026
		LR	0.452	**0.504**	0.408	0.426	0.390	0.052
	1.0	ARF	0.603	0.602	0.600	**0.604**	0.574	0.002
		AHT	**0.573**	0.532	0.545	0.522	0.518	−0.029
		LR	0.482	**0.504**	0.441	0.172	0.433	0.022
0.5336	0.0	ARF	0.483	0.145	0.468	0.000	**0.581**	0.098
		AHT	0.411	0.401	0.407	0.000	**0.518**	0.107
		LR	0.612	0.535	**0.616**	0.000	0.583	0.004
	0.05	ARF	0.749	0.730	0.783	0.733	**0.791**	0.042
		AHT	0.691	0.686	**0.777**	0.664	0.749	0.087
		LR	0.814	**0.817**	0.796	0.767	0.772	0.003
	0.1	ARF	0.758	0.751	**0.803**	0.745	0.792	0.045
		AHT	**0.775**	0.771	0.756	0.757	0.753	−0.005
		LR	0.820	**0.825**	0.798	0.793	0.800	0.006
	1.0	ARF	0.797	0.796	**0.819**	0.795	0.810	0.022
		AHT	0.785	0.786	**0.795**	0.783	0.792	0.010
		LR	**0.831**	0.827	0.800	0.809	0.789	−0.004

in the dataset in Fig. 1b, once again CORAL and SDA present a significant decrease in performance, this time when the dataset is mostly balanced. Given that SDA provides significant decreases in performance for all three models, we can conclude that this method causes negative transfer [16]: it results in a separation of the data that is more difficult to learn than the original. On the other hand, once again, SRARA provides an improvement of around 6%, this time when the dataset is balanced, although with a decrease in performance for lower proportions of malware.

Figures 1c and 1d show the percentages of improvement for AHT. In this case, SDA shows the worst performance when considering both available labels and the proportion of malware, with a consistent decrease in performance of

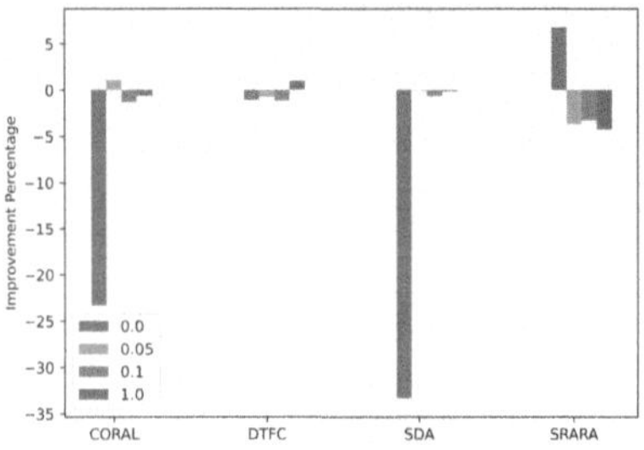

(a) ARF. Available labels

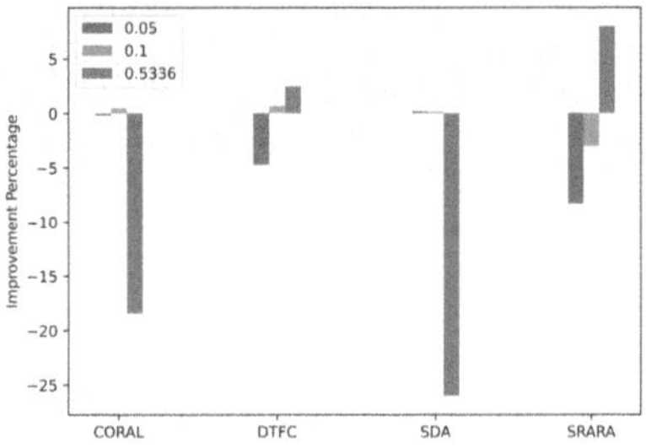

(b) ARF. Malware proportion

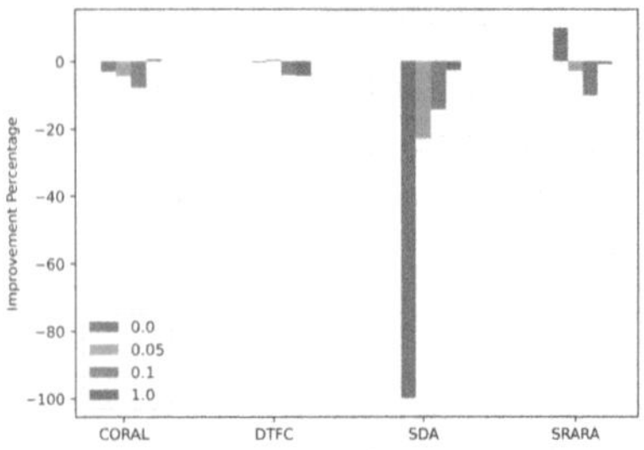

(c) AHT. Available labels

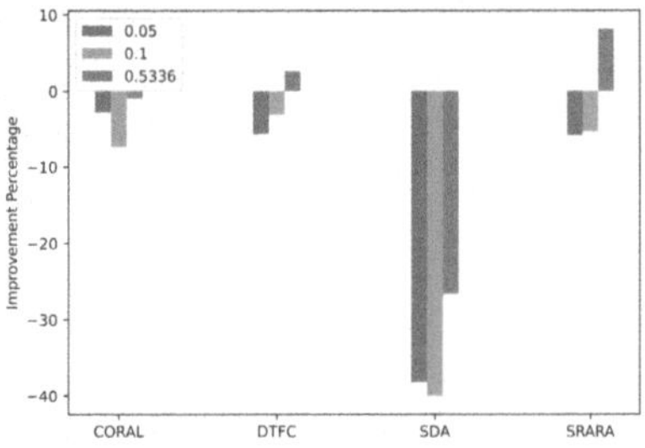

(d) AHT. Malware proportion

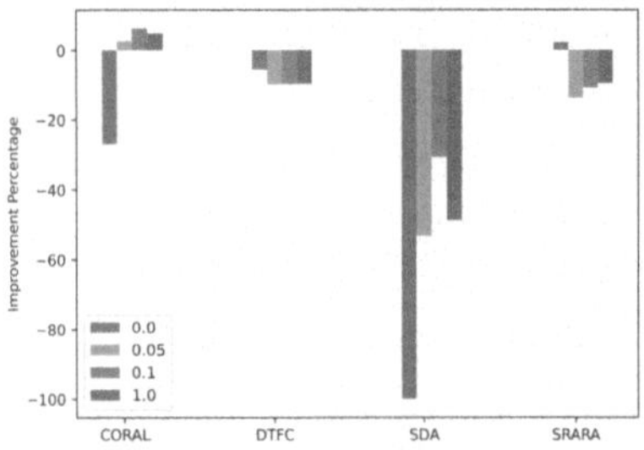

(e) LR. Available labels

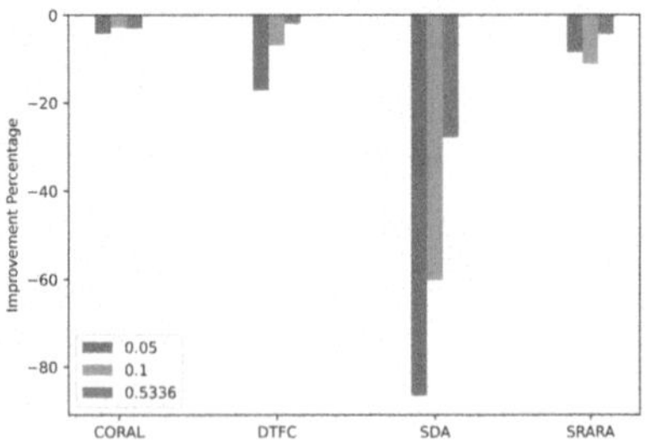

(f) LR. Malware proportion

Fig. 1. Percentages of improvement of TL algorithms for each model, averaged over proportions of malware and available labels.

more than 20% except when the data are fully labelled. Also, SRARA is the model that provides the highest increases in performance in the same setting as ARF: no labelled instances and class balance in the dataset.

Finally, Figs. 1e and 1f show the improvement for LR. LR is the model with the worst results in the application of TL to the problem. There is no average improvement in any case when considering different proportions of malware in the dataset and there are only small (<2%) improvements for CORAL when some labels are available for update and for SRARA when there are none.

5 Conclusion

In this work, we have carried out an evaluation of the application of TL algorithms to improve the performance of online models in the problem of malware detection in the presence of concept drift in a publicly available dataset of Android apps. The results show that, overall, TL algorithms may not be effective in this problem. They provide inconsistent improvements and may, in some cases, decrease performance, although on average, both improvements and degradation tend to be small, lower than 5%. The inconsistency of the results implies that the TL algorithms may have an important dependence on the hyperparameter configuration and/or the nature of the data.

Given the significant decreases in performance in certain cases, the algorithms may be removing relevant information from the data, making classification more difficult. Some algorithms, such as SDA, show a consistent decrease in performance, which is a clear case of negative transfer taking place.

In future work, we intend to study more in depth the phenomenon of negative transfer in both the dataset used in this study and others, in order to determine which characteristics of the data may make the application of TL inadvisable or whether the concept drift in the samples may be incompatible with its performance. In addition, we also intend to study how to select appropriate hyperparameter configurations for the algorithms, given that we believe that the inconsistency of the results may be a symptom of unfavourable configurations.

Acknowledgements. This work is carried out within the framework of the Recovery, Transformation and Resilience Plan funds, financed by the European Union (Next Generation), in the strategic project with key X67 *Data science for an artificial intelligence model in cybersecurity.*

References

1. Bifet, A., Gavaldà, R.: Adaptive learning from evolving data streams. In: Adams, N.M., Robardet, C., Siebes, A., Boulicaut, J.-F. (eds.) IDA 2009. LNCS, vol. 5772, pp. 249–260. Springer, Heidelberg (2009). https://doi.org/10.1007/978-3-642-03915-7_22
2. Ceschin, F., Botacin, M., Gomes, H.M., Pinagé, F., Oliveira, L.S., Grégio, A.: Fast & furious: on the modelling of malware detection as an evolving data stream. Expert Syst. Appl. **212**, 118590 (2023). https://doi.org/10.1016/j.eswa.2022.118590
3. Cox, D.R.: The regression analysis of binary sequences. J. Roy. Stat. Soc. Ser. B (Methodol.) **20**(2), 215–242 (1958)
4. Gibert, D., Mateu, C., Planes, J.: The rise of machine learning for detection and classification of malware: research developments, trends and challenges. J. Netw. Comput. Appl. **153**, 102526 (2020). https://doi.org/10.1016/j.jnca.2019.102526
5. Gomes, H.M., et al.: Adaptive random forests for evolving data stream classification. Mach. Learn. **106**, 1469–1495 (2017)
6. Guerra-Manzanares, A., Bahsi, H., Nõmm, S.: KronoDroid: time-based hybrid-featured dataset for effective android malware detection and characterization. Comput. Secur. **110**, 102399 (2021). https://doi.org/10.1016/j.cose.2021.102399
7. Guerra-Manzanares, A., Luckner, M., Bahsi, H.: Android malware concept drift using system calls: detection, characterization and challenges. Expert Syst. Appl. **206**, 117200 (2022). https://doi.org/10.1016/j.eswa.2022.117200
8. Jiang, W., Gao, H., Lu, W., Liu, W., Chung, F.L., Huang, H.: Stacked robust adaptively regularized auto-regressions for domain adaptation. IEEE Trans. Knowl. Data Eng. **31**(3), 561–574 (2019). https://doi.org/10.1109/TKDE.2018.2837085
9. Kan, Z., Pendlebury, F., Pierazzi, F., Cavallaro, L.: Investigating labelless drift adaptation for malware detection. In: Proceedings of the 14th ACM Workshop on Artificial Intelligence and Security, pp. 123–134. Association for Computing Machinery (2021). https://doi.org/10.1145/3474369.3486873
10. Kumar, S., Janet, B.: DTMIC: deep transfer learning for malware image classification. J. Inf. Secur. Appl. **64**, 103063 (2022). https://doi.org/10.1016/j.jisa.2021.103063
11. Li, H., Chen, Z., Spolaor, R., Yan, Q., Zhao, C., Yang, B.: DART: detecting unseen malware variants using adaptation regularization transfer learning. In: Proceedings of IEEE International Conference on Communications, pp. 1–6 (2019). https://doi.org/10.1109/ICC.2019.8761598
12. Liu, K., Xu, S., Xu, G., Zhang, M., Sun, D., Liu, H.: A review of android malware detection approaches based on machine learning. IEEE Access **8**, 124579–124607 (2020). https://doi.org/10.1109/ACCESS.2020.3006143
13. Lu, J., Liu, A., Dong, F., Gu, F., Gama, J., Zhang, G.: Learning under concept drift: a review. IEEE Trans. Knowl. Data Eng. **31**(12), 2346–2363 (2019). https://doi.org/10.1109/TKDE.2018.2876857
14. Matthews, B.: Comparison of the predicted and observed secondary structure of T4 phage lysozyme. Biochimica et Biophys. Acta (BBA) - Protein Struct. **405**(2), 442–451 (1975). https://doi.org/10.1016/0005-2795(75)90109-9
15. Montiel, J., et al.: River: machine learning for streaming data in Python (2021)
16. Pan, S.J., Yang, Q.: A survey on transfer learning. IEEE Trans. Knowl. Data Eng. **22**(10), 1345–1359 (2010). https://doi.org/10.1109/TKDE.2009.191

17. Sun, B., Feng, J., Saenko, K.: Return of frustratingly easy domain adaptation. In: Proceedings of the Thirtieth AAAI Conference on Artificial Intelligence, AAAI 2016, pp. 2058–2065. AAAI Press (2016)
18. Sun, B., Saenko, K.: Subspace distribution alignment for unsupervised domain adaptation. In: Xie, X., Jones, M.W., Tam, G.K.L. (eds.) Proceedings of the British Machine Vision Conference (BMVC), pp. 24.1–24.10, September 2015. https://doi.org/10.5244/C.29.24
19. Wei, P., Ke, Y., Goh, C.K.: Feature analysis of marginalized stacked denoising autoenconder for unsupervised domain adaptation. IEEE Trans. Neural Netw. Learn. Syst. **30**(5), 1321–1334 (2019). https://doi.org/10.1109/TNNLS.2018.2868709
20. Yosinski, J., Clune, J., Bengio, Y., Lipson, H.: How transferable are features in deep neural networks? In: Proceedings of 28th Annual Conference on Neural Information Processing Systems, vol. 4, pp. 3320–3328 (2014)

A New Training Algorithm for Support Vector Machines

Acélio Sousa(✉), Thiago Alves Rocha, and Ajalmar Rêgo da Rocha Neto

Instituto Federal do Ceará, IFCE, Fortaleza, Ceará, Brazil
acelio.sousa00@aluno.ifce.edu.br, {thiago.alves,ajalmar}@ifce.edu.br

Abstract. We propose a training algorithm for support vector machines based on their decision function, which is a kind of distance measure. We use such a measure to select the support vectors as well as set their Lagrange multiplier values. We compare our proposal with sequential minimal optimization (SMO) and classical quadratic optimization problem (QP) solver in terms of accuracy, precision, recall, and training time for several datasets. In general, the results are equivalent in accuracy; however, our proposal is faster than SMO and QP for all the considered datasets. Besides that, we highlight that our proposal can handle datasets with a large number of patterns in much less time when compared to SMO and classical QP solvers.

Keywords: Machine learning · support vector machines · classification · minimal sequential optimization · training algorithms

1 Introduction

Support Vector Machine (SVM) is a supervised machine learning method that has been applied to both classification and regression tasks. In classification tasks, the SVM training process finds an optimal hyperplane that separates patterns of two different classes. This optimal hyperplane is achieved by applying a training algorithm, in which the support vectors and the bias are found. Support vectors are those patterns that, after the training process, have non-zero Lagrange multipliers [3].

Training a Support Vector Machine involves solving a quadratic optimization problem, typically defined by a quadratic objective function with constraints. Alternative training algorithms include the chunking method [4], which utilizes projected conjugate gradient techniques, the Osuna method [10], and the well-known training method called Sequential Minimal Optimization (SMO) [12]. The problem with classical optimization methods to perform the training of support vector machines on large datasets lies in the fact that it involves dealing with a large square matrix[1] in the objective function of the quadratic optimization

[1] This matrix is square of size N, where N is the number of training patterns.

H. Quintián et al. (Eds.): HAIS 2024, LNAI 14857, pp. 190–201, 2025.
https://doi.org/10.1007/978-3-031-74183-8_16

problem to be solved [8]. While the chunking and Osuna methods try to mitigate this disadvantage by using smaller matrices, which may still be sufficiently large to make solving via classical quadratic optimization methods impractical. Alternative training methods use genetic algorithms [6] or simulated annealing [5]; however, in some methods, the optimization problem constraints are violated.

The SMO algorithm, however, reduces the quadratic programming problem into a series of smaller optimization problems that are solved analytically [12]. However, even with this advantage, it is still computationally slow to use SMO on very large datasets, as it may take a considerable amount of time/processing for the algorithm to converge to its stopping point. A more general way to deal with this type of problem involves, for example, the use of pattern selection techniques or vector quantization to reduce the size of the training set [2,9]. After this process, one way use methods like SMO or the other classics mentioned to carry out the training [12]. However, when applying a vector quantization technique, for example, the resulting dataset is considered a representation of the original dataset. Generally, this representation occurs with losses, and as such, its quality in representation depends on the capability of the applied method. In this context, it can be seen that it is still interesting to find methods that are efficient for dealing with large datasets.

The goal of this work is to present an algorithm for training support vector machines, which is efficient while still satisfying the constraints of the problem. The objective of this work is to present an algorithm for training support vector machines that is efficient and still satisfies the constraints of the QP problem. This is achieved by using the decision function to iteratively adjust the support vectors and their corresponding Lagrange multipliers. The decision function is employed to identify and update the support vectors dynamically during the training process, ensuring that the model meets optimization constraints at each step and provides a better performance in training time.

The remainder of this paper contains a general presentation on support vector machines in Sect. 2. Next, in Sect. 3, we present a description of the SMO algorithm and the classical QP method that will be used for comparison with our proposal. In Sect. 4, we present our proposed training algorithm, called d-SVM. Subsequently, the methodology and results obtained with the computational simulations are shown in Sect. 5. And finally, a conclusion and future work are presented in Sect. 6.

2 Support Vector Machines

Consider a training set $D = \{(\mathbf{x}_i, \mathbf{y_i})\}_{i=1}^{N}$ consisting of N training patterns, where each pattern $\mathbf{x}_i \in \mathbb{R}^d$ with d attributes is associated with a label $y_i \in \{-1, +1\}$ in a binary problem. In training support vector machines, the optimization problem aims to maximize the separation margin $\rho = \frac{c}{||\mathbf{w}||^2}$ between classes, with c as a constant, or equivalently, to minimize $||\mathbf{w}||^2$, where $\mathbf{w}$ represents the weight vector of the decision function.

$$f(\mathbf{x}) = \text{sign}\left(\mathbf{w}^T\mathbf{x} + b\right), \tag{1}$$

where

$$\text{sign}(u) = \begin{cases} +1, & \text{if } u \geq 0 \\ -1, & \text{if } u < 0 \end{cases} \tag{2}$$

and b is the bias [3].

The problem for soft-margin support vector machines is given by

$$\begin{aligned} \text{minimize} \quad & \frac{1}{2}\|\mathbf{w}\|^2 + C\sum_{i=1}^{N}\xi_i \\ \text{subject to} \quad & y_i(\mathbf{w}\cdot\mathbf{x}_i + b) \geq 1 - \xi_i, \quad \forall i = 1,\ldots,N, \\ & \xi_i \geq 0, \quad \forall i = 1,\ldots,N. \end{aligned} \tag{3}$$

where C is a regularization constant. A ξ_i is the i-th slack variable used to allow classification errors to occur.

The dual problem for soft-margin support vector machines is defined as:

$$\text{maximize} \left\{ \sum_{i=1}^{N}\alpha_i - \frac{1}{2}\sum_{i=1}^{N}\sum_{j=1}^{N}\alpha_i\alpha_j y_i y_j K(\mathbf{x}_i,\mathbf{x}_j) \right\} \tag{4}$$

$$\text{subject to} \qquad \sum_{i=1}^{N}\alpha_i y_i = 0 \tag{5}$$

$$0 \leq \alpha_i \leq C \tag{6}$$

In a linear SVM, the kernel function $K(\mathbf{x}_i,\mathbf{x}_j)$ is defined as $\mathbf{x}_i^T\mathbf{x}_j$. Each Lagrange multiplier α_i corresponds to the i-th training pattern $\mathbf{x}_i$ [1]. The optimality conditions for the dual problem are as follows:

$$\mathbf{w} = \sum_{i=1}^{N}\alpha_i\mathbf{x}_i \tag{7}$$

and

$$\sum_{i=1}^{N}\alpha_i y_i = 0. \tag{8}$$

Based on Eq. (7), the decision function presented in Eq. (1) for SVMs can be shown as follows.

$$f(\mathbf{x}) = \text{sign}\left(g(\mathbf{x})\right) \tag{9}$$

where

$$g(\mathbf{x}) = \sum_{i=1}^{N} y_i\alpha_i K(\mathbf{x}_i,\mathbf{x}) + b. \tag{10}$$

where $\mathbf{x}$ is the pattern to be classified, $\mathbf{x}_i$ is the i-th training pattern; while $K(\mathbf{x}_i,\mathbf{x}) = \mathbf{x}_i^T\mathbf{x}$ for a linear SVM. Another interesting point to highlight is that:

$$d(\mathbf{x}_i) = \frac{|g(\mathbf{x}_i)|}{||\mathbf{w}||} \tag{11}$$

represents the distance from any pattern $\mathbf{x}_i$ to the optimal hyperplane $\mathbf{w}$. Thus, $|g(\mathbf{x}_i)|$ can also be considered a type of distance measure, since the value of $||\mathbf{w}||$ is the same for every training pattern [13].

2.1 Solving a QP Problem

In the literature, there are various solvers with implementations of classical methods for solving Quadratic Programming problems. Among these, software packages from languages as Python, Matlab, Scilab, and Octave stand out. In these classical methods, the optimization problem described in Eq. (4) is used in its matrix form as follows

$$\begin{aligned} \min_{\alpha} \quad & L(\boldsymbol{\alpha}) = \frac{1}{2}\boldsymbol{\alpha}^T Q \boldsymbol{\alpha} - \boldsymbol{\alpha}^T \mathbf{1} \\ \text{s.t.} \quad & \boldsymbol{\alpha}^T \mathbf{y} = 0 \\ & 0 \leq \boldsymbol{\alpha}_i \leq C \quad \forall i = 1, \ldots, n \end{aligned} \tag{12}$$

where Q is an $N \times N$ matrix, with its elements described by $q_{i,j} = y_i y_j K(\mathbf{x}_i, \mathbf{x}_j)$ such that $i, j = 1, \ldots, N$. Generally, the matrix Q is dense and semi-positive definite, and if the value of N is high, this matrix can be too large to be stored [7]. Therefore, an iterative algorithm such as SMO can be useful, as it does not require a large amount of memory.

3 Sequential Minimal Optimization (SMO) Algorithm

The Sequential Minimal Optimization (SMO) algorithm, proposed by [11], iteratively optimizes a pair of randomly chosen Lagrange multipliers. In the work [11], there is a rearrangement of Eq. (4) that describes the dual optimization problem in such a way as to separate the pair of Lagrange multipliers to be optimized, thus obtaining an analytical solution for adjusting these multipliers. More details about the SMO algorithm can be found in [12]. The selection of the pair of Lagrange multipliers can be random as initially proposed by [11] or alternatively can be made based on heuristics aimed at maximizing the progress toward an optimal solution [5].

4 Proposal: *d*-SVM

In this section, a new training algorithm for support vector machines is proposed. The support vector machines trained with our algorithm are henceforth referred to as *d*-SVM, as our proposal is based on computing the decision function prior to applying the sign function. More specifically, our proposal is based on computing the function $g(\mathbf{x})$ described in Eq. (10), which can be interpreted as a type of distance measure when considering $|g(\mathbf{x})|$. A pattern that is exactly on the separation hyperplane has a $g(\mathbf{x})$ value of 0, when the pattern is on the side of the positive class $g(\mathbf{x}) > 0$ and, obviously, when it is on the side of the negative class $g(\mathbf{x}) < 0$. The farther from the optimal hyperplane, the higher the value of $|g(\mathbf{x})|$. The idea of the proposal lies in the use of the function $g(\mathbf{x})$ to adjust the Lagrange multipliers. However, for such an adjustment to be performed adequately, an approximate estimate of the function $g(\mathbf{x})$ is required, which in our proposal is obtained based on initial random values for the multipliers[2]. Subsequently, adjustment functions for the Lagrange multipliers are proposed based on the function $g(\mathbf{x})$. The details of our proposal are shown below, and at the end of this section, we present our algorithm.

4.1 Adjustment of the Lagrange Multipliers

In our proposal, all Lagrange multipliers are initially started randomly between 0 and C, following a uniform distribution $U(0, C)$. Satisfying KKT, analyzing the decision function, it is verified that the output/class is defined based on the weighted average[3] of the vectors support for each class. To make this more evident, consider that from the label $y_i \in \{-1, +1\}$, we have

$$g(\mathbf{x}) = \left[\sum_{i \in SV^+} \alpha_i \mathbf{x}_i^T - \sum_{j \in SV^-} \alpha_j \mathbf{x}_j^T\right] \mathbf{x} + b. \tag{13}$$

The above equation can also be seen in terms of direct weighted average values as follows

$$g(\mathbf{x}) = \left[\mu_i^T - \mu_j^T\right] \mathbf{x} + b \tag{14}$$

where SV^+ and SV^- denote the sets of indices of support vector for the positive and negative classes, respectively. The averages $\mu_i^T = \sum_{i \in SV^+} \alpha_i \mathbf{x}_i^T$ and $\mu_j^T = \sum_{j \in SV^-} \alpha_j \mathbf{x}_j^T$ are the weighted averages of the positive and negative classes, respectively. And, based on this weighted average, it is verified which of the two averages (μ_i or μ_j) the pattern $\mathbf{x}$ is more similar to (i.e., when it has the highest value).

4.2 Rule for Adjusting the Lagrange Multipliers

The adjustment rule for the Lagrange multipliers, in our proposal, accounts for the patterns both furthest from and closest to the optimal hyperplane for each class. Specifically, for the positive class ($y_i = +1$ and $i \in SV^+$), we define:

$$g_{\min}^+ = g(\mathbf{x}_{i_{\min}^+}), \quad i_{\min}^+ = \arg\min\{g(\mathbf{x}_i) | i \in SV^+\} \tag{15}$$

$$g_{\max}^+ = g(\mathbf{x}_{i_{\max}^+}), \quad i_{\max}^+ = \arg\max\{g(\mathbf{x}_i) | i \in SV^+\} \tag{16}$$

[2] A constant value can also be used initially, for example, equal to C.

[3] Weighted by the values of the non-zero Lagrange multipliers associated with each of the training patterns.

These indices $i^+_{\min}$ and $i^+_{\max}$ represent the indices of the patterns that are closest and furthest from the optimal hyperplane, respectively. Based on these values $g^-_{\min}$, $g^-_{\max}$, $g^+_{\min}$, and $g^+_{\max}$, computations are used to indicate the relative position of any training pattern in relation to its farthest and nearest peers. For this, the following expressions for the relative positions of patterns of the positive class are used The relative positions r_i for the positive class and r_j for the negative class are given by:

$$r_i = \frac{g(\mathbf{x_i}) - g^+_{\min}}{g^+_{\max} - g^+_{\min}}, \tag{17}$$

$$r_j = \frac{g^-_{\max} - g(\mathbf{x_i})}{g^-_{\max} - g^-_{\min}}, \tag{18}$$

where the values of r_i and r_j are constrained within the range $[0, 1]$. Specifically, r^* equals 0 when the pattern is closest to the optimal hyperplane, and 1 when it is the furthest. With the values of r_i and r_j, the following rules for updating the Lagrange multipliers of the positive and negative classes are applied, respectively:

$$\alpha_i = r_i \cdot 0.1C + (1 - r_i) \cdot C \tag{19}$$

$$\alpha_j = r_j \cdot 0.1C + (1 - r_j) \cdot C \tag{20}$$

After the update, the values of α_i and α_j are in the range $[0.1C, C]$, i.e., the closest patterns have values in this range and the remaining values are set to zero. Assigning a zero value to the other patterns aims to maintain sparsity in the vector of Lagrange multipliers.

Intercept Calculation b: Finally, the intercept b of the SVM is calculated based on the support vectors that strictly lie within the margin (i.e., those for which support $\mathrm{S} = \{i \mid 0 < \alpha_i < C\}$). If such support vectors exist:

$$\mathrm{b} = \frac{1}{|\mathcal{S}|} \sum_{i \in \mathcal{S}} (y_i - g(\mathbf{x_i})) \tag{21}$$

This step calculates the average offset needed to align the predictions with the actual class labels, centering the decision boundary.

4.3 Part Two of Adjustment

In the continuation of our proposed d-SVM algorithm, we refine the adjustment of the Lagrange multipliers (α) using the calculated distances and class centers. This part of the adjustment process is crucial for effectively tailoring the support vector machine to better discriminate between the classes. **Calculation of Weighted Class Centers:** Initially, we calculate the centers of the classes weighted by the corresponding α values. This is done separately for the positive and negative classes using the formula:

$$\mathbf{x}_{\text{pos}} = \frac{\sum_{i:y_i>0} \alpha_i \mathbf{x_i}}{\sum_{i:y_i>0} \alpha_i} \tag{22}$$

$$\mathbf{x}_{\text{neg}} = \frac{\sum_{i:y_i<0} \alpha_i \mathbf{x_i}}{\sum_{i:y_i<0} \alpha_i} \tag{23}$$

These centers represent the "average" position of each class in the feature space, weighted by the influence of each pattern as dictated by its α value. We then compute the real-valued predictions d_{pos} and d_{neg} at these centers using the function predict_real, which evaluates the decision function without applying the sign threshold:

$$d_{\text{pos}} = g(\mathbf{x}_{\text{pos}}), d_{\text{neg}} = g(\mathbf{x}_{\text{neg}}) \tag{24}$$

Final Update α: Next, we identify the indices where adjustments to α are necessary based on their deviation from these central values:

$$\text{ind1} = \{i \mid y_i > 0, g(\mathbf{x_i}) < d_{\text{pos}}\}, \tag{25}$$

$$\text{ind2} = \{i \mid y_i < 0, g(\mathbf{x_i}) > d_{\text{neg}}\} \tag{26}$$

For these identified indices, α values are set to zero to enforce the margin constraints more strictly and enhance model sparsity:

$$\alpha_i = 0, \quad \forall i \in \text{ind1} \cup \text{ind2} \tag{27}$$

After this update, the Lagrange multiplier is adjusted again based on KKT.

Algorithm 1 d-SVM

```
Computation of new values of α:
g(x) ← predict_real(X)
Calculate minimum g⁺_min and maximum g⁺_max g(x) for y = 1
Calculate minimum g⁻_min and maximum g⁻_max g(x) for y = −1
Normalize g(x) in each class and readjust α:
if (y = +1) then
    r_i ← (g(x) − g⁺_min) / (g⁺_max − g⁺_min)
    α_i ← r_i · C/10 + (1 − r_i) · C
else
    r_j ← (g⁻_max − g(x)) / (g⁻_max − g⁻_min)
    α_j ← r_j · C/10 + (1 − r_j) · C

Calculate x_pos and x_neg using α_i for positive and negative classes respectively
d_pos ← g(x_pos)
d_neg ← g(x_neg)
ind1 ← {i | y_i > 0 ∧ g(x_i) < d_pos}
ind2 ← {i | y_i < 0 ∧ g(x_i) > d_neg}
α ← adjust_alphas_wKKT(α, y)

Intercept Calculation b:
Find supports where 0 < α < C
if support vectors exist then
    gx ← g(X[support])
    b ← average(y[support] − gx)
```

5 Computer Simulations

The proposed d-SVM training algorithm, along with the SMO and SVMQP algorithms, all implemented in Python, were compared using various datasets detailed in Table 1. The hyperparameters used in the training process for these algorithms varied across several ranges: the regularization parameter C was tested at values [0.1, 1, 10], the polynomial degree at [1, 2, 3], the gamma parameter at [0.1, 1, 10], and the types of kernels used were radial basis function (rbf) and polynomial.

Table 1. Data sets used in computational simulations.

Dataset	Abbrev	Patterns	Attributes	Data Source
Breast Cancer Wisconsin	BCW	569	30	UCI ML Repo.
Heart Disease	HEA	303	76	UCI ML Repo.
Iris Flower	IFD	150	4	UCI ML Repo.
Pima Indians Diabetes	PID	768	8	Kaggle
Sonar	SON	208	60	UCI ML Repo.
Vertebral Column Pat	VCP	310	6	UCI ML Repo.
Wine	WIN	178	13	UCI ML Repo.
Artificial	ART	20,000	2	Generated
Twitter	TWI	49,999	78	Twitter API

In each of 10 trials, datasets were split into 70% for training and 30% for testing. During training, a grid search with 5-fold cross-validation was used to optimize the kernel hyperparameters and the regularization term C. The models, trained using the complete training set, were evaluated on the test set with linear, polynomial, and RBF kernels. The performance of the support vector machines using these kernels for the d-SVM, SMO, and SVMQP methods is detailed in Tables 2, 3, and 4, showing accuracy, precision, recall, and training time. Analyzing the linear *kernel* in Table2, d-SVM matches SMO in accuracy on the VCP, SONAR, and IFD datasets, and performs better on the HEA and ART datasets. SMO leads on the BCW, PID, and WIN datasets. Compared to SVMQP, d-SVM is either superior or equivalent in accuracy, more efficient, and faster in training. Notably, SMO couldn't train the Twitter dataset within two weeks.

For the polynomial *kernel* (Table 3), d-SVM generally outperforms or equals SMO and SVMQP, especially on the SONAR dataset. Both SMO and SVMQP were unable to train the Twitter dataset within the allotted two weeks.

Table 2. Results for d-SVM, SMO and SVMQP with linear *kernel*.

Method	Accuracy	Precision	Recall	Time
BCW				
d-SVM	95.5 ± 1.6	96.8 ± 1.6	95.9 ± 1.9	2.4 ± 1.3
SMO	97.2 ± 1.0	97.0 ± 1.1	98.5 ± 1.0	303.4 ± 185.9
SVMQP	90.0 ± 2.9	91.1 ± 2.8	90.0 ± 2.9	840.7 ± 436.0
VCP				
d-SVM	76.2 ± 3.3	88.8 ± 4.5	75.3 ± 6.8	5.3 ± 2.9
SMO	76.3 ± 3.2	88.9 ± 4.3	75.3 ± 6.8	164.8 ± 90.8
SVMQP	71.5 ± 3.0	97.4 ± 2.1	59.2 ± 4.2	284.4 ± 153.9
PID				
d-SVM	74.1 ± 2.4	86.7 ± 1.8	70.8 ± 3.4	3.3 ± 1.7
SMO	77.2 ± 1.9	78.3 ± 1.8	89.4 ± 2.0	196.1 ± 108.6
SVMQP	74.2 ± 2.2	86.7 ± 16.7	71.3 ± 3.0	3192.4 ± 1880.2
HEA				
d-SVM	91.3 ± 1.8	86.9 ± 2.1	97.9 ± 2.2	3.4 ± 1.3
SMO	83.0 ± 1.3	79.7 ± 2.7	90.1 ± 3.8	360.1 ± 192.4
SVMQP	82.5 ± 1.7	78.4 ± 18.6	91.03 ± 2.7	8452.9 ± 891.7
SONAR				
d-SVM	74.1 ± 4.2	71.0 ± 4.6	76.9 ± 7.6	1.2 ± 0.4
SMO	75.2 ± 5.7	74.1 ± 8.8	73.1 ± 8.2	61.9 ± 33.8
SVMQP	76.1 ± 6.5	72.5 ± 8.5	79.6 ± 59.6	218.3 ± 114.7
WIN				
d-SVM	96.4 ± 1.8	96.6 ± 1.7	96.4 ± 1.8	1.3 ± 0.7
SMO	99.4 ± 0.89	100.0 ± 0.0	99.1 ± 1.34	11.0 ± 31.7
SVMQP	94.4 ± 2.1	88.8 ± 4.2	99.0 ± 1.91	62.3 ± 39.8
IFD				
d-SVM	100.0 ± 0.0	100.0 ± 0.0	100.0 ± 0.0	2.0 ± 1.0
SMO	100.0 ± 0.0	100.0 ± 0.0	100.0 ± 0.0	21.2 ± 10.8
SVMQP	99.0 ± 1.8	96.3 ± 5.0	100.0 ± 0.0	57.6 ± 12.7
ART				
d-SVM	99.7 ± 0.04	99.8 ± 0.06	99.7 ± 0.08	9.1 ± 2.3
SMO	99.0 ± 0.012	99.1 ± 0.011	98.9 ± 2.7	4889.2 ± 2705
SVMQP	98.8 ± 0.2	98.9 ± 0.2	98.9 ± 2.3	6417.1 ± 3133.8
TWI				
d-SVM	91.6 ± 0.1	98.3 ± 9.6	74.0 ± 0.4	505.1 ± 32.3
SMO	-	-	-	-
SVMQP	-	-	-	-

Table 3. Results for d-SVM, SMO and SVMQP with polynomial *kernel*.

Method	Accuracy	Precision	Recall	Time (s)
BCW				
d-SVM	95.7 ± 1.3	95.9 ± 1.8	96.6 ± 1.1	1.2 ± 1.0
SMO	96.7 ± 1.2	96.1 ± 2.2	98.7 ± 1.0	181.8 ± 60.2
SVMQP	97.0 ± 1.2	97.8 ± 1.3	97.3 ± 2.1	2956.9 ± 1911.9
VCP				
d-SVM	76.4 ± 2.3	87.8 ± 4.4	75.3 ± 6.7	5.3 ± 2.9
SMO	76.3 ± 3.2	88.9 ± 4.3	75.3 ± 6.8	164.9 ± 90.9
SVMQP	75.2 ± 2.9	88.7 ± 3.9	75.3 ± 6.8	616.4 ± 341.8
PID				
d-SVM	75.4 ± 1.8	86.5 ± 5.9	64.5 ± 4.5	3.6 ± 2.2
SMO	76.2 ± 2.4	73.4 ± 7.8	52.3 ± 4.6	402.2 ± 131.7
SVMQP	79.8 ± 3.4	83.4 ± 4.5	88.4 ± 2.1	1385.0 ± 717.7
HEA				
d-SVM	84.7 ± 2.1	80.8 ± 3.4	91.8 ± 1.5	8.2 ± 3.8
SMO	97.5 ± 1.0	97.4 ± 1.8	97.8 ± 1.2	1148.5 ± 219.9
SVMQP	97.9 ± 0.02	98.8 ± 0.02	97.9 ± 2.3	9417.1 ± 5133.8
SONAR				
d-SVM	85.5 ± 2.7	86.1 ± 4.3	80.3 ± 7.0	2.5 ± 0.9
SMO	76.5 ± 3.8	96.3 ± 4.8	51.0 ± 8.4	895.7 ± 606.0
SVMQP	76.1 ± 6.5	72.5 ± 8.5	79.6 ± 5.9	1132.9 ± 541.6
WIN				
d-SVM	96.6 ± 2.2	97.6 ± 2.4	94.0 ± 3.7	1.3 ± 0.6
SMO	96.7 ± 2.8	98.4 ± 2.5	92.6 ± 6.3	26.1 ± 14.4
SVMQP	94.4 ± 2.1	88.8 ± 4.2	99.0 ± 1.9	221.0 ± 122.7
IFD				
d-SVM	100.0 ± 0.0	100.0 ± 0.0	100.0 ± 0.0	1.0 ± 0.2
SMO	100.0 ± 0.0	100.0 ± 0.0	100.0 ± 0.0	37.2 ± 11.9
SVMQP	98.8 ± 1.8	97.0 ± 5.0	100.0 ± 0.0	357.7 ± 21.2
ART				
d-SVM	99.8 ± 0.04	99.8 ± 0.06	99.7 ± 0.08	18.0 ± 10.3
SMO	98.2 ± 0.3	98.2 ± 1.2	99.3 ± 0.7	54358.3 ± 28362.6
SVMQP	98.8 ± 1.8	97.0 ± 5.0	100.0 ± 0.0	64417.0 ± 22313.8
TWI				
d-SVM	90.4 ± 4.2	83.4 ± 9.6	93.4 ± 2.3	7554.9 ± 554.9
SMO	-	-	-	-
SVMQP	-	-	-	-

Table 4. Results for *d*-SVM, SMO and SVMQP with *kernel* rbf.

Method	Accuracy	Precision	Recall	Time
BCW				
d-SVM	96.4 ± 1.25	96.1 ± 1.3	96.6 ± 1.2	3.83 ± 1.06
SMO	95.8 ± 0.8	97.6 ± 1.2	95.7 ± 1.7	1036.3 ± 144.3
SVMQP	97.0 ± 1.25	97.8 ± 1.3	97.4 ± 3	2262.2 ± 1215.8
VCP				
d-SVM	80.0 ± 5.0	85.0 ± 4.0	80.0 ± 5.0	2.0 ± 1.0
SMO	85.1 ± 2.6	90.1 ± 2.9	88.1 ± 3.8	239.8 ± 62.7
SVMQP	83.1 ± 1.7	85.5 ± 2.4	91.1 ± 2.9	1000.1 ± 523.1
PID				
d-SVM	72.3 ± 2.20	82.5 ± 2.2	72.8 ± 3.3	3.9 ± 1.27
SMO	76.7 ± 2.2	71.2 ± 6.1	56.5 ± 6.9	925.5 ± 201.5
SVMQP	70.0 ± 2.9	69.8 ± 2.7	70.0 ± 2.9	8514.6 ± 4614.6
HEA				
d-SVM	97.9 ± 0.0	97.1 ± 0.1	97.0 ± 0.0	7.5 ± 0.01
SMO	97.6 ± 1.1	97.7 ± 1.8	98.5 ± 1.3	1563.2 ± 335.4
SVMQP	89.0 ± 12.4	88.3 ± 12.5	88.1 ± 12.4	18452.9 ± 9921.7
SONAR				
d-SVM	86.5 ± 1.5	86.1 ± 3.9	80.1 ± 6.9	2.0 ± 0.97
SMO	76.5 ± 3.8	96.3 ± 4.8	51.0 ± 8.4	1132.9 ± 606.0
SVMQP	76.8 ± 6.2	77.7 ± 6.4	76.8 ± 62.2	5300.0 ± 2920.0
WIN				
d-SVM	99.4 ± 0.8	1.0 ± 0.0	99.1 ± 1.4	8.4 ± 4.3
SMO	99.6 ± 0.7	99.4 ± 0.0	1.0 ± 0.0	23.3 ± 13.0
SVMQP	86.2 ± 0.4	87.6 ± 4.5	86.2 ± 5.4	223.0 ± 137.1
IFD				
d-SVM	100.0 ± 0.0	100.0 ± 0.0	100.0 ± 0.0	2.9 ± 1.5
SMO	100.0 ± 0.0	100.0 ± 0.0	100.0 ± 0.0	46.8 ± 29.2
SVMQP	100.0 ± 0.0	100.0 ± 0.0	100.0 ± 0.0	357.6 ± 110.8
ART				
d-SVM	99.8 ± 0.4	99.8 ± 0.6	99.8 ± 0.6	4361.0 ± 5.4
SMO	-	-	-	-
SVMQP	-	-	-	-
TWI				
d-SVM	91.7 ± 4.5	89.3 ± 9.7	92.4 ± 3.6	9434.8 ± 553.2
SMO	-	-	-	-
SVMQP	-	-	-	-

With the RBF *kernel* (Table 4), *d*-SVM shows superior or similar performance compared to SMO and SVMQP, achieving higher accuracy on the SONAR, HEA, and WIN datasets. Training the ART and Twitter datasets took over two weeks for both SMO and SVMQP without success. *d*-SVM offers significant efficiency and quicker training times as detailed in Tables 2 and 3.

6 Conclusion

In this work, a training algorithm for support vector machines was proposed, which is efficient from a computational point of view in terms of model training time. In two cases with a large number of ART and TWI standards, for example, it is presented among the training methods evaluated as the only viable option for training models for support vector machines. Therefore, also based on the accuracy obtained, our proposal proves to be an interesting alternative for training support vector machines.

References

1. Boser, B.E., Guyon, I.M., Vapnik, V.N.: A training algorithm for optimal margin classifiers. In: Proceedings of the Fifth Annual Workshop on Computational Learning Theory, pp. 144–152 (1992)
2. Chen, G., Cheng, Y., Xu, J.: Cluster reduction support vector machine for large-scale data set classification. In: 2008 IEEE Pacific-Asia Workshop on Computational Intelligence and Industrial Application, vol. 1, pp. 8–12. IEEE (2008)
3. Cortes, C., Vapnik, V.: Support-vector networks. Mach. Learn. **20**, 273–297 (1995)
4. Cristianini, N., Shawe-Taylor, J.: Support Vector Machines. Cambridge University Press (2000)
5. Dias, M.L.D., Rocha Neto, A.R.: Training soft margin support vector machines by simulated annealing: a dual approach. Expert Syst. Appl. **87**, 157–169 (2017)
6. Ji, W., Liu, D., Meng, Y., Xue, Y.: A review of genetic-based evolutionary algorithms in SVM parameters optimization. Evol. Intel. **14**, 1389–1414 (2021)
7. Kaufman, L.: Solving the quadratic programming problem arising in support vector classification. In: Advances in Kernel Methods, pp. 147–167. MIT Press, Cambridge, MA, USA (1999)
8. Li, B., Wang, Q., Hu, J.: A fast SVM training method for very large datasets. In: 2009 International Joint Conference on Neural Networks, pp. 1784–1789. IEEE (2009)
9. Nalepa, J., Kawulok, M.: Selecting training sets for support vector machines: a review. Artif. Intell. Rev. **52**(2), 857–900 (2019)
10. Osuna, E., Freund, R., Girosi, F.: Decomposition algorithms for training support vector machines. In: IEEE Neural Networks Council Workshop on Support Vector Machines. IEEE (1997)
11. Platt, J.: Sequential minimal optimization: a fast algorithm for training support vector machines. In: Advances in Kernel Methods (1998)
12. Platt, J.C.: Fast Training of Support Vector Machines Using Sequential Minimal Optimization, chap. 12. MIT Press, Cambridge, MA, USA (1998)
13. Rocha Neto, A.: SINPATCO II: Novas Estratégias de Aprendizado de Máquinas para Classificação de Patologias da Coluna Vertebral. Ph.D. thesis, Universidade Federal do Ceará (2011)

Soft Adaptive Segments for Bio-Inspired Temporal Memory

Artem Prokhorenko[1], Evgenii Dzhivelikian[1(✉)], Petr Kuderov[1,2], and Aleksandr Panov[1,2,3]

[1] Moscow Institute of Physics and Technology, Dolgoprudny, Russia
dzhivelikian.ea@phystech.edu
[2] Artificial Intelligence Research Institute, Moscow, Russia
[3] Federal Research Center "Computer Science and Control" of the Russian Academy of Sciences, Moscow, Russia

Abstract. World models for online learning in complex environments are increasingly essential, particularly in partially observable scenarios. Within this domain, biologically inspired models of temporal memory have emerged as a promising class of models. These models extend traditional artificial neural networks by incorporating the idea of dendritic segments into point neurons and leveraging the structural insights from neocortical layers to facilitate efficient online sequence learning. This paper introduces an innovative segment-growing strategy for enhancing the Distributed Hebbian Temporal Memory (DHTM) algorithm. The proposed modifications aim to boost the model's generalization capabilities and introduce a more efficient segment growth approach based on real-time training statistics. Our findings demonstrate that this novel strategy not only reduces the number of segments used, thereby enhancing the model's computational efficiency, but also enhances its predictive accuracy in challenging, noisy environments.

Keywords: temporal memory · bio-inspired learning · online learning

1 Introduction

Temporal Memory (TM) algorithms play a key role in natural language processing, time-series analysis, world models and others [6,22,24]. The idea behind TM is to form a compressed representation of the input and subsequently transform this representation over time to predict future data.

Most known TM algorithms, such as Recurrent Neural Network (RNN) [28] and Hidden Markov Model (HMM) [16], have drawbacks. Loss of long-term dependencies, overfitting, and vanishing gradients are inherent in models with backpropagation learning [5]. Also, there are limitations to Baum-Welch [26] training for models such as HMM, which can lead to slow convergence and difficulties in finding the global maximum [9]. In addition, most traditional memory models do not support online learning, which is very important for tasks where

H. Quintián et al. (Eds.): HAIS 2024, LNAI 14857, pp. 202–213, 2025.
https://doi.org/10.1007/978-3-031-74183-8_17

data is constantly changing or where immediate, test time adaptation to new information is required.

There is an increasing necessity for architectures capable of online sequence learning in partially observable environments, which, as a consequence, should not rely on backpropagation or other learning algorithms that require huge sample buffers. Neurophysiological temporal memory models, such as Hierarchical Temporal Memory (HTM) [17] may serve as a basis for such architecture as they rely only on local learning rules, which are more biologically plausible than backpropagation [4]. HTM framework has already shown to be a prolific source of inspiration for anomaly detection [1,2,31] algorithms, hierarchical agent architectures [15], efficient sparse artificial neural networks [20], and networks able to mitigate catastrophic forgetting [21].

Distributed Hebbian Temporal Memory (DHTM) [13] represents a promising approach of bringing ideas of HTM framework into Hidden Markov Models (HMM) representing a hybrid sequence learning algorithm. DHTM maps the idea of Sparse Distributed Representations to categorical state hidden state variables, neuronal dendritic segments to components of transition matrix for partially coupled HMMs [19] and cortical columns to the emission probability function, similarly to CSCG [18]. DHTM demonstrates the capabilities of learning under highly non-stationary conditions and diminishes the limitations associated with the Baum-Welch classical learning algorithm for HMM, including its low computational and sample efficiency. One of the main drawbacks of the DHTM model is the excessive growth of dendritic segments in noisy environments, which impairs its computational efficiency and predictive quality due to a lack of generalization capabilities. Therefore, we introduce another approach for growing new segments, further incorporating ideas from HTM framework. It will be demonstrated that our proposed method for restricting the formation of segments in the DHTM model can reduce the number of grown segments and improve the model's quality in noisy environments.

2 Related Works

Temporal memory models based on the concept of dendritic segments can be primarily found in the framework of Hierarchical Temporal Memory [17]. The HTM model is based on the structure and function of the neocortex and mimics the functioning of the brain through the use of dendritic segments. Dendritic segment with clustered synapses can trigger NMDA spikes, contributing to the prediction of patterns and sequences. This mechanism allows HTM to continually learn from data streams, mimicking some aspects of human memory and cognition.

There are also many developments in HTM ideas. Extensions to the HTM architecture may involve the addition of Gated Recurrent Unit (GRU) [30] neurons. This made it possible to improve the performance of the model with long-term dependencies for time series analysis [25]. In an unsupervised approach, you can combine Extreme Learning Machine [11] and HTM in one model [29].

HTM may also be used for model-based reinforcement learning algorithms [15]. The Distributed Hebbian Temporal Memory [14] is inherited from HTM and connects it to HMM-like models employing a probabilistic segment model.

Another temporal memory capable for online learning is an ecosystem with cognitive models such as Echo State Networks (ESN) [32] and Liquid State Machines (LSM) [34]. ESN and LSM use a reservoir computing approach, where neurons inside a reservoir process inputs and produce complex nonlinear responses. This approach allows models to adapt to changes in input data and learn online.

Many graph models are based on the belief propagation (BP) algorithm [33]. There are many adaptations of the belief propagation ideas in order to improve the quality of models. For example, integrates BP with GRU [7] and Graph Attention Networks [30], which allowing for efficient online learning and addressing issues with static damping factors [10]. Also, the performance of BP can be improved by removing edges [23].

3 Background

3.1 Belief Propagation and Factorial HMM

Our contribution is a new message passing and graphical model learning algorithm based on belief propagation. The belief propagation algorithm is a message-passing mechanism for inference in graphical models. It is often used in probabilistic models to compute marginals and most likely assignments.

To compute marginal probabilities, a node X_i in a graph sends a message to a node X_j along the edge (i, j) using the following equation:

$$m_{i \to j}(x_j) = \sum_{x_i} \psi_{ij}(x_i, x_j) \prod_{k \neq j} m_{k \to i}(x_i), \tag{1}$$

where $\psi_{ij}(x_i, x_j)$—function representing the relationship between nodes X_i and X_j, and $m_{k \to i}(x_i)$—message from node X_k to X_i. Iterations continue until convergence [33].

The graphical structure learned by the proposed method belongs to the class of Factorial Hidden Markov Models, which extends the concept of HMM by allowing multiple hidden states variables to operate concurrently. The transition probabilities between hidden states in Factorial HMM are the following:

$$P(H_{t+1}|H_t) = \prod_{i=1}^{N} A_i(H_{t,i}, H_{t+1,i}), \tag{2}$$

where N is the number of hidden state variables, and $A_i(H_{t,i}, H_{t+1,i})$ is the transition matrix for each of the hidden variables. The more general formulation of the Factorial HMM also allows dependencies between different hidden variables [19].

The DHTM model is inspired by these approaches and provides powerful means for probabilistic modelling of sequential data.

3.2 Distributed Hebbian Temporal Memory

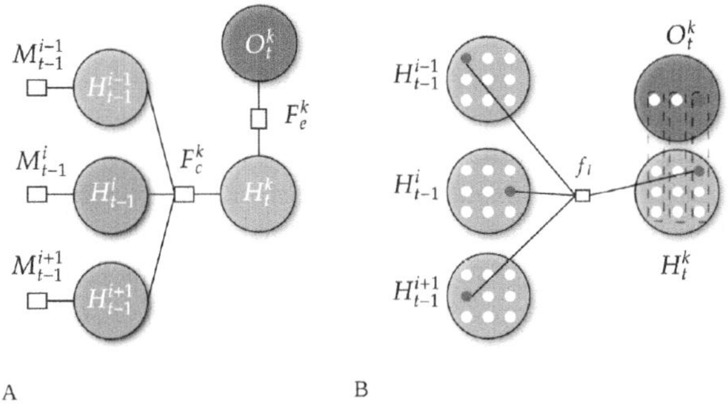

Fig. 1. A. Factor graph of the generative model DHTM learns. B. Internal structure of variables and factors. Each segment corresponds to a context factor value f_l for a combination of states (red circles). Emission factor is fixed that each observation state corresponds to a group of hidden states (column) which could be activated with equal probability, given the observation state active. (Color figure online)

Here, we briefly describe the Distributed Hebbian Temporal Memory algorithm, an extension of which is the subject of our contribution. For more details, see [14].

DHTM implements learning and inference in a factor graph shown in Fig. 1-A for one observation variable. All random variables are categorical. The generative model DHTM may consist of several observation variables, O_t^k, processed in parallel, where t—the current time-step and k—the variable's number. Each hidden variable H_t^k forms an explanation model of the corresponding observation variable O_t^k and is considered independently of other hidden random variables for the current time step. The context factor F_c^k describes the dependency between a subset of previous time-step hidden variables and the current time-step k-th hidden variable H_t^k. Messages from previous time steps are represented by M_{t-1}^i factors. The emission factor F_e^k is fixed, and it sets the hidden variable posterior distribution update rule (Fig. 1-B).

One of the main features of DHTM is that it handles context factor functions as a set of computational units called segments, which are the counterparts of biological dendritic segments of pyramidal neurons. Each segment corresponds to a factor value for a combination of variable states that are arguments of the factor function. Given that only a small fraction of possible combinations are actually used in the model, this design step is analogous to that used for efficient processing of sparse matrices [12]. However, as will be shown in the following sections, not every combination needs a separate segment, that is, some of them may be grouped, further improving the computational efficiency of the algorithm.

4 Methods

In this section, we first outline some aspects of the DHTM algorithm as a setup for our contribution and then describe the method we developed to group factor values for different combinations of states.

Computations of the DHTM segment are depicted in Fig. 2-A. The segment can be viewed as a Bernoulli random variable, the activation probability P_l of which depends on the factor value—f_l, synapse efficiencies—w_u and presynaptic cells (variables' states) activation probabilities m_u. The presynaptic cells form the segment's receptive field, $rec(l)$, which corresponds to state combinations of previous time-step hidden variables. The computations take place during the belief-propagation stage and represent a modified version of the sum-product algorithm to approximately account for dependency between H^i_{t-1} variables, which is not considered by the model itself.

The number of segments in use is determined by the segment-growth stage, which follows the belief-propagation stage. The states of the variables are sampled, and the overlaps between active cells and segments' receptive fields are determined. If there are no segments to match the combination of states, a new one is initialized.

That is, in DHTM, a new segment is constructed for each new combination of sampled states. However, in noisy environments, this results in an excessively large number of segments, which are rarely used and even negatively impact the model's quality.

Usually, in this scenario, pruning is applied to remove noisy segments based on their activation frequency, which, however, may delete important dependencies and deteriorate TM's performance. Moreover, it involves setting hyperparameters, such as a limit on the maximum number of segments or a pruning ratio coefficient, which depend on the environment and cannot be predetermined. In our method, we aimed to develop a more precise method for increasing DHTM's noise tolerance by modifying segments' computation and growth.

4.1 Merging Segments

The central idea involves merging segments with substantially overlapping receptive fields. This is done by setting the overlap activation threshold for a segment during the segment-growth stage lower than the size of the receptive field. In other words, when encountering a new combination of states, we search for the segment with a similar receptive field first. However, this approach requires modifications to the belief-propagation stage, since in that case the segment can be activated in several ways.

The core concept is to sum segment activation probabilities over all possible combinations of states in the receptive field. Each such combination we call a subsegment. However, we leave out combinations that are bigger than the threshold (Fig. 2-B). We do it for several reasons: 1. The contribution to the sum is usually lower the more variables the product includes; 2. it significantly reduces the number of operations. In this case, the number of subsegment combinations

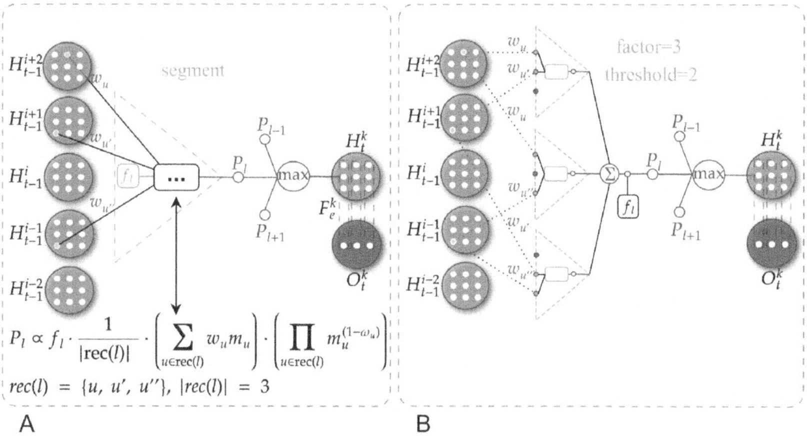

Fig. 2. A. Calculating segment activation probability using factor value f_l, to calculate effective cell excitation by segment l. B. Demonstration of accounting for combinations of subsegments, example for factor size = 3 and thresholds = 2.

taken into account is C^{trsh}_{factor} Then the equation for segment activation probability takes the following form:

$$P_l \propto f_l \cdot \sum_{\substack{\text{rec}^i(l) \\ |\text{rec}^i(l)|=\text{trsh}}} \left(\frac{1}{|\text{rec}^i(l)|} \cdot \sum_{u \in \text{rec}^i(l)} w_u m_u \right) \cdot \left(\prod_{u \in \text{rec}^i(l)} m_u^{(1-\omega_u)} \right) \tag{3}$$

where $\text{rec}^i(l)$ is a subset of cells in the receptive field corresponding to i-th subsegment, $|\text{rec}^i(l)|$ is the number of cells in the subset.

4.2 Adaptive Thresholding

As mentioned, the essence of segments is that they represent a mapping of combinations of variable states into factor values. The collection of segments forms a factor function. By setting an activation threshold lower than the factor size, we simply map all state combinations of a certain size found in the receptive field into one factor value, thereby reducing the number of parameters that define the factor function. This, however, may be too restrictive, and our experiments show that the quality of the model may be further improved if the threshold is adaptively adjusted for each segment.

The threshold at the stage of segment growth determines active segments. The higher the threshold, the fewer active segments there are; thus, the higher the possibility of a new segment, and vice versa.

The approach is based on the idea that the lower the factor value, the less useful the segment is since it is proportional to the frequency of the corresponding combination of states activation. It means that if we have all segments with low factor values, we would like to form a new segment, hoping that it will capture a better combination of states. Raising a segment's threshold inversely to its factor value does exactly that; it increases the probability that a new segment will be grown in the event that there are no high-factor-value segments activated. The initial value for new segments is set to maximum, and therefore the threshold is minimal. If, during the learning process, the factor value decreases, the threshold increases, lowering the segment activation probability.

5 Experiments

DHTM is designed for online learning of the generative model. This is especially useful for Reinforcement Learning model based algorithms, where the test time adaptation is crucial. Therefore, test sequences for our new segment algorithm were gathered in the RL environments, the same, which were used for DHTM testing: Pinball and AnimalAI.

Pinball is a 2D environment created with Godot [3] game engine (Fig. 3-A). It consists of a ball, a field surrounded by walls, and a circle zone in the center capable of deflecting the ball in random directions, introducing stochasticity into the environment. At the beginning of each episode, the ball gets an initial impulse and continues to freely move, interacting with the environment.

Another set of observations was obtained from AnimalAI environment [8] (Fig. 3-B), using a fixed policy. AnimalAI is a configurable 3D environment specially designed to implement various psychological tests for animals.

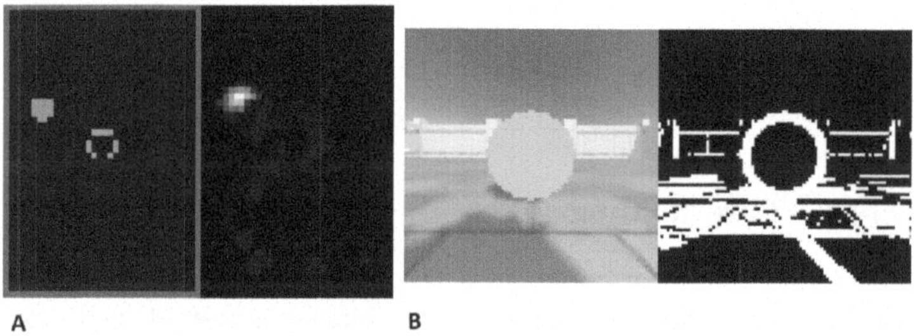

Fig. 3. Examples of raw outputs and its preprocessed version from (right) from A. the Pinball environment, B. AnimalAI

The raw output of each episode step in the environments is an RGB image, which is preprocessed in a way to model the output of a simple event-based camera To test the model's robustness, we also add Gaussian noise to the raw image. This noise introduces random variations, simulating real-world conditions where data might contain some level of inherent noise. The preprocessed image is further fed into the same Winner-Takes-All Hebbian encoder that was used in DHTM experiments. The output of the encoder is 5 and 6 categorical random variables in the Pinball and AnimalAI environments, respectively. Those variables are then fed into the temporal memory.

For each environment, we determined the optimal factor size and threshold to compare the quality of the new segment's computational model with the best old one. We used surprise, which is the negative log-likelihood of observations, and number of segments as the performance metrics [27]. Lower surprise levels and the number of segments correspond to a better and more efficient generative model.

We compared three parameter sets for different levels of noise:

(1) Optimally determined factor size and thresholds for original DHTM segments - red line
(2) Maximum factor size and reduced thresholds, i.e., testing the idea from Sect. 4.1 - blue line
(3) Maximum factor size, reduced threshold at the belief-propagation stage (Sect. 4.1), and adaptive threshold proposed in Sect. 4.2 for segment-growth stage - green curve

The results for the Pinball and AnimalAI environments are presented in Figs. 4 and 5 respectively.

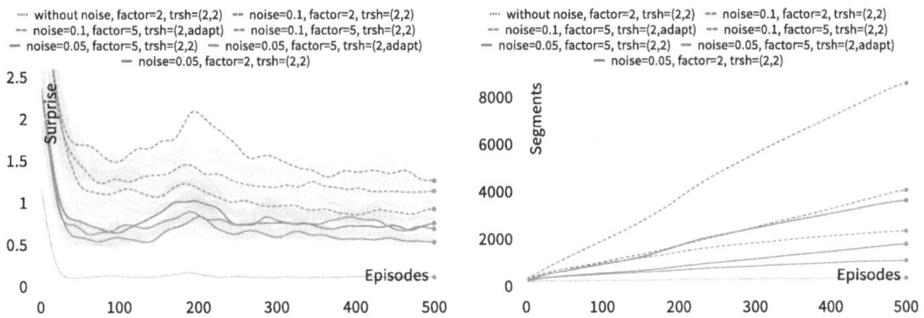

Fig. 4. Pinball environment. Different colors correspond to different variants of the factor size and thresholds: $factor = 2, trsh = (2, 2)$—optimal factor for the original version of DHTM; $factor = 5, trsh = (2, 2)$—fixed threshold (Sect. 4.1); $factor = 5, trsh = (2, adapt)$—adaptive threshold (Sect. 4.2). Differences in line style responsible for noise levels, according to legend

Moreover, we compared the original DHTM (1 - red line), the adaptive version (3 - green line), and the original DHTM using pruning (yellow line). Pruning was based on the maximum number of segments, set according to the number of segments at the last measured episode for the adaptive version. Segments subject to pruning were selected based on the frequency of their use. The corresponding results are presented in Figs. 6 and 7. These results demonstrate a fundamental difference between the method we propose and pruning. We achieve not only a

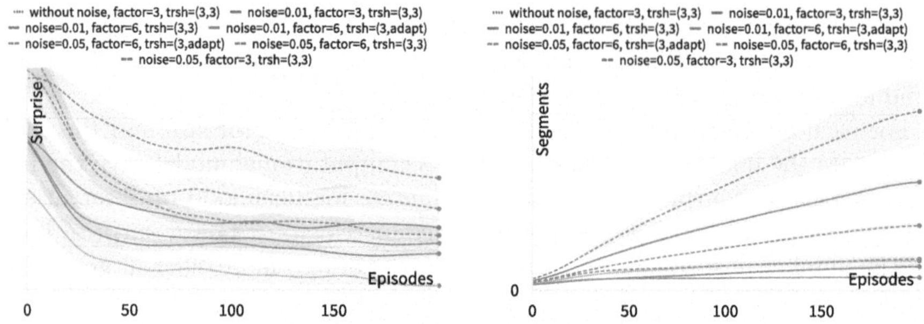

Fig. 5. AnimalAI environment. Color differentiates variants of the factor size and thresholds, the same as in pinball environment. Line style corresponds to different noise levels. (Color figure online)

reduction in the number of segments but also an improvement in quality, whereas pruning only degrades it.

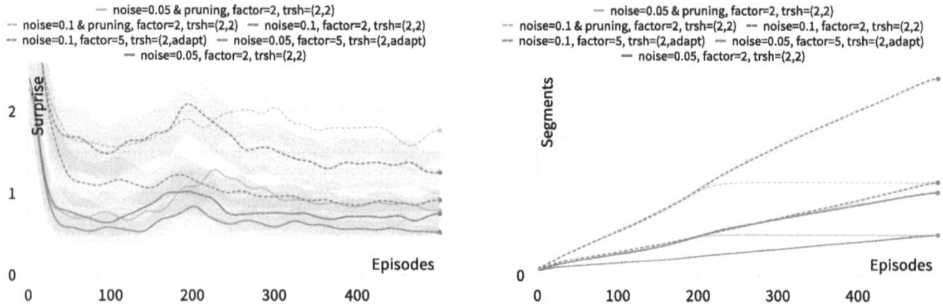

Fig. 6. Pinball environment. Comparison of the original DHTM (red line), the adaptive version (green line), and the original DHTM using pruning (yellow line). Line style corresponds to different noise levels. (Color figure online)

Thus, we managed to significantly reduce the number of segments using thresholds under the size of the factor in noisy environments, and it also improved the quality of the model. It means that using a larger factor size with a lower threshold increases the model's tolerance to noise. Figures also show that the adaptive threshold results in a more robust model but slightly increases the number of grown segments in comparison to a fixed threshold.

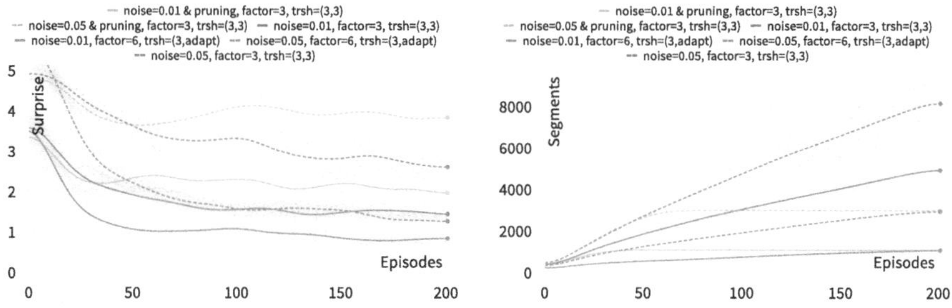

Fig. 7. AnimalAI environment. Comparison of the original DHTM, the adaptive version, and the original DHTM using pruning. Line style corresponds to different noise levels.

6 Conclusion

In this study, we have introduced innovative strategies to enhance the logical framework for constructing and utilizing segments within a biologically plausible DHTM model. Our proposed adjustments focus on augmenting the segment's capacity for generalization through a refined belief propagation threshold mechanism. Additionally, by enabling adaptability in the segment activation threshold, we have successfully amplified the segment count for receptive fields that demand heightened processing power. The implementation of these modifications has yielded significant improvements in the overall quality of the model while simultaneously curtailing the proliferation of new segments. It is evident that the enhancements we have incorporated have greatly fortified the model's efficacy and performance metrics in noisy environments. Moreover, the robustness of our introduced modifications in segment handling within this model paves the way for their seamless integration into other biologically inspired models that share the foundational logic of DHTM.

Acknowledgements. This work was supported by the Ministry of Science and Higher Education of the Russian Federation under Project 075-15-2024-544.

References

1. Ahmad, S., Lavin, A., Purdy, S., Agha, Z.: Unsupervised real-time anomaly detection for streaming data. Neurocomputing **262**, 134–147 (2017). https://doi.org/10.1016/j.neucom.2017.04.070. https://www.sciencedirect.com/science/article/pii/S0925231217309864. Online Real-Time Learning Strategies for Data Streams
2. Bamaqa, A., Sedky, M., Bosakowski, T., Bastaki, B.B.: Anomaly detection using hierarchical temporal memory (HTM) in crowd management. In: Proceedings of the 2020 4th International Conference on Cloud and Big Data Computing, ICCBDC 2020, pp. 37–42. Association for Computing Machinery, New York, NY, USA (2020). https://doi.org/10.1145/3416921.3416940

3. Beeching, E., Debangoye, J., Simonin, O., Wolf, C.: Godot reinforcement learning agents. arXiv preprint arXiv:2112.03636 (2021)
4. Bengio, Y., Lee, D.H., Bornschein, J., Mesnard, T., Lin, Z.: Towards biologically plausible deep learning (2016)
5. Bianchi, F.M., Maiorino, E., Kampffmeyer, M.C., Rizzi, A., Jenssen, R.: An overview and comparative analysis of recurrent neural networks for short term load forecasting. arXiv preprint arXiv:1705.04378 (2017)
6. Chowdhary, K., Chowdhary, K.: Natural language processing. In: Fundamentals of Artificial Intelligence, pp. 603–649 (2020)
7. Chung, J., Gulcehre, C., Cho, K., Bengio, Y.: Empirical evaluation of gated recurrent neural networks on sequence modeling. arXiv preprint arXiv:1412.3555 (2014)
8. Crosby, M., Beyret, B., Shanahan, M., Hernández-Orallo, J., Cheke, L., Halina, M.: The animal-AI testbed and competition. In: Neurips 2019 Competition and Demonstration Track, pp. 164–176. PMLR (2020)
9. Dedieu, A., Gothoskar, N., Swingle, S., Lehrach, W., Lázaro-Gredilla, M., George, D.: Learning higher-order sequential structure with cloned HMMs. arXiv preprint arXiv:1905.00507 (2019)
10. Deng, Y., Kong, S., Liu, C., An, B.: Deep attentive belief propagation: Integrating reasoning and learning for solving constraint optimization problems. In: Advances in Neural Information Processing Systems, vol. 35, pp. 25436–25449 (2022)
11. Ding, S., Xu, X., Nie, R.: Extreme learning machine and its applications. Neural Comput. Appl. **25**, 549–556 (2014)
12. Duff, I.S., Erisman, A.M., Reid, J.K.: Direct Methods for Sparse Matrices. Oxford University Press (2017)
13. Dzhivelikian, E., Kuderov, P., Panov, A.I.: Learning hidden Markov model of stochastic environment with bio-inspired probabilistic temporal memory. In: Biologically Inspired Cognitive Architectures 2023. Studies in Computational Intelligence, vol. 1130, pp. 330–339 (2023)
14. Dzhivelikian, E., Kuderov, P., Panov, A.I.: Learning successor representations with distributed Hebbian temporal memory. arXiv preprint arXiv:2310.13391 (2023)
15. Dzhivelikian, E., Latyshev, A., Kuderov, P., Panov, A.I.: Hierarchical intrinsically motivated agent planning behavior with dreaming in grid environments. Brain Inf. **9**(1), 8 (2022)
16. Eddy, S.R.: What is a hidden Markov model? Nat. Biotechnol. **22**(10), 1315–1316 (2004)
17. Fan, D., Sharad, M., Sengupta, A., Roy, K.: Hierarchical temporal memory based on spin-neurons and resistive memory for energy-efficient brain-inspired computing. IEEE Trans. Neural Netw. Learn. Syst. **27**(9), 1907–1919 (2015)
18. George, D., Rikhye, R.V., Gothoskar, N., Guntupalli, J.S., Dedieu, A., Lázaro-Gredilla, M.: Clone-structured graph representations enable flexible learning and vicarious evaluation of cognitive maps. Nat. Commun. **12**(1), 2392 (2021). https://doi.org/10.1038/s41467-021-22559-5
19. Ghahramani, Z., Jordan, M.: Factorial hidden Markov models. In: Advances in Neural Information Processing Systems, vol. 8 (1995)
20. Hunter, K., Spracklen, L., Ahmad, S.: Two sparsities are better than one: unlocking the performance benefits of sparse–sparse networks. Neuromorphic Comput. Eng. **2**(3), 034004 (2022). https://doi.org/10.1088/2634-4386/ac7c8a
21. Iyer, A., Grewal, K., Velu, A., Souza, L.O., Forest, J., Ahmad, S.: Avoiding catastrophe: active dendrites enable multi-task learning in dynamic environments. Front. Neurorob. **16** (2022). https://doi.org/10.3389/fnbot.2022.846219. https://www.frontiersin.org/articles/10.3389/fnbot.2022.846219

22. Lara-Benítez, P., Carranza-García, M., Riquelme, J.C.: An experimental review on deep learning architectures for time series forecasting. Int. J. Neural Syst. **31**(03), 2130001 (2021)
23. Leisenberger, H., Pernkopf, F., Knoll, C.: Fixing the Bethe approximation: how structural modifications in a graph improve belief propagation. In: Uncertainty in Artificial Intelligence, pp. 1085–1095. PMLR (2022)
24. Moerland, T.M., Broekens, J., Plaat, A., Jonker, C.M., et al.: Model-based reinforcement learning: a survey. Found. Trends® Mach. Learn. **16**(1), 1–118 (2023)
25. Qin, T., Chen, R., Qin, R., Yu, Y.: Improved hierarchical temporal memory for online prediction of ocean time series data. J. Mar. Sci. Eng. **12**(4), 574 (2024)
26. Rabiner, L., Juang, B.: An introduction to hidden Markov models. IEEE ASSP Mag. **3**(1), 4–16 (1986)
27. Rodkin, I., Kuderov, P., Panov, A.I.: Stability and similarity detection for the biologically inspired temporal pooler algorithms **213**, 570–579 (2022)
28. Salehinejad, H., Sankar, S., Barfett, J., Colak, E., Valaee, S.: Recent advances in recurrent neural networks. arXiv preprint arXiv:1801.01078 (2017)
29. Sekh, A.A., Dogra, D.P., Kar, S., Roy, P.P., Prasad, D.K.: ELM-HTM guided bio-inspired unsupervised learning for anomalous trajectory classification. Cogn. Syst. Res. **63**, 30–41 (2020)
30. Veličković, P., Cucurull, G., Casanova, A., Romero, A., Lio, P., Bengio, Y.: Graph attention networks. arXiv preprint arXiv:1710.10903 (2017)
31. Wang, C., Zhao, Z., Gong, L., Zhu, L., Liu, Z., Cheng, X.: A distributed anomaly detection system for in-vehicle network using HTM. IEEE Access **6**, 9091–9098 (2018). https://doi.org/10.1109/ACCESS.2018.2799210
32. Yang, C., Nie, K., Qiao, J., Wang, D.: Robust echo state network with sparse online learning. Inf. Sci. **594**, 95–117 (2022)
33. Yedidia, J.S., Freeman, W.T., Weiss, Y., et al.: Understanding belief propagation and its generalizations. Exploring Artif. Intell. New Millennium **8**(236–239), 0018-9448 (2003)
34. Zhang, Y., Li, P., Jin, Y., Choe, Y.: A digital liquid state machine with biologically inspired learning and its application to speech recognition. IEEE Trans. Neural Netw. Learn. Syst. **26**(11), 2635–2649 (2015)

Assessing Generative Artificial Intelligence in Fundamental Physics with Gaussian Processes

Miguel Cárdenas-Montes[1(✉)], Laura Toribio San Cipriano[1], Jacobo Asorey Barreiro[2], Juan de Vicente[1], and Ignacio Sevilla Noarbe[1]

[1] Centro de Investigaciones Energéticas Medioambientales y Tecnológicas, Avda. Complutense 40, 28040 Madrid, Spain
{miguel.cardenas,laura.toribio,juan.vicente,ignacio.sevilla}@ciemat.es

[2] Departamento de Física Teórica and Instituto de Física de Partículas y del Cosmos (IPARCOS-UCM), Universidad Complutense de Madrid, 28040 Madrid, Spain
jaasorey@ucm.es

Abstract. Generative Artificial Intelligence, particularly Generative Adversarial Networks, has garnered significant attention across diverse sectors, showcasing its ability to create realistic content based on previous examples. While mainstream outcomes of Generative Adversarial Networks rely on human verification —a few new instances are generated to be watched or listened to by humans for checking their realism— the scientific community encounters distinct challenges, especially in Physics. Due to the volume of new instances generated, human-based verification methods may be impractical. This work explores the application of Generative Artificial Intelligence, focusing on conditional Generative Adversarial Networks, to address issues inherent in Astrophysics scenarios where observational data volume is limited, and standalone simulations could be infeasible due to stochastic processes or when examples of interest represent only a fraction of the entire simulation. Human-based supervision of thousands to billions of scientific examples for similarity verification becomes impractical, highlighting a unique barrier of Generative Neural Network in scientific data generation. Generative Adversarial Networks, comprising generator and discriminator networks engaged in a training game, hold promise for generating new data. The discriminator evaluates realism, while the generator aims to produce instances indistinguishable from real data. An extension of this, conditional Generative Adversarial Networks, incorporates additional input (labels) for targeted generation. One the most critical issue of this kind of network is collapse mode, which adversely impacts the quality and diversity of generated instances. In the context of Astrophysics, this work proposes a novel approach. Gaussian Processes are used to evaluate the fit between generated and observed instances, generating similarity measurements and identifying collapse model. This proposal is particularly applied to the generation of galaxies from the Cosmic Evolution Survey (COSMOS).

Keywords: Generative Adversarial Networks · Conditional Generative Adversarial Networks · Gaussian Process · Collapse Mode

H. Quintián et al. (Eds.): HAIS 2024, LNAI 14857, pp. 214–225, 2025.
https://doi.org/10.1007/978-3-031-74183-8_18

1 Introduction

The advent of Generative Artificial Intelligence has revolutionized various sectors by demonstrating its prowess in creating realistic content based on learned patterns from existing examples. However, the new contents still need of human verification for evaluating their realism: images and videos must be visualized and audios must be listen to.

In scientific disciplines, Generative Artificial Intelligence can be employed when confronting the limitations of simulations. For instance, when standalone simulations for all cases of interest are not feasible due the processing time or when the examples of interest are only a tiny part of the bulk of simulations, mainly due to stochastics process. In this context, Artificial Intelligence (AI) -generated datasets through the use of generative neural networks emerge as a promising solution.

While the deployment of Generative Adversarial Networks (GANs) for generating audiovisual content has been a widespread success, the scientific community, for instance in Physics, faces unique challenges. These challenges are exacerbated by the impracticality of human-based verification methods, specially when confronted with vast volume of newly generated instances, which is usually the final target.

This paper delves into the application of GANs, with specific focus on conditional GANs (cGANs), and Gaussian Process to overcome these challenges in scientific scenarios, using an astrophysical problem as a testbed.

While cGANs are innovative solutions, issues such as collapse mode, arising from insufficient variety in training data or network architecture, can compromise the quality and diversity of the generated instances. Therefore, non-human-based supervision mechanisms for evaluating the diversity of the generated instances and metrics for measuring the fitting of generated instances to the true instances or to models based on the true instances are mandatory in the scientific scenario of AI generated dataset.

The scarcity of certain astronomical objects underscores the importance of enlarged datasets with Generative Artificial Intelligence. In Astrophysics, some objects are inherently rare, making it challenging to obtain sufficient observational data. The ability of cGANs to generated instances based on limited examples proves invaluable in addressing this scarcity, enabling researchers to build balanced classifiers.

Recognizing this, our work proposes an approach that integrates Gaussian Processes (GPs) into the evaluation process. GPs serve as a robust tool to assess the fit between the AI-generated instances and observed data. This integration not only provides a measure of similarity but also identifies collapse mode, enhancing the overall reliability of the generated datasets.

The focus of this study is the generation of galaxies of different types, in particular in three colour groups: red, green and blue galaxies (see Sect. 2.1) from The Cosmic Evolution Survey (COSMOS). The main contribution is the use of GPs for measuring similarity of the AI-generated instances compared to true ones, and proposing a methodology for the identification of the collapse mode. Generating realistic galaxies of different colour types serves as a stringent test for the proposed method.

2 Methodology

2.1 Dataset and Relevance of the Problem

Classifying galaxies by type is fundamental for understanding the evolution of galaxies and the Universe. Galaxies exhibit a variety of shapes and structural properties, mainly classified by the Hubble diagram [3,5,6,10]. This classification system is based on morphological properties closely related to other characteristics of galaxies, such as their colour, star formation rate, etc. In particular, colour is a feature used in the classification especially when galaxies are located at greater distances where detailed morphologies are difficult to observe. The dataset was obtained using Cosmohub [2,11].

In particular, in this work we are using a group of 40672 of galaxies from the COSMOS2015 catalogue [7]. We will use information from 10 broad bands: the u band from Canada-France Hawaii Telescope (CFHT u band); the B, V, r, i, z bands from Suprime-Cam/Subaru and the Y, J, H, K_s bands from VIRCAM/VISTA. Specifically, to normalize the magnitudes of the galaxies in these 10 bands, what we have used are their colors, that is, the differences in magnitude between one band and the next: u-B, B-V, V-r, r-i, i-z, Z-Y, Y-J, J-H, and H-Ks. For this work, we will not use the redshift information. We should clarify that although redshift is a very important parameter and that the spectral energy distribution (SED) of galaxies changes with redshift, the catalogs sometimes lack this information. In particular, not all galaxies in our sample contain spectroscopic redshift information. In order to perform a homogeneous analysis we have decided not to use the redshift information in the analysis and to study the results using as less parameters as possible. In addition, we use the galaxy classification of Alarcon et al. (2020) [1]. These authors classify galaxies into three categories: red, green and blue using the best continuum fit to a set of galaxy templates generated by Laigle et al. (2016), Polletta et al. (2007), Bruzual & Charlot (2003) and Ilbert et al. (2013).

Although there is no perfect correspondence in galaxy classification, red galaxies tend to be early-type galaxies, while blue galaxies are late-type galaxies. The fact that red galaxies show less star formation with ageing stellar populations compared to blue galaxies with higher star formation rates may indicate a transformation from blue to red galaxies, while green galaxies are considered a transitional phase in evolution (see e.g. Eales, S. et al. 2018, Casado J. 2015).

Our sample of galaxies comprises 7089 red galaxies, 6032 green galaxies and 27551 blue galaxies. The disparity in the numbers of galaxies within each category is one of the challenges we encountered during the classification process.

In the initial stages of our study, we undertook an exploration of the capacity of a Multilayer Perceptron architecture to accurately classify galaxies into three distinct types: red, green, and blue. To accomplish this, we employed a Multilayer Perceptron (MLP) with a shallow architecture consisting of two dense layers with ReLU activation functions. Each dense layer is followed by a dropout layer to prevent overfitting, and the network concludes with an output layer utilizing softmax activation. Despite its simplicity, this architecture yielded impressive results, achieving an accuracy of approximately 92% on the test set, which constitutes 30% of the dataset. Notably, this accuracy was achieved without the need for imbalance correction techniques. The training process spanned approximately 30 epochs, with early stopping implemented using the `EarlyStoppying` callback, configured with a patience parameter of 5 epochs. This configuration ensures that training halts when the model's performance fails to improve for five consecutive epochs, typically around the 25th epoch, as observed in Fig. 1, which illustrates the evolution of the loss and accuracy metrics throughout the training process.

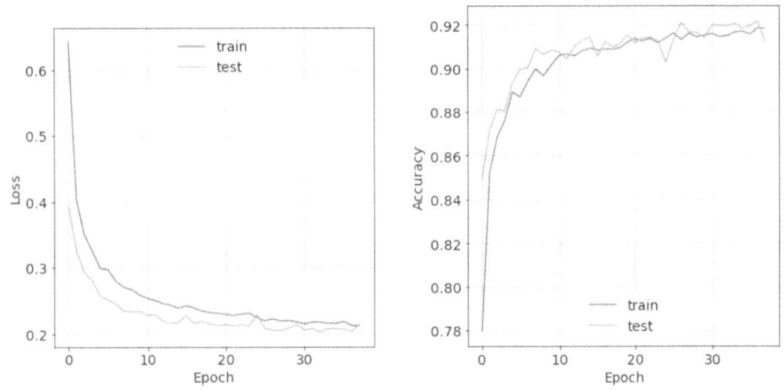

(a) Loss. (b) Accuracy.

Fig. 1. Loss (Fig. 1(a)) and Accuracy (Fig. 1(b)) evolutions for the classification problem of the types of galaxies based in a Multilayer Perceptron architecture.

The confusion matrix depicting the classification results is presented in Fig. 2. Remarkably, the model exhibits high performance, accurately classifying the majority of instances. Few errors occur, primarily among neighboring types of galaxies, with minimal misclassifications observed between red and blue galaxies.

2.2 cGAN

Generative Neural Networks (GANs) consist of a generator network and a discriminator network engaged in a game adversarial process. The generator aims to generate realistic data from random noise, while the discriminator attempts to distinguish between real and generated instances [4]. GANs are trained iteratively through a minimax game where the generator and discriminator learn to improve their respective capabilities leading to the generation of increasingly realistic data.

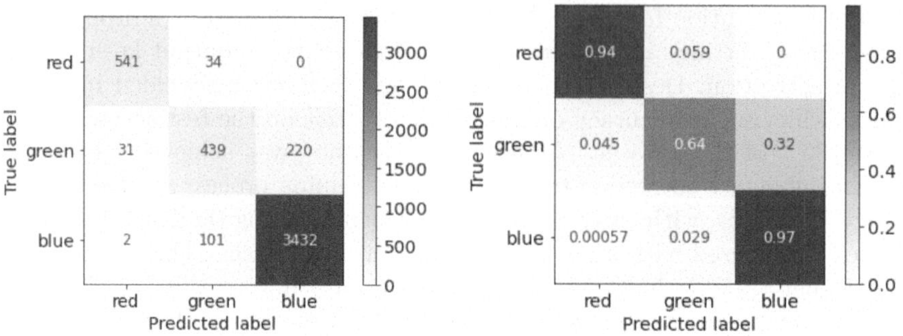

(a) Confusion Matrix. (b) Normalized Confusion Matrix.

Fig. 2. Confusion Matrix (Fig. 2(a)) and normalized Confusion Matrix (Fig. 2(b)) for the classification problem of the types of galaxies in a Multilayer Perceptron architecture.

Conditional Generative Adversarial Networks (cGANs) extend GANs by introducing conditional information during the generation process [8]. Both GANs and cGANs belong to the family of generative models. This allows for targeted generation based on specific conditions, such class labels. In cGANs, the generator receives both random noise and conditional information as input, enabling more controlled and targeted data generation.

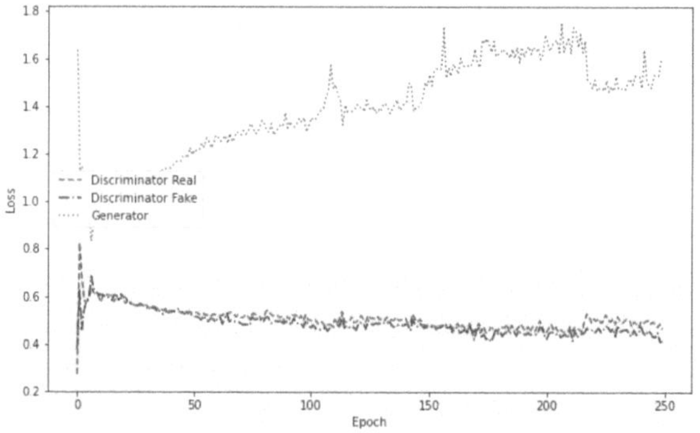

Fig. 3. Evolution of losses for the generator (green dotted), the discriminator loss for fake instances (blue dash-dotted), and the discriminator loss for real instances (red dashed). (Color figure online)

A cGAN is trained during 250 epochs with about 40k galaxy samples. The training of the cGAN is the most computationally intensive part. It takes around 100 s per epoch in a single GPU. However, it should be noted that once the cGAN has been trained, the model can be saved and used to generate instances as needed. Pathological behaviors in the evolution of losses are not observed: discriminator losses for real and fake instances are similar and close to 0.5 (Fig. 3).

Mode collapse is a phenomenon that can occur during the GAN, impacting the diversity and richness of the generated data. This issue arises when the generator of a GAN fails to capture the full range of variability present in the true data distribution. Instead, it converges to a limited set of output, effectively collapsing multiple modes of the data distribution into a smaller subset. As a result, the generator tends to produce repetitive and similar instance, compromising the model's ability to generate diverse and representative samples. Mitigation actions to minimize the mode collapse presence include careful design of the GAN architecture, regularization techniques, and fine-tuning of hyperparameters.

2.3 Gaussian Process

Gaussian Processes (GPs) are a powerful and flexible tool in machine learning, offering a non-parametric approach to capture complex relationships in data. Unlike traditional parametric models that assume a fixed number of parameters, GPs model entire distributions over functions. This enable them to provide not only predictions but also quantifiable uncertainties, making them suitable for applications where uncertainty is inherent. At the core of GPs is the concept of modeling functions as infinitely dimensional multivariante Gaussian distributions [9].

The key feature of GPs is their ability to capture complex patterns and dependencies in data without relying on a predetermined functional form. A GP is defined by a mean function $\mu(x)$ and a covariance function or kernel $k(x_1, x_2)$. The mean function represents the expected value of the function at any given point, while the kernel encodes the covariance structure between different point in the input space. The choice of kernel reflects the assumptions about the underlying data structure, allowing GPs to adapt to various patterns, from smooth trends to abrupt changes.

On the strengths of GPs lies in their Bayesian nature. GPs provide a principled framework for incorporating prior knowledge into the modeling process, updating it as new data becomes available. This Bayesian aspect allows GPs to make predictions not only based on observed data but also taking into account the uncertainty associated to those prediction. As a result, GPs are particularly well-suited for tasks where understanding and quantifying uncertainty are crucial.

In the context of this work, a GP model is trained with a subset of red galaxies. The fitting of the GP model is the most computationally intensive part of utilizing GP. It takes around 325 s. Later, the discrimination process involves evaluating instances of red, green and blue galaxies generated by the cGAN model against the trained GP. The GP model quantifies the uncertainty associated with those predictions. This uncertainty estimation is crucial for evaluating the degree alignment or deviation between the generated instances and the learned patterns of the GP model. Utilizing GPs to assess the deviation between the generated instances and the GP model built on the true instances allows the inspection of potential mode collapse.

The choice of the kernel in the GP model plays a crucial role. Our choice is an additive combination of `Rational Quadratic`, $k_{\text{Rational Quadratic}}(x, x') = \left(1 + \frac{\|x-x'\|^2}{2\alpha\ell^2}\right)^{-\alpha}$ and `White Noise`, $k_{\text{White Noise}}(x, x') = \delta(x, x') \cdot \sigma^2$, kernels.

3 Results and Analysis

In Figs. (4, 5, 6) comparisons between instances of the three classes generated by the cGAN and the GP model of true red galaxies are presented. Due to computational intensity, the model is constructed based on a random subset of 250 true red galaxies. This comparison involves the calculation of the likelihood of each color of the generated instances against the GP model. The likelihood serves as a metric, offering valuable insights into the alignment or deviation of each generated instance with respect to the model and, consequently, the true red galaxies' colors.

An ongoing inquiry in this study revolves around devising a methodology to assess the emergence of collapse mode. As demonstrated in Fig. 4, each generated instance can be juxtaposed against a GP-based model constructed from true instances of the same class. In Fig. 4, four cGAN-generated instances representing red galaxies (class 0) are contrasted with a model derived from 250 true red galaxies. Visual scrutiny enables the evaluation of distinctions among each cGAN-generated instance depicted from Fig. 4(a) to Fig. 4(d).

Furthermore, this process can be automated to eliminate the need for human supervision. This can be achieved through the calculation of the multivariate normal probability density function, thereafter multivariate normal pdf. The multivariate normal pdf provides a quantitative measure of the similarity between each generated instance and the GP model constructed from true instances. The collapse mode can be automatically detected by measuring its dispersion. A low dispersion will point out the presence of repetitive generated instances, indicating potential collapse mode. This automated approach enhances the efficiency of the evaluation process and enables timely intervention to prevent the collapse mode.

The same procedure can be applied to the cGAN-generated instances of other labels. For other labels, it is expected to evaluate the emergence of the collapse model, similar to the process described for label 0 (Fig. 4). Additionally, it is anticipated that the multivariate normal pdf will diverge when compared with the GP-based model of red galaxies (label 0), indicating differences in the distribution of generated instances compared to the true instances used for training the GP model.

In Figs. 5 and 6, four examples of cGAN-generated instances for classes 1 and 2 are juxtaposed with the GP model based on instances of red galaxies (class 0). It is evident that the values of the variables for the generated instances are less likely to belong to the model. This discrepancy is particularly notable in the variables: u-B, B-V, V-r, and r-i.

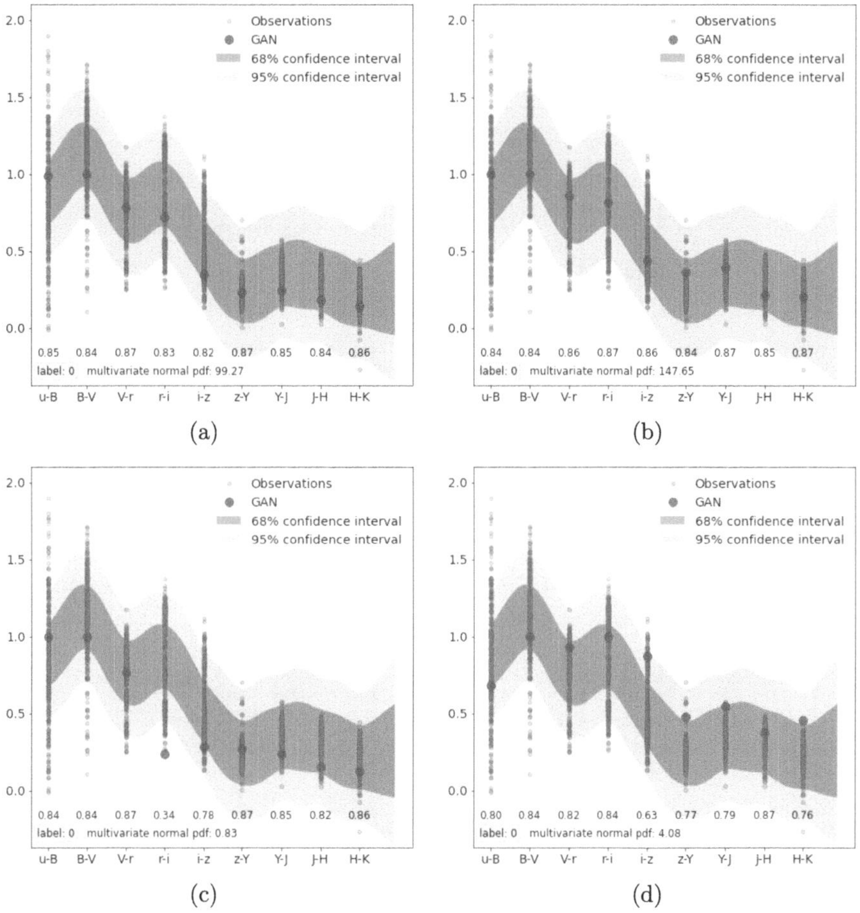

Fig. 4. Comparison between instances of red galaxies (class 0) generated using the cGAN architecture and the GP model based on true red galaxies. The red points denote the `color` values of 250 true red galaxies employed for training the GP model. The GP model, trained with these instances, exhibits 1-sigma and 2-sigma variances plotted in dark blue and light blue, respectively. The green points represent a single red galaxy generated the cGAN. The label of the generated event is displayed in the lower-left corner, the numerical values correspond to the probability density for each `color` according to the GP model assuming each color follows a univariante normal distribution, and the multivariate normal pdf. (Color figure online)

Although this section could be done with the GP model using a different one from the red galaxies, the use of this model also serves to highlight the collapse mode. By comparing the new instances generated with the model of the red galaxies, a greater contrast will be shown, and it will be possible to appreciate if the variety of generated galaxies for each label disperses with the different labels.

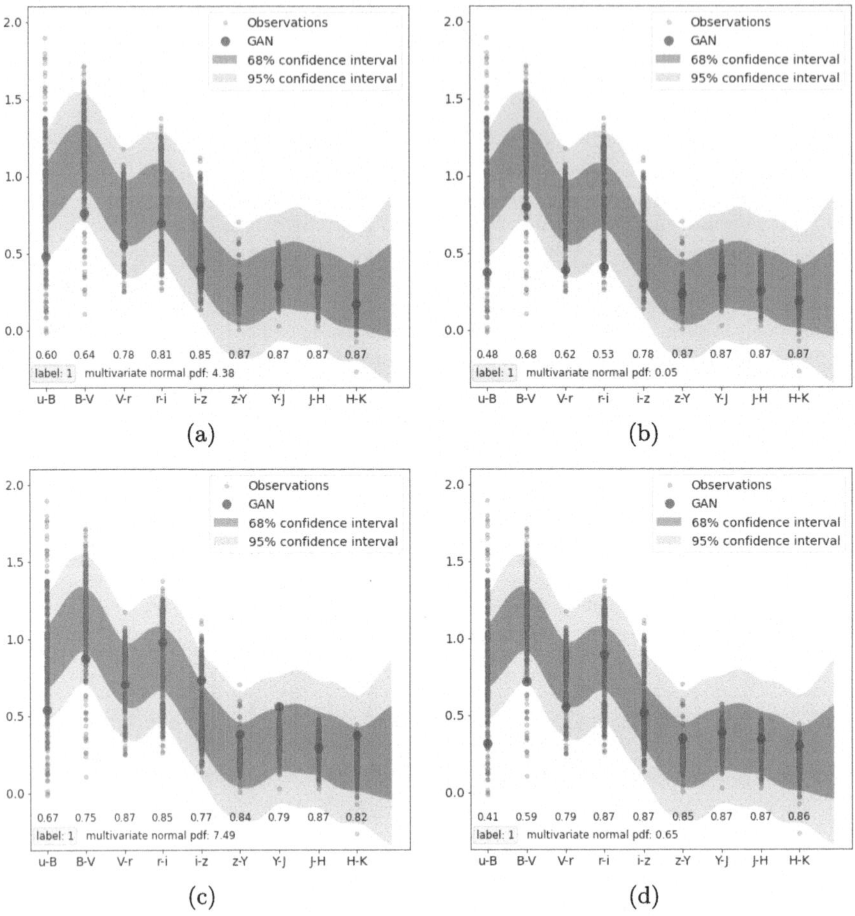

Fig. 5. Comparison between instances of green galaxies (class 1) generated using the cGAN architecture and the GP model based on true red galaxies. The red points denote the `color` values of 250 true red galaxies employed for training the GP model. The GP model, trained with these instances, exhibits 1-sigma and 2-sigma variances plotted in dark blue and light blue, respectively. The green points represent a single red galaxy generated the cGAN. The label of the generated event is displayed in the lower-left corner, and the numerical values correspond to the likelihood scores for each `color` according to the GP model assuming each color follows a univariante normal distribution, and the multivariate normal pdf. (Color figure online)

Considering the analysis of the variance of cGAN generated instances, their likelihood to the Bayesian model based on true red galaxies can be used as a metric about the dispersion of the generated instances as well as about the ability of cGAN to reproduce each type of galaxy. In Fig. 7, the multivariante normal probability density function—joint probability density—of each type of cGAN-generated galaxy to the Bayesian model of true red galaxies is depicted.

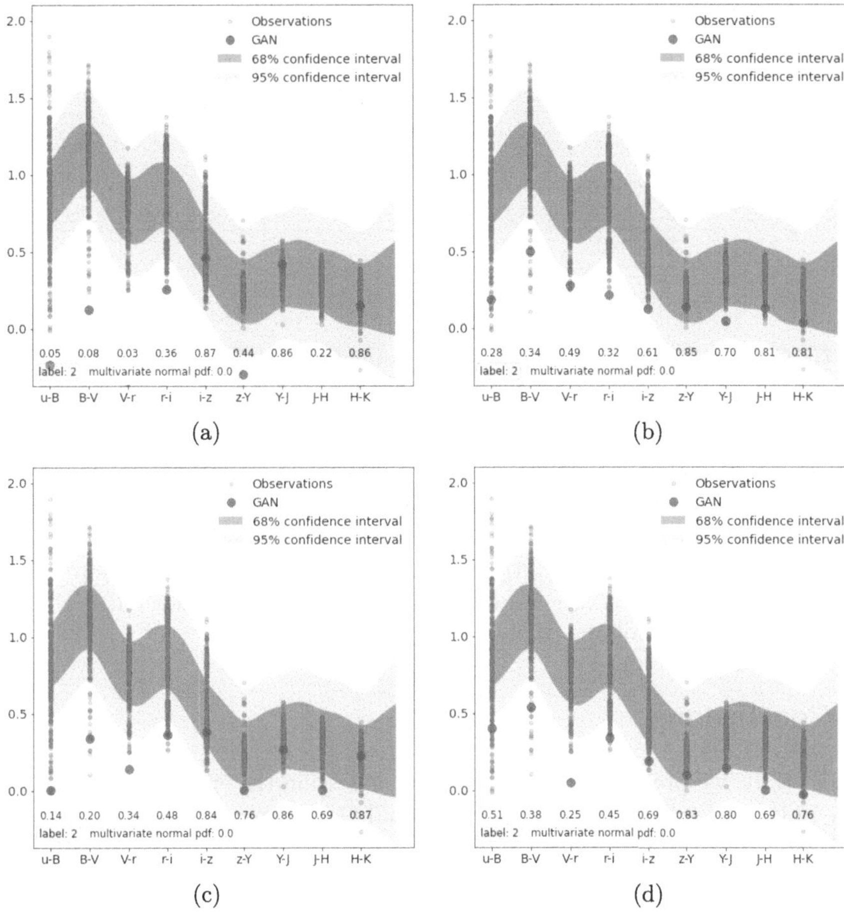

Fig. 6. Comparison between instances of blue galaxies (class 2) generated using the cGAN architecture and the GP model based on true red galaxies. The red points denote the `color` values of 250 true red galaxies employed for training the GP model. The GP model, trained with these instances, exhibits 1-sigma and 2-sigma variances plotted in dark blue and light blue, respectively. The green points represent a single red galaxy generated the cGAN. The label of the generated event is displayed in the lower-left corner, and the numerical values correspond to the likelihood scores for each `color` according to the GP model assuming each color follows a univariante normal distribution, and the multivariate normal pdf. (Color figure online)

As it can be observed the red-type generated galaxies adjust better than the two other galaxy type, the blue-type generated galaxies the lest similar to the Bayesian model. This decreasing similarity from red, to green and blue generated galaxies to the Bayesian model indicates that the cGAN is able to capture the patterns of each type of galaxy, for later reproduce them with a certain variance, at the same time it avoids collapse mode.

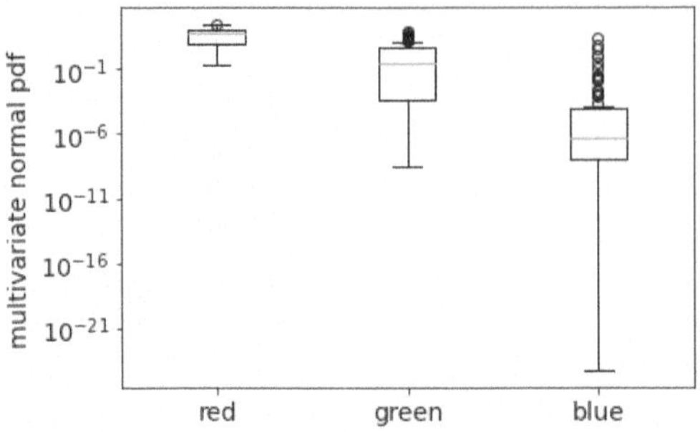

Fig. 7. Boxplots depicting the multivariate normal probability density function for generated red, green, and blue instances as compared to the Bayesian model based on true red galaxies. (Color figure online)

This mechanism allows checking the variance of the generated instances when they are employed as augmented input for other classifiers. By generating augmented datasets with growing variance, the future classifiers become more robust against noise or simply a larger variety of the true instances not currently registered by a reduced volume of observations.

4 Conclusions

In this study, we present a methodology for assessing the emergence of collapse mode in instances generated using conditional Generative Adversarial Networks (cGANs). The evaluation is done based on the capability of Gaussian Process to measure the fitting of AI-generated instances to a GP-model built with true instances. Our approach is applied to a dataset comprising galaxies of red, green, and blue types sourced from the Cosmic Evolution Survey (COSMOS).

The findings demonstrate the viability of our proposed methodology, capable of visually and automatically evaluating the emergence of collapse mode. This is particularly crucial in scenarios where Generative Neural Networks are utilized as generators of scientific data, as the substantial volume of generated data renders human-based supervision impractical.

This study opens up several avenues for future research. One promising direction is the extension of the proposed methodology from 1D data to images, which represent 2D data. This expansion would involve adapting the techniques developed for evaluating collapse mode and measuring the similarity of generated instances to models based on true instances to the realm of image data.

Acknowledgment. MCM is co-funded by the Spanish Ministry of Science and Innovation for funding support through the grant PID2020-113807RA-I00 "SERVICIOS INNOVADORES DE ANALISIS DE DATOS PARA EL EXPERIMENTO CMS".

References

1. Alarcon, A., et al.: The PAU survey: an improved photo-z sample in the COSMOS field. Mon. Not. Roy. Astron. Soc. **501**(4), 6103–6122 (2021). https://doi.org/10.1093/mnras/staa3659
2. Carretero, J., et al.: CosmoHub and SciPIC: massive cosmological data analysis, distribution and generation using a big data platform. In: Proceedings of the European Physical Society Conference on High Energy Physics, 5–12 July, p. 488, July 2017
3. de Vaucouleurs, G.: Classification and morphology of external galaxies. Handbuch der Physik **53**, 275 (1959). https://doi.org/10.1007/978-3-642-45932-0_7
4. Foster, D., Friston, K.: Generative Deep Learning: Teaching Machines to Paint, Write, Compose, and Play. O'Reilly (2023)
5. Hubble, E.P.: Extragalactic nebulae. ApJ **64**, 321–369 (1926). https://doi.org/10.1086/143018
6. Hubble, E.: The Realm of the Nebulae. Yale University Press (1936)
7. Laigle, C., et al.: The COSMOS2015 catalog: exploring the $1<z<6$ universe with half a million galaxies. ApJs **224**(2), 24 (2016). https://doi.org/10.3847/0067-0049/224/2/24
8. Mirza, M., Osindero, S.: Conditional generative adversarial nets. CoRR abs/1411.1784 (2014). http://arxiv.org/abs/1411.1784
9. Rasmussen, C., Williams, C.: Gaussian Processes for Machine Learning. Adaptive Computation and Machine Learning. MIT Press, Cambridge, MA, USA, January 2006
10. Sandage, A.: The Hubble Atlas of Galaxies (1961)
11. Tallada, P., et al.: CosmoHub: interactive exploration and distribution of astronomical data on Hadoop. Astron. Comput. **32**, 100391 (2020). https://doi.org/10.1016/j.ascom.2020.100391. http://www.sciencedirect.com/science/article/pii/S2213133720300457

Implementation of Classical Decision Trees in a Quantum Computing Paradigm

M. P. Cuellar[1(✉)], L. G. B. Ruiz[2], and M. C. Pegalajar[1]

[1] Department of Computer Science and Artificial Intelligence, University of Granada, 18014 Granada, Spain
manupc@decsai.ugr.es, bacaruiz@ugr.es
[2] Department of Computer and Software Engineering, University of Granada, 18014 Granada, Spain
mcarmen@decsai.ugr.es
http://decsai.ugr.es

Abstract. Decision trees are widely known models in Supervised Machine Learning with efficient inference mechanisms and outstanding interpretability. In this article, we design the implementation of classical Inductive Decision Trees under a quantum computing paradigm, and explore the advantages of Quantum Decision Trees designed in the presence of missing and uncertain data. Our findings extend to quantum ensembles analogous to Decision Forests as a Quantum Machine Learning method to improve the interpretability of a type of variational quantum circuits. Our approach provides an improvement in efficiency in the case of probabilistic inference with respect to the classical counterpart, and a general methodology is designed to address multiple classification tasks with Quantum Machine Learning tools, with a focus on the interpretability of quantum models. The theoretical results are supported by experimental simulations using different data sets and state-of-the-art examples.

Keywords: Quantum Decision Trees · Quantum Decision Forests · Quantum Machine Learning

1 Introduction

Quantum Machine Learning [4] (QML) is a research area at the intersection of Artificial Intelligence (AI) and Quantum Computing (QC). Its goal is to either use classical AI to address QC challenges, or to incorporate AI into QC to solve classical or quantum problems. Different pure quantum and hybrid classical/quantum QML models have been proposed in the literature to solve supervised, unsupervised and reinforcement learning tasks [7,8], and they can be

This article was funded by the project QUANERGY (Ref. TED2021-129360B-I00), Ecological and Digital Transition R&D projects call 2022 by MCIN/AEI/10.13039/501100011033 and European Union NextGeneration EU/PRTR.

H. Quintián et al. (Eds.): HAIS 2024, LNAI 14857, pp. 226–237, 2025.
https://doi.org/10.1007/978-3-031-74183-8_19

classified into two categories: Some of them are inspired by well-known classical methods [8] such as Quantum Support Vector Machines (qSVMs), Quantum Neural Networks (qNNs), quantum Generative Adversarial Networks [3] (qGANs), or quantum Policy Iteration [2] to mention a few. Others are pure quantum algorithms such as the Quantum Approximate Optimization Algorithm (QAOA) or the Grover Adaptive Search(GAS) [3]. In any case, all proposals aim to use QC features such as superposition, entanglement or quantum parallelism to produce a significant speedup in terms of algorithmic complexity, or to take advantage of quantum measurement nonlinearity to improve state-of-the-art results by reducing model complexity. This work belongs to the first category. It combines a hybrid approach that explores how to implement classical Inductive Decision Trees (IDT) [5] in a quantum algorithm to solve classification problems, and the advantages that a quantum nature can provide to process imperfect and/or missing data. While the Quantum Decision Trees obtained regard to the quantum implementation of classical IDTs, the inference is performed in a pure quantum state evolution setting.

The proposals presented in this manuscript are based on the design of a procedure to perform a direct implementation of IDTs as a quantum circuit. We design this procedure taking into account three requirements: Simplicity, utilization of the minimum resources needed to represent the tree (measured as the minimum number of qubits), and maintaining the same interpretability as the original IDT. The result provided by the method is called Quantum Decision Tree (QDT), and offers a number of advantages: First, the interpretation of any quantum circuit with the same designed structure as a classical IDT, allowing the explanation and interpretability of a quantum program in a natural human way; Second, a base methodology for the design of quantum circuits that solve different tasks beyond classification, e.g. oracles [6]; and third, a natural way to perform probabilistic inference on the tree with a substantial improvement in algorithmic complexity. Having presented the method, we also explore how the designed QDT can be used to deal with imperfect knowledge. In our case, we take advantage of quantum superposition to represent multiple input feature values simultaneously, and quantum parallelism to evaluate all these values in superposition simultaneously. Our final contribution in this paper extends the approach to construct Quantum Decision Forests (QDFs) together with their aggregation procedure as QDTs superimposed on a quantum circuit, while maintaining the same expressivity as classical Decision Forests (DFs).

A Background in Quantum Computing

In Quantum Computing [6], an arbitrary qubit $|\psi\rangle$ is modeled as an element of a vector subspace in the complex plane $\mathbb{C}^2$. A qubit is always in superposition (linear combination) of the elements of the computational basis vectors $|\psi\rangle = \alpha_0|0\rangle + \alpha_1|1\rangle; \alpha_i \in \mathbb{C}$ with the constraint $\sum_i |\alpha_i|^2 = 1$. Here, $|0\rangle, |1\rangle$ uses Dirac notation to represent the column basis vectors $[1,0]^t, [0,1]^t \in \mathbb{C}^2$, respectively. The computational space of a system containing n qubits is a vector subspace in

$\mathbb{C}^{2^n}$ obtained as the tensor product ($\otimes$) of the basis vectors of each qubit. As an example, the computational basis of a system containing two qubits is $\{|0\rangle \otimes |0\rangle = |00\rangle = [1,0,0,0]^t, |0\rangle \otimes |1\rangle = |01\rangle = [0,1,0,0]^t, |1\rangle \otimes |0\rangle = |10\rangle = [0,0,1,0]^t, |1\rangle \otimes |1\rangle = |11\rangle = [0,0,0,1]^t\}$. A quantum state of n qubits is represented in its computational space as $|\psi\rangle_n = \sum_{i=0}^{2^n-1} \alpha_i |i\rangle, \alpha_i \in \mathbb{C}, \sum_{i=0}^{2^n-1} |\alpha_i|^2 = 1$, where $|i\rangle$ represents the i-th basis vector in binary representation.

Operations on quantum states with n qubits are modeled as complex unitary linear transformations in matrix form $U_{2^n,2^n}$, and their application on a set of qubits is written as $U|\psi\rangle_n$ and computed as a classical matrix multiplication. Each transformation must be reversible, except the *measurement* of the quantum state which makes the quantum state collapse to any of the basis vectors $|i\rangle$ of the computational space with probability $|\alpha_i|^2$.

In this work, we use single-qubit operations to create quantum states representing classical data, and to construct QDTs and QDFs. Of particular relevance is the X/NOT gate (Eq. 1) similar to a classical NOT gate, and the rotation about the x-axis of the Bloch sphere $R_x(\theta)$ (Eq. 2). In this manuscript, multi-qubit operations are limited to controlled gates and, in particular, controlled NOT gates and controlled $R_x(\theta)$ gates. A controlled operation implements a single-qubit gate U on a target qubit when other qubits (*controls*) are in a control state $|0\rangle$ or $|1\rangle$. The mathematical model for a controlled gate operation acting on n qubits, where the n-th qubit is the target and the remaining $\{1...n-1\}$ are controls with control states $|11...1\rangle_{n-1}$, is a block matrix constructed as in Eq. 3 for an arbitrary single-qubit operation U, where $I_{2^{n-1},2^{n-1}}$ represents the identity matrix of size 2^{n-1} and $0_{2^{n-1},2}$ is a zero matrix of size 2^{n-1} rows and 2 columns. An example of a controlled operation is the CNOT gate (Eq. 4). The CNOT operation maps a quantum state $|\psi\rangle = \alpha_0|00\rangle + \alpha_1|01\rangle + \alpha_2|10\rangle\alpha_3|11\rangle$ to $CNOT|\psi\rangle = \alpha_0|00\rangle + \alpha_1|01\rangle + \alpha_3|10\rangle\alpha_2|11\rangle$, i.e., the value of the second qubit is negated iif the value of the first qubit is $|1\rangle$. Assuming an initial quantum state $|q_0q_1\rangle = |q_00\rangle$, the CNOT gate is a key operation in our proposed interpretation of quantum decision trees, since it can be read directly as "*If* $|q_0\rangle = |1\rangle$, *then* $|q_1\rangle = |1\rangle$; *otherwise* $|q_1\rangle = |0\rangle$", in the non-probabilistic case. However, under uncertain data, the result of a CNOT can also be read in terms of the measured state amplitudes as $p(|q_1\rangle = |1\rangle \,|\, |q_0\rangle = |1\rangle) \cdot p(|q_0\rangle = |1\rangle)$, allowing probabilistic inference.

$$X = \begin{pmatrix} 0 & 1 \\ 1 & 0 \end{pmatrix} \tag{1}$$

$$R_x(\theta) = \begin{pmatrix} cos(\theta/2) & -isin(\theta/2) \\ -isin(\theta/2) & cos(\theta/2) \end{pmatrix} \tag{2}$$

$$CU = \begin{pmatrix} I_{2^{n-1},2^{n-1}} & 0_{2^{n-1},2} \\ 0_{2,2^{n-1}} & U \end{pmatrix} \tag{3}$$

$$CNOT = \begin{pmatrix} 1 & 0 & 0 & 0 \\ 0 & 1 & 0 & 0 \\ 0 & 0 & 0 & 1 \\ 0 & 0 & 1 & 0 \end{pmatrix} \tag{4}$$

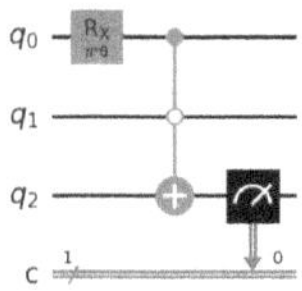

Fig. 1. Example of a quantum circuit with a $R_x(\theta\pi)$ gate acting on qubit q_0 followed by a Toffoli (CCNOT) over target q_2 controlled by $|q_0q_1\rangle = |10\rangle$

A quantum program can be formulated as a sequence of quantum gates applied on qubits in parallel. A quantum circuit is a visual model that facilitates the evaluation of a quantum program. In it, each qubit is assigned a horizontal line, and the qubits are usually grouped into quantum registers. The sequence of operations is read from left to right, and marked with symbols over the qubits involved in the operation. As an example, Fig. 1 shows a circuit with three qubits that implements the program $U = (I \otimes X \otimes I)CCNOT(R_x(\theta)|q_0\rangle \otimes X|q_1\rangle \otimes |q_2\rangle)$. If the initial quantum state is $|000\rangle$ then the resulting quantum state of this circuit is written as $U|000\rangle$ and shown in Eq. 5. Measuring $|q_2\rangle$ in the classical bit c would provide bit 1 or 0 depending on the value of θ, and its expectation using the observable σ_z is represented as $\langle 000|U^\dagger(I^{\otimes 2} \otimes \sigma_z)U|000\rangle$, where $U^\dagger$ represents the complex conjugate transpose of U.

$$U|000\rangle = cos(\theta\pi/2)|000\rangle - isin(\theta\pi/2)|101\rangle \tag{5}$$

Another relevant feature of Quantum Computing in this manuscript is Quantum Parallelism. As we can see in Fig. 1, the parallel structure of qubit lines allows multiple operations to be performed simultaneously on different sets of qubits. This structure has no added value over classical parallelization on multiple CPUs or GPUs; however, when combined with additional features such as superposition and entanglement, it could serve as a powerful tool to evaluate multiple input values simultaneously in a single circuit execution and, in some cases, obtain quantum supremacy. This is the case for well-known quantum algorithms such as Shor's algorithm for integer factorization, Simon's algorithm or Deutsch-Jotza's [6] algorithm. In our work, the advantages of quantum parallelism are combined with the superposition of input feature values as a way to deal with imperfect input classification patterns, and helped to achieve a significant speedup in QDT inference under partial observability with respect to classical IDTs. For example, setting $\theta = 0.5$ in the circuit in Fig. 1 moves $|q_0\rangle$ from $|0\rangle$ to an equiprobable superposition $R_x(0.5\pi)|0\rangle = cos(\pi/4)|0\rangle - isin(\pi/4)|1\rangle$, which means that both values $|q_0\rangle = |0\rangle$ and $|q_0\rangle = |1\rangle$ are processed simultaneously by the circuit. As a result, measuring $|q_2\rangle$ with the observable σ_z provides an expectation value equal to 0, since the probability of $|q_2\rangle = |1\rangle$ results in 0.5.

The final tool from Quantum Computing that we have used in this manuscript is entanglement [6], as a possible avenue for developing quantum-inspired missing value imputation methods. Two qubits are said to be entangled if their values are highly correlated, as for example in the resulting unitary state in Eq. 5. In the possible results after measurement of all qubits $|q_0q_1q_2\rangle \in \{|000\rangle, |101\rangle\}$, we can verify a high correlation between qubits $|q_0\rangle, |q_2\rangle$, since once we know the value of one qubit, then we already know the value of the other without measurement. In our work, the entanglement is performed using $R_x(\theta\pi)$ gates along with $NOT/R_x(\theta\pi)$ multiple control gates. In fact, the construction of a QDT in our approach aims at finding entanglements between class label qubits (target) and input feature values (controls) that serve to predict correct classifications. Thus, we argue that a QDT model could also be used in some situations to perform missing value imputation thanks to the entanglement between input features and the target class.

2 From Classical to Quantum Decision Trees

Our method for encoding a classical IDT as a QDT consists of two steps: 1) a state preparation procedure to map the input feature data to a quantum state; and 2) a quantum circuit containing the IDT logic (antsatz). If there is no uncertainty in the input data, a basis encoding mechanism [8] can be used for state preparation. Otherwise, the uncertainty is encoded in the quantum state amplitudes as the probability that the input feature contains one value or another. Depending on the uncertainty, this can be achieved using angle encoding [8] or more sophisticated methods such as amplitude embedding [1].

Given a dataset containing n input features $\{F_1, F_2, ..., F_n\}$ and a target class C, a QDT must implement a unitary transformation U such that, for a given set of feature values $\{V_1, V_2, ..., V_n\}$ mapped to quantum states $\{|Q_1\rangle, |Q_2\rangle, ..., |Q_n\rangle\}$ and a class label c_l assigned to $|c_l\rangle$, the circuit computes the target quantum state $|Q_1\rangle|Q_2\rangle...|Q_n\rangle|c_l\rangle = U|Q_1\rangle|Q_2\rangle...|Q_n\rangle|0\rangle$. Our approach constructs this unitary operation as a sequence of multiple controlled NOT gates (MCX), where each gate corresponds to a path from the root of the classical IDT to a leaf node. Thus, each MCX operation implements a rule for class value prediction.

The complete procedure for creating a quantum circuit that implements QDT logic from a classical IDT is shown in Algorithm 1. The classical IDT T is an input as well as the interpretation I where $I_{F,v}$ represents the encoding of the binary representation basis for the v value of the F feature. In lines 1–4, the quantum registers for all input and output features are created. Next, line 6 finds the *paths* of T. This operation can be easily performed with a preorder traversal of the tree, and we assume that a path contains a set of (F_i, v_i) pairs along with the target class label. Next, each *path* is implemented as a MCX operation in lines 8–17, and added to the output QDT. The variables *controls* and *states* store the quantum states involved in the MCX and its control state, respectively.

The first thing to remark here is that reaching a particular leaf node in classical IDT is performed in $log(n)$ node evaluations, assuming a balanced tree with n leaf nodes (the worst case for QDT). However, reaching the same leaf node in QDT is realized in $\mathcal{O}(1)$, since it requires a constant number of operations depending on the instruction set of a quantum computer to implement MCX. The main limitation of QDT is that it requires the evaluation of all MCX operations in the circuit to return a result, which is n. However, if we consider a scenario where the inference is probabilistic, all nodes of the classical IDT could be evaluated, while the number of QDT operations remains n. This is a significant efficiency improvement over classical IDT inference.

Algorithm 1: Algorithm to encode a classical Inductive Decision Tree into a Quantum Decision Tree

T: Classical Decision Tree
I : Interpretation/mapping from classical feature values to quantum register basis states

foreach *non-terminal feature* $F_i \in T$ **do**
    Create quantum register $|Q_{F_i}\rangle$ for F_i
end
Create quantum register $|Q_{label}\rangle$ for target class
QDT $= \emptyset$
paths= set of paths from root to leaf nodes in T
foreach *path* $\in$ *paths* **do**
    states = {}
    controls = {}
    c_l = get class label value from path
    q_c = qubit of $|Q_{label}\rangle$ for which I_{C,c_l} is 1
    if q_c *is not None* **then**
        foreach *non-terminal pair* F_i, v_i *in path* **do**
            append $|Q_{F_i}\rangle$ to controls
            append I_{F_i,v_i} to states
        end
        rule = MCX(target=q_c, controlled_by=controls, controlled_states=states)
        QDT = QDT $\bigcup$ {rule}
    end
end
return QDT

The second aspect we want to highlight is that the interpretability of the QDT remains unchanged with respect to the original IDT, since each *path* can be easily located in the QDT circuit as a *MCX* operation. Moreover, we can observe that all QDTs obtained with our procedure contain the same structure: a set of input quantum registers, an output register, and a sequence of *MCX* operations. Thus, our approach allows the interpretability of any quantum circuit with the same structure as a classical IDT. We believe that this is a relevant contribution to the interpretability of quantum circuits in the field of Quantum Machine Learning.

Finally, the inference in a QDT is straightforward and equivalent to DT inference: First, the feature values must be encoded by the state preparation procedure. After that, a single *MCX* will move the corresponding output qubit of the quantum register $|Q_{label}\rangle$ from $|0\rangle$ to $|1\rangle$, and the output register is measured.

Beyond its high interpretability, the main practical advantage of a QDT concerns the natural processing of unknown or imperfect input data. We take advantage of quantum superposition and parallelism to encode different values of an unknown input feature and evaluate all these values simultaneously in the QDT. The main idea is to encode the probability of each feature value in the amplitudes of a quantum register. The output register will then provide the probability of the target class labels considering all established superpositions. As it was mentioned above, our supporting examples use $R_x(\theta\pi)$ rotation gates in the input state preparation step with angle encoding due to its simplicity, although amplitude embedding could also be used. A rotation $R_x(\theta\pi)$ applied as state preparation with $\theta = 0$ leaves a qubit value unchanged in $|0\rangle$ state, while a $\theta = 1$ value negates the qubit as using a NOT gate to $|1\rangle$ state. Any value of $\theta \in (0, 1)$ alters the probability that the qubit is in a nontrivial superposition of $|0\rangle$ and $|1\rangle$. Since a QDT is a direct implementation of a classical DT, its prediction accuracy is also not altered, although it retains the same training limitations in terms of overtraining risk.

2.1 Quantum Decision Forests

We devise two strategies to create a Quantum Decision Forest from a set of existing QDTs in Fig. 2. In either of them, each IDT is implemented in its corresponding Quantum Decision Tree module from QDT_1 to QDT_N using Algorithm 1. In addition, a new module *Aggregation* must be created to return the output register $|C_l\rangle$ from the partial outputs of each tree. In the model in Fig. 2a, all trees are evaluated in parallel, while the model in Fig. 2b executes the QDTs sequentially. The advantage of the parallelized strategy in Fig. 2a is a substantial speedup, since the only bottleneck concerns the evaluation of the QDT with the largest circuit depth; however, its main limitation is that many input feature registers must be replicated to feed each QDT with its inputs, so the number of qubits required from this strategy is substantially larger and therefore not suitable for simulation on contemporary classical computers. On the other hand, the sequential strategy in Fig. 2b requires fewer resources in space, although the time complexity depends on the number of QDTs in the forest.

We have implemented the sequential strategy of Fig. 2b in our example, since it has been tested under simulation on a classical computer. In addition, we have implemented the criterion *Weighted Majority Voting* as an aggregation module for illustrative purposes due to its simplicity. This aggregation procedure returns the most frequent result among the weighted partial results of QDTs, and can be easily implemented in a QDF by replacing the *MCX* lines with Controlled Multiple X-Rotations ($MCR_x(\theta)$) parameterized by θ. Here, θ controls the contribution of the result of each QDT to the final output register $|C_l\rangle$, so that no additional registers are required to store the partial output of each QDT.

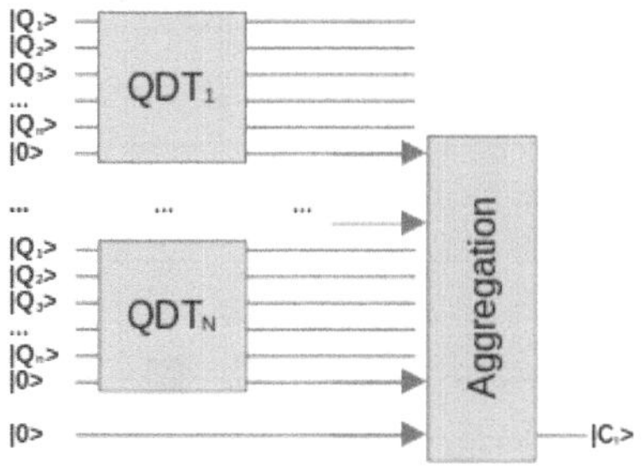

(a) Parallel Quantum Decision Forest.

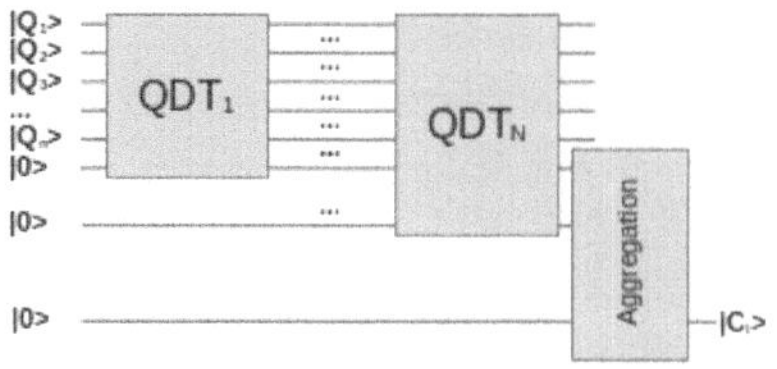

(b) Sequential Quantum Decision Forest.

Fig. 2. Strategies to create Quantum Decision Forests.

3 Experimental Results

We design quantum decision trees using a quantum gating framework under simulation to solve multiclass classification problems. IBM's Python Qiskit library is used to demonstrate our examples and inference tests. All experiments were performed on an Intel(R) Core(TM) i5-9600K CPU desktop computer at 3.70 GHz with 32 GB RAM.

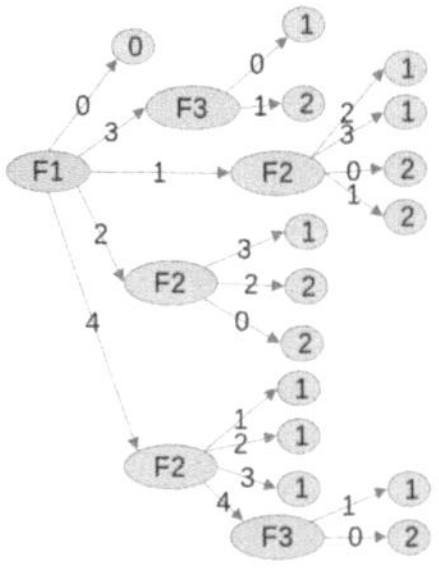

(a) Iris problem.

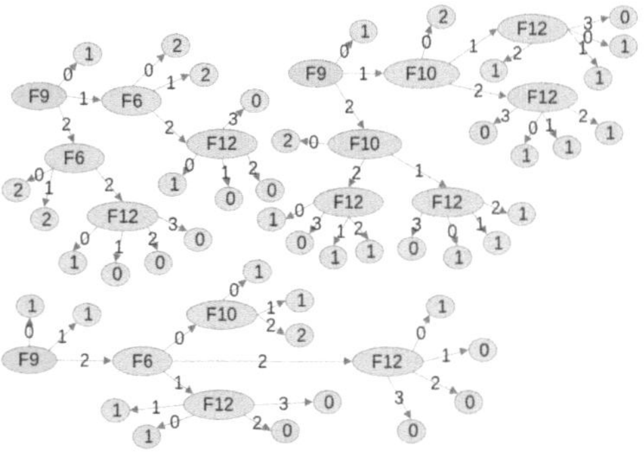

(b) Wine problem.

Fig. 3. Decision Tree and Decision Forest representation of the datasets used.

We used classical reference data sets to experimentally support our findings: The *Iris* classification problem with four features (sepal length, sepal width, petal length, petal width) of three Iris flower types (target class: Setosa, Versicolor, Virginica), and the *Wine* classification dataset containing 13 features and 3 target class labels. The *Iris* problem is used as an example for multiclass QDT coding, with the classical tree depicted in Fig. 3a. On the other hand, *Wine* is used to show Quantum Decision Forest coding, for the classical decision forest

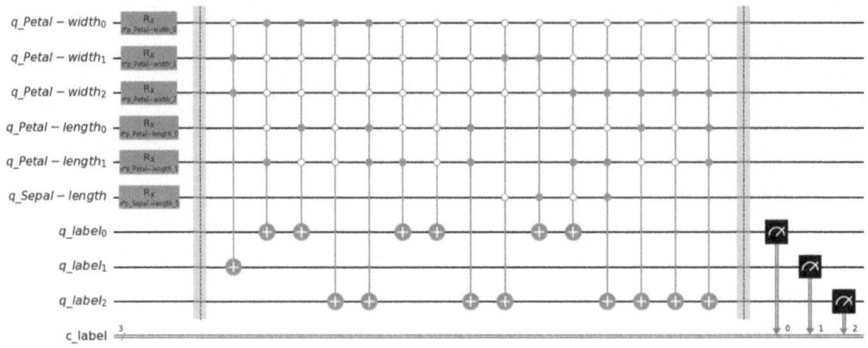

Fig. 4. Quantum Decision Tree for the Iris problem

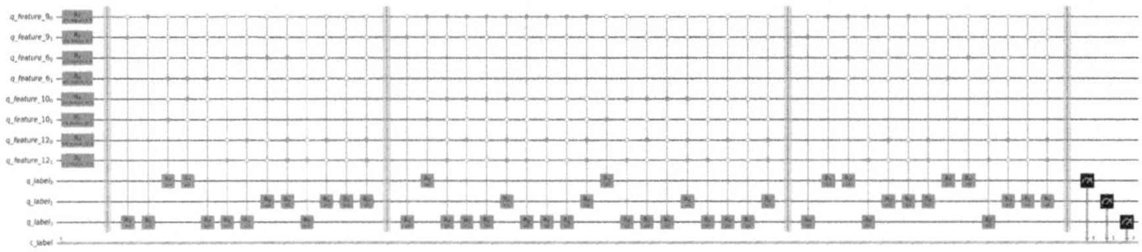

Fig. 5. Quantum Decision Forest for the Wine problem overlapped sequentially

containing three trees in Fig. 3b. The tree was designed to provide 100% accuracy on the *Iris* data set. However, the decision trees in the forest in Fig. 3b provide between 95% and 98% accuracy separately for the *Wine* dataset, and 100% accuracy with the majority voting output aggregation. Our experiments are limited to features with discrete values, so that preprocessing should be applied to discretize features with continuous data, such as the *Iris* and *Wine* datasets. In addition, a mapping from classical data to quantum states is required to achieve full interpretability of the generated QDTs and to devise a mechanism for quantum preparation of the input state. Tables 1 and 2 describe the discretization limits along with an example interpretation that maps each feature value to a quantum ground state for the trees in Fig. 3. The number of quantum registers used to translate an IDT into a QDT is equal to the number of features in a tree plus one output register. If a feature F_i containing n_i values is paired with quantum register Q_i, the number of qubits in the register is $\lceil log_2 n_i \rceil$. The resulting implementation of DT and DF are shown in Figs. 4 and 5, respectively. Here, we can distinguish each path from the root of each tree to their respective leaf nodes implemented as MCX. Experimental simulations concluded that the accuracy of the quantum circuits on the datasets equals the accuracy of the initial classical DTs and reaches an accuracy of 100% in both cases.

The main practical advantage of a QDT concerns the natural processing of unknown or imperfect input data. We take advantage of quantum superposition and parallelism to encode different values of an unknown input feature and

Table 1. Discretization bounds and quantum encoding for the *Iris* dataset.

Feature	Q. Register	Range	Discretization	Basis Encoding
F_1: Petal width	Q_{pw}	$[0, 0.8]$	0	$\|011\rangle$
		$(0.8, 1.55]$	1	$\|100\rangle$
		$(1.55, 1.65]$	2	$\|000\rangle$
		$1.65, 1.75]$	3	$\|010\rangle$
		$(1.75, 2.5]$	4	$\|001\rangle$
F_2: Petal length	Q_{pl}	$[0, 4.85]$	0	$\|01\rangle$
		$(4.85, 4.95]$	1	$\|10\rangle$
		$(4.95, 5.45]$	2	$\|00\rangle$
		$(5.45, 6.9]$	3	$\|11\rangle$
F_3: Sepal length	Q_{sl}	$[0, 5.95]$	0	$\|0\rangle$
		$(5.95, 7.90]$	1	$\|1\rangle$
Target: Label	Q_{label}	Setosa	0	$\|010\rangle$
		Virginica	1	$\|001\rangle$
		Versicolor	2	$\|100\rangle$

evaluate all these values simultaneously in the QDT. The main idea is to encode the probability of each feature value in the amplitudes of a quantum register. The output register will then provide the probability of the target class labels considering all established superpositions. As mentioned above, our supporting examples use $R_x(\theta\pi)$ rotation gates in the input state preparation step with angle encoding due to their simplicity, although amplitude embedding could also be used. A rotation $R_x(\theta\pi)$ applied as state preparation with $\theta = 0$ leaves a qubit value unchanged in the $|0\rangle$ state, while a value $\theta = 1$ negates the qubit as using a NOT gate and moves it to the $|1\rangle$ state. Any value of $\theta \in (0, 1)$ alters the probability that the qubit is in a nontrivial superposition of $|0\rangle$ and $|1\rangle$. As an example, consider the pattern *(p(Sepal-length = 0/1) = 0.5, p(Petal-length = 0) = 1, p(Petal-width = 4) = 1)* for the data set *Iris*. This pattern corresponds to $|Q_{pw}\rangle|Q_{pl}\rangle|Q_{sl}\rangle = |001\rangle_{pw}|01\rangle_{pl}R_x(0.5\pi)|0\rangle_{sl}$. The rules that are triggered in this case correspond to the 11th and 12th *MCXs* in Fig. 4, which compute $p(label = Versicolor|Petal - width = 4, Petal - length = 0, Sepal - length = 0) \cdot p(Sepal - length = 0)$ and $p(label = Virginica|Petal - width = 4, Petal - length = 0, Sepal - length = 1) \cdot p(Sepal - length = 1)$. The result is thus $p(label = Versicolor) \approx 0.5, p(label = Virginica) \approx 0.5$. Since a QDT is a direct implementation of a classical DT, its prediction accuracy is also not altered, although it retains the same training limitations regarding possible overtraining.

Another example in the *Iris* data set concerns possible applications for missing value imputation. Consider the pattern *(p(Petal width = 2) = 1)* to predict *label = Versicolor*, while the other features are supposed to be unknown. Let us assume that the goal is to perform missing value imputation of the feature *Petal length*. An input state could be conceived as $|Q_{pw}\rangle|Q_{pl}\rangle|Q_{sl}\rangle =$

Table 2. Discretization bounds and quantum encoding for the *Wine* dataset.

Feature	Q. Register	Range	Discretization	Basis Encoding
F_6: Total phenols	Q_{f6}	$[0, 1.58]$	0	$\|01\rangle$
		$(1.58, 1.71]$	1	$\|10\rangle$
		$(1, 71, \infty)$	2	$\|00\rangle$
F_9: Proanthocyanins	Q_{f9}	$[0, 3.49]$	0	$\|01\rangle$
		$(3.49, 3.92]$	1	$\|10\rangle$
		$(3.92, \infty]$	2	$\|00\rangle$
F_{10}: Color intensity	Q_{f10}	$[0, 0.83]$	0	$\|01\rangle$
		$(0.83, 0.97]$	1	$\|10\rangle$
		$(0.97, 1]$	2	$\|00\rangle$
F_{12}:diluted wines	Q_{f12}	$[0, 679]$	0	$\|01\rangle$
		$(679, 706.5]$	1	$\|10\rangle$
		$(706.5, 724.5]$	2	$\|00\rangle$
		$(724.5, \infty)$	3	$\|11\rangle$
Target: Label	Q_{label}	Cultivar 1	0	$\|010\rangle$
		Cultivar 2	1	$\|001\rangle$
		Cultivar 3	2	$\|100\rangle$

$|000\rangle_{pw}(R_x(0.5\pi) \bigotimes R_x(0.5\pi))|00\rangle_{pl_1} R_x(0.5\pi)|0\rangle_{sl}$. The possible rules that can be triggered are the 6th, 7th, 8th *MCXs* in Fig. 4. The measurement on the $|Q_{pl}\rangle$ and $|Q_{label}\rangle$ registers is performed on the output quantum state described as $|Q_{pl}\rangle|Q_{label}\rangle = \alpha_0|00\rangle_{pl}|100\rangle_{label} + \alpha_1|01\rangle_{pl}|100\rangle_{label} + \alpha_2|11\rangle_{pl}|001\rangle_{label}$, which means that the value $|Q_{pl}\rangle = |11\rangle$ would lead to a classification of *label* = *Virginica* and the remaining values to *label* = *Versicolor* with the same probability. Since the pattern contains *label* = *Versicolor*, we could replace the missing value with $|Q_{pl}\rangle = |00\rangle$ or $|Q_{pl}\rangle = |01\rangle$.

4 Conclusions

This work addresses the representation and learning of Decision Trees and their extension to Decision Forests under a Quantum Computing paradigm. In the results, we have shown how well-known and widely used quantum gates can be used to translate a classical DT into a quantum circuit in a simple way, without loss of interpretability. In our opinion, this is an important step forward for the analysis and explanation of the behaviour of certain types of quantum programs. Moreover, the use of quantum mechanisms such as superposition and quantum parallelism provide relevant advantages to deal with imperfect knowledge regarding the output inference process for a given input pattern. We have found that an important speed-up could be achieved under a massively probabilistic inference mechanism in a QDT with respect to the classical counterpart, and also that possible applications to develop new techniques for missing value imputation could be a focus of future research using quantum entanglement. Besides, extending QDTs to Quantum Decision Forests was also found an easy task that can be performed with minimum modifications to each QDT in the forest and the implementation of the output aggregation procedure.

Acknowledgements. This work was performed in cooperation with the IEEE Computer Society Task Force in Quantum Computational Intelligence (URL at https://cmte.ieee.org/quantum-computational-intelligence/).

References

1. Araujo, I.F., Park, D.K., Petruccione, F., da Silva, A.J.: A divide-and-conquer algorithm for quantum state preparation. Sci. Rep. **11**, 6329–6341 (2021). https://doi.org/10.1038/s41598-021-85474-1
2. Cherrat, E.A., Kerenidis, I., Prakash, A.: Quantum reinforcement learning via policy iteration. Quant. Mach. Intell. **5**, 1–18 (2023). https://doi.org/10.1007/s42484-023-00116-1
3. Combarro, E.F., Gonzalez-Castillo, S.: A practical guide to Quantum Machine Learning and Quantum Optimization. Packt, Birmingham (2023)
4. Ganguly, S.: Quantum Machine Learning: An Applied Approach. Apress, New York (2021)
5. Quinlan, J.R.: Induction of decision trees. Mach. Learn. **1**(1), 81–106 (1986). https://doi.org/10.1023/A:1022643204877
6. Sutor, R.: Dancing with Qubits. Packt, Birmingham (2019)
7. Umer, M.J., Sharif, M.I.: A comprehensive survey on quantum machine learning and possible applications. Int. J. E-Health Med. Commun. **13**(5), 1–17 (2022). https://doi.org/10.4018/IJEHMC.315730
8. Wittek, P.: Quantum Machine Learning: What Quantum Computing Means to Data Mining. Elsevier, Amsterdam (2014)

Machine Learning Methods as Robust Quantum Noise Estimators

Jon Gardeazabal-Gutierrez(✉), Erik B. Terres-Escudero, and Pablo García Bringas

Deusto University, Bilbao, Spain
jon.g.g@deusto.es

Abstract. Access to quantum computing is steadily increasing each year as the speed advantage of quantum computers solidifies with the growing number of usable qubits. However, the inherent noise encountered when running these systems can lead to measurement inaccuracies, especially pronounced when dealing with large or complex circuits. Achieving a balance between the complexity of circuits and the desired degree of output accuracy is a nontrivial yet necessary task for the creation of production-ready quantum software. In this study, we demonstrate how traditional machine learning (ML) models can estimate quantum noise by analyzing circuit composition. To accomplish this, we train multiple ML models on random quantum circuits, aiming to learn to estimate the discrepancy between ideal and noisy circuit outputs. By employing various noise models from distinct IBM systems, our results illustrate how this approach can accurately predict the robustness of circuits with a low error rate. By providing metrics on the stability of circuits, these techniques can be used to assess the quality and security of quantum code, leading to more reliable quantum products.

Keywords: Quantum Computing · Noise Estimation · Quantum Noise · Quantum Software · Quantum Security

1 Introduction

Quantum computing has recently emerged as a promising alternative to traditional computing, particularly given its optimized processing capabilities for specific optimization problems, which can yield exceptional results [1,2]. Such challenges are prevalent in various market scenarios, including route optimization for logistics [3] or drug discovery [4]. By leveraging the inherent properties of quantum states, quantum computers can exponentially reduce the complexity of costly algorithmic routines, making them indispensable for industries in the future. However, due to its nascent state, the integration of quantum subroutines into current software is not a trivial task, especially hindered by the lack of accessibility to quantum computers.

Quantum microservices have presented themselves as a promising solution to these challenges, offering platforms designed for software developers to seamlessly

H. Quintián et al. (Eds.): HAIS 2024, LNAI 14857, pp. 238–247, 2025.
https://doi.org/10.1007/978-3-031-74183-8_20

integrate quantum microservices into their final products [5,6]. Additionally, to avoid repeating the mistakes of early software development and to minimize technical debt in the long term, several researchers have advocated for the development of software quality metrics [7]. These metrics aim to provide developers with additional insights into the quality of their quantum software. Specifically, this paper focuses on circuit stability, a critical quality metric, particularly in terms of software security.

To measure this property, this paper builds upon the results presented in [8]. The primary contribution of the paper lies in providing a more suitable circuit processing pipeline to fully take advantage of the potential of traditional machine learning (ML) methods as quantum noise estimators. To achieve this, we replace the complex data extraction from IBM systems with a simpler gate counting strategy, employing ideal and noisy outputs to understand the relationship between circuit structure and resulting discrepancies in the measurements. Our results demonstrate that when circuits are appropriately processed as inputs for the ML model, the outcomes exhibit low error rates. Additionally, we introduce a novel circuit processing technique where gates are transformed into an embedding space, enabling us to treat circuits as images and employ neural networks for noise estimation. In contrast to our prior work, where these models showed suboptimal performance, we achieve competitive accuracy with traditional ML models even in low data regimes.

The structure of this paper is outlined as follows: Subsect. 1.1 provides a brief introduction to key concepts in the field of quantum computing; Subsect. 1.2 shows existing results related to quantum noise and estimation algorithms; Sect. 2 introduces the methodology employed to adapt ML methods for quantum circuits; Sect. 3 details the methods and setup employed for conducting the experiments; Sect. 4 presents the obtained results with a brief discussion on their advantages and their limitations; and finally, Sect. 5 concludes the paper with a brief summary of the work and outlines future lines of research.

1.1 Quantum Computing

Quantum computing differs itself from traditional software by employing a probabilistic representation of the states instead of finite and static states. A quantum state is described by a vector in which each coordinate represents the square root of the probability of the system collapsing to its respective state. Formally, a quantum state composed of n qubits is represented by the expression (e.g., a state $|5\rangle$ would be represented as $|101\rangle$).

$$\sum_{i=0}^{2^n} \alpha_i |i\rangle = \alpha_1 |\overbrace{0\ldots00}^{n}\rangle + \alpha_2|0\ldots01\rangle + \cdots + \alpha_{2^n}|1\ldots11\rangle \tag{1}$$

where $(\alpha_1, \alpha_2, \ldots, \alpha_{2^n}) = \alpha \in \mathbb{R}^{2^n}$ are the coefficients of each state, verifying that $\|\alpha\|_2 = 1$.

A fundamental property of quantum states is entanglement, which occurs when a quantum state cannot be decomposed into a product of two separate states. This indivisibility implies that traditional computers require exponential time complexity to simulate the transformation of subsequent quantum gates, as each transformation implies multiplying the state by an exponentially large matrix relative to the number of qubits. In contrast, if this property were not fulfilled, traditional computers could exploit state separation to compute the product of the two smaller states separately, thus forfeiting the desired quantum advantage. A well-known example of entanglement is found in Bell states, with one such state expressed as $\frac{1}{\sqrt{2}}(|00\rangle + |11\rangle)$.

Formally, a NISQ (Noisy Intermediate-Scale Quantum) computer is a system that operates by transforming an initial state $|0\ldots0\rangle$ through operations given by quantum gates. The set of possible quantum gates, denoted as $\mathbb{G}$, is constrained based on the specific computer used. Thus, a quantum circuit $\mathbf{C} \in \mathbb{G}^{n \times m}$ can be described as a grid-like structure, where each row represents the path taken by one of the n qubits during execution, and each column contains the gates to be applied to the circuit sequentially. Each cell in this grid structure may be empty, indicating no transformation, or contain a quantum gate, which may involve one (e.g., Hadamard or rotation gates) or multiple qubits (e.g., CNOT or Toffoli gates). According to this formulation, the theoretically expected result when executing the circuit $\mathbf{C}$ is a probability vector in $\mathbb{R}^{2^n}$. However, due to practical limitations, this probability is approximated by a series of consecutive forward passes, involving measurements of the final state and aggregation of the results into a vector representing the distribution of each reported state.

The current state-of-the-art in quantum computers is represented by NISQ devices. However, as their name suggests, these computers are prone to obtaining imprecise results, heavily influenced by various noise sources that undermine result accuracy [9]. Two well-known gate-independent noise sources are T_1 and T_2. The T_1 value arises due to state loss in the system, measuring the time for a qubit to transition from a high-energy state $|1\rangle$ to collapse to a $|0\rangle$ state. Similarly, the T_2 value measures the dephasing time, representing the duration during which a quantum superposition naturally collapses to either $|0\rangle$ or $|1\rangle$. Another significant noise source arises from imperfect gates, where weak calibration can cause states to deviate from the expected values, potentially resulting in drastically different outcomes [10].

1.2 Related Work

Quantum noise is a well-documented phenomenon that can significantly affect the accuracy of circuit results if not properly addressed [9,11]. As mentioned in the previous section, the origins of this noise are multifactorial, leading to non-trivial heuristics for estimating whether a circuit will produce a confident enough output distribution compared to the theoretical benchmark [9,10]. However, this quality metric is of critical importance, as executions in low robustness environments can yield erroneous results.

To tackle this issue, two main directions are being studied. The first branch focuses on the hardware aspects that give rise to noise, aiming to enhance the stability and robustness of quantum computers while minimizing the misalignment introduced by quantum gates. The second branch, represented by error correction codes, draws on traditional techniques to prevent information loss or modification from impacting the entire system [12]. These methods have already demonstrated their ability to deliver more accurate outputs at the expense of requiring additional qubits to serve as redundancy for computations [13]. However, both approaches primarily concentrate on reducing noise during execution. Neither technique adequately addresses the challenge of determining whether a circuit will perform poorly under a specific noise model.

In order to solidify the quality of quantum circuits for production-ready software, a novel branch of noise estimation has recently emerged. This branch, referred to as quantum noise estimation algorithms, focuses on developing algorithms that can estimate the deviation from theoretical to practical quantum states within a specific quantum system without the need for either simulation or execution on a real quantum system. This estimation involves the development of a function $\mathcal{N} : \mathbf{C} \rightarrow \mathbb{R}$, which maps a circuit to a scalar value, quantifying the distance between real and practical errors.

Currently, literature on this topic is scarce, however, two approaches have already been proposed. The first method was introduced by Aseguinolaza et al., advocating for the use of an ad-hoc formula to measure the fidelity output of quantum circuits. The authors analyzed the noise effects in several well-known quantum algorithms, demonstrating how their metric can determine result robustness [14]. A second approach was presented by Alvarado et al., where they utilized a linear method to measure the estimated difference between theoretical and actual outputs, based on IBM models [8]. This approach aims to provide a quality metric for incorporation into a quantum micro-service pipeline, serving as a security measure for developers.

2 Methodology

This section describes the process employed to clean and process the quantum circuits to allow machine learning methods to estimate the noise. This section starts by introducing the process employed to generate the training data. Then, it details the transformation process employing for using the data for traditional methods focused on tabular data. Finally, it details the process employed to transform the circuits into a well-suited data shape for conventional neural networks.

Dataset Generation. To create a large and representative dataset of distinct quantum circuits, we generated 35,000 random quantum circuits using the quantum gates available on IBM machines. These 35,000 samples were divided into seven chunks of 5,000 circuits each, with each chunk containing circuits of varying qubit counts, ranging from 4 to 10 qubits. The depth of each circuit was selected from a uniform distribution, spanning from short circuits with only 2 columns to deeper instances with up to 50 columns.

Tabular Data Adaptation. Similar to the approach employed in [8], we utilize a function N^T_{Emb}, defined as the mapping of the circuit to its gate count, which provides a more suitable space for tabular methods. While we collected gate errors from IBM machines, we opted not to incorporate them in this work. This decision stems from the increased data complexity associated with individual errors across multiple gates and qubits. Therefore, we hypothesize that by limiting the amount of information fed to the circuits, models can improve their learning dynamics, extracting simpler yet more robust relationships between circuit composition information and obtained noise measurements.

Neural Network Data Adaptation. In the aforementioned work, we also employed neural networks to estimate noise; however, the experiments resulted in the neural networks being unable to learn. We attributed this outcome to the tabular nature of the data, which is known to be unsuitable for these approaches. To address this limitation, we propose transforming quantum circuits into low-dimensional image-like samples. Given the grid-like structure of a circuit $\mathcal{C}$ with a depth D and Q qubits, we define a function $\mathcal{N}^I_{Emb} : \mathbb{G}^{D\times Q} \rightarrow \mathbb{R}^{E\times D\times Q}$ to project the given circuit into a low-dimensional representation using an embedding dimension of E.

This projection function $\mathcal{N}^I_{Emb}$ consists of two sequential transformations. The first transformation maps the circuit from the gate space $\mathbb{G}$ to the space of natural numbers $\mathbb{N}$, simplifying each circuit into a more manageable space. This transformation can be achieved by assigning each unique gate to a consecutive integer, thus establishing a mapping of distinct gates to consecutive integers. Given the poor performance observed by neural networks when operating in such spaces, we apply an additional learnable embedding to this set, enabling each gate to be represented by a vector in $\mathbb{R}^E$. With this formulation, neural networks should be better equipped to leverage circuit information for optimal noise estimation.

3 Experimental Setup

IBM offers a variety of quantum computers for academic use, each featuring a distinct noise model. To evaluate the quantum computer's impact on our approach, we selected two backends for experimentation: IBM Cairo and IBM Hanoi, both capable of handling circuits with up to 27 qubits. Due to the substantial queue required to compute measurements on a dataset as extensive as the one proposed in this work using real machines, we chose to simulate the results. We employed the Qiskit Aer simulator [15], conducting 1000 shots for each circuit in both noisy and ideal executions. The distance between these two outputs has been measured using the cosine distance (Fig. 1).

Due to the inherent high costs of computing a large set of circuits, we chose to evaluate the robustness of these methods against different training sizes. We conducted experiments using two training split sizes: 1% and 80%. Each training split was obtained by randomly sampling the specified size of random samples from the aforementioned 35,000 generated circuits[1]. No additional data augmentation techniques were employed during training. Two metrics were used to compute the error between the estimated noise and the actual computed noise, namely, the Mean Absolute Error (MAE) and the Root Mean Squared Error (RMSE).

To compare our results, we employ tabular-based methods under $\mathcal{N}^T_{Emb}$, and neural networks under the $\mathcal{N}^I_{Emb}$ projection. The chosen tabular methods include Linear Regression, Histogram-based Gradient Boosting [16], and XGBoost [17]. For neural network models, we selected a dense neural network and a convolutional neural network. No hyperparameter tuning operation was conducted for any algorithm.

Both neural networks have approximately 130,000 parameters. The dense neural network comprises 3 layers with 80, 40, and 1 neurons, respectively. The convolutional neural network consists of 2 convolutional layers, each with 16 channels, followed by 3 dense layers with the same structure as the aforementioned neural network. Both networks were trained using the Mean Square Error loss with the Adam Optimizer for 100 epochs. The learning rate was set to 0.001, halving every 5 epochs during the first 50 epochs.

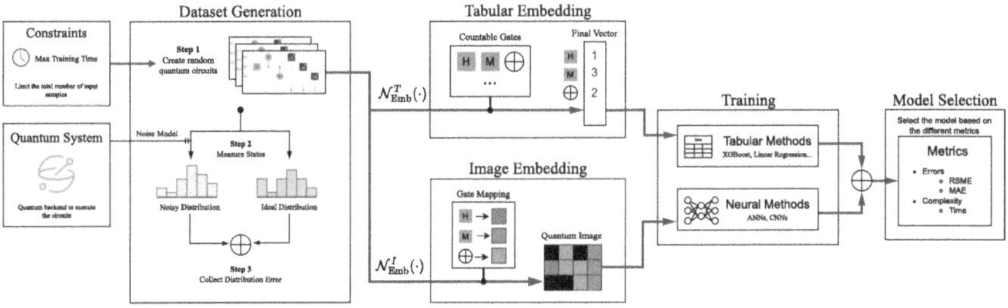

Fig. 1. Schema detailing the process followed to obtain the data and train the different models.

4 Results and Discussions

The results of the error for all training methods are presented in Table 1. Under these results, our initial hypothesis on the accuracy of these methods in estimating noise is verified. It comes as no surprise to observe that linear regression, which closely resembles our prior approach, yields the least optimal results. This method only captures linear dependencies between the number of gates and the error, neglecting further relationships within the circuits. This defect is particularly clear in the data related to IBM Hanoi, where the model has an almost double error rate. In contrast, all other methods attain competitive results, with XGBoost yielding the most precise outcomes.

[1] Dataset repository: https://github.com/Jongarde/Qserv_dataset.

Table 1. MAE and RSME of the ideal and noisy outputs of the quantum circuits under all ML methods. Each cell contains the error when employing a train split size of 1% (left-side of the arrow), and the error when employing an 80% split size (right-side of the arrow)

Algorithm	IBM Cairo		IBM Hanoi	
	MAE	RSME	MAE	RSME
XGboost	0.082 → 0.073	0.120 → 0.106	0.051 → 0.042	0.083 → 0.073
Hist Gradient Boost	0.081 → 0.070	0.117 → 0.102	0.050 → 0.039	0.081 → 0.069
Linear Regression	0.093 → 0.086	0.122 → 0.115	0.090 → 0.083	0.116 → 0.107
Dense NN	0.081 → 0.074	0.111 → 0.106	0.058 → 0.043	0.088 → 0.071
Convolutional NN	0.086 → 0.073	0.117 → 0.110	0.066 → 0.042	0.096 → 0.074

Nevertheless, a clear pattern can be observed when analyzing the learned heuristics of tabular-based ML methods, as most of them heavily rely on gates related to the total qubit count of the circuit, indicating a strong correlation between this value and the total system's noise. While this effect was expected, as higher qubit counts imply greater entanglement and thus more decoherence-related noise, the impact of this variable surpasses initial hypotheses. To further analyze this effect, we examine the effect of removing gates related to the qubit count (e.g. reset or measure), and presented the results in Table 2. A clear down-trend in all algorithms is appreciated. This effect is particularly pronounced when looking into the results of IBM Hanoi, where the amount of qubits serves as the leading noise indicator. Interestingly, under this framework, Gradient Boosting methods fail to establish previous patterns relating the qubit count to other gates, causing Linear Regression to transition from the least accurate among all methods to the one with the highest accuracy.

Moreover, our results also prove how employing non-tabular inputs for neural network-based approaches can yield competitive results. While these models previously underperformed when incorporating additional variables from the IBM noise models in [8], the reduced amount of extra information has led to increased accuracy. The results show competitiveness against gradient boosting methods, especially in both low and high data regimes. Due to the data processing pipeline, where circuits are transformed into image representations, the information regarding the number of qubits cannot be hidden and is therefore not included in Table 2.

One crucial characteristic of a reliable noise estimator for production-ready software is the speed of computing this metric. Given the simple design of the selected algorithms and the small size of the parameters in the neural networks, our models can perform extremely quickly, even computing hundreds or thousands of instances per second. These timing results are presented in Table 3, where we measure the time taken to obtain the results of training and testing in each respective set of circuits. The speed advantages are clearly evident in traditional machine learning methods, as they can process up to 10,000 instances

Table 2. MAE and RSME of the ideal and noisy outputs of the quantum circuits under tabular methods with `reset` and `measure` gates removed. Each cell contains the error when employing a train split size of 1% (left-side of the arrow), and the error when employing an 80% split size (right-side of the arrow).

Algorithm	IBM Cairo		IBM Hanoi	
	MAE	RSME	MAE	RSME
XGboost	0.102 → 0.094	0.132 → 0.121	0.138 → 0.113	0.178 → 0.154
Hist Gradient Boost	0.098 → 0.091	0.127 → 0.117	0.130 → 0.110	0.168 → 0.149
Linear Regression	0.095 → 0.092	0.122 → 0.119	0.124 → 0.111	0.161 → 0.150

per second. This effect is particularly noticeable when using linear regression methods. However, when seeking a more robust method, XGBoost can achieve competitive accuracies while maintaining high prediction speeds. In comparison, these models achieve much faster training speeds than neural networks, given the costly training loop required to update these models. Moreover, between standard neural networks and convolutional neural networks, convolutional require twice as much computation time for both training and inference.

Table 3. Time in seconds of execution of the training and prediction process under each method. We showcase the results under the 1% and the 80% training splits.

Algorithm	Training		Prediction	
	1%	80%	1%	80%
XGboost	0.086	2.940	0.068	0.062
Hist Gradient Boost	0.225	1.437	0.242	0.088
Linear Regression	0.016	0.258	0.015	0.016
Dense NN	5.417	413.916	2.085	0.428
Convolutional NN	10.720	729.841	3.684	0.843

5 Conclusion

In this study, we investigate the reliability of machine learning methods in obtaining accurate noise estimations in quantum circuits. To accomplish this, we created a large dataset of circuits with varying numbers of qubits, gates, and depth. Subsequently, we computed the distances between noisy and ideal output distributions, leveraging two distinct noise models extracted from IBM backends. Through a well-suited data processing pipeline that solely relies on the gate counts of the circuits, we trained three well-known ML models to estimate this noise metric. Additionally, recognizing the limited capability of neural networks to handle tabular data, we expanded the pipeline to obtain image representations of the circuits, which are particularly good suit for convolutional neural networks. Our results demonstrate the robustness of these methods in providing accurate heuristics for estimating the fidelity of the circuit's output. Moreover, given the speed offered by these algorithms, these techniques are particularly appropriate for robust production systems requiring high throughput. We envision a future line of focused on integrating the concepts developed in this paper into a production-ready tool for analyzing quantum software and quantum code.

Acknowledgements. The authors would like to acknowledge the partial financial support by Ministry of Science (project QSERV-UD, PID2021-124054OB-C33), and also to the Basque Government (projects TRUSTIND - KK-2020/00054, and REMEDY - KK-2021/00091). Additionally, the authors wish to acknowledge the selfless support from IBM, who generously provided their quantum computing equipment for the project. Finally, it is important to also express gratitude for the support and drive that the regional government of Bizkaia is providing in all matters related to the development of quantum technologies as a driving force for progress of the Society of this historic territory.

References

1. Hogg, T., Portnov, D.: Quantum optimization. Inf. Sci. **128**(3–4), 181–197 (2000)
2. Moll, N., et al.: Quantum optimization using variational algorithms on near-term quantum devices. Quant. Sci. Technol. **3**(3), 030503 (2018)
3. Sales, J.F.A., Araos, R.A.P.: Adiabatic quantum computing for logistic transport optimization, *arXiv preprint* arXiv:2301.07691 (2023)
4. Blunt, N.S., et al.: Perspective on the current state-of-the-art of quantum computing for drug discovery applications. J. Chem. Theory Comput. **18**(12), 7001–7023 (2022)
5. Garcia-Alonso, J., Rojo, J., Valencia, D., Moguel, E., Berrocal, J., Murillo, J.M.: Quantum software as a service through a quantum API gateway. IEEE Internet Comput. **26**(1), 34–41 (2021)
6. Alvarado-Valiente, J., et al.: Quantum services generation and deployment process: a quality-oriented approach. In: Fernandes, J.M., Travassos, G.H., Lenarduzzi, V., Li, X. (eds.) QUATIC 2023. CCIS, vol. 1871, pp. 200–214. Springer, Cham (2023). https://doi.org/10.1007/978-3-031-43703-8_15
7. Piattini, M., Murillo, J.M.: Quantum software engineering landscape and challenges. In: Serrano, M.A., Pérez-Castillo, R., Piattini, M. (eds.) Quantum Software Engineering, pp. 25–38. Springer, Cham (2022). https://doi.org/10.1007/978-3-031-05324-5_2
8. Alvarado-Valiente, J., et al.: Improving the quality of quantum services generation process: controlling errors and noise. In: García Bringas, P., et al. (eds.) HAIS 2023. LNCS, vol. 14001, pp. 180–191. Springer, Cham (2023). https://doi.org/10.1007/978-3-031-40725-3_16
9. Resch, S., Karpuzcu, U.R.: Benchmarking quantum computers and the impact of quantum noise. ACM Comput. Surv. (CSUR) **54**(7), 1–35 (2021)
10. Bravyi, S., Englbrecht, M., König, R., Peard, N.: Correcting coherent errors with surface codes. Npj Quantum Inf. **4**(1), 55 (2018)

11. Clerk, A.A., Devoret, M.H., Girvin, S.M., Marquardt, F., Schoelkopf, R.J.: Introduction to quantum noise, measurement, and amplification. Rev. Mod. Phys. **82**, 1155–1208 (2010). https://link.aps.org/doi/10.1103/RevModPhys.82.1155
12. Knill, E., Laflamme, R.: Theory of quantum error-correcting codes. Phys. Rev. A **55**(2), 900 (1997)
13. Calderbank, A.R., Shor, P.W.: Good quantum error-correcting codes exist. Phys. Rev. A **54**(2), 1098 (1996)
14. Aseguinolaza, U., Sobrino, N., Sobrino, G., Jornet-Somoza, J., Borge, J.: Error estimation in current noisy quantum computers, *arXiv preprint* arXiv:2302.06870 (2023)
15. Qiskit Contributors: Qiskit: An open-source framework for quantum computing (2023)
16. Shi, Y., Ke, G., Chen, Z., Zheng, S., Liu, T.-Y.: Quantized training of gradient boosting decision trees. Adv. Neural Inf. Process. Syst. **35**, 18 822–18 833 (2022)
17. Chen, T., Guestrin, C.: XGBoost: a scalable tree boosting system. In: Proceedings of the 22nd ACM SIGKDD International Conference on Knowledge Discovery and Data Mining, pp. 785–794 (2016)

Deep Learning

The Impact of Data Annotations on the Performance of Object Detection Models in Icon Detection for GUI Images

Mădălina Dicu[1](✉), Enol García González[2], Camelia Chira[1], and José R. Villar[2]

[1] Faculty of Mathematics and Computer Science, Babeş-Bolyai University, Str. Mihail Kogălniceanu nr. 1, 400084 Cluj-Napoca, Romania
{madalina.dicu,camelia.chira}@ubbcluj.ro

[2] Department of Computer Science, University of Oviedo, C. Jesús Arias de Velasco, s/n, 33005 Oviedo, Spain
{garciaenol,villarjose}@uniovi.es

Abstract. Detecting icons in Graphical User Interfaces (GUIs) is essential for effective application automation. This study examines the impact of different annotation methods on the performance of object detection models for icon detection in GUIs. We compared manual, automated, and hybrid annotations using three models: Faster R-CNN, YOLOv8, and YOLOv9. The results show that manual annotations achieve the highest accuracy, with YOLOv9 reaching an Average Precision (AP) of 68.23% and Faster R-CNN achieving 61.82%. Hybrid methods that combine automated annotations with manual corrections also show significant improvements, though they do not perform as well as manual annotations alone. These findings underscore the importance of high-quality, consistent annotations for training effective detection models. While we used HTML code for automated annotations to simplify the process, we encountered inconsistencies that affected model performance. This highlights the need to develop better hybrid methods tailored to specific tasks, ensuring efficiency and accuracy in data annotation.

Keywords: icon detection · deep-learning models · annotation impact

1 Introduction

In today's digital age, our activities increasingly depend on computers and smartphones, making automation essential for saving time and effort [5]. Graphical User Interfaces (GUIs) are now central to many applications, requiring precise detection of UI elements for effective automation [1]. Icons, in particular, play a crucial role in enabling users to navigate applications intuitively [9]. However, detecting these icons accurately presents significant challenges as GUIs grow more complex.

H. Quintián et al. (Eds.): HAIS 2024, LNAI 14857, pp. 251–262, 2025.
https://doi.org/10.1007/978-3-031-74183-8_21

Creating high-quality datasets for training object detection models is critical but time-consuming. We encountered substantial difficulties due to the extensive time required for manual labeling. This issue is compounded by the lack of comprehensive datasets specifically designed for GUIs. Most existing datasets focus on mobile interfaces, leaving a gap for desktop and web-based GUIs. Studies have primarily addressed mobile UI elements, as seen in the work of Xie et al. [15] and Gu et al. [6], but there is a significant need for datasets that cover a broader range of GUI environments.

To address this gap, we proposed extracting websites and using HTML code to automate the labeling process. HTML contains structured information about GUI elements, making it reliable for generating accurate annotations. This method aimed to streamline the annotation process, reducing the time and effort required while maintaining high accuracy. Automated techniques have shown promise in various contexts [3], and we adapted these techniques to our specific needs. Our study evaluates the impact of different annotation methods on the performance of object detection models for icon detection in desktop GUIs. By comparing manual, automated, and hybrid annotation techniques, we aim to determine how annotation quality influences model performance using Faster R-CNN, YOLOv8, and YOLOv9 models.

The study shows that high-quality manual annotations significantly boost object detection model performance in GUI icon detection, with YOLOv9 achieving the best results. Hybrid methods, combining automated annotations with manual corrections, improve performance but are still inferior to purely manual annotations. Despite similar website structures, automated annotations were inconsistent, negatively impacting accuracy. This highlights the necessity of thoroughly understanding the data to tailor the automation process effectively.

The structure of this paper is as follows: Sect. 2 reviews related work on data annotation and object detection. Section 3 outlines our methodology, covering data collection, annotation processes, and the models used. Section 4 presents the experimental results and their initial analysis. Section 5 discusses our findings, and Sect. 6 concludes the paper.

2 Related Work

Data annotation is crucial for developing object detection models, directly impacting performance. While high-quality annotations are known to be essential, the specific impact of varying annotation quality on object detection models for GUIs needs systematic evaluation.

Everingham et al. [4] demonstrated that annotation quality significantly influences model performance in the PASCAL Visual Object Classes (VOC) challenge. Chen et al. [3] emphasized the necessity of manual refinement for correcting automated annotations. However, these studies do not specifically address GUI elements.

Detecting GUI elements, such as buttons and icons, presents unique challenges due to design variability. Xie et al. [15] improved detection accuracy in mobile applications using detailed annotations, but their focus was on mobile UIs, leaving desktop GUIs less explored.

Gu et al. [6] used detailed OCR annotations in their "Adaptively Prompt Tuning" (APT) method to enhance mobile UI element detection, showing that precise annotations can compensate for language and context differences. Xiao et al. [14] highlighted that precise annotations improve UI automation and metadata generation, while Selcuk et al. [11] confirmed that accurate annotations are critical for YOLO models in mobile UI detection.

Despite these advancements, there is a need for comprehensive studies that evaluate the impact of different annotation methods on object detection models for desktop GUIs. Understanding how annotation quality affects model performance in these contexts is essential for developing efficient and accurate detection systems.

3 Methodology

In this section, we detail our methodology for examining the impact of annotation methods on icon detection. We describe the data collection and annotation processes, outline the object detection models used in our study, and explain the experimental setup and evaluation metrics. Finally, we present our proposed approach for comparing different annotation scenarios to determine the most effective method for training accurate and efficient icon detection models.

3.1 Data Collection and Annotation

To study the impact of annotations on icon detection, we utilized websites to create a comprehensive dataset with icon annotations. We selected templates from various websites, focusing on corporate websites, administration interfaces, desktop applications, blogs, portfolios, and online stores to represent a diverse set of user interfaces. Our approach aimed to inspect the impact of annotations, starting with the idea that we needed similar templates or templates from the same area. To ensure a variety of styles, we selected templates from both WordPress and Envato.

Automatic Annotation Process. For automatic labeling, we leveraged the HTML and CSS code of websites, focusing primarily on the HTML code, which contains marked information identifying element types on the web page. The automated system traversed all interface aspects in the HTML code to determine whether they belonged to any classes defined in the dataset. To build a comprehensive dataset, we needed to generate an image of the website and obtain the position and size of elements. We used web test environments such as Selenium or Cypress to load the web page in a browser and access its graphical representation, code, and browser-calculated attributes like position and size.

The detailed annotation process for each web page included in the dataset was as follows:

1. Load the web page in the browser.
2. Obtain a snapshot of the complete web page.
3. Traverse the tree of components of the web page and for each one:
   (a) Check if it is identified as one of the classes defined in the dataset.
   (b) If it is an element defined in the dataset:
      i. Get the position and size attributes calculated by the browser.
      ii. Store the information about the annotation (image, class, position, and size).

This process was carried out on 32 websites selected from web development templates of known technologies. Although templates were taken from the same source, the tags from which we extracted the annotations were not identical. Additionally, some icons were either not annotated or annotated incorrectly as a different class, such as images instead of icons. Automatic annotation took on average 1 min per image. Figure 1 presents an image from our dataset.

Fig. 1. Example image from the dataset generated after processing websites

Manual Annotation Process. For manual annotation, we used the images obtained from the automatic annotation process. Using the Label Studio tool [12], we annotated these images according to predefined characteristics, ensuring consistency and accuracy. These characteristics included defining the size and position attributes of icons. The differences between manual and automatic annotation involved adding some unmarked icons, removing incorrect annotations, or correcting the boundaries of existing annotations. Manual annotation took 5 min per image.

Hybrid Annotation Process. The hybrid annotation process involved reviewing the automatically annotated data to verify accuracy. We used the images from the automatic annotation process and checked that the annotations matched the dataset standards. Missing or incorrect annotations were corrected or added, maintaining a high level of precision and consistency. The hybrid approach ensured that the final dataset maintained a high standard of annotation quality. Hybrid annotation took 2 min per image.

Overall, the dataset consisted of annotations from 146 images, resulting from the combination of automatic, manual, and hybrid annotations. From each site, we built our dataset by creating images with different content, leading to the final total of 146 images from the initial 32 sites. All images have a width of 1920 pixels, reflecting the resolution of the capturing computer, though the height varies depending on the content. All images are in PNG format. We noticed from the beginning that the annotations given in the HTML code were not always consistent. Although not many changes were necessary, it was essential to review and correct these annotations to ensure the dataset's accuracy.

3.2 Object Detection Models

In this section, we describe the three models employed in our study: Faster R-CNN, YOLOv8, and YOLOv9.

Faster Region-based Convolutional Neural Network (Faster R-CNN) [10] is an advanced object detection algorithm using Convolutional Neural Networks (CNNs). It introduces the Region Proposal Network (RPN) to efficiently generate object proposals, which are then refined and classified by a detection network. As a two-stage detector, it offers high accuracy but demands more computational resources.

You Only Look Once Version 8 (YOLOv8) [7] enhances object detection with a real-time, end-to-end approach. It features the C2f module for improved accuracy and an anchor-free model with a decoupled head, optimizing objectness, classification, and regression tasks. YOLOv8 is fast and efficient, ideal for processing large icon datasets.

You Only Look Once Version 9 (YOLOv9) [13] introduces further optimizations, including an enhanced attention mechanism and improved feature pyramid networks (FPN). It uses a novel training strategy that combines supervised and unsupervised learning, boosting performance with less labeled data. YOLOv9 retains the one-stage processing pipeline, offering high accuracy and speed for real-time detection, making it suitable for our icon detection and annotation tasks.

3.3 Experiment Setup

For our experiments, we utilized established architectures for the models discussed previously. For the Faster R-CNN model, we used a pre-trained ResNet50 architecture as the backbone. The model was trained over 100 epochs with a batch size of 2. Stochastic Gradient Descent (SGD) was employed as the optimizer, with a learning rate set at 0.005. These parameters are the best obtained after exhaustive experimentation with different values.

For the YOLO models, we adopted architectures proposed by Ultralytics. Specifically, we used the YOLOv8m and yolov9c.pt models [7]. Both YOLO models were trained over 100 epochs with a batch size of 2, using SGD as the optimizer. The learning rate for the YOLO models was set at 0.01.

The choice of learning rates, optimizer, and number of epochs was based on common defaults for these models, providing a reliable starting point. The small batch size was necessary due to the limited number of images in our dataset. Despite the high number of epochs, all models were configured to save the best-performing model during training to prevent overfitting. All experiments were conducted using the Google Colaboratory platform [2].

3.4 Evaluation Metrics

To evaluate the performance of the models, we considered several metrics:

- **Intersection over Union (IoU)**: This metric evaluates the overlap between the actual and predicted bounding boxes by measuring the ratio of their intersection area to their union area. For our evaluations, IoU was set to 0.5.
- **Average Precision (AP)**: This metric is derived from the precision-recall curve, representing the model's ability to correctly identify objects of interest. Precision is calculated by dividing the number of correct positive predictions by the total number of positive predictions. The recall is determined by dividing the number of correct positive predictions by the total number of actual positive instances in the dataset [8].
- **Confidence Thresholds**: These thresholds filter model predictions based on their confidence scores, influencing precision and recall metrics. For our evaluations, we used confidence thresholds of 0.50, 0.25, and 0.20. Lower confidence thresholds are necessary for YOLO models to perform optimally.

3.5 Proposed Approach

We designed four scenarios to systematically test and compare the models using various annotation approaches.

- **Scenario 1: Automatic Annotation.** In the first scenario, we utilized the automatic annotations obtained through the process described in the Data Collection and Annotation section. This scenario serves as a baseline to understand the effectiveness of the automated annotation process in training our object detection models.
- **Scenario 2: Hybrid Annotation.** In the second scenario, we employed a hybrid annotation method. Starting with the automatically annotated data, we manually verified and corrected any incorrect or missing annotations. This scenario aims to combine the efficiency of automatic annotation with the accuracy of manual correction, providing a potentially more robust dataset for training.

- **Scenario 3: Mixed Annotation for Training and Validation.** The third scenario involved using the annotations from Scenario 1 (automatic annotation) for training the models. However, for validation and testing, we used the manually verified and corrected annotations from Scenario 2. This approach helps in assessing the models' performance when there is a discrepancy between the training data quality and the validation/testing data quality.
- **Scenario 4: Manual Annotation** In the fourth and final scenario, we used exclusively manual annotations. This scenario serves as the gold standard for comparison, highlighting the performance of the models when trained and evaluated with the highest quality annotations available.

Each of these scenarios was designed to provide insights into how different annotation methods affect the performance of object detection models, specifically in the context of icon detection. By comparing the results across these scenarios, we can determine the trade-offs between annotation efficiency and accuracy, and identify the optimal approach for training robust and reliable detection models.

4 Results

This section presents the results obtained from training the icon detection models on GUI images and provides an initial analysis of the findings.

In preparation for the experiments, the data was split with a ratio of 80% for training, 10% for validation, and 10% for testing. The distribution of images and the number of annotations are shown in Table 1. While the number of images remains the same across all experiments, the number of annotations varies. Scenario 1 has the fewest training annotations due to the limitations of the automatic annotation method, which often resulted in missing or mispositioned annotations. This also affects Scenario 3. Scenarios 2 and 4 have the same number of annotations, as manual annotation is considered the standard, covering all icons in the dataset.

Table 1. Distribution of the dataset for the conducted experiments

Experiment	Number of images				Number of annotations			
	Total	Train	Valid	Test	Total	Train	Valid	Test
Scenario 1	146	118	14	14	3140	2580	291	269
Scenario 2	146	118	14	14	3588	2944	369	275
Scenario 3	146	118	14	14	3224	2580	369	275
Scenario 4	146	118	14	14	3588	2944	369	275

The performance of the Faster R-CNN, YOLOv8, and YOLOv9 models was evaluated in the four annotation scenarios using Average Precision (AP) at three confidence thresholds (50%, 25%, and 20%) (Table 2).

Table 2. Average Precision results for the 4 proposed scenarios and the 3 models at Confidence Thresholds of 0.50, 0.25, and 0.20

Scenario	Model	Confidence threshold		
		50	25	20
Scenario 1	**Faster RCNN**	37.96	38.86	38.98
	YOLOv8	0.00	0.83	0.83
	YOLOv9	0.19	3.69	3.69
Scenario 2	**Faster RCNN**	45.76	47.06	47.06
	YOLOv8	0.05	3.15	3.15
	YOLOv9	29.87	49.28	49.28
Scenario 3	**Faster RCNN**	23.00	24.82	25.26
	YOLOv8	0.00	0.00	0.00
	YOLOv9	0.00	1.39	1.39
Scenario 4	**Faster RCNN**	59.95	61.56	61.82
	YOLOv8	2.71	34.96	34.96
	YOLOv9	65.27	68.23	**68.23**

In Scenario 1, which relied solely on automatic annotations, the performance was suboptimal due to missing and misplaced annotations. However, the Faster R-CNN model achieved an AP of 38.98% at the 20% confidence threshold, indicating a moderate level of accuracy. In contrast, YOLOv8 and YOLOv9 exhibited significantly lower APs, both under 4%. These results suggest that the quality of automatic annotations is insufficient for training effective object detection models. Notably, the Faster R-CNN model demonstrated a surprising level of adaptability to the inconsistencies present in the validation and test data, an adaptability that YOLO-based models lacked.

Scenario 2, which combined automatic and manual annotations in a hybrid model, demonstrated substantial performance improvements. The AP of Faster R-CNN increased to 47.06%, while YOLOv9's AP rose significantly to 49.28%. YOLOv8 also showed some improvement, although it remained relatively low. These results indicate that the hybrid approach, which incorporates manual verification and correction, significantly enhances dataset quality and, consequently, model performance.

In Scenario 3, where automatic annotations were used for training and manually verified annotations for validation, all models experienced a significant drop in performance. This scenario yielded the weakest results, illustrating the direct impact of missing annotations on model training. The moderate results of Faster R-CNN observed in Scenario 1 were significantly degraded in this scenario due to the annotation quality. This highlights the adverse effects of inconsistencies between the training and validation data quality, emphasizing the critical need for consistent annotation standards throughout the dataset.

Scenario 4, which used exclusively manual annotations, yielded the highest performance across all models. Faster R-CNN improved its AP by nearly 15% compared to its next best result, and YOLOv9 improved by almost 19%, achieving the best overall result. These outcomes confirm the superiority of high-quality manual annotations in training effective object detection models, demonstrating their critical role in achieving optimal performance. Additionally, this scenario underscores the importance of consistency in annotation quality. Despite the hybrid method's manual intervention, the consistently high-quality manual annotations, classified by the same criteria, had a significant impact. This suggests that for annotations derived from HTML code, adapting these annotations to the type of website is necessary to achieve a unified annotation style, especially when creating a comprehensive dataset.

Figure 2 graphically represents an example of labeling for each scenario presented in the experimentation.

(a) Scenario 1 (b) Scenario 2 (c) Scenario 3 (d) Scenario 4

Fig. 2. Example of the labeling. The best model from each scenario has been taken for this example.

5 Discussion

The experimental results highlight the importance of annotation quality for object detection models, particularly in GUI icon detection. Key findings include:

Scenario 1, using only automatic annotations, showed poor performance due to missing and mispositioned annotations. This was evident in YOLOv8 and YOLOv9, with Faster R-CNN performing moderately better but still insufficient. These results indicate that relying solely on automatic annotations can lead to significant inaccuracies that impair model performance.

Scenario 2, combining automatic and manual annotations, significantly improved performance. This hybrid approach balances automation efficiency with manual correction, resulting in substantial performance gains for both Faster R-CNN and YOLOv9. The findings suggest that integrating human oversight in the annotation process can effectively bridge the gap between fully automated and manual methods, enhancing dataset quality and model accuracy.

Scenario 3 demonstrated the negative impact of inconsistent annotation standards between training and validation data, leading to the weakest performance across all models. This highlights the necessity of maintaining consistent annotation practices throughout the dataset to ensure that models can generalize effectively. Inconsistent data quality can severely hinder a model's ability to perform well in real-world applications.

Scenario 4, using exclusively manual annotations, achieved the highest performance across all models. This underscores the value of precise, consistent manual annotations for effective model training. The superior results of both Faster R-CNN and YOLOv9 in this scenario demonstrate that manual annotation remains the gold standard for achieving optimal model performance.

In addition to the above findings, it was observed that YOLOv9 consistently outperformed YOLOv8 across all scenarios, indicating its robustness to variations in annotation quality. Faster R-CNN also performed well, particularly in scenarios with higher-quality annotations. These results suggest that while advanced models like YOLOv9 and Faster R-CNN can mitigate some deficiencies of lower-quality annotations, they still heavily rely on the precision and consistency provided by manual annotations.

Figure 3 graphically represents the relationship between the time spent labeling the dataset images and the quality of the trained models. The dashed orange line represents the average time required to label each dataset image in the three scenarios. The solid blue lines represent the Average Precision target for each model. Manual labeling has better results when compared to AP, but it also significantly increases the time needed to generate the images. The hybrid method achieves more efficient results by comparing the time spent on labeling with the AP obtained.

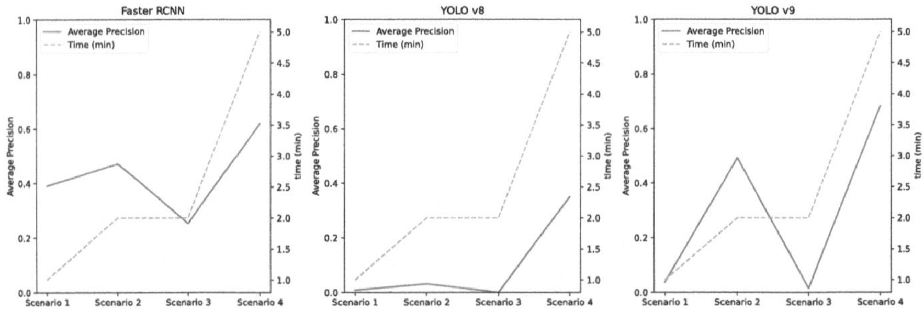

Fig. 3. Average Precision obtained compared with the average time needed to label each dataset image.

Based on these results, we recommend the following best practices for future annotation efforts:

- **Prioritize Manual Annotations:** Whenever feasible, use manual annotations to ensure the highest quality and consistency. This is particularly important for creating training datasets for complex models.

- **Incorporate Hybrid Approaches:** If the manual annotation is not entirely feasible, use a hybrid approach that combines automatic and manual methods. Ensure that manual verification is thorough to correct any inaccuracies in the automated annotations.
- **Maintain Consistency:** Ensure that the quality of annotations is consistent across the entire dataset. Avoid using different annotation methods for training and validation data to prevent performance degradation.
- **Adapt Annotations to Context:** For annotations derived from HTML code, adapt the annotations to the specific type of website to achieve a unified annotation style. This is especially important when creating comprehensive datasets that span multiple contexts. This principle can also be extended to other domains such as images and different data types, where contextual adaptation ensures that annotations are relevant and consistent across varying conditions and scenarios.

6 Conclusion and Future Work

This study underscores the critical impact of annotation quality on the performance of object detection models in GUI icon detection. Scenario 4, which utilized manual annotations, achieved the highest performance, with YOLOv9 attaining the best result with an AP of 68.23%, followed by Faster R-CNN with an AP of 61.82%. In contrast, YOLOv8 showed the lowest performance, achieving an AP that was half of the best result. The hybrid annotation approach also demonstrated significant improvements, illustrating the advantages of combining automated and manual methods. However, the performance was still lower than that of the manual annotations, indicating that successful automation requires a comprehensive understanding of the data to establish general annotation criteria. The necessity for consistent annotations was further validated by Scenario 3, where inconsistencies in training data were shown to significantly impact performance.

Future work will focus on exploring automated annotation refinement techniques and developing adaptive annotation strategies tailored to GUI image contexts. The objective is to create an automated annotation method that leverages website HTML code to generate datasets, which can be adapted for both icon detection and other UI elements. This approach aims to enhance the efficiency and accuracy of annotation processes, contributing to the advancement of object detection models in complex GUI environments.

Acknowledgements. This research has been funded by the Spanish Ministry of Economics and Industry –grant PID2020-112726RB-I00–, the Spanish Research Agency –grant PID2023-146257OB-I00–, and Missions Science and Innovation project MIG-20211008 (INMERBOT). Also, by Principado de Asturias, grant SV-PA-21-AYUD/2021/50994, and by the Council of Gijón through the University Institute of Industrial Technology of Asturias grants SV-21-GIJON-1-19, SV-22-GIJON-1-19, SV-22-GIJON-1-22, SV-23-GIJON-1-09, and SV-23-GIJON-1-17. Finally, this research has also been funded by Fundación Universidad de Oviedo grants FUO-23-008 and FUO-22-450.

References

1. Altinbas, M.D., Serif, T.: GUI element detection from mobile UI images using YOLov5. In: Awan, I., Younas, M., Poniszewska-Marańda, A. (eds.) MobiWIS 2022. LNCS, vol. 13475, pp. 32–45. Springer, Cham (2022). https://doi.org/10.1007/978-3-031-14391-5_3
2. Bisong, E., Bisong, E.: Google colaboratory. Building machine learning and deep learning models on google cloud platform: a comprehensive guide for beginners, pp. 59–64 (2019)
3. Chen, J., et al.: Object detection for graphical user interface: old fashioned or deep learning or a combination? In: Proceedings of the 28th ACM joint meeting on European Software Engineering Conference and Symposium on the Foundations of Software Engineering, pp. 1202–1214 (2020)
4. Everingham, M., Van Gool, L., Williams, C.K., Winn, J., Zisserman, A.: The pascal visual object classes (VOC) challenge. Int. J. Comput. Vision **88**, 303–338 (2010)
5. Fröhlich, P., Baldauf, M., Meneweger, T., Tscheligi, M., de Ruyter, B., Paternó, F.: Everyday automation experience: a research agenda. Pers. Ubiquit. Comput. **24**, 725–734 (2020)
6. Gu, Z., Xu, Z., Chen, H., Lan, J., Meng, C., Wang, W.: Mobile user interface element detection via adaptively prompt tuning. In: Proceedings of the IEEE/CVF Conference on Computer Vision and Pattern Recognition, pp. 11155–11164 (2023)
7. Jocher, G., Chaurasia, A., Qiu, J.: YOLO by Ultralytics (2023). https://github.com/ultralytics/ultralytics. Accessed 10 June 2024
8. Padilla, R., Netto, S.L., Da Silva, E.A.: A survey on performance metrics for object-detection algorithms. In: 2020 International Conference on Systems, Signals and Image Processing (IWSSIP), pp. 237–242. IEEE (2020)
9. Passini, S., Strazzari, F., Borghi, A.: Icon-function relationship in toolbar icons. Displays **29**(5), 521–525 (2008)
10. Ren, S., He, K., Girshick, R., Sun, J.: Faster R-CNN: towards real-time object detection with region proposal networks. Adv. Neural Inf. Process. Syst. **28** (2015)
11. Selcuk, B., Serif, T.: A comparison of YOLOv5 and YOLOv8 in the context of mobile UI detection. In: Younas, M., Awan, I., Grønli, T.M. (eds.) MobiWIS 2023. LNCS, vol. 13977, pp. 161–174. Springer, Cham (2023). https://doi.org/10.1007/978-3-031-39764-6_11
12. Tkachenko, M., Malyuk, M., Holmanyuk, A., Liubimov, N.: Label Studio: Data labeling software (2020-2022). https://github.com/heartexlabs/label-studio. Open source software https://github.com/heartexlabs/label-studio
13. Wang, C.Y., Yeh, I.H., Liao, H.Y.M.: YOLOv9: learning what you want to learn using programmable gradient information. arXiv preprint arXiv:2402.13616 (2024)
14. Xiao, S., et al.: UI semantic component group detection: grouping UI elements with similar semantics in mobile graphical user interface. Displays **83**, 102679 (2024)
15. Xie, M., Feng, S., Xing, Z., Chen, J., Chen, C.: UIED: a hybrid tool for GUI element detection. In: Proceedings of the 28th ACM Joint Meeting on European Software Engineering Conference and Symposium on the Foundations of Software Engineering, pp. 1655–1659 (2020)

Bayesian Model Selection Pruning in Predictive Maintenance

David Solis-Martin[1,2(✉)], Juan Galan-Paez[1,2], and Joaquin Borrego-Diaz[1]

[1] Computer Science and Artificial Intelligence Department, Seville University, Seville, Spain
{dsolis,juangalan,jborrego}@us.es
[2] Datrik Intelligence S.A., Seville, Spain
{david.solis,juan.galan}@datrik.com

Abstract. Deep Neural Network architecture design significantly impacts the final model performance. The process of searching for optimal architectures, known as Neural Architecture Search (NAS), involves training and evaluating an important number of models. Therefore, mechanisms to reduce the resources required for NAS are highly valuable.

This work proposes a methodology to prune the Bayesian Optimization process used in NAS. With this aim, an estimator has been trained to predict the future performance of a model by just observing few training and validation epochs. To build such an estimator, the authors developed a dataset containing information (hyperparameters and performance curves) of multiple architectures trained on 62 different predictive maintenance datasets. The results of a simulated BO process used for NAS highlight a reduction in the optimization time of more than 50% with a minimal loss (around 2%) in the performance of the best model found.

Keywords: Learning Curves · Neural Architecture Search · Predictive Maintenance · Bayesian Optimization

1 Introduction

The foray of Deep Learning (DL) into many fields of industry has been quite strong in recent years. DL has achieved impressive results in image processing, natural language processing, and audio processing. Additionally, in less-known industrial contexts such as Predictive Maintenance (PM), it has also achieved successful results.

It is a fact that neural architecture design is essential to extract useful features for the specific task involved, which impacts the performance of the final model. Throughout the research history of neural networks, different high-level architectures have been designed, such as feedforward networks (FFN), convolutional neural networks (CNN), recurrent neural networks (RNN), and transformers.

H. Quintián et al. (Eds.): HAIS 2024, LNAI 14857, pp. 263–274, 2025.
https://doi.org/10.1007/978-3-031-74183-8_22

However, the specific configuration of hyperparameters (number of layers, type of layers, activation functions, number of neurons, learning rate, etc.) for each architecture requires a lot of experience to be set effectively.

In this context, a known approach is to use an optimization process to search for optimal architectures, which is known in the literature as Neural Architecture Search (NAS). NAS involves training and evaluating multiple models (tens or hundreds of them) during the search process. Obviously, it is resource-intensive and time-consuming. For example, NASNet [12] utilizes 2,000 GPU days using reinforcement learning, and AmoebaNet-A [9] uses 3,150 GPU days using evolutionary learning. Therefore, mechanisms to reduce the resources needed for NAS are very valuable.

In the mentioned optimization process, the input to the objective function f is the model architecture and training hyperparameters, whereas the output is the performance of the model trained using the provided settings. Bayesian Optimization (BO) is a method that performs especially well in scenarios where f is expensive to evaluate. A typical application of BO in machine learning is model selection [10], where the generalization performance of a statistical model cannot be analytically determined and must be empirically evaluated. For example, BO can be used to choose the parameter λ and the kernel bandwidth h for an SVM. BO has also been applied in NAS previously. For example, in NASBOT [5], the use of BO for NAS is proposed with a new distance metric in the space of neural network architectures.

Human experts in machine learning typically inspect performance curves during the training process to quickly terminate runs with poor hyperparameter settings. This practice significantly speeds up manual hyperparameter optimization. In the context of machine learning, learning curves are used to assess the performance of a learning algorithm with respect to a certain resource, such as the number of training examples or the number of training iterations. Learning curves have important applications in several areas of machine learning, including data acquisition, early stopping of model training, and model selection.

This work focuses on using learning curves to discard unpromising models during NAS with BO. To illustrate the proposed methodology, a dataset of 61,000 learning curves has been generated. This dataset was created using 62 different datasets from multiple tasks (failure detection, fault diagnosis, and prognosis) in the context of predictive maintenance. The datasets were obtained by searching different research repositories, related bibliography, and the internet in general, for public datasets in the context of predictive maintenance, covering the years between 2010 and 2022. All datasets found were included in the experiment set. The only requirement that a dataset has to meet to be included in the study is that it must be a time series dataset. The datasets span multiple engineering domains, systems and components, such as electrical components, drive technology, mechanical components, and materials, among others. For each dataset, NAS was performed on four different architectures: Feedforward Networks (FFN), Deep Convolutional Networks (DCN), Recurrent Neural Networks

(RNN), and Transformers. The NAS process was conducted using BO, with each run consisting of 100 iterations. Figure 1 shows a sample of learning curves from the dataset.

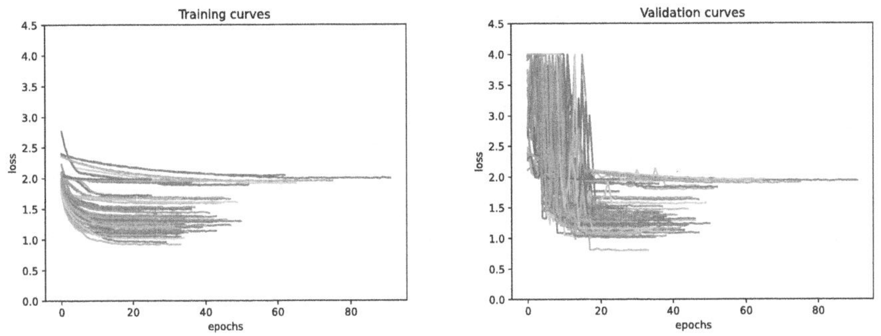

Fig. 1. Example of learning curves used in this work. On the left are the training performance curves, and on the right are the validation performance curves, both for the same model settings. As can be seen, the validation curves are particularly noisy during the first epochs.

1.1 Related Work

NAS is typically structured with an *outer loop* that searches for optimal network hyperparameters and an *inner loop* that optimizes the model parameters (i.e., the network weights) using those hyperparameters. This work focuses on implementing early stopping mechanisms within the *inner loop* to improve efficiency.

In [1], following the idea of [3], learning curves are used to early stop the training of selected networks. They employ an estimator to predict the final performance of the current model. If the estimation is worse than the best performance obtained so far, the training of that model is stopped. They apply this approach to the Hyperband [8] optimization algorithm. Similarly, the authors of [7] apply Bayesian networks to estimate learning curves during hyperparameter optimization using Hyperband. It is worth noting that the Hyperband search algorithm is a search procedure that does not take former performances into account when deciding the next points in the search space to visit.

In the context of Bayesian Optimization (BO), several methods have been proposed to increase overall efficiency by scheduling the search and implementing early stopping in the inner loop for each hyperparameter set tested when no further improvement is expected. For example, in BOHB [4], HyperBand and Bayesian Optimization are combined. HyperBand [8] aims to speed up random search by applying an early-stopping strategy through adaptive resource allocation (iterations, data samples, or number of features). In this way, BOHB leverages learning from previously sampled configurations of Bayesian Optimization and discards unpromising solutions from HyperBand.

An idea similar to ours was published in [2]. The authors used a Bayesian model to estimate when the model being trained during a BO iteration had converged. Consequently, the training was stopped earlier, avoiding a number of unnecessary training epochs. However, with this method, a model without potential to surpass the current best model could still be trained for a considerable number of epochs.

This work goes a step further by training each model for a fixed, lower number N of epochs. During these N epochs, the learning curves are monitored and used by a previously trained network to estimate the final performance of the model. If the estimation indicates that the model performance is significantly worse than the best obtained so far, the training of the model is stopped. This approach aims to ensure that poorly performing models are trained for only N epochs.

2 Final Performance Estimators

The key element of the proposed methodology is a model capable of estimating the final validation performance y_T that a neural To build the estimator, in the first approach, the first N observed train and validation performance points taken from the learning curves are used:

$$y(N) = \{\{y_0^{train}, y_1^{train}, \ldots, y_N^{train}\}, \{y_0^{val}, y_1^{val}, \ldots, y_N^{val}\}\}$$

Therefore, the training set to build such a model will be composed of the former training and validation performances and their corresponding targets:

$$\mathcal{S}_{\mathcal{LC}} = \{(y(N)^1, y_T^1), (y(N)^2, y_T^2), \ldots, (y(N)^M, y_T^M)\}$$

where M is the number of samples in the dataset.

Note that the number of training epochs for each model could be different (see Fig. 1). This variation is due to the models being trained using an early stopping criterion. This is quite different from other works, where the number of epochs is always the same.

In the second approach, we study how the information of the hyperparameters impacts the learning curve estimator. Thus, the hyperparameters h^i will be included as part of the estimator. Since the dataset contains various types of architectures and only a general learning curve estimator is trained, the hyperparameter vector is paired with a one-hot vector that determines whether each hyperparameter was set for that network. Thus, the training set for this estimator will be of the form:

$$\mathcal{S}_{\mathcal{LC}+\mathcal{H}} = \{((y(N)^1, h^1), y_T^1), ((y(N)^2, h^2), y_T^2), \ldots, ((y(N)^M, h^M), y_T^M)\}$$

2.1 Estimator Architectures

In this work, a neural network has been used as a final performance estimator, specifically, an RNN with Bidirectional Long Short-Term Memory (Bi-LSTM) cells comprising 128 units. Following the Bi-LSTM cells, two fully connected layers with 128 and 64 neurons each, using ReLU activation, were added. Additionally, Batch Normalization was applied after the Bi-LSTM cells. The input shape varies between 2 and 9 observed epochs of training and validation performance curves. The full architecture has been depicted in Fig. 2.

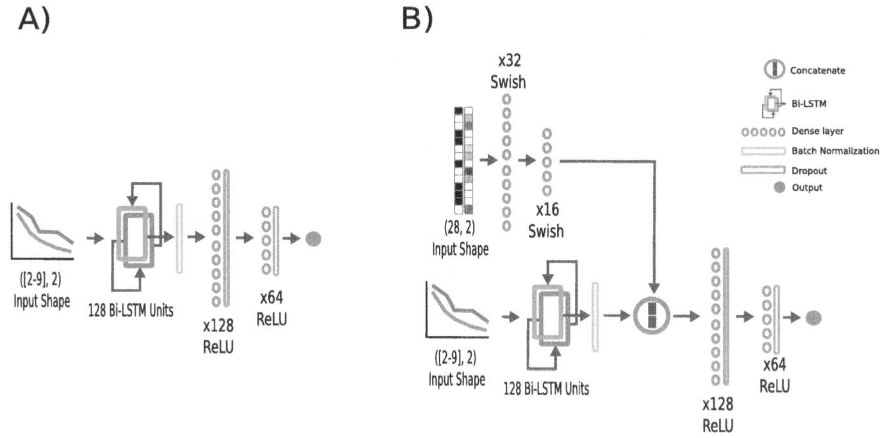

Fig. 2. Performance estimator architectures. A) Estimator architecture using only observed training and validation performance curves. B) Estimator architecture using performance curves and network hyperparameters.

To study the impact of network hyperparameters, a conditioned network is designed. The hyperparameters define the network architecture used to create the learning curve. Since the dataset was created considering different types of networks (FFN, CNN, RNN, and transformer), some parameters are not applicable to all architectures (see Table 1). To address this issue, a one-hot vector mask was added to indicate which of the 28 network hyperparameters are relevant for each network. The hyperparameter vector and mask, with a dimension of 28×2, pass through two fully connected layers with 32 and 16 neurons, respectively. These layers use the Swish activation function. The output of the last fully connected layer is appended to the output of the Bi-LSTM cells before being fed into the two final network dense layers. Tables 2 and 3 summarize the full architectures of both approaches.

2.2 Training Procedure

The performance estimators are trained to predict the final validation loss value. Depending on the nature of the task, regression or classification, the loss could be the mean squared error or the cross-entropy error, respectively.

The dataset of performance curves is split into training, validation, and test sets. To avoid overfitting, the split was carried out by dataset. The performance curves of 30% of the datasets, selected randomly, were reserved for the test set. The remaining 70% of the datasets were further split, with 70% used as the training set and 30% as the validation set. Additionally, a cross-validation approach with 3 folds was used. To validate the results across different test sets and network initializations, the experiments were conducted 6 times using different random seeds.

Table 1. Hyperparameters used to condition the performance estimator. Some hyperparameters are not applicable, depending on the type of network.

Hyperparameter	Description	MLP	CNN	RNN	Transformer
MLP Activation	Activation Function	✓			
Batch Normalization	Use batch normalization	✓	✓	✓	✓
Bidirectional	Bidirectional RNN			✓	
Block Size	Number of convolutional blocks		✓		
Rnn Cell Type	Recurrent cell type			✓	
Conv Activation	Convolution Activation Function		✓		
Dense Activation	Dense Block Activation Function		✓	✓	
Dilation Rate	Convolution Activation Rate		✓		
Dropout	Dropout Regularization Rate	✓	✓	✓	✓
F1, F2, F3	MS-CNN Convolution Size		✓		
FC1, FC2	Dense Layer Size		✓	✓	✓
Filters	Convolution Filters		✓		
Kernel Size	Convolution Kernel Size		✓		
L1, L2	L1 y L2 Regularization Rates	✓	✓	✓	✓
Dense Dim	Dense Block Parameters		✓	✓	✓
Model Dim	Total Model Parameters	✓	✓	✓	✓
MS Blocks	Number of MS-CNN Blocks		✓		
Conv Blocks	Number of Convolutional Blocks		✓		
Layers	Number of layers	✓	✓	✓	✓
Heads	Number of transformer heads				✓
Output Dim	Output dimension	✓	✓	✓	✓
RNN Units	Number of RNN Units			✓	
Segment Size	Patch Segment Size				✓

Early stopping was applied when the performance of the networks ceased to improve on the validation set for eight consecutive epochs. Additionally, a learning rate decay [11] was applied by a factor of 0.1 when there was no improvement in validation performance for five consecutive epochs.

The Adam optimizer [6] was employed as the optimizer, with an initial learning rate set to 0.0001.

2.3 Estimators Performance

Figure 3 shows the performance of both estimators depending on the number of observed training epochs. As expected, with a higher number of observed training epochs, the error of the estimator decreases. It is also observed that the use of network hyperparameters improves the performance, especially when the number of observed epochs is reduced.

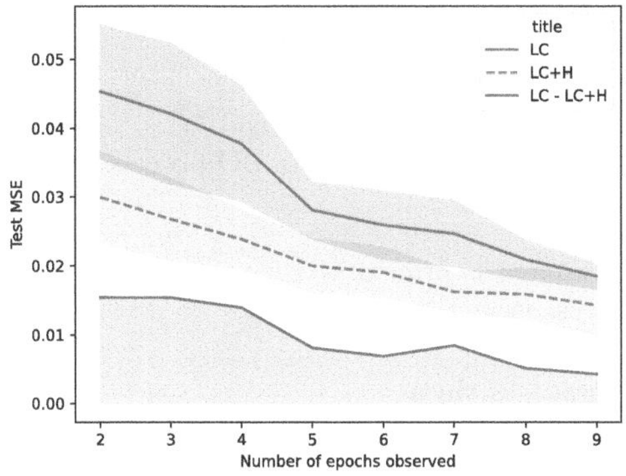

Fig. 3. Efficiency of the final performance estimators. LC: Performance of the estimator using only performance curves. LC+H: Performance of the estimator using both performance curves and network hyperparameters. LC - LC+H: Difference between the performance of the two estimators.

3 Early-Stopping During NAS with BO

Once the final performance estimator has been trained, it is possible to validate its effectiveness in reducing the number of epochs during BO. Running the BO process for the different architectures on each of the 62 datasets is highly time-consuming, and was already carried out to build the learning curves dataset. Thus, in this preliminary work, the BO process is simulated using the traces obtained from the formerly executed experiments. Specifically, the experiments run in the test set for each dataset are traversed in the same order as they were trained. This is described in Algorithm 1.

Figure 4 presents the results of the simulation. In terms of the percentage of time saved, both estimators save between 42% and 65%, approximately. The inverse trend is mainly due to the fact that with fewer observed epochs, more epochs will be discarded when a non-promising architecture is found.

During the simulation, it is possible to measure how often the best solution (ground truth) is found by the estimator. In this case, there is an increasing trend: with a higher number of observed epochs, the likelihood of not pruning the optimal execution increases.

Input: $E(\cdot)$: Final performance estimator
BO: Bayesian Optimization experiment records
N: Number of observed epochs
Output: Best Loss

```
Initialize variables: best_loss ← ∞, best_hyperparameters ← NaN;
for 1 to 100 do
    h ← next hyperparameter set taken (in same order) from a formerly
    executed BO process;
    lc ← train and validation performance curves for the N first epochs;
    estimated_loss ← E(lc, h);
    if estimated_loss < best_loss * 2 then
        /* The experiment is run until the end */
        final_loss ← actual loss obtained in BO process
    end
    else
        /* The experiment is pruned */
        final_loss ← estimated_loss
    end
    if final_loss < best_loss then
        best_loss ← final_loss;
    end
end
```

Algorithm 1: Early Stopping within BO simulation

Lastly, the mean loss obtained depending on the number of observed epochs can be computed. In general, the increase in loss is low, around 2% on average in the worst cases, when observing only two epochs.

The impact of the hyperparameters is limited. Results show that even with a low number of observed epochs, there is only a slight improvement in the average loss obtained by the BO process. While the performance estimator makes better predictions when is extended with network features, these differences seem to be diluted when the estimator is used in the BO process. This is expected, given the greater variation in the estimator performance observed in Fig. 3 when only a few data points are considered. When both estimator approaches (with and without network features) converge, the amount of discarded training is similar, resulting in almost equal average performance of the BO processes.

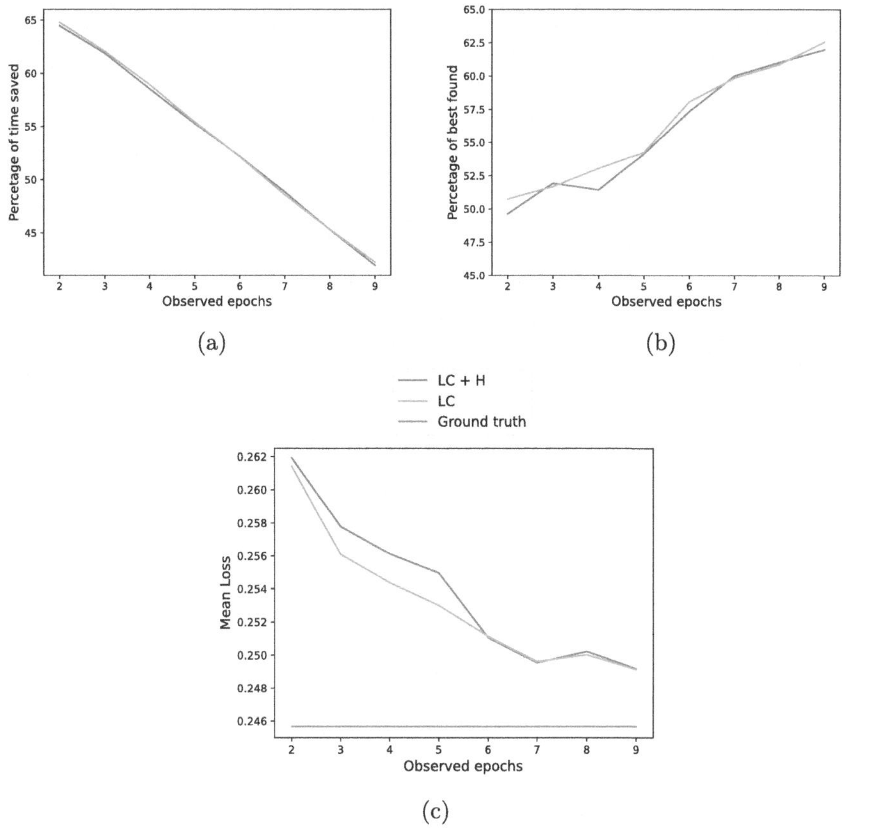

Fig. 4. BO early-stopping simulation results. a) Percentage of time saved with respect to the number of observed epochs. b) Percentage of times that the best solution (ground truth) is found. c) Average mean loss obtained depending on the number of observed epochs.

4 Conclusions and Future Work

This work uses a dataset of training and validation performance curves created by the authors to develop an early-stopping approach applied to a BO process for NAS. Results show that using an estimator to predict the future performance of a model based on a few observed training and validation performance epochs is feasible. This estimator, when applied to a BO process for NAS, can significantly reduce computation time with minimal impact on the performance of the final model.

This preliminary study gains its insights through a simulated approach. Therefore, the next immediate step is to corroborate these findings with a real BO execution process.

Additionally, other points of improvement have been identified. In this work, the estimator has been trained to make estimations with a fixed number N of observed epochs. In some cases, with a few more executions, it becomes evident that a model will not perform well. Thus, estimating future performance at each epoch could help stop other executions that were not detected earlier. In some sense, this approach will converge with the method proposed in [2].

Regarding the hyperparameters used to condition the estimator, it could be interesting to include additional hyperparameters, such as meta-attributes about the dataset and the involved task. Studying how these meta-attributes could impact the estimator would be an interesting avenue for academic research.

Finally, it should be noted that the current method does not fully exploit the potential knowledge and adaptation capabilities of the performance curves generated during application to a new dataset. Incorporating few-shot learning to leverage these performance curves in ongoing experiments could be another area for improvement.

Acknowledgments. This work has been supported by Proyecto PID2019-109152GB-I00 financiado por MCIN/ AEI /10.13039/501100011033 (Agencia Estatal de Investigación), Spain and by the Ministry of Science and Education of Spain through the national program "Ayudas para contratos para la formación de investigadores en empresas (DIN2019-010887 / AEI / 10.13039/50110001103)", of State Programme of Science Research and Innovations 2017–2020.

A Appendix

A.1 Performance Estimator Architectures

Table 2. Network architecture used to train the performance estimator based on **3** observed training curve points.

Layer type	Output Shape	Param #
LC Input	**3**, 2	0
Bi-LSTM	3, 128	26112
BN	3, 128	512
Flatten	384	0
MLP (ReLU)	128	49280
Dropout	128	0
MLP (ReLU)	64	8256
Dropout	64	0
Output	1	65
Total params: 84,225 Trainable params: 83,969 Non-trainable params: 256		

Table 3. Network architecture used to train the performance estimator based on **3** observed training curve points (LC Input) and the **28** possible network hyperparameters (H Input). The highlighted rows define the additional layers added to condition the model to the network hyperparameters.

Layer	Layer type	Output Shape	Param #	Connected to
1	LC Input	**3**, 2	0	
2	H Input	**28**, 2	0	
3	Flatten	56	0	2
4	MLP (Swish)	32	1824	3
5	MLP (Swish)	16	528	4
6	Bi-LSTM	3, 128	26112	1
7	BN	3, 128	512	6
8	Flatten	384	0	7
9	Concatenate	400	0	5, 8
10	MLP (ReLU)	128	51328	9
11	Dropout	128	0	10
12	MLP (ReLU)	64	8256	11
13	Dropout	64	0	12
14	Output	1	65	13
Total params: 88,625				
Trainable params: 88,369				
Non-trainable params: 256				

References

1. Baker, B., Gupta, O., Raskar, R., Naik, N.: Accelerating neural architecture search using performance prediction. arXiv preprint arXiv:1705.10823 (2017)
2. Dai, Z., Yu, H., Low, B.K.H., Jaillet, P.: Bayesian optimization meets Bayesian optimal stopping. In: International Conference on Machine Learning, pp. 1496–1506. PMLR (2019)
3. Domhan, T., Springenberg, J.T., Hutter, F.: Speeding up automatic hyperparameter optimization of deep neural networks by extrapolation of learning curves. In: Twenty-Fourth International Joint Conference on Artificial Intelligence (2015)
4. Falkner, S., Klein, A., Hutter, F.: BOHB: robust and efficient hyperparameter optimization at scale. In: International Conference on Machine Learning, pp. 1437–1446. PMLR (2018)
5. Kandasamy, K., Neiswanger, W., Schneider, J., Poczos, B., Xing, E.P.: Neural architecture search with Bayesian optimisation and optimal transport. Adv. Neural Inf. Process. Syst. **31** (2018)
6. Kingma, D.P., Ba, J.: Adam: a method for stochastic optimization. arXiv preprint arXiv:1412.6980 (2014)
7. Klein, A., Falkner, S., Springenberg, J.T., Hutter, F.: Learning curve prediction with Bayesian neural networks. In: International Conference on Learning Representations (2022)

8. Li, L., Jamieson, K.G., DeSalvo, G., Rostamizadeh, A., Talwalkar, A.: Hyperband: Bandit-based configuration evaluation for hyperparameter optimization. In: ICLR (Poster), p. 53 (2017)
9. Real, E., Aggarwal, A., Huang, Y., Le, Q.V.: Regularized evolution for image classifier architecture search. In: Proceedings of the AAAI Conference on Artificial Intelligence, vol. 33, pp. 4780–4789 (2019)
10. Snoek, J., Larochelle, H., Adams, R.P.: Practical Bayesian optimization of machine learning algorithms. Adv. Neural Inf. Process. Syst. **25** (2012)
11. You, K., Long, M., Wang, J., Jordan, M.I.: How does learning rate decay help modern neural networks? arXiv preprint arXiv:1908.01878 (2019)
12. Zoph, B., Vasudevan, V., Shlens, J., Le, Q.V.: Learning transferable architectures for scalable image recognition. In: Proceedings of the IEEE Conference on Computer Vision and Pattern Recognition, pp. 8697–8710 (2018)

Neonates Crying Detection Through Feature Extraction and Machine Learning Methods

Lucía Núñez-Calvo[1], Nuria Velasco-Pérez[1], Samuel Lozano-Juárez[1], Álvaro Herrero[1], Juan Arnaez[2,3,4], and Daniel Urda[1(✉)]

[1] Grupo de Inteligencia Computacional Aplicada (GICAP), Departamento de Digitalización, Escuela Politécnica Superior, Universidad de Burgos, Avda Cantabria s/n, 09006 Burgos, Spain
{lncalvof,nuriavp,sljuarez,ahcosio,durda}@ubu.es

[2] Unidad Neonatal, Hospital Universitario de Burgos, Avda Islas Baleares 3, 09006 Burgos, Spain

[3] Neurología Neonatal, Fundación NeNe, Calle Eloy Gonzalo, 3, 28010 Madrid, Spain
juan.arnaez@neurologianeonatal.org

[4] Profesor Sociedad Iberoamericana de Neonatología (SIBEN), New Jersey, USA

Abstract. Analyzing how a newborn reacts to different stimuli is crucial to diagnose possible neurological conditions. In this sense, a key factor that expert clinicians assess in newborns is the presence of crying under nociceptive stimuli, since the absence of this factor under the stimulation procedure increases the chances of developing neonatal encephalopathy. To this end, this work tackles this problem by using Machine Learning techniques to detect infant cry events from audios recorded during nociceptive stimulation of 63 newborns at the "Hospital Universitario de Burgos". Particularly, this work analyzes the performance of several well-known machine learning models (Multi-Layer Perceptron, Support Vector Machines and Long-Short Term Memory network) after preprocessing the audios with two feature extraction techniques (Mel Frequency Cepstral Coefficients and Linear Predictive Coding). Promising results are obtained in the analysis carried out achieving a F1-score of 0.93, a result that shows the potential of this approach in improving pediatric diagnosis, neonatal care, and the diagnose of other health problems through cry analysis.

Keywords: Deep learning · Machine learning · Audio analysis · Classification · Feature extraction · Neonatal encephalopathy

1 Introduction

Neonatal encephalopathy (NE) is a clinical syndrome that affects newborns from 35 weeks of gestation or more and has a certain relationship with the level of development of the country. While in developed countries the incidence of babies with NE is less than two babies per thousand (live) births, in underdeveloped

H. Quintián et al. (Eds.): HAIS 2024, LNAI 14857, pp. 275–285, 2025.
https://doi.org/10.1007/978-3-031-74183-8_23

countries the incidence is more than eight babies per thousand (live) births [1]. This disease causes approximately 20% of cases of cerebral palsy in infancy and is the leading cause of death in term infants. For this reason, finding both treatments and early detection of this disease has a great impact on both survival and improving the quality of life of babies.

For newborns presenting NE early in life (within six hours of birth), controlled therapeutic hypothermia for neonatal encephalopathy has been shown to slow metabolic processes in the brain, decrease swelling and brain damage [2]. However, if this treatment is incorrectly applied to neonates who do not meet the criteria for this treatment, unnecessary and potentially serious complications may result. Therefore, it is crucial to check the newborn's condition in the first six hours of life by different neurological examinations [3]. However, assessments vary between centres and even within the same team [4]. To avoid erroneous or inconsistent diagnoses, specialists are now being guided by telemedicine, which allows real-time contact between specialists to discuss whether a baby has NE and, if so, to what degree [5].

According to the Garcia-Alix's score scale [6], there are multiple aspects that must be taken into account to determine the presence of NE in a newborn like the status of alertness, posture, or spontaneous motor activity, among others. However, García-Alíx and other authors agree that alertness is one of the most important [7,8]. In order to tackle this problem, advanced tools are now available, such as Deep Learning (DL) and Machine Learning (ML), which have the main feature of being able to automate and improve processes such as the detection and classification of certain diseases. In concrete, there are many articles that present different models for disease detection and improvement [9,10]. More precisely, authors in [11] focus on the evaluation of different ML algorithms to detect diseases with health data. In their work, 48 articles applying different algorithms for single disease prediction were reviewed, concluding that by applying these novel techniques, disease predictions become more accurate and efficient compared to traditional statistical methods.

Concerning the status of alertness, infant cry events is one of the associated items that clinicians focus on during nociceptive stimuli. In this sense, the authors aim at providing a concise and uniform assessment of alertness of babies through the collection of audios of newborns and the use of DL and ML techniques, since there are previous studies supporting the use of such techniques [12–15]. Therefore, the purpose of this study is to explore the ability of ML and DL to identify and classify the sound responses produced by a newborn to a stimulus by analysing its cry. To achieve this goal, authors present a feature extraction procedure based on two well-known techniques such as Mel Frequency Cepstral Coefficients (MFCC) or Linear predictive coding (LPC), allowing us to extract relevant features from time-varying audios. Then, three well-known classifiers such as Multilayer Perceptron (MLP), and Support Vector Machine (SVM), are trained and evaluated in an audio recording dataset of infant cry consisting of 63 audios collected at the "Hospital Universitario de Burgos".

The rest of the paper is organised as follows. Section 2 presents the data that has been used for both training and evaluation of the models and audios were labelled. A description of the feature extraction methods and classifiers employed in this work is included in Sect. 3, together with some details of the experimental design. Finally, results are included in Sect. 4, and some conclusions and future work are provided in Sect. 5.

2 Dataset

This research study began in 2023 with the acquisition of different videos provided by the maternity ward of the University Hospital of Burgos (HUBU). The newborns shown in each of the videos are less than twenty-four (24) hours old and are characterised by being premature or having experienced complications during birth. All videos were acquired with the written consent of their parents, who voluntarily provided their data in order to contribute to the advancement of the study.

First of all, it is important to note what the data we use in this project contain and why such data are important. The cohort provided by the HUBU consists of a total of 63 videos in which different stimulations are performed on newborns. To assess the level of alertness, neonatologists recorded the routine checks they performed on each newborn. During these assessments, the doctors looked for specific signs of alertness, such as the duration of the baby's crying. A small pinch can be used to observe the newborn's response, and the type of cry, whether it stops abruptly or whether, in cases where a crying reaction would be expected, the baby does not respond in this way.

The study uses videos with a sampling rate of 44.1 kHz and of different lengths, from videos as short as thirty seconds to videos over ten minutes long. Some videos only capture a single test during the check-up, while other videos, which are much longer, document the entire test. For this reason, as will be seen below, a greater number of non-crying moments are available. The first step in processing the audio was to separate it from the original video, i.e. to extract the audio and store it in a directory system equal to the one containing the videos. Since the videos are available in different formats, it has been necessary to create an extraction process that is adapted to each of them.

On the other hand, each of the audio files has been manually labelled. For the creation of these labels, a vector has been generated with a length equal to the number of seconds that each audio file has, in which a 1 represents that the baby is crying in each second of the audio and a 0 that the baby is not crying, regardless of the sound that is heard when the baby is not crying. Therefore, a binary classification setting is generated indicating whether the newborn is crying or not on each second of the audio. Moreover, it should be noted that this labeling simply responds to the moments in time when a cry is heard, without taking into account the intensity of this sound.

This labelling system has allowed to extract full clear audios in which newborns are crying or not crying, to further employ feature extraction techniques and for model training and evaluation. Besides, this labelling procedure will allow to generate visual representations of the time instants in which the baby is perceived to be crying.

3 Methods and Experimental Design

This section describes the feature extraction methods employed to preprocess the audio recordings and extract relevant features characterizing the audios. Besides, some brief details of the three well-known classifiers used in this study to develop accurate models with the intention of identifying newborn alertness based on the infant's sound response to different stimuli, together with the experimental design carried out for the analysis.

3.1 Feature Extraction

Two well-known feature extraction methods for audio prepocessing were employed to compare the results obtained with different classifiers, which are next described.

- Mel Frequency Cepstral Coefficients (MFCC). It is a complex process by which an audio signal is transformed from its original time domain to a representation that mimics the human perception of sound. The first step has been to load the audio files with a specific sample rate, in this case a sample rate of 44100 Hz has been set. This sampling rate is that of each file in the dataset. The second step has been to divide the audio into one-second segments, where each of these segments have a length equal to the previously defined sampling rate. Each of these segments is checked for sufficient length, at least 2048 samples. This step has been carried out in order to apply the Hamming window correctly, and subsequently the Discrete Fourier Transform (DFT). After this check, the process is continued by extracting, in this case, thirteen MFCC coefficients for each segment. The choice of this number of coefficients is given by the objective pursued by the project. This value provides a balance between information and computational efficiency, being sufficient for speech processing tasks. Finally, the result obtained is an average of the coefficients over time for each segment, so that each second of audio becomes an independent instance with fixed-length characteristics. In this way, the models are subsequently provided with consistent data for training.
- Linear Predictive Coding (LPC). It is a technique widely used in audio signal processing, like the previous technique, this technique also focuses on speech synthesis and speech recognition. The first step has been to load the audio files with a sampling rate equal to 44100 Hz. Then, the pre-emphasis filter has been applied to improve the signal to noise ratio. This filter follows the formula where alpha is greater than 0 and less than 1.0. Typical values for alpha are between 0.95 and 0.97, on this occasion a value of alpha = 0.97

has been selected with the intention of amplifying the high frequencies to not introduce excessive distortion into the signal. Afterwards, the audio has been segmented into one-second fragments and a Hamming window was applied to each segment. After the windowing, the next step was to apply the autocorrelation technique. In this case, the most relevant part for the LPC coefficients has been selected, i.e. the part related to the centre of the forward autocorrelation has been extracted. This step has been intended to capture the temporal structure of the signal, making it possible to determine the current samples from the previous samples. Since the LPC coefficients model the signal according to the linear combination of past samples, this is a fundamental step. Finally, the Toeplitz equation is solved using the Levinson-Durbin algorithm to obtain the LPC coefficients. These coefficients are stored in a list of vectors in which the length of each vector is equal to the number of coefficients previously defined, in this case the number of coefficients has been defined equal to 10.

3.2 Classifiers

In this study, a comparison has been made between two well-known classifiers: a Multi-Layer Perceptron (MLP) and Support Vector Machines (SVM), both non-linear models which are based on neural networks and kernels, respectively. Next, a more detailed description is provided:

- Multi-Layer Perceptron (MLP). It is a fundamental structure in the field of ANNs due to the variety of solutions it presents for use in the field of machine learning. Its main characteristic is that it is capable of solving problems that are not linearly separable, which is also its main limitation [16]. This model consists of at least one input layer, one hidden layer and one output layer, each layer being connected to the next by neurons. For the MLP model developed in this work, the L2 regulation parameter has been defined with a value of 0.01, which allows a balance between the model's ability to correctly fit the data and to avoid the risk of overfitting. Next, the artificial network was defined as a single hidden layer and 300 neurons. The choice of a single hidden layer is due to the limited amount of data available to date, the need to create a model with high computational efficiency and to meet the requirement of minimal risk of overfitting. Finally, an adaptive learning rate has been defined. This rate has the particularity of decreasing when the training results do not show an improvement.
- Support Vector Machines (SVM). They belong to the category of kernel-based classifiers because the method they implement is the creation of a hyperplane for the separation of the defined spaces. The main objective of this algorithm is to maximise the margin that exists between the classes and the hyperplane. This margin is defined as the smallest distance between the training points closest to the plane, known as support vectors, and the hyperplane. Achieving a robust margin enhances the model's ability to generalise unseen data, leading to increased confidence in the classification [17]. In particular, the SVM

model has been defined with an radial basis function (RBF) kernel since it has been shown to provide good results in classifying infant cry [12]. This kernel manages to project the data in an infinite dimensional space, being able to handle non-linear and multidimensional data. Therefore, by using the RBF kernel, the data is projected into a higher dimensional space where it is more likely to find a hyperplane that separates the classes. Then, the regularisation parameter has been set to one, achieving a balance between the error tolerance and the complexity of the model. Finally, it must be taken into account that SVM produces as a result distances to the hyperplane, and not probabilities, so a very important step has been the application of a method that calibrates the outputs to convert them into probabilities. This has been achieved by setting the probability parameter included in the Scikit-learn library that creates the SVM model to True, to obtain probabilities on the model outputs instead of mere labels. This configuration makes it possible to interpret the SVM predictions in a more intuitive way. Instead of a simple binary classification indicating whether the baby is crying or not, the probabilities give an output between 0 and 1. This output is important to gradually observe changes in the baby's behaviour and to see how the probability of the baby crying varies.

3.3 Experimental Design

A very important aspect for the validation of results and the real verification of how the models respond, is the validation with new data. To this end, features have been extracted from fifty-eight (58) audio files out of the sixty-three (63) available, reserving the remaining five audio files for a visual qualitative evaluation.

Within the 58 audios, for both MFCC and LPC feature extraction method, an average of the coefficients over time has been obtained for each segment, so that each second of the audio becomes an independent instance with fixed-length features. This ensures that the models subsequently receive consistent data for training. Then, the two classifiers considered in this work are trained using the Scikit-learn Python library. A 5-fold cross-validation strategy is employed, which splits the complete data into 5 folds of equal sizes. Classifiers are iteratively trained in a process where 4 out of the 5 folds are used for the training process and the left apart fold (test set) is used purely for evaluating the performance of the models. The test set rotates on each iteration.

To evaluate the performance of the Machine Learning and Deep Learning models, presented in the previous section, it is essential to use quantitative metrics. These metrics allow an objective and accurate assessment of the true performance of the models by providing concrete numerical values that facilitate the understanding of the models' performance.

The precision metrics used in this project are defined below and are also summarised in the Fig. 1:

- F1-score. This value is the harmonic mean between the recall and precision values.

- Accuracy. This value expresses the proportion of correct predictions out of the total number of predictions made. This metric is useful to get a general idea of the model's performance, but be aware that this result may not be sufficiently accurate. In unbalanced ensembles this value may give a result close to one which would be interpreted as a good result, but this may be because it is conditioned by the predominant class.
- Area Under the ROC Curve (AUC). The ROC curve is constructed from the true positive rate (TPR), also known as recall, and the false positive rate (FPR). In the generated graph, the Y-axis would correspond to the TPR and the X-axis to the FPRs. The AUC value summarises the information from the ROC curve into a single metric, i.e., a numerical value. For a perfect classifier this value would be equal to one, while an AUC of 0.5 would represent a random classifier. Thus, the closer the AUC is to one, the better the model is classifying.
- Confusion matrix, this matrix clearly, and concisely represents the performance of the model. It shows a comparison between the predictions made by the model and the actual values. With this metric, it is possible to effectively compare whether the model's performance is being effective on unbalanced sets by looking at the percentage of data that is misclassified in each class.

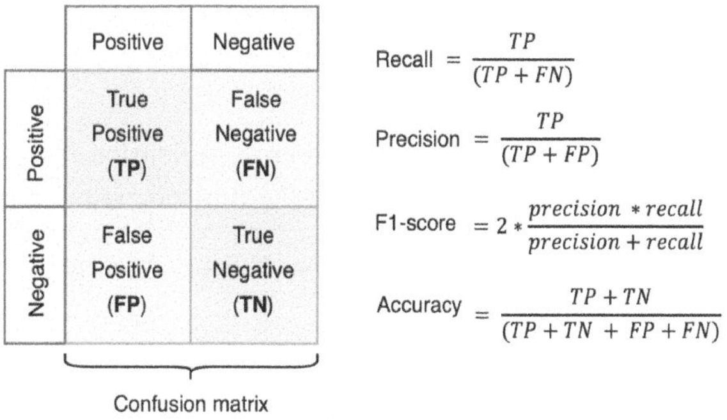

Fig. 1. Quantitative metrics.

4 Results

Both quantitative and qualitative analyses have been carried out to assess the effectiveness and accuracy of the models and feature extraction techniques analyzed.

First, the quantitative results focus on performance metrics such as accuracy, F1-score and AUC. To this end, Table 1 presents the performance of the different classifiers and feature extraction methods considered in this work. With these metrics it can be observed that the models that generate better classifications are those that have been trained with MFCC features. In terms of AUC, classifiers that are trained with MFCC features tend to perform, in average, around 5% better than those trained using the LPC features. Concerning models' accuracy, the MLP model trained with the MFCC extracted features achieved the highest accuracy of 89%. Finally, the table also includes the F1−score for both the negative and positive class. In general, it can be observed that the class that is predicted better by classifiers is the positive class (crying). Furthermore, and as commented before with the AUC values, one can see that classifiers trained with the MFCC features tend to perform better, in terms of F1−score, than those trained with the LPC features. Additionally, it can be highlighted that classifiers trained with the MFCC features achieve more robust and consistent F1−score metric in the negative class (no crying), since the LPC extracted feature ends up seriously affecting the performance of classifiers (almost 10% worse F1−score for the negative class).

The qualitative results include a visual evaluation of the cry event classification. These visual ratings have been created in several ways. For this purpose, the models have been evaluated with the 5 audio files that were reserved for qualitatively test the classification efficiency of the models. For this task, a system capable of predicting, in real time, the probability that the baby is crying in each second of the audio file has been implemented. This analysis is carried out in three steps: feature extraction using MFCC, probability prediction with a previously trained model, and final visualisation of the results in a graph representing the probability of crying over time.

Table 1. Average performance results through cross-validation for the different classifiers and feature extraction methods analyzed.

Model	Features	F1-score Cry	F1-score Not cry	Accuracy	AUC
MLP	MFCC	0.71	0.93	0.89	0.95
MLP	LPC	0.61	0.90	0.84	0.91
SVM	MFCC	0.70	0.93	0.88	0.94
SVM	LPC	0.64	0.92	0.87	0.90

Figure 2 presents a qualitative evaluation of the trained classifiers (MLP in the mid column and SVM on the right column). In order to be able to clearly and visually check whether the result provided by the classifiers is as expected or not, a first column has been added on the left of the image to visualize the ground truth of the 5 videos left apart from the training process (rows in the image). It should be noted that these first results contain only a probability of 0 in case no crying is heard or 1 in case crying is heard, without distinguishing between the types of crying that are perceived. Overall, both classifiers are performing reasonably good. For instance, in the fourth video there are two short periods of time right before the middle of the audio when the baby is crying.

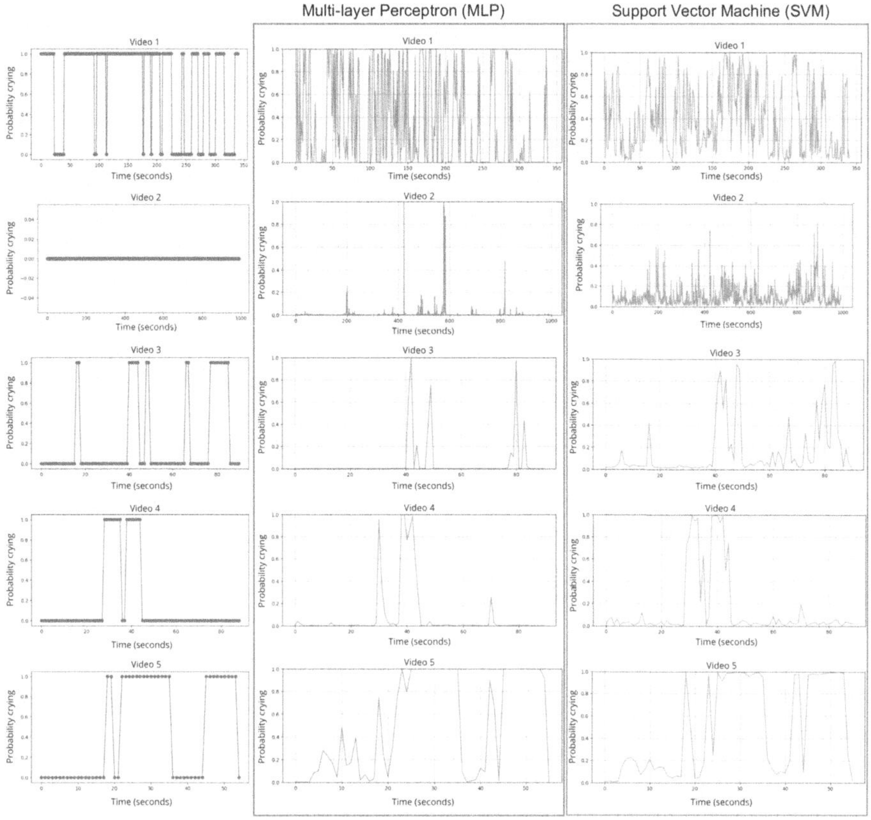

Fig. 2. Qualitative evaluation of the trained classifiers on five audios (rows) that were left apart from the training process with respect to the ground truth (left column).

Consequently, both the MLP and SVM classifiers are outputting higher probabilities (close to 1) in the same period of time in contrast to the rest of the audio recording, where both classifiers are predicting a nearly 0 probability.

5 Conclusions

This paper has presented a ML-based approach in order to detect infant crying events in audio recordings. As discussed throughout this work, early detection of NE is essential to be able to treat the neonate as quickly as possible and thus significantly improve long-term adverse effects [18]. For this reason, this study has shown the relevance of using ML and DL algorithms in solving audio analysis problems, especially in the context of child health. The data employed in this work was facilitated by the "Hospital Universitario de Burgos" consisting of 63 audio recordings associated to nociceptive stimuli performed to neonates. These audio recordings were then employed to develop two well-known classifiers,

MLP and SVM, after employing two different feature extraction techniques to preprocess the audios, such as MFCC and LPC.

Looking at the results obtained, and taking into account that the number of samples is not too large, in particular the number of crying samples, very promising classifications results have been achieved. This suggests that such models could potentially be used in the future to detect infant crying in clinical settings and aid in the diagnosis of NE. It is also important to note that models considered in this study achieved promising results by using data from a typical or representative clinical environment, which could make this approac generalisable to other hospitals or clinical settings, strengthening the reliability and usefulness of ML and DL techniques.

As future work, authors intend to increase the audio samples in order to develop more complex DL classifiers and to outperform the baseline results obtained in this work. Besides, it would be interesting to employ computer vision techniques to characterize the videos associated to these audios and develop a higher-level ML-based model that can learn the hidden patterns in the audio and video characterizations that drive predictions of the status of alertness.

Acknowledgements. This research is part of the SITAD-NPCN project funded in 2022 in the "Desafío Universidad-Empresa" call by the "Plan de Transferencia de Conocimiento Universidad - Empresa (Plan TCUE) 2021–2023".

References

1. Garcia-Alix, A., Arnaez, J., Arca, G., Martinez-Biarge, M.: Hypoxic-ischaemic encephalopathy code: a systematic review for resource-limited settings. Anales de Pediatría (Engl Ed) **100**(4), 275–286 (2024)
2. Tagin, M.A., Woolcott, C.G., Vincer, M.J., Whyte, R.K., Stinson, D.A.: Hypothermia for neonatal hypoxic ischemic encephalopathy: an updated systematic review and meta-analysis. Arch. Pediatr. Adolesc. Med. **166**(6), 558–566 (2012)
3. Arnaez, J., Garcia-Alix, A., Calvo, S., Lubian-Lopez, S., Grupo de Trabajo E-E.: Care of the newborn with perinatal asphyxia candidate for therapeutic hypothermia during the first six hours of life in Spain. Anales de Pediatría **89**(4), 211–221 (2018)
4. Olsen, S.L., et al.: Optimizing therapeutic hypothermia for neonatal encephalopathy. Pediatrics **131**(2), e591–e603 (2013)
5. Laptook, A.R.: Initiating therapeutic hypothermia during transport for encephalopathy: current state and future direction. J. Perinatol. **33**(3), 169–170 (2013)
6. Garcia-Alix, A., et al.: Development, reliability, and testing of a new rating scale for neonatal encephalopathy. J. Pediatr. **235**, 83–91 (2021)
7. Kurinczuk, J.J., White-Koning, M., Badawi, N.: Epidemiology of neonatal encephalopathy and hypoxic-ischaemic encephalopathy. Early Hum. Dev. **86**(6), 329–338 (2010)
8. Sarnat, H.B., Sarnat, M.S.: Neonatal encephalopathy following fetal distress: a clinical and electroencephalographic study. Arch. Neurol. **33**(10), 696–705 (1976)

9. Kohli, P.S., Arora, S.: Application of machine learning in disease prediction. In: 2019 International Conference on Advances in Computing, Communication and Control (ICAC3), pp. 1–5. IEEE (2019)
10. Hwang, K., Wang, L., Wang, L., Chen, M., Hao, Y.: Disease prediction by machine learning over big data from healthcare communities. IEEE Access **5**, 8869–8879 (2017)
11. Uddin, S., Khan, A., Hossain, M., et al.: Comparing different supervised machine learning algorithms for disease prediction. BMC Med. Inform. Decis. Mak. **19**(1), 281 (2019)
12. Ashwini, K., Durai Raj Vincent, P.M., Srinivasan, K., Chang, C.-Y.: Deep learning assisted neonatal cry classification via support vector machine models. Front. Publ. Health **9**, 670352 (2021)
13. Ji, C., Bamunu Mudiyanselage, T., Gao, Y., Pan, Y.: A review of infant cry analysis and classification. EURASIP J. Audio Speech Music Process. (2021)
14. Bashiri, A., Hosseinkhani, R.: Infant crying classification by using genetic algorithm and artificial neural network. Acta Medica Iranica **58**(10), 531–539 (2020). Received 11 Apr 2020; Accepted 28 Sept 2020
15. Ithaya Rani, P., Pavan Kumar, P., Moses Immanuel, V., Tharun, P., Rajesh, P.: Baby cry classification using machine learning. Int. J. Innov. Sci. Res Technol. **7**(3), 677–681 (2022). IJISRT22MAR645
16. Álvarez-Morales, M., Patiño-Morales, J.I., Gutiérrez-Zabala, E.A., Cortés-Torres, J.H.: Clima organizacional, estilo de liderazgo y satisfacción laboral en empresas del sector agropecuario. Revista de Psicología Universidad de Antioquia **7**(2), 67–80 (2015)
17. Cáceres, J.M.R.: Tutorial sobre máquinas de vectores soporte (SVM). ResearchGate (2014)
18. Wu, Y.: Clinical features, diagnosis, and treatment of neonatal encephalopathy. Literature review current through: May 2024. This topic last updated 30 Jan 2024

Differentiable Prototypes with Distributed Memory Network for Continual Learning

Min-Seo Kwak[1], Hyung-Jun Moon[2], and Sung-Bae Cho[1](✉)

[1] Department of Computer Science, Yonsei University, Seoul 03722, Republic of Korea
{rhkraltj103,sbcho}@yonsei.ac.kr

[2] Department of Artificial Intelligence, Yonsei University, Seoul 03722, Republic of Korea
axtabio@yonsei.ac.kr

Abstract. Deep learning models demonstrate outstanding performance across various fields but need to continuously learn new knowledge while preserving previously learned one. The main challenge in continual learning is catastrophic forgetting caused by semantic drift. Existing approaches to this problem often store portions of previously learned data or prototypes, but their effectiveness heavily depends on heuristics, and storage requirements grow rapidly with increasing data. In this paper, we propose a new method that enables end-to-end learning of prototypes. This method selects the prototypes with a distributed memory network to eliminate the dependency on specific algorithms and allow automatic updates to prevent obsolescence. The distributed storage of prototypes spreads information widely across memory, which is controlled with feature compactness and separateness to minimize the memory usage. To prevent the semantic shift, encoded features are stored in the buffer and a decoder reconstructs the data. Experiments on continual learning setup with MNIST, permuted MNIST, and fashion-MNIST show the competitive performance against the state-of-the-art models. For a buffer size of 500, performance improvement reaches to 0.04%p, 1.45%p, and 5.4%p for MNIST, permuted MNIST, and fashion-MNIST, respectively.

Keywords: Continual Learning · Class-Incremental Learning · Memory Network · Prototypes

1 Introduction

Continual learning (CL) is a novel learning setup for an environment where data are presented sequentially, and a model continually learns new tasks. The main challenge in CL lies in catastrophic forgetting caused by semantic drift [1], which refers to the change in class representation as the model learns a new task. To prevent semantic drift, it is essential to preserve previously learned knowledge, and one effective strategy is to store previous data [2–5]. However, the performance of the model strongly depends on the effectiveness of the sample selection heuristic or algorithm, and the capacity of the storage increases rapidly as the amount of input data grows. In particular, this approach may be impractical when the access to the previous data is restricted due to privacy

H. Quintián et al. (Eds.): HAIS 2024, LNAI 14857, pp. 286–298, 2025.
https://doi.org/10.1007/978-3-031-74183-8_24

concerns, say for medical records. On the other hand, instead of saving exemplars of previous data, an alternative strategy involves storing a prototype of each class [6, 7]. This method uses memory space more efficiently because it is smaller in size compared to storing input samples, but the selection and update processes of prototypes still rely on heuristics.

In order to address these issues, we propose a new method that stores prototypes in an end-to-end manner via a memory network. This method eliminates dependency on specific algorithms or heuristics, and automatically updates prototypes to prevent them from becoming obsolete over time. When storing the prototypes externally, we use a distributed storage instead of a one-to-one correspondence with memory slots, spreading the information widely across the memory. By controlling this with feature compactness and separateness [8], the proposed method can store multiple prototypes while minimizing memory usage. To prevent the shift of the feature extractor when a new task comes, the encoded features are stored in the buffer instead of raw data and are used to regenerate the data through a decoder. The proposed method does not use an additional generative model, thereby reducing memory storage overhead, and the learning process of the generative model is simplified as it is trained simultaneously with the main model. We will conduct experiments on MNIST, permuted MNIST, and fashion-MNIST to show the competitive performance against the state-of-the-art methods.

2 Related Works

Prototype in Continual Learning. In continual learning, the prototypes can prevent the forgetting of previous knowledge by utilizing very small additional storage. By combining the prototypes with NCM (nearest class mean) classifier, some methods reduce bias towards the most recently learned tasks [2]. There are also some studies that have successfully mitigated forgetting without replay, by leveraging the prototypes. PASS [6] maintains decision boundaries using prototypes, and PRD [7] preserves the relative distance between the prototypes of new and previous classes.

Most of the previous studies used a single value as a prototype [2, 6, 7, 9], often utilizing the class mean for the prototype. In contrast, CPP [10] employed multi-centroid prototypes, arguing that the distribution of the feature space may not be convex or isomorphic. One of the main challenges in using prototypes in CL is that previously stored prototypes may become invalid as the feature extractor updates. To solve this problem, COPE [9] updates the prototypes based on momentum using the data of the previous task. PRD [7] uses a relation distillation term for updates. In our work, prototypes are updated without additional complex methods.

Memory Network. Memory networks are widely used to capture long-term dependencies due to their ease of reading and writing. Memory networks were initially introduced in the field of question answering. With the development of memory networks, their applications have expanded to video object segmentation [11, 12], object tracking [13], and anomaly detection [8]. Memory networks can automatically record prototypes and are easily trained in an end-to-end manner. Particularly in the field of anomaly detection, the performance has been improved by recording prototypical normal patterns in memory networks.

In continual learning, memory networks have been utilized to learn prompts for pre-trained vision transformers. However, a pre-trained model may not always available for real-world applications. Inspired by the capability of memory networks to automatically select prototypes, we incorporate memory networks into continual learning to memorize the prototypes. The proposed method is fundamentally different to the previous methods, as memory networks are employed to select multiple prototypes.

3 Proposed Method

3.1 Problem Definition and Overview

We focus on class-incremental learning (CIL), where model learns from a sequence of tasks. At each task t, model is trained on a dataset $D_t = \{(x_t^i, y_t^i)\}_{i=1}^{n_t}$ where x_t^i and y_t^i are the i th sample and label respectively and n_t denotes the number of samples in task t. C_t represents the class set in D_t, which satisfies $y_t^i \in C_t$ and there are no overlapping classes among the tasks. After training task t, the model is evaluated on all previously seen classes $\{C_1, C_2, \ldots, C_t\}$, where t is the number of tasks.

As shown in Fig. 1, the proposed model consists of four components: encoder f_e, memory module f_m, decoder f_d and classifier g. The encoder extracts feature from the input, with which prototypes are retrieved from the memory, and the memory is updated. The feature and memory items are combined and fed into the decoder and classifier, which are represented by $f_d(f_m(f_e(x)))$ and $g(f_m(f_e(x)))$, respectively. The decoder is for image generation, and the classifier is for image classification.

3.2 Initial Learning and Inference

The model uses a convolutional autoencoder for the encoder and decoder. For the first task (D_1), the proposed method involves learning for f_e, f_m, f_d, and g. The encoder receives input x and extracts feature $z = f_e(x)$ of size $H \times W \times C$, where H, W, and C denote height, width, and the number of channels, respectively. The feature z is converted into individual queries $\{z_n\}_{n=1}^{N}$ of shape $1 \times 1 \times C$, where $N = H \times W$. These queries are used to read and update the memory module.

Memory Module. The memory network in its initial state is in the form of a $K \times C$ matrix, where K represents the memory size and C is the dimension of the memory, which is the same as the dimension of the feature z. A row vector of the matrix becomes a memory item. The memory consists of K memory items $\{m_k\}_{k=1}^{K}$ of size $1 \times 1 \times C$, which is equal to the dimension of query. Each memory item stores a prototypical feature. The memory network matrix is initialized with random values between 0 and 1 when it is created.

Memory Read. For each query z_n, we compute cosine similarities with memory items $m_1, \ldots, m_K$ and apply a softmax function. Similarity between z_n and m_i is as follows:

$$w^{n,i} = \frac{\exp\left((m_i)^T z_n\right)}{\sum_{i'}^{K} \exp\left((m_{i'})^T z_n\right)}. \tag{1}$$

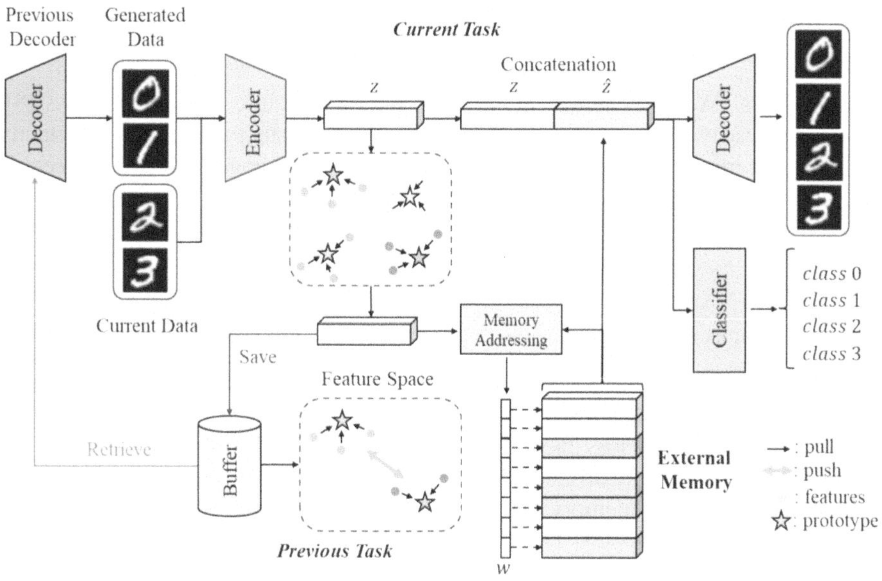

Fig. 1. Overview of the proposed method.

Then, we calculate the weighted average memory items using $w^{n,i}$:

$$\hat{z}^n = \sum_{i'=1}^{K} w^{n,i'} m_{i'}. \tag{2}$$

By reading memory for all queries, we can get new feature of size $H \times W \times C$. Since the new feature is created using memory items, it accurately retains previously learned features. Therefore, we concatenate this new feature with original feature and feed the combined feature into decoder and classifier after memory update.

Memory Update. After extracting $\hat{z}$, the memory update process is performed to reflect the information of the current task. For each memory item m_i, we find all queries that the most similar memory item is m_i, and the index set of these queries is U^i.

The similarity mentioned here is the same as $w^{n,i}$. Afterwards, the cosine similarity between m_i and z_n is computed, followed by the application of softmax function:

$$v^{n,i} = \frac{\exp\left((m_i)^T z_n\right)}{\sum_{n'}^{K} \exp\left((m_i)^T z_{n'}\right)}. \tag{3}$$

The dimension of the softmax differs from that of the previous $w^{n,i}$. Then, we renormalize $v^{n,i}$ using the queries in U^i:

$$v'^{n,i} = \frac{v^{n,i}}{max_{n' \in U^i} v^{n',i}}. \tag{4}$$

We update each memory item by weighted average of the relevant queries:

$$m_i \leftarrow f\left(m_i + \sum_{k \in U^i} v'^{k,i} z_k\right), \tag{5}$$

where $f(\cdot)$normalizes the vector using the L2 norm. By this process, prototypes of the features are automatically stored in the memory.

Memory Loss. We use feature compactness loss and feature separateness loss [8]. Employing these two losses ensures that similar features cluster together while distinctly separating different features. Feature compactness loss encourages a feature to become closer to the nearest memory item:

$$L_{compact} = \sum_{n=1}^{N} \|z_n - m_p\|_2, \tag{6}$$

where $p = \underset{i \in K}{\operatorname{argmax}}\, w^{n,i}$ denotes the index of the memory item that has the highest cosine similarity with the feature z_n. Since similar features are mapped to the same memory item, it allows for the use of a smaller memory size.

Feature separateness loss facilitates the distancing of dissimilar memory items, thereby allowing for a more diverse selection of prototypes. Each query z_n is encouraged to be close to its nearest memory item m_p and distant from its second nearest memory item m_q:

$$L_{separate} = \sum_{n=1}^{N} \left[\|z_n - m_p\|_2 - \|z_n - m_q\|_2 + \alpha\right]_+, \tag{7}$$

where α represents the margin, and $q = \underset{i \in K, i \neq p}{\operatorname{argmax}}\, w^{n,i}$ is the index of the second nearest memory item. The final memory loss is as follows:

$$L_{memory} = L_{compact} + L_{seperate}$$

Total Training Loss. The total training loss for the initial task is:

$$L = L_{rec} + L_{cls} + \lambda L_{memory}, \tag{8}$$

where L_{rec} is the reconstruction loss, defined as $L_{rec} = \sum_{t}^{T} \hat{x} - x_2$ with $\hat{x}$ representing the reconstructed image by decoder f_d and x is the original image. L_{cls} is the classification loss, which utilizes cross-entropy. After the model training is completed, B instances of z per class are stored for subsequent tasks, and the overall model is stored for regenerating the encoded representation.

3.3 Subsequent Learning and Inference

After completing the learning of the initial task, we preserve the previous knowledge using knowledge distillation to prevent semantic drift of the previous encoder. Since the z used in all modules is dependent on the encoder, preserving the knowledge of the encoder is essential to avoid confusion with previous knowledge. To effectively transfer the knowledge of a previous model, knowledge distillation is employed. In the proposed method, logit distillation and feature distillation are applied.

Logit distillation is performed in the label space to ensure that predictions closely resemble those of the previous model:

$$L_{ld} = -\sum_{i=1}^{|c_{t-1}|} \hat{p}_i\left(\widetilde{x_{t-1}^i}\right) log p_i\left(\widetilde{x_{t-1}^i}\right) \tag{9}$$

where input $\widetilde{x_{t-1}^i}$ consists of data from previously generated tasks, and $|c_{t-1}|$ represents the number of classes up to task $(t-1)$. At this time, since we cannot access the previous x_{t-1}, we use the decoder learned from the previous task. The decoder takes z as input and reconstructs the previous data, so we store B instances of z for each class from the previous task and utilize them for the current task. $\widehat{p_i}$ denotes the probability of the i th class as predicted by the previous model, and p_i is the probability of the i th class as predicted by the current model:

$$\hat{p}_i\left(\widetilde{x_{t-1}^i}\right) = \frac{e^{\hat{o}_i(x)/T}}{\sum_{j=1}^{n} e^{\hat{o}_j(x)/T}}, p_i\left(\widetilde{x_{t-1}^i}\right) = \frac{e^{o_i(x)/T}}{\sum_{j=1}^{n} e^{o_j(x)/T}}, \tag{10}$$

where T is the temperature parameter, $\hat{o}$ is the logits from the previous model's classifier, and o is the logits from the current model's classifier.

Feature distillation is employed to prevent changes in encoder:

$$L_{fd} = \sum_{i=1}^{n_m} f_e^{t-1}\left(x_t^i\right) - f_e^t\left(x_t^i\right)_2, \tag{11}$$

where f_e^{t-1} and f_e^t denote the encoders of the old model and the new model, respectively. Therefore, the distillation loss is as follows:

$$L_{distillation} = L_{fd} + L_{ld}$$

The loss for subsequent tasks after the first task is as follows:

$$L = L_{rec} + L_{cls} + \lambda L_{memory} + L_{distillation} \tag{12}$$

After the model is trained, the prototypes of previous classes are automatically updated, and the prototypes of new classes are added to the memory network. The buffer for previously learned classes is updated to reflect changes in the encoder. To update the buffer, generated data is used, and the encoder outputs for B samples of the currently learned classes are newly stored in the buffer.

4 Experiments

The proposed method enables end-to-end learning and can store multiple prototypes in a distributed manner, allowing for more accurate retention on class information. We evaluate the effectiveness of the proposed method in a CL setting in this section.

4.1 Experimental Setup

Datasets. Three datasets of MNIST, permuted MNIST (P-MNIST), and fashion-MNIST (F-MNIST) are used. MNIST consists of handwritten digits from 0 to 9, P-MNIST is a variant of the MNIST images with their pixels shuffled according to a consistent rule to create new images, and F-MNIST is composed of 10 classes related to fashion. Dividing the datasets so that two consecutive classes form one task yields a total of 10 classes for each dataset, which are trained in a class incremental learning setting with 5 tasks.

Evaluation Metric. The methods are evaluated with average accuracy, which is calculated by averaging accuracies across all incremental steps.

Baseline Methods. There are 8 baseline methods: 5 replay-based and 3 non-replay-based methods. The replay-based methods include iCaRL [2], BiC [14], WA [15], DER [3], and BEEF [4]. Unlike the comparative methods, the proposed model stores not the original images but their encoded form. Non-replay-based methods include LwF [16], EWC [17], and PASS [6]. We use the implementation of the PyCIL framework for the baseline methods and the hyperparameters. ResNet-20 [18] is used as the backbone.

Implementation Details. The encoder and decoder of the proposed method are each composed of 6 convolution layers. Except for the last layer of the decoder, each layer is followed by batch normalization and a leaky ReLU activation. The final layer of the decoder uses tanh activation. The memory is a 2-dimensional tensor with a memory size of 100 and a memory dimension of 32. The classifier consists of two linear layers with a LeakyReLU activation in between. The proposed method is trained by AdamW optimizer with a learning rate of 0.001. The size of feature z is $7 \times 7 \times 32$. We empirically find the optimal hyperparameters as $\lambda = 0.01$, and $\alpha = 1$. All the methods are trained for 100 epochs.

4.2 Performance Evaluation

The experimental results are summarized in Table 1. The comparative methods employing replay (iCaRL, BiC, WA, DER, and BEER) are tested with buffer sizes of 100, 300, and 500. The proposed method not only outperforms the methods that do not store original samples, but also shows superior performance compared to those that do. Note that the proposed method uses regenerated images. Except for P-MNIST with buffer sizes of 300, the proposed method performs the best in all other experiments. Especially, the proposed method demonstrates superior results on the F-MNIST, where the performance is improved by 2.39%p, 0.53%p, and 5.4%p for memory sizes of 100, 300, and 500, respectively.

We also conduct a comparative analysis of iCaRL, WA, DER, and the proposed model after the final task. Fig. 2 compares the experimental methods across three datasets under the condition of a memory size of 500, according to the tasks. As observed in the experiments, the proposed method produces comparable performance across the three datasets. However, in the later tasks of F-MNIST dataset, it shows lower performance than DER, WA, and iCaRL. Nevertheless, it achieves a significant increase in average accuracy, as shown in Table 1, by maintaining high accuracy in the initial tasks. Based on these results, the proposed method has a strong initial learning capability, which helps it achieve higher average accuracy overall. This suggests that the method is particularly effective at quickly adapting to new tasks with high accuracy.

Table 1. Average accuracy on MNIST, P-MNIST, and F-MNIST. *B* denotes the buffer size.

	MNIST			Permuted MNIST			Fashion-MNIST		
B	100	300	500	100	300	500	100	300	500
LwF		94.52			78.78			51.8	
EWC		47.94			42.78			45.78	
PASS		90.27			64.86			68.19	
iCaRL	86.53	94.31	95.07	73.41	86.53	89.65	64.12	76.75	79.14
BiC	70.61	80.78	83.7	88.66	**94.96**	94.94	60.20	66.83	74.18
WA	95.57	97.79	98.31	88.12	89.06	92.55	67.57	79.35	81.06
DER	94.9	97.9	98.17	80.13	89.89	92.35	65.7	77.06	79.64
BEEF	86.53	94.31	95.07	88.8	93.85	95.47	68.24	71.83	74.2
Ours	**96.72**	**98.33**	**98.35**	**90.01**	91.2	**96.92**	**70.63**	**79.88**	**86.46**

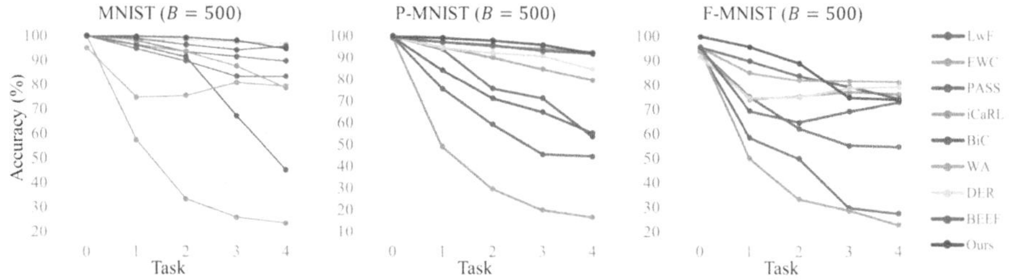

Fig. 2. Accuracy curves for three benchmark datasets.

4.3 Ablation Study

We conduct an ablation study using the MNIST dataset to investigate the effects of knowledge distillation and feature related loss in continual learning. The experiments are conducted by individually removing feature distillation, logit distillation, feature compactness loss, and feature separateness loss. The buffer size used in the experiment is 300, and the memory size is 300.

Removing feature distillation results in a performance decline of 9.03%p as shown in Table 2, suggesting that maintaining encoder to improve model performance is crucial, as feature distillation plays a pivotal role in preserving prototypes of previous tasks.

Eliminating logit distillation leads to a performance drop of 2.52%p. Interestingly, models without any form of distillation performs better than those with only logit distillation, implying that maintaining feature space is essential for performance. Figure 3 shows that iCaRL, WA, and DER exhibit class overlap in their representations of t-SNE visualization, whereas the proposed method demonstrates more discriminative features, attributable to the incorporation of feature compactness and feature separateness losses. These discriminative features help in reducing misclassification and preventing from forgetting the previous tasks.

For feature related loss, the combined use of feature compactness and feature separateness losses yields the best results. Notably, employing only feature compactness loss, without feature separateness loss, results in all features becoming too similar, which significantly impaired performance.

Table 2. Ablation study of knowledge distillation and feature related loss.

Ablated Components	L_{fd}	L_{ld}	$L_{compact}$	$L_{separate}$	Average accuracy
feature distillation		√	√	√	89.33
logit distillation	√		√	√	95.84
distillation			√	√	92.72
feature compactness loss	√	√		√	94.97
feature separateness loss	√	√	√		90.47
feature related loss	√	√			94.81
All	√	√	√	√	98.36

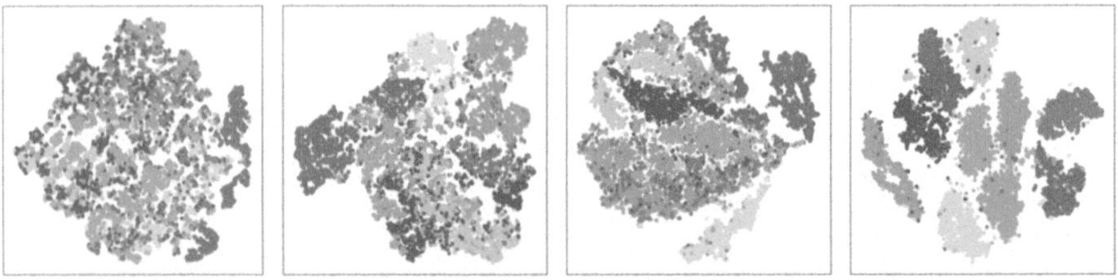

(a) iCaRL (b) WA (c) DER (d) Ours

Fig. 3. t-SNE visualization of class representation on the MNIST with buffer size of 300.

Effects of Memory. To investigate the effect of memory, we conduct experiments with a model without the memory network, under the same settings as the proposed method. The experiments utilize MNIST dataset with a buffer size of 300 and a memory size of 100. Figure 4 shows the t-SNE results and the confusion matrix after learning all tasks: (a) represents the results of the model without memory network from the proposed method, and (b) is the proposed method. The t-SNE results at the left-hand side are color-coded by class labels, while those at the right-hand side are marked in green for correctly classified instances and in red for incorrectly classified ones.

Because of knowledge distillation and replay, it seems that the learned features are well distinguished between classes in both (a) and (b). However, when examining the classification results, it appears that features are poorly classified (b). It seems that the prototypes of classes stored in memory prevent misclassification. Looking at the confusion matrix, it is evident that there is a greater bias towards the last task in the absence of memory compared to when memory is present.

4.4 Method Analysis

Automatic Selection of Prototype. To observe the update of prototypes, we visualize the output (prototypes) from the memory. With MNIST dataset, we visualize the memory output generated at the end of each task to investigate these updates, as shown in Fig. 5. After training on task 2, it is observed that the positions of the representations for class 0 and class 1 have shifted. The memory network automatically updates the prototypes for class 0 and class 1 without any additional process. Furthermore, it demonstrates the capability to accommodate the prototypes for classes 0, 1, 2, and 3 without requiring an increase in the size of the memory network.

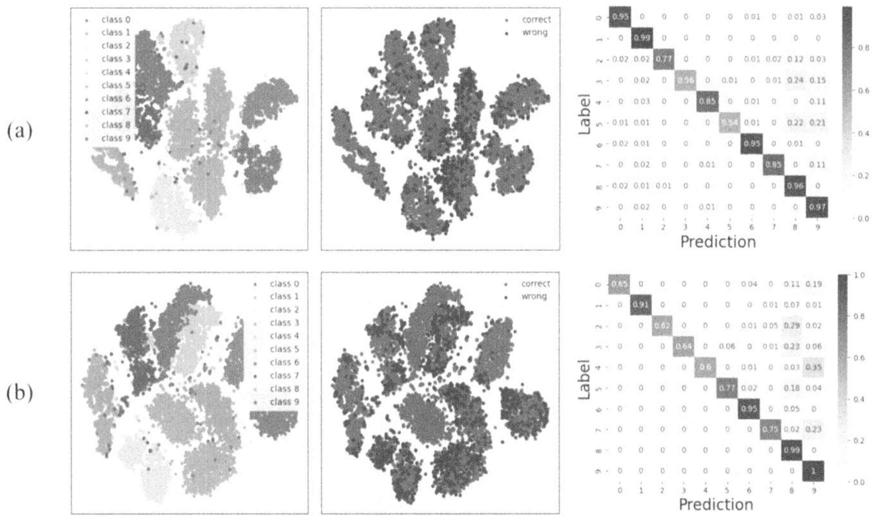

Fig. 4. t-SNE visualization and confusion matrix after the final task. (a) is the proposed method and (b) is proposed method without memory. The left image represents classes by color, the middle image shows whether the answer is correct, and the right image is confusion matrix.

Effects of Memory Size. The effect of the memory size is evaluated by gradually increasing it from very small size. We use MNIST dataset and employ a buffer size of 300 in a CIL setting. As illustrated in Fig. 6, from 10 to 50, there is a tendency

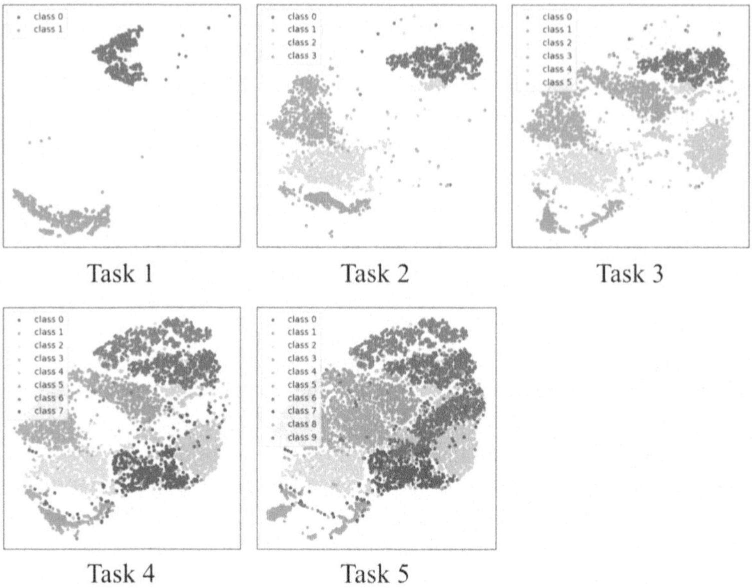

Fig. 5. Visualization of memory output after training each task.

for performance to increase as memory size increases. However, there is negligible performance improvement beyond a memory size of 50. This suggests that a memory size 50 is sufficient to adequately store the feature for MNIST dataset. Conversely, an excessively large memory size leads to underfitting, resulting in poorer performance. For MNIST dataset, the optimal results appear to be achieved around a memory size of 100.

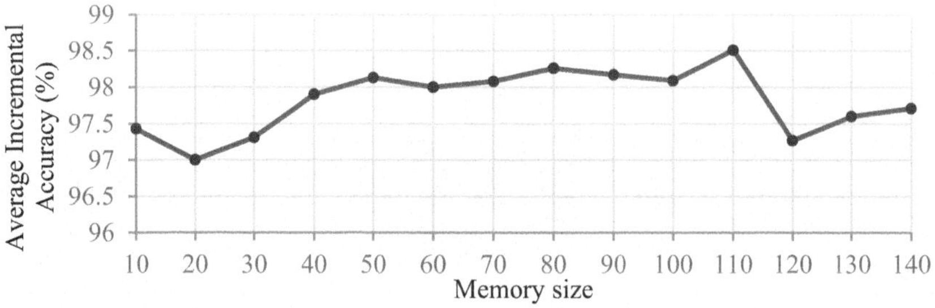

Fig. 6. The effects of memory size.

5 Concluding Remarks

We have proposed a new method for CIL, which automatically selects critical information in an end-to-end manner. We effectively select and update prototypes utilizing memory network. This method avoids storing original data by saving and restoring encoded samples. Experimental results have demonstrated superior performance across three datasets compared to the baseline models. We have conducted the research solely on using the autoencoder, one of the simplest generative models.

In the future, we need to improve its performance in later tasks, especially on the F-MNIST dataset, for retaining knowledge from earlier tasks while still learning new ones. This trade-off between initial accuracy and long-term retention is a critical aspect to consider in further developments and optimizations of the method [19]. We will focus on enhancing the memory retention strategies to ensure consistent performance across all tasks [20].

Acknowledgements. This work was supported by the Yonsei Fellow Program funded by Lee Youn Jae, IITP grant funded by the Korea government (MSIT) (No. RS-2022-II220113, Developing a Sustainable Collaborative Multi-modal Lifelong Learning Framework), and Air Force Defense Research Sciences Program funded by Air Force Office of Scientific Research.

References

1. Yu, L., et al.: Semantic drift compensation for class-incremental learning. In: CVPR, pp. 6982–6991 (2020)
2. Rebuffi, S.A., Kolesnikov, A., Sperl, G., Lampert, C.H.: iCaRL: incremental classifier and representation learning. In: CVPR, pp. 2001–2010 (2017)
3. Yan, S., Xie, J., He, X.: DER: dynamically expandable representation for class incremental learning. In: CVPR, pp. 3014–3023 (2021)
4. Wang, F.Y., et al.: BEEF: bi-compatible class-incremental learning via energy-based expansion and fusion. In: ICLR, vol. 11 (2022)
5. Kim, T.H., Moon, H.J., Cho, S.B.: Gradient regularization with multivariate distribution of previous knowledge for continual learning. In: Yin, H., Camacho, D., Tino, P. (eds.) Intelligent Data Engineering and Automated Learning – IDEAL 2022. IDEAL 2022. LNCS, vol. 13756. Springer, Cham (2022). https://doi.org/10.1007/978-3-031-21753-1_35
6. Zhu, F., Zhang, X.Y., Wang, C., Yin, F., Liu, C.L.: Prototype augmentation and self-supervision for incremental learning. In: CVPR, pp. 5871–5880 (2021)
7. Asadi, N., Davari, M., Mudur, S., Aljundi, R., Belilovsky, E.: Prototype-sample relation distillation: towards replay-free continual learning. In: ICML, pp. 1093–1106 (2023)
8. Park, H., Noh, J., Ham, B.: Learning memory-guided normality for anomaly detection. In: CVPR, pp. 14372–14381 (2020)
9. De Lange, M., Tuytelaars, T.: Continual prototype evolution: learning online from non-stationary data streams. In: ICCV, pp. 8250–8259 (2021)
10. Li, Z., et al.: Steering prototypes with prompt-tuning for rehearsal-free continual learning. In: WACV, pp. 2523–2533 (2024)
11. Xie, H., Yao, H., Zhou, S., Zhang, S., Sun, W.: Efficient regional memory network for video object segmentation. In: CVPR, pp. 1286–1295 (2021)

12. Liang, S., Shen, X., Huang, J., Hua, X.S.: Video object segmentation with dynamic memory networks and adaptive object alignment. In: ICCV, pp. 8065–8074 (2021)
13. Cai, J., et al.: MeMOT: multi-object tracking with memory. In: CVPR, pp. 8090–8100 (2022)
14. Wu, Y., et al.: Large scale incremental learning. In: CVPR, pp. 374–382 (2019)
15. Zhao, B., Xiao, X., Gan, G., Zhang, B., Xia, S.T.: Maintaining discrimination and fairness in class incremental learning. In: CVPR, pp. 13208–13217 (2020)
16. Li, Z., Hoiem, D.: Learning without forgetting. In: IEEE Transactions on Pattern Analysis and Machine Intelligence, vol. 40, no. 12, pp. 2935–2947 (2017)
17. Kirkpatrick, J., et al.: Overcoming catastrophic forgetting in neural networks. In: Proceedings of the National Academy of Sciences, vol. 114, no. 13, pp. 3521–3526 (2017)
18. He, K., Zhang, X., Ren, S., Sun, J.: Deep residual learning for image recognition. In: CVPR, pp. 770–778 (2016)
19. Moon, H.J., Cho, S.B.: Contrastive learning of multivariate gaussian distributions of incremental classes for continual learning. In: Ferrández Vicente, J.M., Val Calvo, M., Adeli, H. (eds.) Artificial Intelligence for Neuroscience and Emotional Systems. IWINAC 2024. LNCS, vol. 14674, pp. 518–527. Springer, Cham (2024). https://doi.org/10.1007/978-3-031-61140-7_49
20. Moon, H.J., Cho, S.B.: A subgraph embedded GIN with attention for graph classification. In: Quaresma, P., Camacho, D., Yin, H., Gonçalves, T., Julian, V., Tallón-Ballesteros, A.J. (eds) Intelligent Data Engineering and Automated Learning – IDEAL 2023. IDEAL 2023. LNCS, vol. 14404, pp. 356–367. Springer, Cham. https://doi.org/10.1007/978-3-031-48232-8_33

Evolutionary Computation and Optimization

Efficient Continuous Sign Language Recognition with Temporal Shift and Channel Attention

Nguyen Tu Nam[1] and Hiroki Takahashi[2(✉)]

[1] Graduate School of Informatics and Engineering, The University of Electro-Communications, Tokyo, Japan
g2340024@gl.cc.uec.ac.jp

[2] Graduate School of Informatics and Engineering, Artificial Intelligence Exploration Research Center, Meta-Networking Research Center, The University of Electro-Communications, Tokyo, Japan
rocky@inf.uec.ac.jp

Abstract. The field of vision-based Continuous Sign Language Recognition (CSLR) offers a promising solution to bridge the communication gap between the hearing and Deaf and Hard of Hearing (DHH) communities by enabling the translation of sign language videos into written or spoken language. Current state-of-the-art CSLR approaches often rely on complex deep learning architectures to capture the spatial and temporal features of sign language, but these complex models often come at a significant computational cost. Our work proposes an efficient framework that leverages the Temporal Shift Module (TSM) and Squeeze-and-Excitation (SE) module to enhance temporal modeling and feature representation. The TSM empowers 2D Convolutional Neural Networks (CNNs) to effectively capture temporal features without increasing computational resources, while the SE module adaptively selects informative features. Our proposed framework is designed to be both accurate and efficient. We evaluate our framework on the PHOENIX14 and PHOENIX14-T datasets, achieving competitive recognition performance compared to prior works while requiring only a small increase in computational resources.

Keywords: Continuous Sign Language Recognition · Neural Network · TSM · SE Net · Channel attention

1 Introduction

Sign language is the natural method of communication between DHH communities. It uses a complex combination of manual and non-manual elements, such as hand gestures, facial expressions, in order to communicate. The complexity of sign languages presents a significant challenge for smooth communication between normal-hearing and DHH people. In an effort to bridge this communication barrier, the accurate recognition of sign language gestures has been the

H. Quintián et al. (Eds.): HAIS 2024, LNAI 14857, pp. 301–311, 2025.
https://doi.org/10.1007/978-3-031-74183-8_25

subject of extensive research and development in recent years. Different from isolated sign language recognition [10,30,31], which translates a single video segment into a single gloss, CSLR translates a video into a series of glosses to express a sentence, making it more closely aligned with real-life scenarios.

Extracting spatial-temporal features is a crucial aspect that has been extensively explored in CSLR to overcome its challenges. Initially, researchers relied on handcrafted features [12,22,32] or Hidden Markov Models. However, recent advancements have seen the integration of CNNs for feature extraction, combined with Long Short-Term Memory (LSTM) [18,24,27] or transformers [3,9,34] to capture long-term temporal information, along with Connectionist Temporal Classification (CTC) for alignment. Some studies have utilized 2D CNNs to process individual frames separately, which may not effectively capture temporal dynamics. In contrast, others have employed 3D CNNs [1,25] to extract richer information. Furthermore, the inclusion of multimodal approaches has gained traction to enhance recognition accuracy and feature richness in CSLR. For instance, two-stream networks [8] with one stream dedicated to RGB images and another to optical flow images have shown promising results. Additionally, leveraging cues [4,5,36,37] such as hand shape, facial expressions, and human posture as inputs in multimodal models has been explored to improve performance. Nevertheless, these studies often require significant computational resources due to the complexity of the models and the diverse data sources being integrated.

In this work, we propose an efficient deep learning framework for CSLR that incorporates specialized modules to enhance temporal modeling and feature representation capabilities while maintaining computational efficiency. More specifically, we leverage the TSM to enable existing 2D CNNs to effectively capture temporal dependencies in a parameter-efficient manner. Additionally, we integrate the SE module to compute channel-wise attention maps, allowing the network to selectively emphasize the most informative features. Our framework achieves competitive recognition performance on challenging sign language datasets while requiring fewer computational resources compared to complex state-of-the-art methodologies, though it does use slightly more resources than the baseline 2D CNN approach.

2 Related Work

CSLR is an active area of research in computer vision and human-computer interaction, that aims to interpret sign language from video sequences and translate them into text or speech to bridge the communication gap between the deaf and hearing communities. The advent of deep learning has revolutionized CSLR, leading to a shift from manually engineered features to learned features facilitated by CNNs.

A typical framework for CSLR consists of two main components: a feature extractor and an alignment module [24]. The feature extractor, typically CNNs, is responsible for learning and extracting meaningful spatial and temporal features from the input video sequences. These learned features capture the intricate patterns and dynamics of sign language gestures, serving as a rich representation of the visual information. The alignment module, on the other hand, takes the extracted features and aligns them with the corresponding text output. This module often utilizes CTC, a powerful technique that allows for the alignment of the input features with the output labels without requiring explicit segmentation of the video frames of CSLR datasets.

However, a common challenge faced by the alignment module is its tendency to overfit, while the feature extractor may not be adequately trained [7,8,29]. To address these issues, researchers have explored various strategies to improve the performance of CSLR systems. One approach involves using iterative training methods [8,29] to reduce overfitting, although this often results in longer training times. Another effort involves using 3D CNNs [1,25] to capture spatio-temporal features in sign language videos. Several studies have used a two-stream approach, one for RGB and another for depth information. While this approach can achieve high accuracy, it often requires a large number of parameters, leading to increased computational complexity. Some researchers have used (2+1)D CNNs [13,33] as feature extractors, with 2D CNNs for spatial information and 1D CNNs for temporal information. This approach has achieved remarkable recognition performance. More recent methods aim to enhance the feature extractor. For instance, Min et al. [24] used alignment losses as a form of knowledge distillation to improve results. Building on this idea, Hu et al. [18,19] further enhanced the approach by introducing additional modules that emphasize sign movements. Nonetheless, the work of Hu et al. [18,19] still requires a large number of resource due to its continued reliance on 3D CNNs. Our proposed approach eliminates the need for computationally expensive 3D CNNs by employing 2D CNNs with the TSM and SE module, thereby enhancing the spatial-temporal modeling capabilities of the feature extractor while maintaining a lightweight and efficient architecture.

3 Proposed System Architecture

Our methodology follows a well-established non-iterative framework VAC [24] that consists of several crucial components. These components include a 2D CNN feature extractor, a 1D CNN for short-term information extraction, and Bidirectional LSTM (BiLSTM) model for capturing long-term dependencies. Together, these components contribute to the prediction process facilitated by a classifier. To ensure consistency with previous studies and allow for fair comparisons with existing methodologies, we have chosen ResNet18 [15] as the 2D CNN feature extractor. ResNet18 has been pre-trained on the ImageNet [11] dataset. In addition to these foundational components, we have introduced two novel enhancements through the incorporation of the TSM modules and the SE module. As illustrated in Fig. 1, we integrate TSM modules after layers two, three, and four of ResNet18. The outputs of these modules are fused with the original features using a learned weighting coefficient. We have also placed the SE module after the Convolution layer of each residual block in the ResNet18

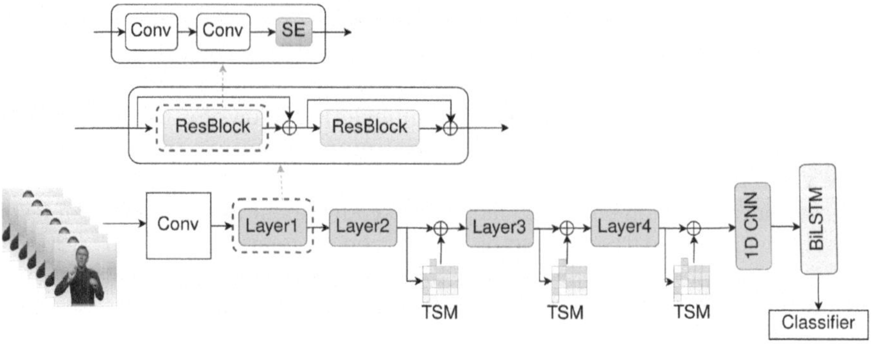

Fig. 1. Illustration of our proposal framework. ResNet18 is pre-trained with ImageNet. SE modules are put on each ResBlock and TSMs with learnable coefficient are put after layer two to layer four.

model. In the following subsections, we will provide a detailed explanation of the TSM and SE modules, highlighting their unique features and contributions to the overall performance of our CSLR framework.

3.1 TSM

Traditional video analysis methods often involve performing computationally intensive tasks, such as convolutions, on each individual frame. This could potentially consume a significant amount of processing time and computational resources. To address these limitations, the TSM [23] has emerged as a powerful technique. This innovative approach uses shift operations within existing 2D CNNs to process video frames more efficiently. By rearranging the feature channels along the temporal dimension, TSM captures and models the temporal dependencies in the data. The key strength of TSM lies in its ability to improve the accuracy of video comprehension without introducing additional parameters or computations.

For simplicity and intuition, let's consider a normal 1-D convolution operation with a kernel size of 3. We can express the convolution operator $C = \mathrm{Conv}(A, B)$ as:

$$C_i = a_1 B_{i-1} + a_2 B_i + a_3 B_{i+1} \tag{1}$$

where the weight $A = (a_1, a_2, a_3)$ and a 1-D vector input B. This convolution operation can be broken down into two steps: shifting and multiplying-accumulating. The formulas for these are:

$$B_i^{-1} = B_{i-1}, \quad B_i^0 = B_i, \quad B_i^{+1} = B_{i+1} \tag{2}$$

$$C = a_1 B^{-1} + a_2 B^0 + a_3 B^{+1} \tag{3}$$

In the TSM, the shifting input B by $-1, 0, +1$ can be done without any multiplication and the second step is merged into the following 2D convolution, so it doesn't add any extra cost compared to 2D CNN based models. The TSM leverages this concept to process video frames efficiently, capturing temporal information and leading to enhanced accuracy and computational efficiency.

3.2 SE Net

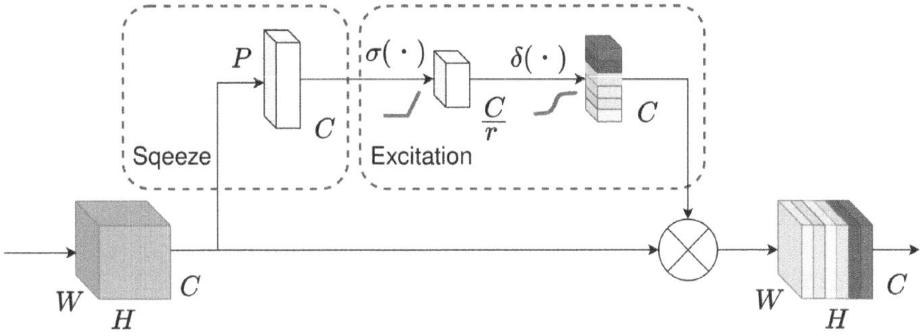

Fig. 2. Illustration of SE module.

The SE module was introduced by Hu et al. [16]. It is a channel-wise attention mechanism in computer vision designed to enhance the representational power of CNNs by selectively emphasizing or suppressing different channels of the feature maps. The module achieves this by following a two-step process: squeeze and excitation. Figure 2 provides an illustration of the SE module, detailing its internal structure and operation.

The squeeze operation aims to capture the global spatial context of each channel in a feature map. It accomplishes this by summarizing the local spatial information learned by each convolutional filter within its receptive field. This is typically done using global average pooling, although global max pooling or other pooling methods can also be employed. The squeeze operation can be mathematically expressed as:

$$s = P(u_c) \tag{4}$$

where u_c represents the input feature map for the c-th channel, and P denotes the squeeze operation. The excitation operation, on the other hand, aims to generate channel-wise attention weights. This is achieved by passing the output of squeeze step $1\times 1\times C$, where C is the number channels of the input feature maps, through two Fully Connected (FC) layers with nonlinear activation functions. The first FC layer reduces the dimensionality by a factor $r = 16$, followed by a ReLU activation, and the second FC layer restores the dimensionality, followed by a Sigmoid activation:

$$e = \sigma(W_2\delta(W_1 s)) \tag{5}$$

where W_1 and W_2 are the weights of the fully connected layers, δ represents the ReLU activation function, and σ denotes the sigmoid activation function. The output e is a vector containing the channel-wise attention weights $[e_1, e_2, \ldots, e_C]$.

Finally, the learned attention weights are applied to the input feature maps through channel-wise multiplication. This process acts as a dynamic gating mechanism, adjusting contribution of each channel based on its determined significance. Despite its lightweight and simple design, the SE module effectively refines the feature representation. By integrating the SE module, our proposed framework improves the overall performance of the network without incurring significant computational cost. Specifically, the inclusion of the SE module results in a minimal computational overhead, requiring approximately only 0.0009 GFLOPs (Giga Floating-Point Operations) per image.

4 Experimental Setup

4.1 Datasets

We employ the multi-signer sets from the PHOENIX14 [22] and PHOENIX14-T [2] datasets in our experiments. These datasets were compiled from daily German weather forecast broadcasts. Each dataset comprises a sequence of video frames with a resolution of 210 pixels. The PHOENIX14 dataset involves the participation of 9 signers, divided into three subsets, with 5672, 540, and 629 video samples for training, development (Dev), and testing (Test) purposes, respectively. Similarly, the PHOENIX14-T datasets provide 7096 videos samples for training, 519 for development and 642 for testing.

4.2 Implementation Details

Our training settings follow recent studies [18,24] for comparison. Input video frames are randomly cropped to 224×224 pixels after being resized from 210×256 pixels to 256×256 pixels with 20% temporal rescaling and 50% horizontal flipping. The models were trained 40 epochs, batch size is 2, Adam optimizer with learning rate of 10^{-4} reduced by 5 at the 20th and 35th epochs, weight decay of 10^{-4}.

We evaluate our models using CTC loss (L_{CTC}) and Word Error Rate (WER) as the evaluation metric. The WER is calculated as the sum of the total insertions, deletions, and substitutions, divided by the total words in the reference sentence. A lower WER indicates better performance and higher values indicate more errors in the model's output compared to the reference sentence. Equation 6 and Fig. 3 illustrate the calculation method and provide an example of WER, where REF denotes the reference sentence and PRE represents the prediction sentence generated by the model.

$$\text{WER} = \frac{\text{insertions} + \text{deletions} + \text{substitutions}}{\text{reference}} \times 100\% \tag{6}$$

REF:	spaeter	regen	UEBERALL	region	*****
PRE:	******	regen	KOMMEN	region	nacht

Fig. 3. An example of WER

We adopt the Visual Enhancement loss (L_{VE}) and Visual Alignment loss (L_{VA}) for visual supervision, assigning weights of $\theta_1 = 1.0$ and $\theta_2 = 25$ to them, following the use of VAC [7]. The overall loss can be formulated as:

$$L_{Total} = L_{CTC} + \theta_1 \cdot L_{VE} + \theta_2 \cdot L_{VA} \tag{7}$$

All experiments were conducted on a system running Ubuntu 22.04, equipped with a single GeForce RTX 4090 graphics card and 64 GB of RAM. The software environment consisted of PyTorch version 2.0.1, CUDA version 11.8, python 3.9.

5 Experiments Result

Our proposed deep learning framework incorporating the TSM and SE modules was evaluated on the challenging PHOENIX14 and PHOENIX14-T datasets for German sign language recognition. Table 1 shows the performance of our approach with various state-of-the-art methods, including those utilizing RGB-only information and additional modalities (such as pose, optical flow). Our proposed framework achieves competitive performance compared to other RGB-based methods on both PHOENIX14 and PHOENIX14-T datasets with accuracy are 19.9/19.9 and 19.3/20.6 respectively. Remarkably, our framework maintains a balance between accuracy and efficiency, requiring only a small increase in resource consumption when incorporating SE and TSM modules. In comparison to the state-of-the-art CorrNet which uses only RGB data, our framework has slightly smaller model size. Table 2 shows a comparison of the GFLOPs for our model and CorrNet, considering videos with the fewest, mean, and maximum number of frames in the PHOENIX14 dataset test set. Specifically, our model takes only 22.5 s on average, whereas CorrNet takes 32.3 s, where averaged over 10 runs, excluding the time to read and transfer data, focusing on inference time.

Furthermore, our ablation studies to measure the effect of TSM and SE modules individually are displayed in Table 3, using the PHOENIX14 dataset. The data showed that performance dropped on both the development and test sets, as indicated by a rise in the WER, when either SE or TSM was excluded, demonstrating the importance of these modules for achieving optimal performance.

Table 1. Performance comparison with state-of-the-art methods on PHOENIX14 and PHOENIX14-T datasets

Methods	WER (%)			
	PHOENIX14		PHOENIX14-T	
	Dev	Test	Dev	Test
RGB Only				
SFL [26]	26.2	26.8	25.1	26.1
FCN [6]	23.7	23.9	23.3	25.1
Joint-SLRT [3]	-	-	24.6	24.5
VAC [24]	21.2	22.3	-	-
CMA [28]	21.3	21.9	-	-
SignBT [35]	-	-	22.7	23.9
SMKD [14]	20.8	21.0	20.8	22.4
SEN [19]	19.5	21.0	19.3	20.7
SSSLR [20]	20.9	20.8	20.5	22.3
TLP [17]	19.7	20.8	19.4	21.2
Cornet [18]	**18.8**	**19.4**	**18.9**	**20.5**
Ours	19.9	19.9	19.3	20.6
Additional Modalities				
CNN-LSTM-HMM [21]	26.0	26.0	22.1	24.1
DNF [8]	23.1	22.9	-	-
STMC [36]	21.1	20.7	19.6	21.0
C^2SLR [37]	20.5	20.4	20.2	20.4
TwoStream-SLR [5]	**18.4**	**18.8**	**17.7**	**19.3**

Table 2. Comparison of GFLOPs between CorrNet and our model for videos with minimum, mean, and maximum frames in the PHOENIX14 test dataset set.

	Min Frames	Mean Frames	Max Frames
CorrNet [18]	226	7556	1310
Our	203	7286	1290

Table 3. Ablation studies for effectiveness of proposal modules on the PHOENIX14 dataset.

Proposal Framework	Dev (%)	Test (%)
w/o SE	20.1	20.9
w/o TSM	20.4	20.7
w/ SE & TSM	19.9	19.9

6 Conclusion

In this paper, we presented an efficient deep learning framework for CSLR that incorporates the TSM and SE modules. The TSM allows existing 2D CNNs to model temporal dependencies in video data by shifting channels along the temporal dimension, without any additional parameters or computations. The SE module complements this by calculating attention weights for each channel to highlight the most informative features in the network's learned representations. We evaluated our method on the challenging PHOENIX14 and PHOENIX14-T datasets for German Sign Language recognition. Experimental results show that our framework achieves competitive performance compared to previous state-of-the-art RGB-based methods, while requiring a small increase of computational resources. To further enhance the feature representations, future research could investigate integrating additional modalities such as body pose, hand movement or facial expressions, as well as explore explainable deep learning techniques to gain further insights into our proposed approach. Moreover, exploring explainable deep learning methods may offer a deeper understanding of our model's effectiveness. This investigation might result in a stronger and more easily understandable model.

References

1. Ariesta, M.C., Wiryana, F., Zahra, A., et al.: Sentence level Indonesian sign language recognition using 3D convolutional neural network and bidirectional recurrent neural network. In: 2018 Indonesian Association for Pattern Recognition International Conference (INAPR), pp. 16–22. IEEE (2018)
2. Camgoz, N.C., Hadfield, S., Koller, O., Ney, H., Bowden, R.: Neural sign language translation. In: Proceedings of the IEEE Conference on Computer Vision and Pattern Recognition, pp. 7784–7793 (2018)
3. Camgoz, N.C., Koller, O., Hadfield, S., Bowden, R.: Sign language transformers: joint end-to-end sign language recognition and translation. In: Proceedings of the IEEE/CVF Conference on Computer Vision and Pattern Recognition, pp. 10023–10033 (2020)
4. Caridakis, G., Asteriadis, S., Karpouzis, K.: Non-manual cues in automatic sign language recognition. In: Proceedings of the 4th International Conference on Pervasive Technologies Related to Assistive Environments, pp. 1–4 (2011)
5. Chen, Y., Zuo, R., Wei, F., Wu, Y., Liu, S., Mak, B.: Two-stream network for sign language recognition and translation. Adv. Neural. Inf. Process. Syst. **35**, 17043–17056 (2022)
6. Cheng, K.L., Yang, Z., Chen, Q., Tai, Y.W.: Fully Convolutional Networks for Continuous Sign Language Recognition. In: Vedaldi, A., Bischof, H., Brox, T., Frahm, J.M. (eds.) ECCV 2020, pp. 697–714. Springer, Cham (2020). https://doi.org/10.1007/978-3-030-58586-0_41
7. Cui, R., Liu, H., Zhang, C.: Recurrent convolutional neural networks for continuous sign language recognition by staged optimization. In: Proceedings of the IEEE Conference on Computer Vision and Pattern Recognition, pp. 7361–7369 (2017)
8. Cui, R., Liu, H., Zhang, C.: A deep neural framework for continuous sign language recognition by iterative training. IEEE Trans. Multimedia **21**(7), 1880–1891 (2019)

9. De Coster, M., Van Herreweghe, M., Dambre, J.: Sign language recognition with transformer networks. In: 12th International Conference on Language Resources and Evaluation, pp. 6018–6024. European Language Resources Association (ELRA) (2020)
10. De Coster, M., Van Herreweghe, M., Dambre, J.: Isolated sign recognition from RGB video using pose flow and self-attention. In: Proceedings of the IEEE/CVF Conference on Computer Vision and Pattern Recognition, pp. 3441–3450 (2021)
11. Deng, J., Dong, W., Socher, R., Li, L.J., Li, K., Fei-Fei, L.: ImageNet: a large-scale hierarchical image database. In: 2009 IEEE Conference on Computer Vision and Pattern Recognition, pp. 248–255. IEEE (2009)
12. Freeman, W.T., Roth, M.: Orientation histograms for hand gesture recognition. In: International Workshop on Automatic Face and Gesture Recognition, vol. 12, pp. 296–301. Citeseer (1995)
13. Han, X., Lu, F., Yin, J., Tian, G., Liu, J.: Sign language recognition based on $R(2+1)$ d with spatial-temporal-channel attention. IEEE Trans. Hum. Mach. Syst. **52**(4), 687–698 (2022)
14. Hao, A., Min, Y., Chen, X.: Self-mutual distillation learning for continuous sign language recognition. In: Proceedings of the IEEE/CVF International Conference on Computer Vision, pp. 11303–11312 (2021)
15. He, K., Zhang, X., Ren, S., Sun, J.: Deep residual learning for image recognition. In: Proceedings of the IEEE Conference on Computer Vision and Pattern Recognition, pp. 770–778 (2016)
16. Hu, J., Shen, L., Sun, G.: Squeeze-and-excitation networks. In: Proceedings of the IEEE Conference on Computer Vision and Pattern Recognition, pp. 7132–7141 (2018)
17. Hu, L., Gao, L., Liu, Z., Feng, W.: Temporal lift pooling for continuous sign language recognition. In: Avidan, S., Brostow, G., Cissé, M., Farinella, G.M., Hassner, T. (eds.) ECCV 2022, pp. 511–527. Springer, Cham (2022). https://doi.org/10.1007/978-3-031-19833-5_30
18. Hu, L., Gao, L., Liu, Z., Feng, W.: Continuous sign language recognition with correlation network. In: Proceedings of the IEEE/CVF Conference on Computer Vision and Pattern Recognition, pp. 2529–2539 (2023)
19. Hu, L., Gao, L., Liu, Z., Feng, W.: Self-emphasizing network for continuous sign language recognition. In: Proceedings of the AAAI Conference on Artificial Intelligence, vol. 37, pp. 854–862 (2023)
20. Jang, Y., et al.: Self-sufficient framework for continuous sign language recognition. In: ICASSP 2023-2023 IEEE International Conference on Acoustics, Speech and Signal Processing (ICASSP), pp. 1–5. IEEE (2023)
21. Koller, O., Camgoz, N.C., Ney, H., Bowden, R.: Weakly supervised learning with multi-stream CNN-LSTM-HMMs to discover sequential parallelism in sign language videos. IEEE Trans. Pattern Anal. Mach. Intell. **42**(9), 2306–2320 (2019)
22. Koller, O., Forster, J., Ney, H.: Continuous sign language recognition: towards large vocabulary statistical recognition systems handling multiple signers. Comput. Vis. Image Underst. **141**, 108–125 (2015)
23. Lin, J., Gan, C., Han, S.: TSM: temporal shift module for efficient video understanding. In: Proceedings of the IEEE/CVF International Conference on Computer Vision, pp. 7083–7093 (2019)
24. Min, Y., Hao, A., Chai, X., Chen, X.: Visual alignment constraint for continuous sign language recognition. In: Proceedings of the IEEE/CVF International Conference on Computer Vision, pp. 11542–11551 (2021)

25. Neto, G.M.R., Junior, G.B., de Almeida, J.D.S., de Paiva, A.C.: Sign language recognition based on 3D convolutional neural networks. In: Campilho, A., Karray, F., ter Haar Romeny, B. (eds.) ICIAR 2018. LNCS, vol. 10882, pp. 399–407. Springer, Cham (2018). https://doi.org/10.1007/978-3-319-93000-8_45
26. Niu, Z., Mak, B.: Stochastic fine-grained labeling of multi-state sign glosses for continuous sign language recognition. In: Vedaldi, A., Bischof, H., Brox, T., Frahm, J.M. (eds.) ECCV 2020. LNCS, vol. 12361, pp. 172–186. Springer, Cham (2020). https://doi.org/10.1007/978-3-030-58517-4_11
27. Papadimitriou, K., Potamianos, G.: Multimodal locally enhanced transformer for continuous sign language recognition, pp. 1513–1517 (2023)
28. Pu, J., Zhou, W., Hu, H., Li, H.: Boosting continuous sign language recognition via cross modality augmentation. In: Proceedings of the 28th ACM International Conference on Multimedia, pp. 1497–1505 (2020)
29. Pu, J., Zhou, W., Li, H.: Iterative alignment network for continuous sign language recognition. In: Proceedings of the IEEE/CVF Conference on Computer Vision and Pattern Recognition, pp. 4165–4174 (2019)
30. Rastgoo, R., Kiani, K., Escalera, S.: Real-time isolated hand sign language recognition using deep networks and SVD. J. Ambient. Intell. Humaniz. Comput. **13**(1), 591–611 (2022)
31. Sincan, O.M., Tur, A.O., Keles, H.Y.: Isolated sign language recognition with multi-scale features using LSTM. In: 2019 27th Signal Processing and Communications Applications Conference (SIU), pp. 1–4. IEEE (2019)
32. Sun, C., Zhang, T., Bao, B.K., Xu, C., Mei, T.: Discriminative exemplar coding for sign language recognition with Kinect. IEEE Trans. Cybern. **43**(5), 1418–1428 (2013)
33. Wang, F., Du, Y., Wang, G., Zeng, Z., Zhao, L.: (2+1)D-SLR: an efficient network for video sign language recognition. Neural Comput. Appl. **34**(3), 2413–2423 (2022)
34. Xie, P., Zhao, M., Hu, X.: PiSLTRc: position-informed sign language transformer with content-aware convolution. IEEE Trans. Multimedia **24**, 3908–3919 (2021)
35. Zhou, H., Zhou, W., Qi, W., Pu, J., Li, H.: Improving sign language translation with monolingual data by sign back-translation. In: Proceedings of the IEEE/CVF Conference on Computer Vision and Pattern Recognition, pp. 1316–1325 (2021)
36. Zhou, H., Zhou, W., Zhou, Y., Li, H.: Spatial-temporal multi-cue network for continuous sign language recognition. In: Proceedings of the AAAI Conference on Artificial Intelligence, vol. 34, pp. 13009–13016 (2020)
37. Zuo, R., Mak, B.: C2SLR: consistency-enhanced continuous sign language recognition. In: Proceedings of the IEEE/CVF Conference on Computer Vision and Pattern Recognition, pp. 5131–5140 (2022)

Solving the Clustered Minimum Routing Tree Problem Using Prüfer-Coding Based Hybrid Genetic Algorithms

Cosmin Sabo(✉), Bogdan Teglas, Petrică C. Pop, and Adrian Petrovan

Technical University of Cluj-Napoca, North University Center of Baia Mare, Dr. V. Babes 62A, 430083 Baia Mare, Romania
{cosmin.sabo,petrica.pop}@mi.utcluj.ro, adrian.petrovan@ieec.utcluj.ro

Abstract. The clustered minimum routing tree problem (CluMRTP) extends the classical minimum routing tree problem by considering a graph with vertices divided into a given number of clusters. The scope of the CluMRTP is to find a minimum-cost routing tree ensuring that each cluster forms a connected subgraph. In this work, we present Prüfer encoding-based hybrid genetic algorithms (HGAs) developed to address the CluMRTP. Our approach involves a macro-level genetic algorithm (GA) framework, employing the Prüfer code to generate trees linking the clusters, which is coupled with local-level algorithms to derive a feasible solution for the CluMRTP corresponding to a tree which spans the clusters. Preliminary computational results are reported on a set of 78 benchmark instances. These results serve to showcase the efficiency of our novel solution approaches. The achieved computational results demonstrate that our innovative hybrid genetic algorithms are strongly competitive compared with the current state-of-the-art algorithms.

Keywords: Hybrid genetic algorithms · minimum routing tree problem · clustered minimum routing tree problem

1 Introduction

The problem of determining a spanning tree with minimum cost in a weighted and connected graph, denoted by MST, is a significant and very well investigated problem in computer science. As pointed out by Pop [21], several extensions of the MST problem have been considered in the literature: the Steiner tree problem, the k-minimum spanning tree problem (k-MST), the minimum routing tree (MRT) problem, etc. The MRT problem in a weighted and connected graph looks for a spanning tree with the property that its routing cost, i.e., the total cost of the paths among all pairwise vertices, is minimal. MRT is an NP-hard problem and has many interesting real-world applications. For a state-of-the-art of the MRT problem, we refer to Masone et al. [13].

CluMRTP extends the classical minimum routing tree problem. The CluMRTP is defined on a graph where all nodes are divided into predefined clusters,

H. Quintián et al. (Eds.): HAIS 2024, LNAI 14857, pp. 312–323, 2025.
https://doi.org/10.1007/978-3-031-74183-8_26

seeking a spanning tree T fulfilling the following criteria: ensuring connectivity within each cluster's induced sub-graphs and minimizing the total cost of the paths between all the vertices in T. The CluMRTP's hierarchical structure is crucial for many network design problems encountered in many areas such as communications, design of agricultural irrigation systems, transportation, etc.

Lin and Wu [11] examined for the first time the CluMRTP and a related problem called the minimum inter-cluster routing cost clustered tree problem (Inter-CluMRCT). The same authors described a 2-approximation algorithm for the CluMRTP for complete weighted graphs with edge weights fulfilling the triangle inequality. Trung et al. [27] proposed a multifactorial evolutionary algorithm (MFEA) by investigating genetic operators that constitute a feasible solution to the CluMRTP in two levels: the first level builds spanning trees for graphs within the clusters, while the second level constructs a spanning tree linking the clusters. Thang et al. [26] developed an MFEA that used a representation of the population based on a probabilistic distribution model adopted to online learning and genetic operators applied as well at two levels. Thang and Bin [25] described a hybrid multi-tasking algorithm called the multifactorial firefly algorithm, that includes the high exploitation ability of the firefly algorithm into an MFEA to strengthen the self-evolution of every task when facing low-similarity tasks, while enhancing the inter-task knowledge transfers by providing higher-quality feasible solutions of the CluMRTP. Recently, Long et al. [12] described a multi-population multitasking evolutionary method with adaptive knowledge transfer whose main feature is implementing a mechanism for efficient knowledge transfer among sub-problems when solving them at the same time.

The CluMRTP belongs to the category of generalized network design problems (GNDPs), which naturally expands the standard network design problems. In these optimization problems, the original graph's vertices are divided into a specified number of clusters, and feasibility restrictions are defined in terms of these clusters rather than individual nodes. A closely related problem to the CluMRTP is the clustered shortest-path tree problem (CluSPTP), which aims to find a shortest-path spanning tree from a given source node to all other nodes in the graph, ensuring that every cluster is a connected sub-graph. For more information concerning the CluSPTP, we refer to Petrovan et al. [16,17] and Cosma et al. [3,4]. Another problem related to the CluMRTP, the generalized minimum spanning tree problem (GMSTP) was described first by Myung et al. [15]. The scope of the GMSTP is to seek a minimum cost tree, ensuring that it covers a specific set of vertices containing precisely a single vertex from each cluster. For further details on the GMSTP and its variants, we refer to Pop et al. [19,21]. Based especially on their real-world applications the GNDPs have been intensively studied, see for example the generalized traveling salesman problem (GTSP) and its variants [22], the generalized vehicle routing problem (GVRP) and its variants [2,10,18,20], the selective graph coloring problem [7,9], etc. For additional information on the class of GNDPs, we refer to Feremans et al. [8] and Pop [23].

This paper presents innovative hybrid genetic algorithms designed to solve the CluMRT problem. Our approach involves breaking down the primary problem into two distinct subproblems: a global-level subproblem and a local-level subproblem. The first one focuses on generating global trees that span the clusters using a Prüfer encoding genetic algorithm (GA). The second subproblem focuses on determining the minimum cost routing tree for each tree spanning the clusters generated by the GA. The local-level subproblem is efficiently solved using two heuristic approaches.

Our study addresses the CluMRTP by designing two-level hybrid genetic algorithms. In this way, we make use of the hierarchical structure of the problem, providing computational efficiency and high-quality feasible solutions. The contributions of this paper include: i) the design of efficient Prufer encoding-based hybrid genetic algorithms tailored to the CluMRTP, ii) the development of two heuristic algorithms to determine minimum cost routing trees within clusters, and iii) preliminary computational experiments showcasing the performance of our HGAs compared to the existing state-of-the-art methods.

The remaining of our paper has the following structure: in Sect. 2, we define the investigated problem, and Sect. 3 outlines our innovative solution approaches. This approach integrates a framework that includes a macro-level Prüfer based encoding GA, employed to produce trees connecting the clusters, with two micro-level heuristic algorithms that determine a corresponding feasible solution to the CluMRT problem. In Sect. 4, we perform a comparative study to assess the effectiveness of our designed solution approaches against existing approaches from the literature. Finally, in Section V, we draw conclusions and outline potential future research directions.

2 Definition of the Clustered Minimum Routing Tree Problem

We consider an undirected complete graph $G = (V, E)$ with the set of nodes $V = \{v_1, v_2, ..., v_n\}$ and the set of edges $E = \{\{v_i, v_j\}|\ v_i, v_j \in V,\ i \neq j \in \{1, 2, ..., n\}\}$. Additionally, we define a cost function $c : E \rightarrow R_+$, which assigns a positive value $c_e = c(u, v)$ to each edge $e = (u, v) \in E$, value referred to as the edge cost.

The complete vertex set V is partitioned into k nonempty subsets of nodes $V_1, ..., V_k$ and referred to as *clusters*. Consequently, the fulfillment of the following conditions is required:

1. $V = V_1 \cup V_2 \cup ... \cup V_k$
2. $V_r \cap V_s = \emptyset$ for all $r, s \in \{1, ..., k\}$ and $r \neq s$.

Given the hierarchical structure of the investigated problem, we distinguish two kinds of spanning trees: trees connecting the clusters called *global spanning trees* and trees of G with the property that removing $k - 1$ inter-cluster edges there are formed exactly k subtrees, each spanning the vertices of the clusters V_i, with $i \in \{1, ..., k\}$. This kind of tree is called a clustered spanning tree.

Given a subset of nodes S, then we will denote by $G[S]$ the sub-graph induced by S, consisting of the vertex set S and edges whose endpoints belong to S. Given a spanning tree T of G and two vertices $v_i, v_j \in V$, there is a unique path between v_i and v_j, and we will denote its cost by $d_T(v_i, v_j)$.

The *clustered minimum routing tree (CluMRT) problem* seeks for a tree T that meets the properties:

1. T includes all the vertices of G;
2. All the induced subgraphs $T[V_i]$, for all $i \in \{1, ..., k\}$ have to be connected;

and the total cost TC of all the paths between any two nodes of G is minimized, i.e.

$$TC = \sum_{v_i, v_j \in V} d_T(v_i, v_j) \rightarrow \min.$$

In Fig. 1, we present a feasible solution of the CluMRTP in the case of the instance $6berlin52 - 2 \times 3$ consisting of 52 vertices partitioned into 6 clusters.

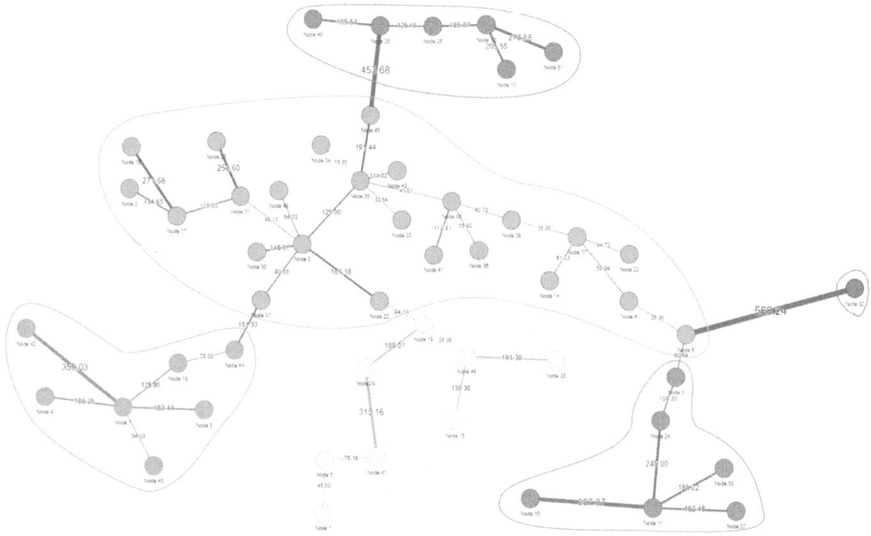

Fig. 1. An illustration of a solution of the CluMRTP

3 The Proposed Hybrid Genetic Algorithms

A widely known technique for addressing complex optimization problems involves dividing them into smaller, more manageable sub-problems and solving each separately. This approach has successfully tackled difficult problems, such as Pop et al. [19,20].

The scope of this section is to present our new HGAs for CluMRTP, which are obtained by decomposing the original problem into two smaller sub-problems:

1. A global-level subproblem aimed at generating global trees spanning the clusters using a Prüfer based encoding GA;
2. A local-level subproblem focused on identifying the connections between vertices within the same cluster, corresponding to a predefined global spanning tree. The local-level subproblem is solved effectively using two different heuristic approaches for every tree spanning the clusters. The links among vertices from different clusters are defined keeping into account the structure of the investigated problem.

Our innovative two-level hybrid GAs are tailored to the hierarchical structure of the CluMRTP, where the graph's vertices are divided into a predefined number of clusters. Our approaches offer computational benefits by utilizing effective algorithms for solving the two subproblems and integrating their results to produce feasible solutions of the CluMRTP.

3.1 The Global-Level Subproblem

To describe the global-level subproblem corresponding to the CluMRTP, we employed a methodology which is similar to the one introduced by Pop et al. [23] for GMSTP. We consider the graph G_{global}, which is derived from graph G by replacing all vertices within each cluster V_j with a single supernode representing that cluster, $\forall\ j \in \{1, ..., k\}$. We refer to this graph as the *global graph.* We define the global graph $G_{global} = (V_{global}, E_{global})$ as outlined: each cluster of the underlying graph G is a vertex of V_{global}, $V_{global} = \{V_1, ..., V_k\}$ with $|V_{global}| = k$, and the edges of the G_{global} are defined among every pair of the global graph nodes: $E_{global} = \{(V_i, V_j) \mid 1 \leq i < j \leq k\}$.

For the CluMRTP, we employ a GA applied to the corresponding global graph G_{global} to generate a set of trees that span the clusters. This approach significantly reduces the size of the solution space of the original CluMRTP. Such a tree that spans the clusters of the graph is called a *global spanning tree.*

Multiple clustered spanning trees are associated with a global tree spanning the clusters. In Sect. 3.3, we will present two heuristic approaches that determine such trees with the aim of minimizing the corresponding routing cost.

3.2 The Genetic Algorithm

For the CluMRTP, we adopted an effective representation at the level of the global graph G_{global} in which the chromosome corresponding to each global spanning tree is encoded as a unique Prüfer sequence of length $k-2$, where k is the number of vertices in G_{global}. This encoding method is well-suited for representing all possible global trees, as even after undergoing genetic operations, we can ensure that the resulting chromosomes remain global spanning trees.

The Prüfer sequence is generated by iteratively removing vertices from the tree until only two vertices remain. At each step i, the leaf with the smallest label is eliminated, and the i-th element of the Prüfer is determined by the label of this leaf's neighbor. Considering a labeled tree with vertices labeled as $1, 2, ..., k$, associated to the clusters $V_1, V_2, ..., V_k$, applying the described Prüfer encoding algorithm will result a sequence $(a_1, a_2, ..., a_{k-2})$ with $a_i \in \{1, ..., k\}$.

The algorithm that reconstructs the unique labeled tree with k vertices from a given Prüfer string of length $k-2$, is called the Prüfer decoding algorithm, see for further details [17].

The fitness function associated with every chromosome in our GA population is determined by the routing cost of the clustered spanning tree corresponding to the global spanning tree defined by the chromosome. This cost will be found based on two different heuristic approaches described in Subsect. 3.3. Our aim is to find a clustered spanning tree whose routing cost is minimized.

Our initial population was generated using completely random chromosomes to maintain population diversity.

We used the following genetic operators in our proposed GA:

- an elite tournament selection method with 3 rounds and an elitist value of 0.05;
- a standard uniform crossover;
- a swap mutation operator.

Based on extensive computational experiments, we have opted for the next parameters of the GA: the size of the population is proportional to the number of clusters. Specifically, we calculate the population size by multiplying the number of clusters by a factor equal to 100 for a number of clusters up to 15 and 200 for a larger number of clusters. This approach ensures that the population size scales appropriately with the complexity of the problem, allowing the algorithm to explore a sufficient number of potential solutions. The evolutionary process of the populations continues as long as there is a favorable improvement in the fitness value of the best chromosome. This means that as long as the best solution for the population is improving, the algorithm continues to evolve. However, if there is no improvement in the fitness value over a span of 10 epochs, the evolutionary process is halted. This stopping criterion prevents unnecessary computations when no further improvements are being made, ensuring computational efficiency. Throughout the evolutionary process, the probability of mutation and elitism is maintained at a constant rate of 0.05.

This mutation rate helps introduce variability into the population without significantly disrupting high-quality solutions, thereby balancing exploration and exploitation. Also, elitism has been chosen based on previous studies showing this percentage as a reasonable balance between convergence and evolution.

3.3 The Local-Level Subproblem

In this subsection, we present our effective heuristic approaches for determining a corresponding clustered tree, given a tree that spans the clusters.

To find the connections between vertices within the same cluster we use the following methods:

- Shortest-Path Tree Cluster generation, for each cluster V_j of G, with $j \in \{1, ..., k\}$, we determine the shortest-path tree T_j within the cluster V_j using the Dijkstra's algorithm and then the routing cost of T_j: $\sum_{u,v \in V_j} d_{T_j}(u, v)$.
- Using the described Prüfer based GA representation, we encode the clusters using Prüfer sequences used in the genetic algorithm to optimize the global tree spanning all clusters. The Prüfer representation allows for an efficient and unique tree encoding, which is critical for the GA's operations, such as selection, crossover, and mutation. The GA iteratively improves the population of solutions to find the Minimum Routing Tree (MRT) with the best routing cost for the given clusters. The specific parameters and settings for the GA, such as population size, mutation rate, and selection method, are detailed in the previous subsection.

To identify the best connections between clusters, we use the following two approaches:

- For each pair of clusters, we calculate the shortest edge connecting any vertex in one cluster to any vertex in the other cluster. This method directly minimizes inter-cluster connection costs by selecting the shortest possible edge between the clusters.
- We compute the centroid for each cluster, which is the average position of all vertices within the cluster. The centroids are then used to establish connections between clusters, effectively treating the centroids as representative points for the clusters. The edges are then formed based on these centroid positions to connect the clusters.

By combining these approaches for intra-cluster and inter-cluster connections, we develop four hybrid genetic algorithms: HGA1 combines the Shortest Path within the clusters with Shortest Edge determination, HGA2 combines the Shortest Path within the clusters with the Centroid method, HGA3 finds the MRT within the clusters coupled with Shortest Edge determination, and HGA4 that finds the MRT within the clusters coupled with the Centroid method.

4 Preliminary Computational Results

This section presents the preliminary experimental results achieved by our new hybrid Prüfer based encoding GAs.

To evaluate the effectiveness of our designed hybrid Prüfer based encoding GAs, we adapted the instances from the dataset MOM-lib [14] introduced in the case of the Clustered TSP. The MOM-lib [14] dataset was used as a benchmark set of instances in previous studies for the GTSP [22], the clustered GTSP [1], the CluSPTP [3,4] and the CluMRTP [12,25,26].

Our proposed hybrid-based GAs were coded in Python and have been evaluated on a PC with Intel 9, 12-Core 3.4 GHz, 32 GB RAM, and Windows 11 Education operating system. In our designed HGAs, we ran 30 independent trials for every instance.

To assess the performance of our hybrid Prüfer based encoding GAs, we compared them against the state-of-the-art algorithm for CluMRTP, namely the multi-population multitasking evolutionary scheme with adaptive knowledge transfer [12].

In Tables 1 and 2, we provide the best solutions achieved by our designed HGAs for 78 instances of different types of the CluMRTP, comparing them with the best existing results reported by Long et al. [12].

Our tables have the following structure: the first column includes information regarding the instances, the following column includes the best found solutions (BF) achieved by Long et al. [12], the following four columns include the best found solutions achieved by our developed hybrid GAs, and the gap has been calculated as the percentage improvement between the best existing solution provided by Long et al. [12] and the minimum value obtained from our best solution across the four algorithms. The symbol "-" means that Long et al. [12] did not provide solutions for those instances. The improved solutions obtained by our developed hybrid GAs are marked in bold.

The results summarised in our tables show significant improvements in the routing costs for various instances. In our study, we compared the performance of our designed Heuristic Genetic Algorithms (HGAs) with the state-of-the-art (SOTA) algorithm provided by Long et al. [12]. The results demonstrate that our algorithms consistently outperformed SOTA across multiple instances. Specifically, HGA1 significantly improved, surpassing SOTA in 74.36% of the instances. HGA2 also showed considerable enhancement in 39.74% of cases. HGA3 performed strongly as well, with 61.54% of instances improved. Although HGA4 had a relatively lower improvement rate of 11.54%, it still outperformed SOTA. Our proposed HGAs demonstrated superior performance in almost all instances except for three that did not surpass SOTA. This highlights the robustness and effectiveness of our proposed approaches across a diverse set of instances.

Table 1. Comparison results for solving the CluMRT problem

Instance name	Long et al. [12]	HGA1	HGA2	HGA3	HGA4	Gap%
4berlin52-2x2	1051389.87	**1039731.67**	1210305.84	1089259.75	1418063.59	1.11
4eil51-2x2	62584.06	**59906.64**	70460.21	67797.01	102700.18	4.28
4eil76-2x2	155639.12	**134126.12**	178227.96	**149087.59**	207271.44	13.82
4pr76-2x2	35624262.12	**31257138.87**	40429546.17	35759652.91	42782558.89	12.26
5berlin52	1065365.53	**1029451.27**	1188418.89	1126188.71	1766211.1	3.37
5eil76	154584.39	**143990.01**	165923.83	157172.45	207772.05	6.85
5i120-46	5872060.92	**5084097.23**	**5408568.89**	**5617945.3**	6306739.79	13.42
5i60-21	1552213.62	**1464234.45**	1735127.47	1603706.51	2033904.23	5.67
5i65-21	1840023.43	**1693533.19**	1965295.54	**1811712.36**	2239075.78	7.96
5i70-21	2094221.8	**1943306.19**	2314848.74	2136501.83	2616976.25	7.21
5i75-22	2351060.04	**2337499.52**	**2263911.77**	**2228531.46**	2498817.61	5.21
5i90-33	3038360.59	**2882220.01**	**2844031.8**	**2991520.48**	3148876.67	6.4
5pr76	37203819.04	**36296349.54**	**35209979.1**	38280010.05	42479055.55	5.36
5st70	217040.51	**197159.79**	230867.9	**216628.55**	242672.81	9.16
6berlin52-2x3	1131075.44	**1125075.73**	1215733.75	**1090108.14**	1459744.19	3.62
6pr76-2x3	34171917.3	**31740320.35**	36299135.07	34437271.32	39218181.48	7.12
6st70-2x3	209653.7	**202496.29**	213084.41	222690.84	238841.63	3.41
7i45-18	816149.64	**796168.16**	891879.92	882500.49	1122358.16	2.45
8berlin52-2x4	1132854.91	**1119996.29**	1212888.48	**1123513.5**	1238374.07	1.14
9eil101-3x3	300158.6	**277586.63**	**284359.38**	**284714.22**	404496.13	7.52
9eil51-3x3	65638.3	**64330.45**	68296.18	67468.71	72221.25	1.99
9eil76-3x3	154738	**153059.55**	155383.06	**150850.83**	172630.46	2.51
9pr76-3x3	34598209.16	**31670456**	35250900.73	**34197247.51**	39806131.37	8.46
10a280	9689592.22	**7811553.22**	**8296617.05**	**8296617.05**	**9373826.22**	19.38
10berlin52	1056227.28	1093007.81	1079591.54	**1026047.7**	1478868.67	2.86
10berlin52-2x5	1169916.36	1235481.47	**1157898.26**	1178413.96	1211474.08	1.03
10eil51	**64137.10**	65320.79	69200.62	66565.37	71744.13	-1.85
10eil76	153310.57	**148747.97**	161990.38	**147571.92**	170017.74	3.74
10gil262	7246054.16	**5305668.87**	**5982799.83**	**6083687.09**	**7084774.46**	26.78
10i120-46	7390900.1	**6780221.43**	**6934608.15**	**7078794.82**	7895083.85	8.26
10i300-109	25940385.45	**23254486.32**	**23172593.89**	26251469.4	31024787.43	10.67
10i30-17	330157.48	**329709.48**	364921.58	343340.09	381428.24	0.14
10i45-18	759532.77	762356.06	**747194.79**	788054.45	1001303.07	1.62
10i60-21	1576303.94	**1555612.9**	1740078.26	1684092.27	1766740.36	1.31
10i65-21	**1892625.14**	1913607.39	2042344.27	1971443.56	2415919.56	−1.11
10i70-21	2277009.06	**2206272.22**	2369158.7	2291511.13	2544062.84	3.11
10i75-22	2800776.04	**2601311.95**	2837571.34	**2777122.63**	3571683.84	7.12
10i90-33	3197549.02	**3081400.41**	**3136075.28**	**3098041.41**	4484013.1	3.63
10kroB100	12877213.43	**12190223.83**	14046459.76	13542937	14922291	5.33
10lin318	150762957.7	**145082403.5**	**146313633.4**	156933537.3	192357365.4	3.77
10pr76	34377643.13	34503369.43	35479413.23	**32525672.63**	38087962.68	5.39
10rat99	676065.63	**611791.96**	699606.39	690264.37	735063.59	9.51
10st70	**197382.59**	200717.05	217129.79	205865.78	224020.01	−1.69

Table 2. Comparison results for solving the CluMRT problem

Instance name	Long et al. [12]	HGA1	HGA2	HGA3	HGA4	Gap%
12eil51-3x4	66043.73	**64830.3**	66518.46	66189.62	69107.19	1.84
12eil76-3x4	159577.76	**151288.79**	160625.27	**154598.62**	168176.17	5.19
12pr76-3x4	34866708.32	**34181950.9**	36021436.22	**33352570.82**	36695480.07	4.34
12st70-3x4	199786.87	**187388.83**	207765.6	**197217.34**	212598.27	6.21
15berlin52	1106747.67	**1048787.11**	**1070684.07**	**1022406.98**	1268467.67	7.62
15eil76	155439.92	163664.63	156261.24	**151784.95**	171601.53	2.35
15pr76	32920336.14	**31892409.4**	33083053.23	**32759374.95**	36057472.47	3.12
15pr76-3x5	35418463.94	40037235.54	35933183.12	**33307403.5**	36486498.72	5.96
16eil51-4x4	**63003.12**	63336.56	69673.1	66467.77	75074.26	-0.53
16eil76-4x4	154003.97	**142683.46**	**151023.67**	**152504.75**	163850.04	7.35
16lin105-4x4	10493779.77	**9263013.72**	**10396121.55**	**9633264.07**	12058919.24	11.73
16st70-4x4	199924.92	**193851.47**	213889.01	203375.68	224054.53	3.04
18pr76-3x6	33863448.15	34888922.06	34777062.64	**33558091.09**	35952971.28	0.9
20eil51-4x5	64188.84	**61814.08**	65670.68	**62689.78**	66368.94	3.7
20eil76-4x5	157327.27	**144891.2**	162258.57	159471.04	170460.47	7.9
20i300-111	46115904.39	**39780315.45**	**40666943.47**	**40338531.46**	**43515232.41**	13.74
25a280	8980106.12	9240876.57	**8017802.4**	**7969981.39**	**8613956.31**	11.25
25eil101	285229.63	333589	**276569.14**	**273044.43**	305660.16	4.27
25eil101-5x5	281875.61	**277490.99**	291197.17	**277930.23**	292472.08	1.56
25eil51-5x5	64171.19	**63788.98**	**64036.28**	**63235.31**	69928.33	1.46
25eil76-5x5	155518.75	**150255.64**	**152538.36**	**143838.39**	163770.26	7.51
25gil262	6732771.46	7393453.17	**5853962.17**	**5781629.31**	**6353343.31**	14.13
25lin105	9630356.28	**9135914.75**	**9438506.16**	**9143528.03**	9800213.07	5.13
25lin318	179428238.6	**154515239.11**	**156628289.39**	**151906354.27**	**161499846.51**	15.34
25rat99	652800.46	**649778.84**	656418.35	**637802.74**	715070.7	2.3
25rat99-5x5	666495.33	**603066.87**	**649095.15**	**628293.25**	698217.94	9.52
30kroB100-5x6	13504077.52	17292508.35	**13258967.12**	13632335.85	**13104149.73**	2.96
35kroB100-5x5	13143045.01	13696002.68	13519719.02	**12756456.27**	14101081.6	2.94
36eil101-6x6	294313.7	**274800.79**	**278851.27**	**281232.09**	345268.05	6.63
42rat99-6x7	673126.76	694335.04	**643188.94**	**633511.44**	**628677.88**	6.6
50eil101	285339.55	**277841.26**	**271345.87**	**277120.12**	**285055.33**	4.9
50kroA100	13360184.17	14318912.87	**12981140.36**	**12235294.96**	13758406.04	8.42
50lin105	9504846.36	**9181718.45**	**9405749.58**	**9307245.64**	9511668.23	3.4
50rat99	663188.65	729756.97	688594.14	**658443.94**	721692.41	0.72
75lin105	-	**9185130.80**	**9122316.17**	**9098234.64**	**9450360.14**	–

5 Conclusions and Further Research Directions

The clustered minimum routing tree problem (CluMRTP) is an interesting variant of the minimum routing tree problem and has important real-world applications. We designed hybrid two-level Prüfer based genetic algorithms (GAs) by decomposing the original problem into two subproblems: a global-level subproblem and a local-level subproblem. The global-level subproblem determines global trees spanning the clusters using a Prüfer based encoding GA, while the local-level subproblem finds sub-optimal or optimal solutions of the CluMRTP corresponding to a predefined global tree which spans the clusters making use of two heuristic approaches.

Our hybrid genetic algorithm demonstrates high efficiency and competitiveness in solving the CluMRT problem. Future research will explore alternative encoding methods and assess the scalability of our approach on larger problem instances.

Acknowledgements. This work was supported by the project "Collaborative Framework for Smart Agriculture"–COSA that received funding from Romania's National Recovery and Resilience Plan PNRR-III-C9-2022-I8, under grant agreement 760070.

References

1. Cosma, O., Pop, P.C., Cosma, L.: A hybrid based genetic algorithm for solving the clustered generalized traveling salesman problem. In: García Bringas, P., et al. Hybrid Artificial Intelligent Systems, HAIS 2023, LNCS, vol. 14001, pp. 352–362. Springer, Cham (2023). https://doi.org/10.1007/978-3-031-40725-3_30
2. Cosma, O., Pop, P.C., Pop Sitar, C.: A two-level based genetic algorithm for solving the soft-clustered vehicle routing problem. Carpathian J. Math. **38**(1), 117–1280 (2022)
3. Cosma, O., Pop, P.C., Zelina, I.: An effective genetic algorithm for solving the clustered shortest-path tree problem. IEEE Access **9**, 15570–15591 (2021)
4. Cosma, O., Pop, P.C., Zelina, I.: A novel genetic algorithm for solving the clustered shortest-path tree problem. Carpathian J. Math. **36**(3), 401–414 (2020)
5. D'Emidio, M., Forlizzi, L., Frigioni, D., Leucci, S., Proietti, G.: On the clustered shortest-path tree problem. In Proceedings of Italian Conference on Theoretical Computer Science, pp. 263-268 (2016)
6. D'Emidio, M., Forlizzi, L., Frigioni, D., Leucci, S., Proietti, G.: Hardness, approximability and fixed-parameter tractability of the clustered shortest-path tree problem. J. Comb. Optim. **38**, 165–184 (2019)
7. Demange, M., Monnot, J., Pop, P.C., Ries, B.: On the complexity of the selective graph coloring problem in some special classes of graphs. Theoret. Comput. Sci. **540–541**, 82–102 (2014)
8. Feremans, C., Labbe, M., Laporte, G.: Generalized network design problems. Eur. J. Oper. Res. **148**(1), 1–13 (2003)
9. Fidanova, S., Pop, P.C.: An improved hybrid ant-local search for the partition graph coloring problem. J. Comput. Appl. Math. **293**, 55–61 (2016)
10. Ghiani, G., Improta, G.: An efficient transformation of the generalized vehicle routing problem. Eur. J. Oper. Res. **122**, 11–17 (2000)
11. Lin, C.-W., Wu, B.Y.: On the minimum routing cost clustered tree problem. J. Comb. Optim. **33**(3), 1106–1121 (2017)
12. Long, N.B., Anh, D.T., Ban, H.-B., Binh, H.T.T.: A multipopulation multitasking evolutionary scheme with adaptive knowledge transfer to solve the clustered minimum routing cost tree problem. Inf. Sci. **657**, 119961 (2024)

13. Masone, A., Nenni, M.E., Sforza, A., Sterle, C.: The minimum routing cost tree problem. State of the art and a core-node based heuristic algorithm. Soft Comput. **23**, 2947–2957 (2019)
14. Mestria, M., Ochi, L.S., de Lima Martins, S.: GRASP with path relinking for the symmetric Euclidean clustered traveling salesman problem. Comput. Oper. Res. **40**(12), 3218–3229 (2013)
15. Myung, Y.S., Lee, C.H., Tcha, D.W.: On the generalized minimum spanning tree problem. Networks **26**, 231–241 (1995)
16. Petrovan, A., Pop, P.C., Sabo, C., Zelina, I.: A two-level hybrid based genetic algorithm to solve the clustered shortest-path tree problem using the Prüfer code. In: García Bringas, P., et al. Hybrid Artificial Intelligent Systems, HAIS 2022, LNCS, vol. 13469, pp 323–334. Springer, Cham (2022). https://doi.org/10.1007/978-3-031-15471-3_28
17. Petrovan, A., Pop, P.C., Sabo, C., Zelina, I.: Novel two-level hybrid genetic algorithms based on different Cayley-type encodings for solving the clustered shortest-path tree problem. Expert Syst. Appl. **215**, 119372 (2023)
18. Pintea, C., Chira, C., Dumitrescu, D., Pop, P.C.: Sensitive ants in solving the generalized vehicle routing problem. Int. J. Comput. Commun. Control **6**(4), 734–741 (2011)
19. Pop, P.C., Matei, O., Sabo, C., Petrovan, A.: A two-level solution approach for solving the generalized minimum spanning tree problem. Eur. J. Oper. Res. **265**(2), 478–487 (2018)
20. Pop, P.C., Fuksz, L., Horvat Marc, A., Sabo, C.: A novel two-level optimization approach for clustered vehicle routing problem. Comput. Ind. Eng. **115**, 304–318 (2018)
21. Pop, P.C.: The generalized minimum spanning tree problem: an overview of formulations, solution procedures and latest advances. Eur. J. Oper. Res. **283**(1), 1–15 (2020)
22. Pop, P.C., Cosma, O., Sabo, C., Pop Sitar, C.: A comprehensive survey on the generalized traveling salesman problem. Eur. J. Oper. Res. **314**(3), 819–835 (2024)
23. Pop, P.C.: Generalized Network Design Problems. Modeling and Optimization. De Gruyter Series in Discrete Mathematics and Applications, Germany (2012)
24. Thanh, P.D.: CluSPT instances, Mendeley Data v2. https://doi.org/10.17632/b4gcgybvt6.2
25. Thang, T.B., Binh, H.T.T.: A hybrid multifactorial evolutionary algorithm and firefly algorithm for the clustered minimum routing cost tree problem. Knowl.-Based Syst. **241**, 108225 (2022)
26. Thang, T.B., Long, N.B., Hoang, N.V., Binh, H.T.T.: Adaptive knowledge transfer in multifactorial evolutionary algorithm for the clustered minimum routing cost problem. Appl. Soft Comput. **105**, 107253 (2021)
27. Trung, T.B., Thanh, L.T., Hieu, L.T., Thanh, P.D., Binh, H.T.T.: Multifactorial evolutionary algorithm for clustered minimum routing cost problem. In: Proceedings of the Tenth International Symposium on Information and Communication Technology, pp. 170–177 (2019)

Diversity Population Metrics in Diploid and Haploid Genetic Algorithm Variants

Adrian Petrovan[1(✉)], Oliviu Matei[1], Petrica C. Pop[2], and Cosmin Sabo[2]

[1] Department of Electrical Engineering, Electronics and Computer Science, Technical University of Cluj-Napoca, Cluj-Napoca, Romania
{adrian.petrovan,oliviu.matei}@ieec.utcluj.ro

[2] Department of Mathematics and Computer Science, Technical University of Cluj-Napoca, Cluj-Napoca, Romania
{petrica.pop,cosmin.sabo}@mi.utcluj.ro

Abstract. Genetic Algorithms (GAs) are powerful optimization techniques inspired by the principles of natural selection and genetics. One critical aspect of their success lies in the diversity of solutions within their populations. Diversity ensures exploration of a broader solution space, preventing premature convergence to sub-optimal solutions. Consequently, the evaluation and maintenance of diversity metrics in GA populations have garnered significant attention in the field of evolutionary computation. This article presents the efficiency of diploid genetic algorithms against the haploid variant through measures of population diversity.

Keywords: diploid genetic algorithm · diversity metrics · entropy

1 Introduction

1.1 Overview of Genetic Algorithms

On the scene of optimization tools the evolutionary algorithms (EAs) stand out as powerful and versatile problem solvers. The huge amount of research undertaken in this area confirms the increased importance of these algorithms on obtaining efficient solutions to numerous problems in the real world. Inspired by natural selection [8], EAs leverage populations of candidate solutions through a selection, recombination and mutation process. This method favor solutions with better qualities, progressively guiding the search towards optimal solutions [28]. A series of approaches can be found under this very large concept, such as *genetic algorithms*, *evolution strategies* or *evolutionary programming*. When we are discussing in general about diversity we refers to the presence of a variety of different elements within a group, organization, community, or society. These elements can include demographic diversity, cognitive diversity or experiential diversity. The population diversity is a critical factor in the effectiveness of GAs. Maintaining a diverse population is essential to prevent premature convergence [17,22].

H. Quintián et al. (Eds.): HAIS 2024, LNAI 14857, pp. 324–338, 2025.
https://doi.org/10.1007/978-3-031-74183-8_27

Numerous studies have emphasized the importance of population diversity in GAs, highlighting that high diversity is essential to avoid local optima and to ensure the algorithm's adaptability to changing environments [37,44]. In [7] is presented a stochastic algorithm used for generating feasible initial population for the vehicle routing problem with time windows problem (VRPTW). Yu et al. [45] presents a solution to improve the diversity of the GAs performance by introducing improvements on crossover and mutation techniques.

The objectives of this study was to measure the diversity of populations in the case of HGA and DGA. In this sense, two experiments were carried out, as follows: in the first experiment we calculated for the diploid genetic algorithm its fitness values for each individual chromosome, as well as the fitness of the phenotype of the diploid individual, and in the second experiment we calculated the entropy haploid and diploid individual in each generation of GA.

1.2 Solutions on Maintaining Population Diversity in GAs

Several methods have been considered in the literature in order to preserve population diversity in GAs such as:

- Methods based on increasing the population randomness by using high mutation rate or immigration (injection) of new random individuals [5,26];
- Niching approaches, as suggested by De Jong [9], were designed to mitigate the impact of genetic drift caused by the selection operator in the traditional genetic algorithm (GA). Fitness sharing approaches, initially suggested by Holland [19] and subsequently enhanced by many researchers, are widely recognized and extensively employed niching techniques. Additional details regarding the primary characteristics and advancements of this approach are presented by Schlierkamp et al. [38].
- The restricted mating strategy imposes certain constraints, such as limitations or incentives, to choose both an individual and its mate. The initial tactics were developed using similarity relations between the parents [10]. While these strategies have demonstrated their ability to enhance GA performance, they come with a high computational cost. Galan et al. [14] proposed a method with two key characteristics: it allows for the definition of mating preferences based on either similarity between individuals or the fitness of individuals, and it can be easily implemented in a self-adaptive manner, where each individual in the population has its own mating preference.
- Collingwood et al. [6] proposed maintaining population diversity by utilizing multiploid individuals with polyploid chromosomes. This idea was inspired by the observation that many organisms in nature have polyploid genotypes, which consist of multiple sets of chromosomes with different mechanisms for determining dominant genes. One of the earliest investigations was conducted by Goldberg and Smith [15], who explored the utilization of diploid representations and dominance operators in GAs to enhance performance in dynamic contexts.

1.3 Distinction Between Diploid and Haploid Variants

In nature, the cells contain various numbers of chromosomes, varying from 1 to 64. This feature is known as *ploidy* [36,40]. *Haploid cells* contain only one complete set of chromosomes [16]. The most common type of haploid cells are gametes, or sex cells, but they are not the only ones. When the haploid sexual cells, produced by meiosis [21], come together and are fertilized, the offspring has a complete set of chromosomes and becomes a diploid cell. This means that in an organism there can coexist both haploid and diploid cells. *Diploid cells* have two sets of chromosomes. In most diploid organisms every cell, except for gametes, will be diploid and contain both sets of chromosomes.

The idea of using a diploid representation in genetic algorithms was first proposed by Goldberg and Smith in the late 1980 s. Their initial work on DGAs focused on the development of a general-purpose diploid representation that could be used to solve a wide range of optimization problems. They proposed a diploid structure with tri-allelic representation of 1, 0 and i that consisted by two chromosomes, each of which encoded a different set of candidate solutions. In 1995, Ng and Wong [29] published a paper that criticized the Goldberg and Smith representation for dominance. They suggested an improved representation by introducing a tetra-allelic dominance scheme that included the potential alleles 1, 0, i, and o. In 1990, Hillis [18] suggested an interesting application of diploidy for the creation of sorting sequences.

DGA's have been used also under several different names:

- *bi-chromosome* or *bi-chromosomal* genetic algorithm (BCGA). Cheng et al. [4] are the first ones who used the term *bi-chromosome genetic algorithm*. Rinehart et al. [27] used the bi-chromosome representation for complex graph scheduling of tasks, Wu et al. [43] used for DGA the same terminology in their article for the semiconductor manufacturing.
- *pseudo-meiosis* genetic algorithm. In 1994 Yukiko and Nobue [46] proposed a diploid genetic algorithm called "pseudo-me-iosis" which aimed to maintain population diversity. Their approach was specifically applied to the non-stationary travelling salesman problem (NSTSP) and they demonstrated that their preliminary results are under further investigation as a pseudo-meiosis genetic algorithm framework for other problems domain. Attea and Al-Rahman [1] adopt and applied the pseudo-meiosis mechanism proposed by Yukiko and Nobue [46] in solving the multiple container packing problem, and in 2006, Attea in [2] presented the effect of pseudo-meiosis GA on bit-coding stationary genetic search. In both works, the authors concluded that diploid representation may increase the ability of GA toward finding better solutions.
- *diploid*. Over time, this attribute of genetic algorithms seems to become a standard name, although *pseudo-meiosis* or *bi-chromosome* rises once in a while. This term, primarily indicates a certain type of genetic structure or representation within the genetic algorithm. The term "*diploidy*", derived from *diploid*, which itself comes from the Greek words "di" (meaning two)

and "ploidēs" (meaning fold). The concept of *diploidy* is related to genetics and refers to the state of having two sets of chromosomes in the cell nucleus. Organisms that exhibit *diploidy*, including most animals and plants, have pairs of homologous chromosomes-one inherited from each parent. Pop et al. effectively applied DGAs to solve the generalized traveling salesman problem [34], the generalized minimum spanning tree problem [35], and the family traveling salesman problem [33]. Dulebenets [12] introduces a Diploid Evolutionary Algorithm (DEA) that aids cross-docking operators in creating cost-effective truck schedules. Petrovan et al. [32] discussed the benefits of DGAs compared to classical GAs that use real-coded chromosome representation. They also conducted a study on the crossover operators in DGAs [31]. In a recent study, Dulebenets [13] introduced an adaptive polyploid memetic algorithm for efficiently scheduling trucks at a cross-docking terminal.

The haploid genetic algorithm variants model populations with single sets of chromosomes, akin to haploid organisms such as bacteria or gametes. In these variants, reproduction typically involves asexual mechanisms. Diversity metrics in haploid populations often focus on the uniqueness of individual chromosomes or genotypes, as there are no pairs to recombine. While haploid populations may exhibit faster convergence due to the absence of recombination overhead, they may also face challenges in maintaining diversity over generations, potentially limiting their exploration capability of the solution space.

2 Diversity Measurements and Evaluation

Diversity measurement and evaluation are essential in the optimization process of genetic algorithms (GAs) to prevent premature convergence and enhance search effectiveness [3]. Wong et al. [42] proposed a probabilistic rule-driven adaptive model (PRAM) and a repelling approach to maintain diversity in GAs [42] and emphasized elitism and diversity in solutions when addressing multi-objective optimization problems using GAs [24]. The literature presents a large amount of metrics and approaches to quantify the degree of diversity of a population in GAs, such as: *Hamming distance* calculation, *Fitness variance* calculation and *Entropy* based diversity calculation. In our paper we have used the evaluation of the diversity by computing the population entropy.

Entropy is a fundamental concept used in various fields, including information theory, statistics, and thermodynamics. In the context of diversity and distance measures, entropy provides a way to quantify uncertainty, randomness, or diversity within a system or distribution. Entropy-based measures are commonly employed in evolutionary computation, machine learning, and data analysis to assess the diversity of populations or distributions and to quantify the dissimilarity between them. One of the key components of information theory is Shannon entropy, which is defined in terms of probabilities of events or messages [41]. The information entropy, defined by Shannon, is a dimensionless logarithmic function that characterizes the uncertainty within a system [23]. Shannon entropy $H(X)$

of a discrete random variable X with probability function $p(x)$ is defined as:

$$H(X) = -\sum_{x \in X} p(x) \log_2(p(x)) \tag{1}$$

where: X is the set of possible outcomes of the random variable; $p(x)$ is the occuring probability of outcome $x \in X$.

3 Computation Methods

The research will investigate the impact of diploid representations on genetic diversity within the population over time. The following experimental tests will be performed: one focusing on the fitness values of individual chromosomes and phenotypes, and the other measuring the entropy of haploid and diploid individuals across generations.

Due the specific nature of the benchmark functions, the genes are represented by real numbers and the solutions space is $\mathbb{R}^D$. For the HGA, the individual is represented as:

$$I_h = (c_1, c_2, \ldots, c_D) \tag{2}$$

where D is the dimension of the benchmark function, and c_i are real numbers, $i = 1, \ldots, D$.

In the case of DGA the individual consists of two coupled haploid chromosomes as follows:

$$I_d = (C_1, C_2) = \Big((c_1^1, c_2^1, \ldots, c_D^1), (c_1^2, c_2^2, \ldots, c_D^2)\Big). \tag{3}$$

The fitness of an diploid individual is based on the phenotype and it can be defined in various ways. Due to the infinity of genetic values for each locus of a chromosome, it is improper to establish a principle of confinement based strictly on the analyzed values. In this sense, the phenotype of an individual encoded by real values is determined based on the average of the values for each locus of an individual as:

$$phen_i = average(c_i^1, c_i^2), i = 1, \ldots, D. \tag{4}$$

Thus, the fitness of an individual is:

$$f = F(phen_1, \ldots, phen_D). \tag{5}$$

This kind of phenotype assures an even influence of the both chromosomes of the individual on the mating and survival chances of each individual.

The fitness were calculated for four benchmark functions described in Sect. 3.1. The results were represented graphically in Sect. 4. In all experiments, the values of the parameters used by each algorithm were chosen to be the same: the population size was 2000 individuals for DGA and double (4000) for HGA, the mutation rate was $p_m = 0.05$ and the number of generations for each run was 200. In both GAs, haploid and diploid ones, the selection was made by the roulette wheel technique and the two point crossover with probability $p_c = 1.0$ was used for the creation of the offspring. The crossover operator used was arithmetic crossover (AX).

Two different tests were carried out, one for the size of a chromosome of 25 genes and the other for a double size of 50 genes. Both of our implemented algorithms utilized the roulette wheel selection operator [30] due to its non-intrusive nature compared to deterministic operators, as explained in more detail in [25]. This operator enables the population to experience a more robust evolution. In the process of roulette wheel selection, similar to other selection procedures, the fitness function evaluates and assigns a fitness value to potential solutions or chromosomes. The fitness level is utilized to assign a chance of selection to each individual chromosome.

3.1 Proposed Benchmark Function

In order to compare the investigated HGAs and DGAs in an unbiased manner, and to validate this comparison, we used in this study a collection of four test functions with diverse properties in terms of modality, regularity, separability, and valley landscape. The test functions used in our computational experiments are presented hereafter, together with their main mathematical characteristics.

1. **Schwefel's function** [39] defined as:

$$F_1(x_i) = 418.9829 \times D - \sum_{i=1}^{D} x_i sin(\sqrt{|x_i|}) \tag{6}$$

subject to $-500 \leq x_i \leq 500$, for $i = 1, ..., D$. The considered Schwefel function is continuous, differentiable, separable, scalable, multimodal, has many local optima and the global minimum is located at $x^\star = (420.9687, ..., 420.9687)$ and $F_1(x^\star) = 0$.

2. **Ackley's function** [20] defined as:

$$F_2(x_i) = -20\, exp\Big(-0.2\sqrt{\frac{1}{D}\sum_{i=1}^{D} x_i^2}\Big) - exp\Big(\frac{1}{D}\sum_{i=1}^{D}\cos(2\pi x_i)\Big) + 20 + e \tag{7}$$

subject to $-32 \leq x_i \leq 32$, for $i = 1, ..., D$. The considered Ackley function is continuous, differentiable, non-separable, scalable, multimodal, and has one global minimum $F_2(x^\star) = 0$ at $x^\star = (0, ..., 0)$.

3. **Rastrigin's function** [11] defined as:

$$F_3(x_i) = 10D + \sum_{i=1}^{D}\Big(x_i^2 - 10\cos(2\pi x_i)\Big) \tag{8}$$

subject to $-5.12 \leq x_i \leq 5.12$, for $i = 1, ..., D$. Rastrigin's function is continuous, differentiable, convex, separable, multimodal, and has one global minimum $F_3(x^\star) = 0$ at $x^\star = (0, ..., 0)$.

4. **Sphere function** [20] defined as:

$$F_4(x_i) = \sum_{i=1}^{D} x_i^2 \tag{9}$$

subject to $-5.12 \leq x_i \leq 5.12$, for $i = 1, ..., D$. The Sphere function is continuous, convex, differentiable, separable, scalable, unimodal, and has one global minimum $F_5(x^\star) = 0$ at $x^\star = (0, ..., 0)$.

4 Experimental Results

In Figs. 1, 3, 5 and 7 we illustrate through the obtained results the diversity and convergence of developed GAs under selected benchmark functions (Scwefel, Ackley, Rastrigin and Sphere), as follows: subfigure (a) shows the convergence of the HGA and the DGA, single run results, under genetic conditions presented in Sect. 3. In Figs. 2, 4, 6 and 8 are illustrated the averaged values of diversity and convergence of developed DGA under selected benchmark functions. The conclusions that emerge from these graphic representations are:

- In the case of HGA, the solutions carried by the best, mean and worst individual converge constantly to the function optimum. This constant convergence shows the absence of a significant variation of the selected individuals over generations. This leads to a rapid convergence of the population towards the minimum of the objective function.
- In the case of DGA, single run, subfigure (b), it is observed that for the same individuals, best, mean and worst have aggressive variations over generations. This means that the population 'suffer' from a massive diversity of the individuals. This phenomenon should not be seen as a negative one, in fact it contributes, by preserving diversity, limiting the rapid convergence of the population towards the optimal objective function.

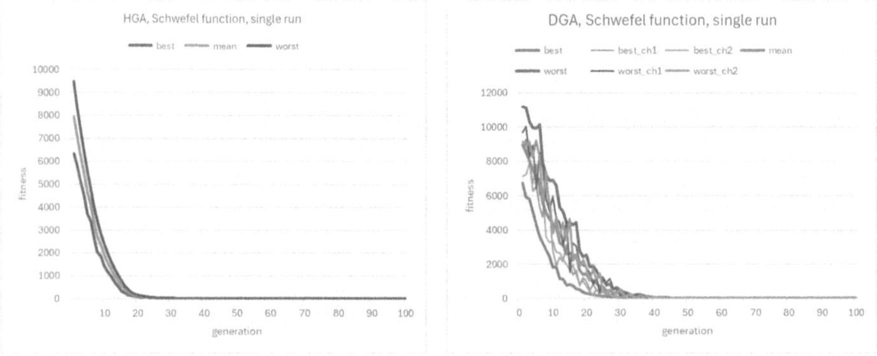

(a) HGA (b) DGA

Fig. 1. Single run results of HGA & DGA for Schwefel function

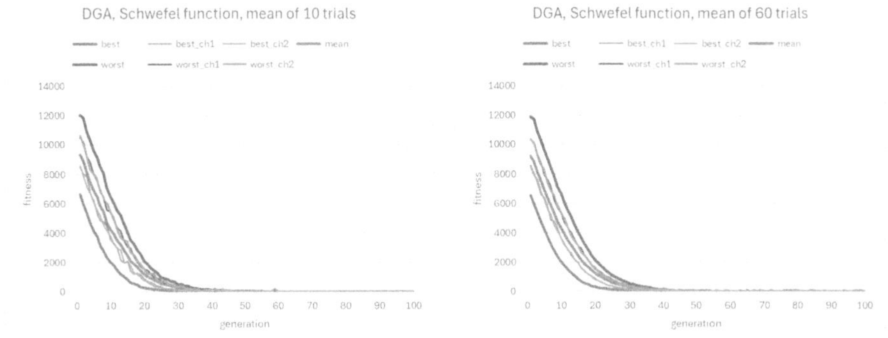

(a) DGA, 10 runs (b) DGA, 60 runs

Fig. 2. Multiple run results of HGA & DGA for Schwefel function

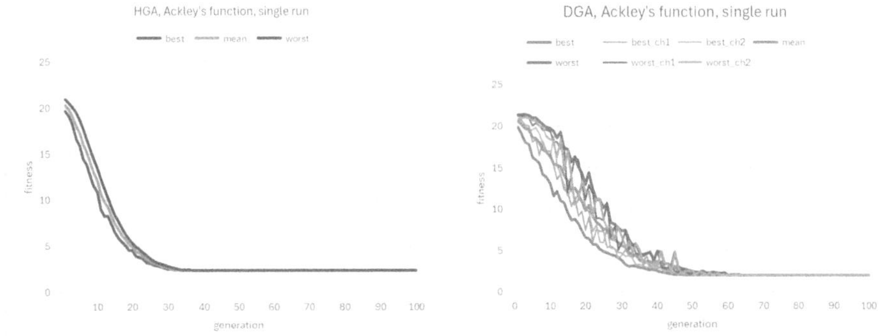

(a) HGA (b) DGA

Fig. 3. Single run results of HGA & DGA for Ackley function

- From Figs. 2, 4, 6 and 8 we observe that, if we calculate the average values of multiple trials, the convergence curves of the best, mean and worst becomes uniform, without significant variations. This result explain and validate the slower convergence behavior of DGA in relation to HGA.

In Figs. 9, 10, 11, 12, 13, 14, 15 and 16 we illustrate through the obtained results calculated using the formula (1) the variation of the entropy of the population over generations for the developed GAs evaluated by selected benchmark functions (Scwefel, Ackley, Rastrigin and Sphere). The tests was performed for

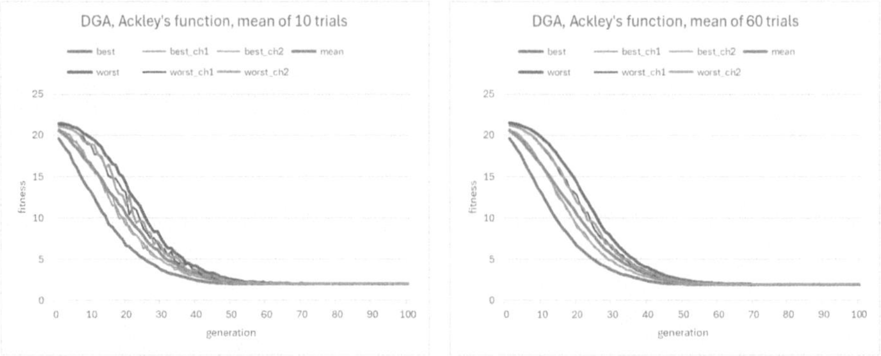

(a) DGA, 10 runs (b) DGA, 60 runs

Fig. 4. Multiple run results of HGA & DGA for Ackley function

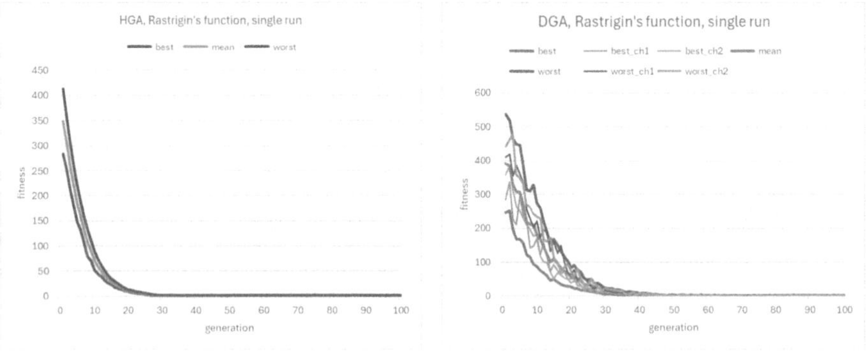

(a) HGA (b) DGA

Fig. 5. Single run results of HGA & DGA for Rastrigin function

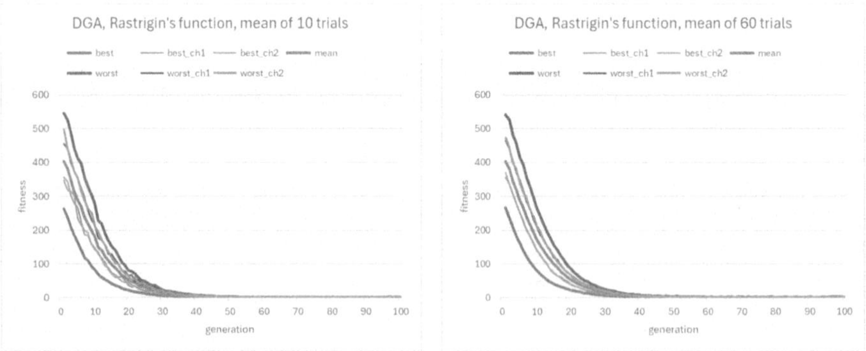

(a) DGA, 10 runs (b) DGA, 60 runs

Fig. 6. Multiple run results of HGA & DGA for Rastrigin function

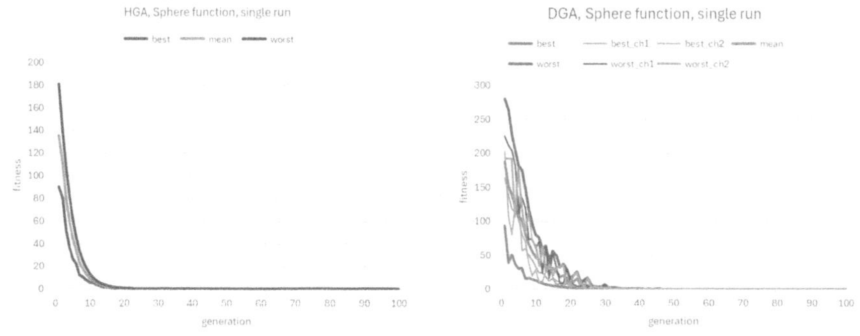

(a) HGA

(b) DGA

Fig. 7. Single run results of HGA & DGA for Sphere function

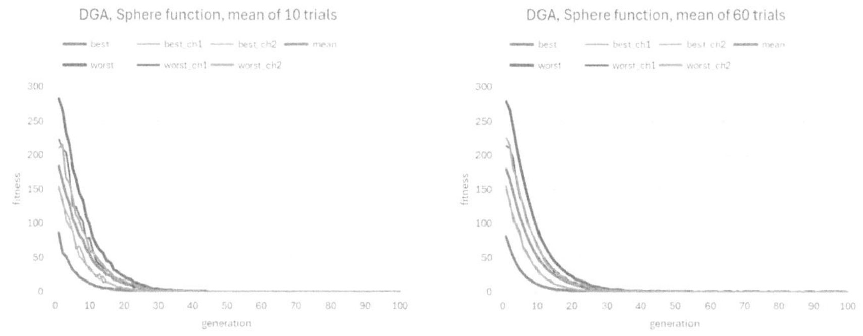

(a) DGA, 10 runs

(b) DGA, 60 runs

Fig. 8. Multiple run results of HGA & DGA for Sphere function

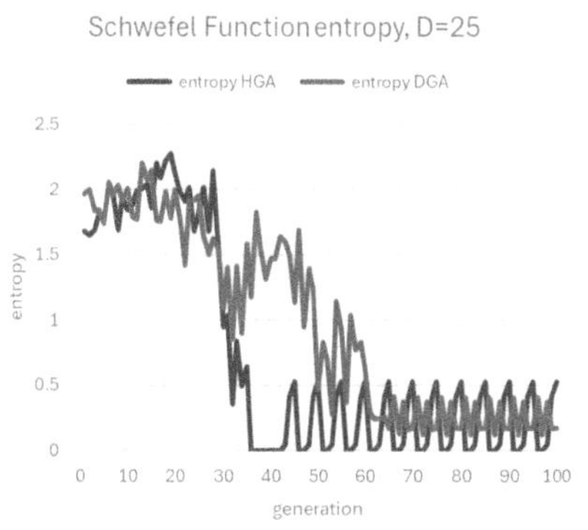

Fig. 9. Schwefel function, $D = 25$

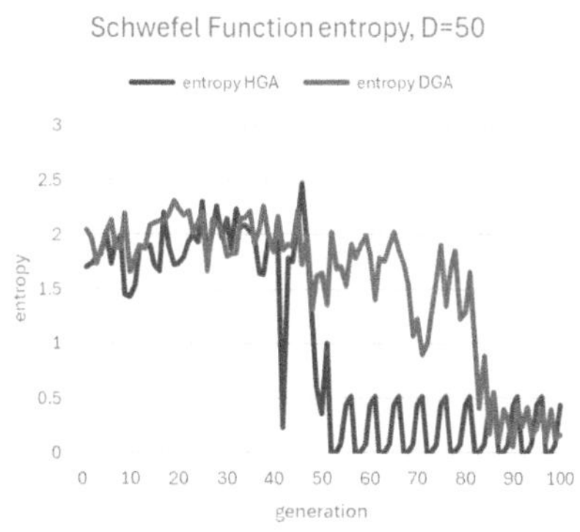

Fig. 10. Schwefel function, $D = 50$

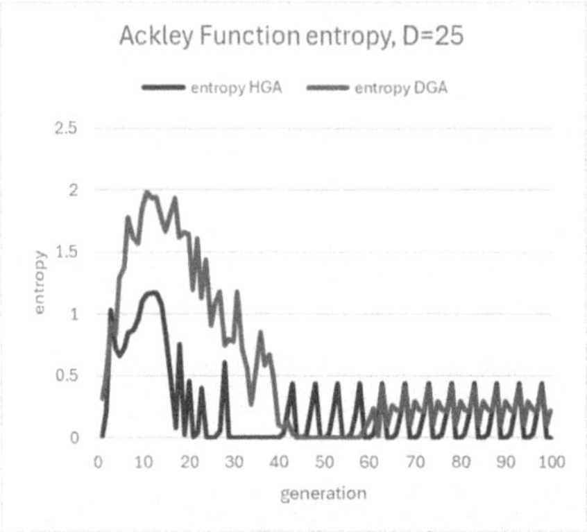

Fig. 11. Ackley function, $D = 25$

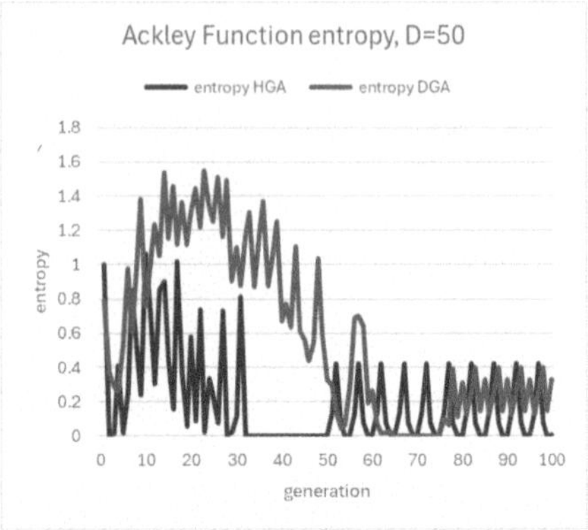

Fig. 12. Ackley function, $D = 50$

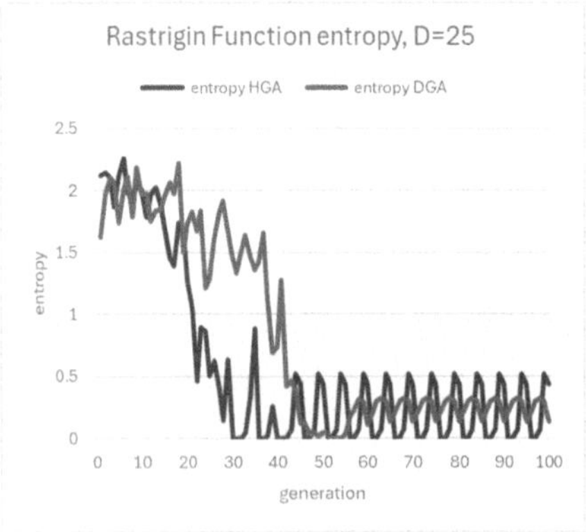

Fig. 13. Rastrigin function, $D = 25$

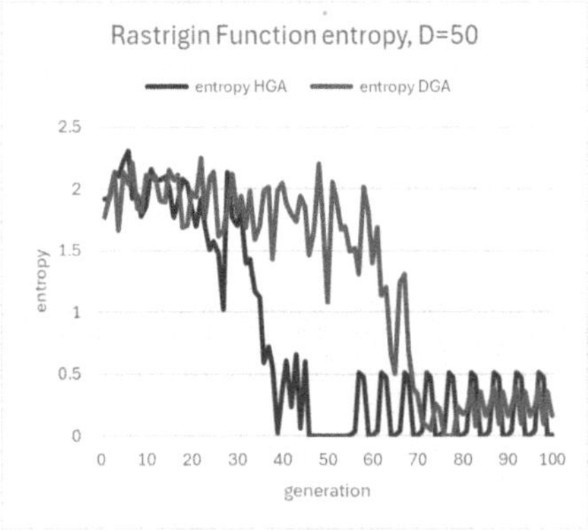

Fig. 14. Rastrigin function, $D = 50$

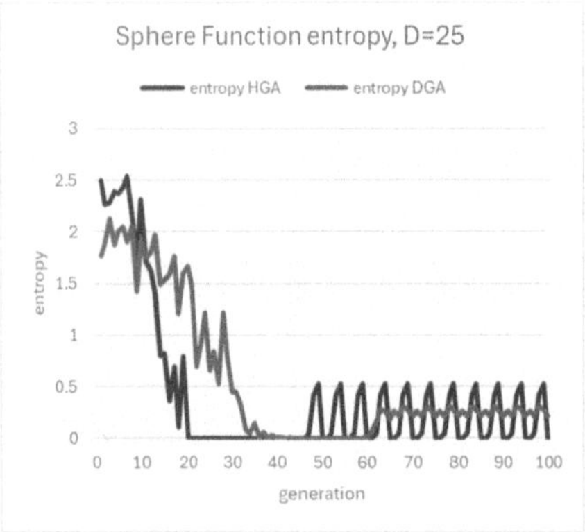

Fig. 15. Sphere function, $D = 25$

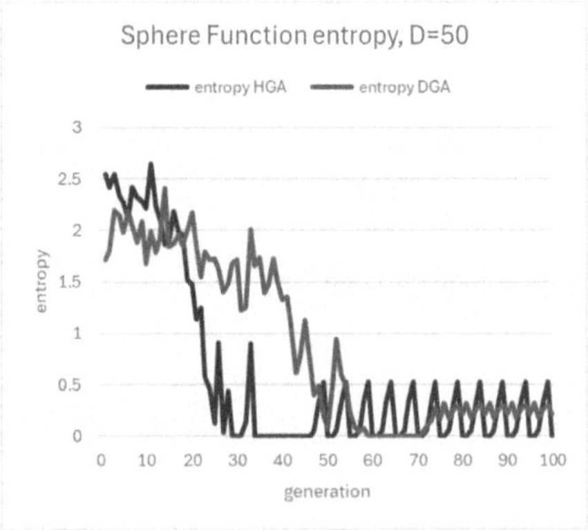

Fig. 16. Sphere function, $D = 50$

each mentioned benchmark function on two dimensions ($D = 25$ and $D = 50$). The conclusions that emerge from these graphic representations are:

- For both performed tests for each benchmark function, the entropy (diversity) of the population is higher for DGA populations than HGA populations.
- From the entropy results obtained in the case of DGA, it can be seen that they indicate an increased diversity of the population, a much larger number of generations than in the case of HGA populations.
- The results validates the previous observations regarding the slower convergent nature of DGA compared to HGA, precisely due to the diversity of the population.

5 Conclusions

In this study, the main objective was to determine and measure the diversity of diploid and haploid GA populations. From the obtained results, we conclude that in the case of DGAs the populations of individuals over the generations are much more diverse than in the case of HGAs. This is due to the fact that in the case of diploid individuals fitness is determined by their phenotype and not by the component chromosomes. The experiments carried out had a uniform character, they used genetic operators of selection, crossing and mutation that did not put too much pressure on the individuals. In conclusion, through the prism of the obtained results, we have validated that the diversity of the DGA populations 'surpasses' the diversity of the HGA populations.

References

1. Al-Rahman, D.I.A., Attea, B.A.: Solving multiple-container packing problems using pseudo-meiosis genetic algorithm. J. Eng. **11**(3), 455–466 (2005)
2. Attea, B.A.: The effect of pseudo-meiosis genetic algorithm on bit-coding stationary genetic search. Iraqi J. Sci. **47**(1), 160–165 (2006)
3. Burks, A.R., Punch, W.F.: An efficient structural diversity technique for genetic programming. In: Proceedings of the 2015 Annual Conference on Genetic and Evolutionary Computation, pp. 991–998 (2015)
4. Cheng, C., Lee, W., Miltenburg, J.: A bi-chromosome genetic algorithm for minimizing intercell and intracell moves. Group Technology and Cellular Manufacturing: A State-of-the-Art Synthesis of Research and Practice, pp. 205–219 (1998)
5. Cobb, H.G., Grefenstette, J.J.: Genetic algorithms for tracking changing environments. Technical Report, Naval Research Lab Washington DC (1993)
6. Collingwood, E., Corne, D., Ross, P.: Useful diversity via multiploidy. In: Proceedings of IEEE International Conference on Evolutionary Computation, pp. 810–813. IEEE (1996)
7. Cruz-Chávez, M.A., Martínez-Oropeza, A., et al.: Feasible initial population with genetic diversity for a population-based algorithm applied to the vehicle routing problem with time windows. Math. Probl. Eng. **2016**, 3851520 (2016)
8. Darwin, C.: On the Origin of Species by Means of Natural Selection, or the Preservation of Favoured Races in the Struggle for life. Murray, London (1859)

9. De Jong, K.A.: An Analysis of the Behavior of a Class of Genetic Adaptive Systems. University of Michigan (1975)
10. Deb, K., Goldberg, D.E.: An investigation of niche and species formation in genetic function optimization. In: Proceedings of the Third International Conference on Genetic Algorithms, pp. 42–50 (1989)
11. Dieterich, J.M., Hartke, B.: Empirical review of standard benchmark functions using evolutionary global optimization. arXiv preprint arXiv:1207.4318 (2012)
12. Dulebenets, M.A.: A diploid evolutionary algorithm for sustainable truck scheduling at a cross-docking facility. Sustainability **10**(5), 1333 (2018)
13. Dulebenets, M.A.: An adaptive polyploid memetic algorithm for scheduling trucks at a cross-docking terminal. Inf. Sci. **565**, 390–421 (2021)
14. Galán, S.F., Mengshoel, O.J., Pinter, R.: A novel mating approach for genetic algorithms. Evol. Comput. **21**(2), 197–229 (2013)
15. Goldberg, D., Smith, R.: Nonstationary function optimization using genetic algorithms with dominance and diploidy. In: Proceedings of Second International Conference on Genetic Algorithms and their Application, pp. 59–68 (1987)
16. of Health, N.I., et al.: Talking glossary of genetic terms. national human genome research institute web site (2017)
17. Herrera-Poyatos, A., Herrera, F.: Genetic and memetic algorithm with diversity equilibrium based on greedy diversification. arXiv preprint arXiv:1702.03594 (2017)
18. Hillis, W.D.: Co-evolving parasites improve simulated evolution as an optimization procedure. Physica D **42**(1–3), 228–234 (1990)
19. Holland, J.H.: Adaptation in Natural and Artificial Systems. The University of Michigan Press, Ann Arbor (1975)
20. Jamil, M., Yang, X.S.: A literature survey of benchmark functions for global optimization problems. arXiv preprint arXiv:1308.4008 (2013)
21. John, B.: Meiosis, vol. 22. Cambridge University Press, Cambridge (2005)
22. Li, X., Epitropakis, M.G., Deb, K., Engelbrecht, A.: Seeking multiple solutions: an updated survey on niching methods and their applications. IEEE Trans. Evol. Comput. **21**(4), 518–538 (2016)
23. Lin, S.K.: Gibbs paradox and the concepts of information, symmetry, similarity and their relationship. Entropy **10**(1), 1–5 (2008)
24. Long, Q., Wu, C., Wang, X., Jiang, L., Li, J., et al.: A multiobjective genetic algorithm based on a discrete selection procedure. Math. Prob. Eng. **2015**, 349781 (2015)
25. Matei, O.: Evolutionary computation: principles and practices. Risoprint (2008)
26. Matei, O., Pop, P.C., Sas, J.L., Chira, C.: An improved immigration memetic algorithm for solving the heterogeneous fixed fleet vehicle routing problem. Neurocomputing **150**, 58–66 (2015)
27. Michael, R., Vida, K., Shuvr, S.: A modular genetic algorithm for scheduling task graphs. United States (2003)
28. Michalewicz, Z.: Genetic algorithms+ data structures= evolution programs. Springer Science & Business Media (2013)
29. Ng, K.P., Wong, K.C.: A new diploid scheme and dominance change mechanism for non-stationary function optimization. In: Proceedings of the 6th International Conference on Genetic Algorithms, pp. 159–166. Morgan Kaufmann Publishers Inc., San Francisco, CA, USA (1995). http://dl.acm.org/citation.cfm?id=645514.657904

30. Pencheva, T., Atanassov, K., Shannon, A.: Modelling of a roulette wheel selection operator in genetic algorithms using generalized nets. Int. J. Bioautomation **13**(4), 257 (2009)
31. Petrovan, A., Matei, O., Erdei, R.: A Behavioural Study of the Crossover Operator in Diploid Genetic Algorithms. In: Herrero, Á., Cambra, C., Urda, D., Sedano, J., Quintián, H., Corchado, E. (eds.) 15th International Conference on Soft Computing Models in Industrial and Environmental Applications (SOCO 2020), SOCO 2020, Advances in Intelligent Systems and Computing, vol. 1268, pp 79–88. Springer, Cham (2021). https://doi.org/10.1007/978-3-030-57802-2_8
32. Petrovan, A., Pop-Sitar, P., Matei, O.: Haploid versus diploid genetic algorithms. a comparative study. In: Pérez García, H., Sánchez González, L., Castejón Limas, M., Quintián Pardo, H., Corchado Rodríguez, E. (eds.) HAIS 2019. LNCS (LNAI), vol. 11734, pp. 193–205. Springer, Cham (2019). https://doi.org/10.1007/978-3-030-29859-3_17
33. Pop, P., Matei, O., Pintea, C.: A two-level diploid genetic based algorithm for solving the family traveling salesman problem. In: Proceedings of the Genetic and Evolutionary Computation Conference, pp. 340–346. ACM (2018)
34. Pop, P., Oliviu, M., Sabo, C.: A Hybrid diploid genetic based algorithm for solving the generalized traveling salesman problem. In: Martínez de Pisón, F.J., Urraca, R., Quintián, H., Corchado, E. (eds.) HAIS 2017. LNCS (LNAI), vol. 10334, pp. 149–160. Springer, Cham (2017). https://doi.org/10.1007/978-3-319-59650-1_13
35. Pop, P.C., Matei, O., Sabo, C., Petrovan, A.: A two-level solution approach for solving the generalized minimum spanning tree problem. Eur. J. Oper. Res. **265**(2), 478–487 (2018)
36. Rieger, R., Michaelis, A., Green, M.M.: Glossary of Genetics: Classical and Molecular. Springer Science & Business Media (2012)
37. Rui, L., Qin, Y., Li, B., Gao, Z.: Context-based intelligent scheduling and knowledge push algorithms for AR-assist communication network maintenance. Comput. Model. Eng. Sci. **118**(2), 291–315 (2019)
38. Schlierkamp-Voosen, D., Mühlenbein, H.: Strategy adaptation by competing subpopulations. In: Davidor, Y., Schwefel, HP., Männer, R. (eds.) Parallel Problem Solving from Nature - PPSN III, PPSN 1994, LNCS, vol. 866. Springer, Berlin, Heidelberg (1994). https://doi.org/10.1007/3-540-58484-6_264
39. Schwefel, H.P.: Numerical Optimization of Computer Models. Wiley, Inc, Hoboken (1981)
40. Thorgaard, G.H.: Ploidy manipulation and performance. Aquaculture **57**(1–4), 57–64 (1986)
41. Witten, E.: A mini-introduction to information theory. La Rivista del Nuovo Cimento **43**(4), 187–227 (2020)
42. Wong, Y.Y., Lee, K.H., Leung, K.S., Ho, C.W.: A novel approach in parameter adaptation and diversity maintenance for genetic algorithms. Soft. Comput. **7**, 506–515 (2003)
43. Wu, X., Chu, C.H., Wang, Y., Yan, W.: Concurrent design of cellular manufacturing systems: a genetic algorithm approach. Int. J. Prod. Res. **44**(6), 1217–1241 (2006)
44. Younes, A., Basir, O., Calamai, P.: A hybrid evolutionary approach for combinatorial problems in dynamic environments. In: 2006 Canadian Conference on Electrical and Computer Engineering, pp. 1595–1600. IEEE (2006)

45. Yu, Z., Ni, M., Wang, Z., Zhang, Y., et al.: Dynamic route guidance using improved genetic algorithms. Math. Probl. Eng. **2013**, 765135 (2013)
46. Yukiko, Y., Nobue, A.: A diploid genetic algorithm for preserving population diversity - Pseudo-Meiosis GA. In: Davidor, Y., Schwefel, HP., Männer, R. (eds.) Parallel Problem Solving from Nature - PPSN III, PPSN 1994, LNCS, vol. 866, pp 36–45. Springer, Berlin (1994). https://doi.org/10.1007/3-540-58484-6_248

Early Failure Detection for Air Production Unit in Metro Trains

Amelia Zafra[1(✉)], Bruno Veloso[2,3], and João Gama[2,3]

[1] Department of Computer Science and Numerical Analysis, Andalusian Research Institute in Data Science and Computational Intelligence (DaSCI), University of Cordoba, Cordoba, Spain
azafra@uco.es

[2] Laboratory of Artificial Intelligence and Decision Support, INESC TEC, Porto, Portugal
{bruno.m.veloso,joao.gama}@inesctec.pt

[3] School of Economics, University of Porto, Porto, Portugal

Abstract. Early identification of failures is a critical task in predictive maintenance, preventing potential problems before they manifest and resulting in substantial time and cost savings for industries. We propose an approach that predicts failures in the near future. First, a deep learning model combining long short-term memory and convolutional neural network architectures predicts signals for a future time horizon using real-time data. In the second step, an autoencoder based on convolutional neural networks detects anomalies in these predicted signals. Finally, a verification step ensures that a fault is considered reliable only if it is corroborated by anomalies in multiple signals simultaneously. We validate our approach using publicly available Air Production Unit (APU) data from Porto metro trains. Two significant conclusions emerge from our study. Firstly, experimental results confirm the effectiveness of our approach, demonstrating a high fault detection rate and a reduced number of false positives. Secondly, the adaptability of this proposal allows for the customization of configuration of different time horizons and relationship between the signals to meet specific detection requirements.

Keywords: Predictive maintenance · Anomaly detection · Time series prediction

1 Introduction

Predictive Maintenance (PdM) utilizes data, sensors, and analytics to predict equipment failures, facilitating timely maintenance to prevent such occurrences. This approach is highly significant in industry as it allows for dynamic maintenance scheduling, reducing operational issues, maintenance costs, unplanned downtime, and extending equipment lifespan.

In recent years, interest in PdM has surged alongside advancements in machine learning and deep learning. Esteban et al. [8] provide a general data

H. Quintián et al. (Eds.): HAIS 2024, LNAI 14857, pp. 339–351, 2025.
https://doi.org/10.1007/978-3-031-74183-8_28

mining perspective on PdM, while Davari et al. [4] focus on machine learning and deep learning in the railway industry. Divya et al. [7] and Nunes et al. [17] highlight critical research areas in PdM, including failure prediction, remaining useful life estimation, and root cause analysis. Focusing on failure prediction, a relevant task in PdM, this work proposes an unsupervised learning approach to anticipate failures that tackles open challenges [17], such as the demand for novel unsupervised and semi-supervised learning models that operate without labeled data, enable early fault detection, and handle time series data from sensorized systems. Our methodology integrates the time series forecasting [11] and anomaly detection [18]. First, a predictive model forecasts future time series of signals received by sensors for a future time horizon. Subsequently, an anomaly detection model identifies unusual patterns in these predicted signals, indicating potential future failures. Finally, a critical verification step is include to ensure that potential faults are corroborated by multiple signals concurrently within the same time-frame.

To evaluate the proposal, we address a real-world problem: predicting failures in APUs installed on the roofs of Metro vehicles [2]. These units perform critical functions, such as maintaining the vehicle's height regardless of passenger load. Due to their high demand and lack of redundancy, any failure necessitates immediate train removal for repair, causing trip interruptions. Traditional maintenance criteria often miss these failures, negatively impacting both the operating company and customers. Anticipating such breakdowns can prevent trip cancellations and vehicle removal, making it highly valuable. Previous works [2,6,16] have addressed this problem but could not anticipate failures in advance. Our experimental results, which evaluate various configurations, time horizons, and models, show that the proposal efficiently forecasts failures in advance (one and three hours ahead) with high precision and a reduced number of false alarms. The main advantages of our proposal include:

- It works in two steps to anticipate future failures. First, time series forecasting is used to generate future signals. Then, these signals are analyzed by an anomaly detection method.
- It incorporates a fault validation mechanism to mitigate false positives in the anomaly detection algorithm, requiring activation across multiple signals to confirm a real fault.
- It utilizes time series data in an unsupervised learning environment, making it adaptable to real-world applications, especially where temporally managed sensor data lacks labeling.

Finally, to demonstrate the effectiveness of our approach in detecting future anomalies, we conducted an experimental study using APU data collected from the Porto metro. The study evaluated several configurations for time series prediction and anomaly detection. We explored various prediction time horizons and tested different models to comprehensively assess their performance. This approach allowed us to analyze how well our method anticipates and identifies anomalies across different scenarios.

The paper is structured as follows: Sect. 2 describes related work, Sect. 3 presents the proposed methodology to predict failures in advanced. Section 4 the experimental setting and discussion of results are shown and finally, Sect. 5 details the conclusions reached and future work.

2 Related Work

Anomaly detection has garnered significant research attention for failure detection in PdM, particularly in recent years [18]. A common approach involves reconstructing normal behavior by encoding segments of training time series into a lower-dimensional latent space, allowing for the calculation of an anomaly score by comparing reconstructed segments with original values. Several studies related to railway anomaly detection have explored this method. Chen et al. [3] introduced a semi-supervised approach using GANs to detect foreign objects on railway tracks, Kang et al. [12] proposed a CNN-based system for detecting surface defects on railway insulators, and Kang et al. [13] developed an LSTM autoencoder method to identify anomalies in subway brake operating units.

From another perspective, models based on prediction, distance, or statistical analysis can also be found. For instance, Kang et al. [14] used a Bayesian statistical model to detect anomalies in train speed. Manco et al. [15] developed an application to forecast based on diagnosis and explain door failures in metro trains. Filios et al. [9] predicted stoppages in packing machines using ARIMA and Prophet algorithms. Baptista et al. [1] incorporated the ARMA algorithm and other statistical features for event prediction using K-Nearest Neighbour, Random Forest, and Support Vector Machine. Zhang et al. [22] proposed a supervised method for abnormal passenger flow detection constructing a graphical model to capture the spatial distribution of anomalies, while Shi et al. [19] introduced a density peak clustering approach for identifying frequent failures in Rail Vehicle Door Systems. Lastly, we highlight other studies have tackled the same issue using the MetroPT dataset. Barros et al. [2] developed rules for APU monitoring and anomaly detection, utilizing peak frequency analysis on sensor data. Davari et al. [6] proposed a PdM framework with deep learning and Sparse Autoencoder-based unsupervised learning, effectively reducing false alarms. Lastly, Ayat et al. [16] introduced a Random Forest-based framework for APU failure detection and classification, employing supervised learning.

Previous research indicates widespread adoption of anomaly detection in PdM related to railways. Our proposal introduces novel advancements in the field compared to previous models by working with unlabeled data, using time series representations, and performing early detection. Additionally, we enhance detection accuracy by combining anomalous results across multiple signals to minimize false positives.

3 Proposed Framework for Early Failure Detection

This section outlines the overall architecture of our proposal for forecasting faults, as illustrated in Fig. 1. Initially, real-time signals acquired from sensors are utilized by the time series forecasting method to predict future signal values, considering different time horizons. Subsequently, the anomaly detection model uses the predicted signals to assess the likelihood of future anomalies. This framework operates within an unsupervised learning framework to anticipate future failures. In the following sections, we detail the main components of the proposal.

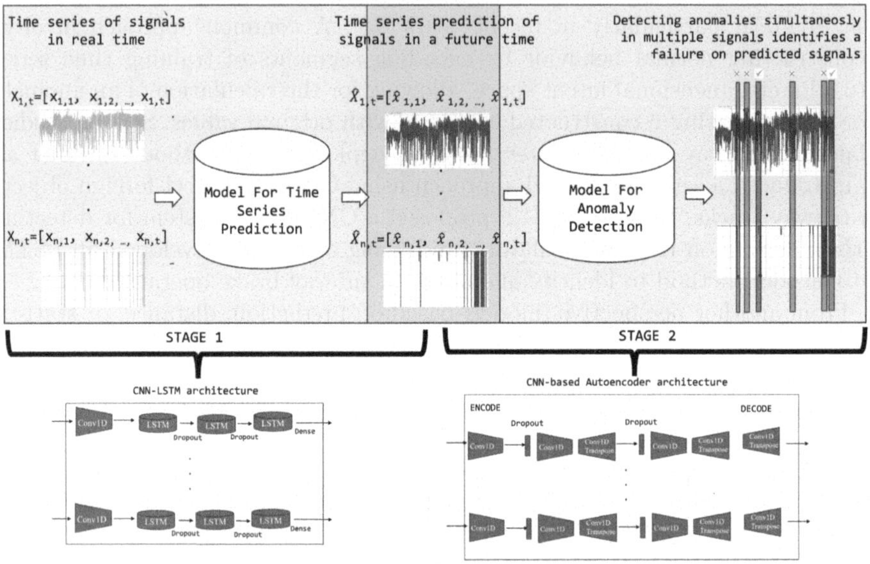

Fig. 1. Architectural overview of the proposed framework to failure prediction in advance

3.1 Model for Forecasting Time Series

The time series forecasting problem involves predicting future values of a sequence of data points based on historical observations. Let $\{x_1, x_2, \cdots, x_t\}$ denote the time series data, where x_t represents the value observed at time t. The objective is to predict future values x_{t+h} for a given horizon h, where h represents the number of time steps into the future.

Thus, the time series forecasting problem can be formulated as follows: given a time series dataset $\{x_1, x_2, \cdots, x_t\}$ and a forecasting horizon h find a function f that maps historical observations $\{x_1, x_2, \cdots, x_t\}$ to predict values $\hat{x}_{t+h}$. The objective is to minimize the discrepancy between the predicted values $\hat{x}_{t+h}$ and the actual values x_{t+h} for all future time steps.

For solving this problem, we select in our framework a deep learning model based on hybrid CNN-LSTM framework (Fig. 1). An hybrid model has been used in similar contexts [20]. Our model consists of a sequence of a convolutional layer and LSTM blocks, which are integrated using a fully connected layer to generate the final output. Initially, the input data is passed through a one-dimensional convolutional layer, which extracts features and produces a two-dimensional output vector with 32 filters and a kernel size of 2. We apply the ReLU activation function to introduce non-linearity. Subsequently, the output vector is fed into three LSTM layers to capture temporal dependencies, designed to memorize historical data and relative long-term dependencies. Leveraging historical data records at time t, our model can make predictions considering various time horizons. Each LSTM layer processes feature maps extracted by preceding layers. To mitigate overfitting, a dropout layer is inserted after the first LSTM layer, randomly disabling a fraction of neurons during training. Finally, the output of the LSTM layers feeds into two dense output layers, producing final predictions. The first dense layer employs 30 units with ReLU activation, while the second dense layer employs a hyperbolic tangent (tanh) activation function. In our model, each signal is predicted independently and the future signal will be the input the next stage of our proposed framework. We note that in this step, the prediction is solely used to anticipate the future.

3.2 Anomaly Detection

The anomaly detection problem involves detecting anomalies in the predicted signals using an unsupervised model. As depicted in Fig. 1, we chose an Autoencoder. Autoencoders are a specific type of feedforward neural network in which the input matches the output. They compress the input into a lower-dimensional code and then reconstruct the output from this representation.

The proposed CNN-based autoencoder involves the repeated application of 1D convolutional layers and their transpose. Dropout is employed to mitigate potential overfitting. Specifically, the model begins with a 1D convolutional layer with 32 filters and a kernel size of 7, followed by a dropout layer for regularization. Then, another 1D convolutional layer with 16 filters and the same kernel size is applied, followed by a transposed convolutional layer with the same number of filters and kernel size to reconstruct the original input. Another dropout layer is employed for regularization before the subsequent transposed convolutional layer. Finally, the last transposed convolutional layer, with a single filter, produces the final output.

To enhance the reliability of detected errors, our proposal incorporates an additional step. This involves analyzing anomalies detected in each predicted signal independently and determining that an error will occur only if a failure is detected simultaneously in different signals. Integrating this final step aims to improve accuracy in future failure detection and mitigate errors.

4 Experimental Setup

The experimentation carried out aims to demonstrate the effectiveness of the proposed framework in anticipating failures. This section will describe the dataset, the experimental setup, and the performance measures used, as well as discuss the experiments and the results obtained. Specifically, the study aims to address the following Research Questions (RQ). **RQ1:** What is the performance of the proposed model to predict signals in different time horizons? We will evaluate the performance of the prediction method for stage 1 (RQ1.1), as well as the utilization of different prediction time horizons to predict signals (RQ1.2). **RQ2:** What is the performance of the proposed model to detect anomalies from previously predicted signals? We will analyze the performance of the proposed model for stage 2 (RQ2.1), as well as the impact of working with predictions at different time intervals (RQ2.2). Finally, **RQ3:** What is the performance of the proposal to detect in detecting anomalies in the future? Based on the conducted studies, we will assess whether the proposed framework is competitive in supporting future fault detection.

4.1 Dataset

The MetroPT dataset [5] contains information from Porto's urban metro public transportation service. It benchmarks PdM models for tasks like online anomaly detection, failure prediction, and remaining useful life prediction. Data is collected from analog and digital sensors in the APU of a train. The APU is a vital component of the compressor, responsible for converting power from an electric motor into kinetic energy by compressing and pressurizing air. Its performance is crucial for various actions such as braking, door opening and closing, and bioreactor usage. The dataset, collected from February to July 2020, includes 16 signals logged at 1 Hz, with data transmitted to a remote server every five minutes via GSM.

After a correlation study between the signals, this study uses 6 analog and 3 digital sensors. Analog sensors consists of real values and they are: 1) *TP2:* Pressure on the compressor. 2) *TP3:* Pressure generated at the pneumatic panel. 3) *H1:* The valve activates when the pressure switch reads above the operational threshold of 10.2 bar. 4) *DV_pressure:* Pressure exerted due to pressure drop generated when air dryer towers discharge water. 5) *Oil_Temperature:* Temperature of the oil present on the compressor and 6) *Motor_Current:* Compressor load. Digital sensors consists of binary values and they are: 1) *COMP:* Electrical signal of the air intake valve on the compressor. 2) *Towers:* Signal that indicates which tower is drying the air and which tower is draining the humidity removed from the air and 3) *Oil_Level:* Signal that indicates when the oil level on the compressor falls below the expected values.

The dataset is unlabeled, but failure reports provided by the company (MetroPT dataset [5]) are available in Table 1. This allows for evaluating the effectiveness of anomaly detection algorithms. The four failures indicated in [5] are shaded in the table for ease of identification. These failures are supplemented with the failures identified in the work of Davari et al. [6]. Among the errors examined in this reference, those that were a continuation of the same failure have been grouped together as a single failure, as they occur sequentially over time; these are marked with the symbol • in the table. Additionally, maintenance periods reported in [5] have been included, encompassing the hour before and after maintenance, as the signals also display anomalous behavior during regular operation. These failures are listed at the end and are marked with ⊕.

Table 1. Failures report

Nr.	Start Time	End Time	Failure	Severity
1	4/12/2020 11:50	4/12/2020 23:30	Air leak	High stress
2•	4/18/2020 00:00	4/19/2020 01:30	Air leak	High stress
3	4/29/2020 03:20	4/29/2020 22:20	Air leak	High stress
4	5/13/2020 14:00	5/13/2020 23:59	Air leak	High stress
5•	5/18/2020 05:00	5/20/2020 20:59	Air leak	High stress
6	5/23/2020 09:50	5/23/2020 10:10	Air leak	High stress
7	5/29/2020 23:30	5/30/2020 6:00	Air Leak	High stress
8	6/01/2020 15:00	6/01/2020 15:40	Air leak	High stress
9	6/03/2020 10:00	6/03/2020 11:00	Air leak	High stress
10	6/5/2020 10:00	6/7/2020 14:30	Air Leak	High stress
11	7/08/2020 17:30	7/08/2020 19:00	Air leak	High stress
12	7/15/2020 14:30	7/15/2020 19:00	Air Leak	High stress
13	7/17/2020 04:30	7/17/2020 05:30	Air leak	High stress
14⊕	6/08/2020 15:00	6/08/2020 17:00	Air leak	High stress
15⊕	7/15/2020 23:00	7/16/2020 01:00	Air leak	High stress

4.2 Experimental Configuration

Models have been developed in Python. We use the scikit-learn library and TensorFlow Keras as a deep learning framework to implement models. Finally, the optuna library is used to automatically optimize the models' parameters. Data sampled are analyzed every 60 seconds, corresponding to values evaluated every minute. A window size of 60 samples, equivalent to 1 hour, is utilized to train the model. Finally, various options are considered for the time horizon, including predictions one and three hours in advance. CNN-LSTM model uses adaptive moment estimation as optimizer to train the autoencoder models. The initial learning rate is set to 0.0001 and the loss is evaluated with mean absolute error. In our study, 40% is used for training, 30% for validation, and finally, 30% for testing. The CNN-based AutoEncoder utilizes the mean absolute error for each subsequence. If the error surpasses a predefined threshold, which is set to the maximum mean absolute error value in the training (normal) dataset, we classify the example as an anomaly.

The experiments were carried out using a computer that has the following specification: Intel Core i7-9700 CPU @ 3.00 GHz and 64 GB RAM with GPU: Nvidia GTX 1080 Ti. Different experiments are repeated 10 times with different seeds and average values are shown in the results.

4.3 Performance Measure

For predicting the time series, we use the Root Mean Square Error (RMSE) that measures the average magnitude of the differences between predicted and real values in the signal.

$$RMSE = \sqrt{\frac{1}{n}\sum_{i=1}^{n}(\text{actual}_i - \text{predicted}_i)^2} \text{ ; n is the number of data points}$$

For anomaly detection. In accordance with the specifications provided by [21], a failure is defined as a time interval ($start - end$). This definition follows the evaluation protocol outlined below: True Positive (TP): the predicted failure interval overlaps with the observed failure interval. False Positive (FP): the predicted failure interval does not overlap with the observed failure interval. True Negative (TN): there is no predicted failure, and there is no observed failure. False Negative (FN): there is no predicted failure, but there is an observed failure. The overall goal is to minimize the number of false alarms (FP) and missed failures (FN), aiming to prevent failures during operational contexts and unnecessary maintenance actions. From these values, we calculate the F-measure that combines precision (P) and recall (R) into a single score. It is defined as the harmonic mean of P and R:

$$F_{measure} = \frac{2 \times \text{P} \times \text{R}}{\text{P} + \text{R}} \text{ ; where } P = \frac{TP}{TP + FP}, \text{ and } R = \frac{TP}{TP + FN}$$

5 Experimental Results

In this section, we will conduct experimental studies to address the posed RQs. The objective is to demonstrate that the proposal enables effective anticipation of fault detection. To achieve this, we will analyze the results of each of the two stages in which the proposal is divided.

5.1 Study of Time Series Prediction Results

In this study, our goal is to evaluate the performance of the time series prediction model. Predicted signals should be as accurate as possible compared to the originals. Table 2 shows RMSE values for predicting the signal one and three hours ahead as the time horizon. The presented results display the average test outcomes alongside the standard deviation of all executions conducted in each experiment. RMSE is calculated using normalized signal data to provide a more robust and reliable performance evaluation of predictive models. The study includes the hybrid model (CNN+LSTM), as well as solely LSTM-based and CNN-based models. This evaluation allows us to determine if there are significant differences between these architectures and confirm if the results

Table 2. Average RMSE for predicting time series with a time horizon of the next one and three hours with statistical tests for comparison

	ONE HOUR IN ADVANCED						THREE HOURS IN ADVANCED					
	CNN+LSTM		LSTM		CNN		CNN+LSTM		LSTM		CNN	
Signal	RMSE	SD	RMSE	SD	RMSE	SD	RMSE	SD	RMSE	SD	RMSE	SD
TP2	**0.5727**	**0.0362**	0.6198	0.0099	0.7929	0.0074	0.6318	0.0084	**0.6235**	**0.0135**	0.7026	0.0250
TP3	0.4195	0.0163	**0.3835**	**0.0001**	0.4924	0.0984	**0.4816**	**0.0739**	0.4970	0.0012	0.5511	0.0455
DV_{pres}	**0.0194**	**0.0043**	0.0362	0.0099	0.0385	0.0032	**0.0291**	**0.0044**	0.0350	0.0057	0.0874	0.0013
H1	0.7833	0.0003	**0.7743**	**0.0427**	0.8467	0.0641	**0.8158**	**0.0051**	0.8351	0.0075	0.9901	0.0358
$Motor_{cur}$	**0.7744**	**0.0232**	0.8236	0.0059	0.8293	0.0490	0.8248	0.0104	**0.8216**	**0.0017**	0.9259	0.0161
Oil_{temp}	**0.2216**	**0.0035**	0.2235	0.0011	0.2669	0.0014	**0.3090**	**0.0083**	0.3224	0.0161	0.3608	0.0193
Oil_{level}	**0.2034**	**0.3131**	0.5943	0.0097	0.4580	0.0090	**0.4848**	**0.0036**	0.4852	0.0032	**0.4848**	**0.0414**
COMP	0.4220	0.0175	**0.4207**	**0.0414**	0.4604	0.0352	0.4851	0.0074	**0.4644**	**0.0091**	0.5394	0.0273
Towers	**0.2274**	**0.0122**	0.2285	0.0036	0.2592	0.0082	**0.2756**	**0.0061**	0.2810	0.0018	0.3116	0.0157
Avg. Ranking	1.4444		1.6667		2.8889		1.444444		1.777778		2.777778	
Friedman's χ^2=13.5556, p-value=0.001139 Corrected Friedman's χ^2=24.4000, p-value=1.526e-05							Friedman's χ^2=8.6667, p-value=0.013124 Corrected Friedman's χ^2=7.4286, p-value=0.005225					
Wilcoxon	LSTM+CNN vs LSTM		LSTM+CNN vs CNN		LSTM vs CNN		LSTM+CNN vs LSTM		LSTM+CNN vs CNN		LSTM vs CNN	
p-value	1.0000		0.00391		0.00781		0.65234		0.00781		0.00781	

Bold values represent the model that achieves the best scores.

Bold values represent the model that achieves the best scores.

obtained effectively replicate the signals in the future to ensure the effectiveness in detecting future failures (RQ1.1).

Results show differences in predicting different signals, with more difficulties in predicting certain signals (for example, H1 and TP2 have higher errors). We remind that both in the prediction model and in the displayed results, signal values are normalized to facilitate result comparison and draw meaningful conclusions. Initially, CNN+LSTM and the LSTM-only architecture exhibit similar performance, with slight differences in the errors achieved. The CNN-based model alone shows poorer results. It is noteworthy that in all results, deviations are small, indicating consistent results across different executions. For a more rigorous comparison of the results, we use the Wilcoxon's Test [10]. With a 99% of level confidence ($p-values$ are shown in Table 2), we can confirm that there are no significant differences between the results obtained by CNN+LSTM model compared to only the LSTM model. However, both approaches outperform the results obtained with the CNN architecture. Applying the Friedman's test [10], Table 2 shows the average ranking for each proposal considering the prediction of all signals. It can be seen that hybrid model obtains the lowest ranking. The test indicates that there are differences, and a Shaffer post-test, with 99% confidence, confirms that CNN statistically achieves worse results than the other two proposals, with a corrected p-value of 0.0029 for comparisons with LSTM-CNN and LSTM. This highlights the limitation of a CNN-based architecture for predicting signals. While CNN architectures can extract spatial features, they struggle to capture temporal features of time-series data as they lack memory of previous patterns. Thus, they are not suitable for time-series data. In contrast, LSTM models can effectively process time-series data and enhance model generalization through their gate structure. Therefore, it is more appropriate to use an LSTM-based model, demonstrating the robustness of this approach for solving the problem.

Similar results are observed when predicting three hours ahead as the time horizon. However, overall, the errors in predicting all signals increase, suggesting less accuracy in signal prediction. Wilcoxon and Friedman tests indicate no significant differences between the hybrid model and LSTM, while differences are noted in the results achieved by CNN, which performs significantly worse (the p-value along with the statistics are shown in Table 2). In both cases, the ranking from the Friedman test places the hybrid model in a superior position. The Shaffer post-test, conducted with 95% confidence, indicates significant differences between CNN and the other two proposals, with corrected p-values of 0.014 and 0.034 for comparisons with LSTM-CNN and LSTM, respectively.

Table 3. Detecting faults using signal predictions one hour in advance

Signal	TP	FP	FN	Detected faults
TP2	2	7	13	F12, F13
TP3	1	35	14	F5
DV_{pres}	1	6	14	F12
H1	3	25	12	F4, F10, F11
$Motor_{cur}$	1	69	14	F12
Oil_{temp}	5	25	10	F2, F5, F7, F10, F12
Oil_{level}	14	2	1	[F1-F7], [F9-F15]
COMP	14	34	1	[F1-F12], [F14-F15]
Towers	15	130	0	[F1-F15]
Intersection	**15**	**7**	**0**	**[F1-F15]**

5.2 Study of Anomaly Detection

In this study, our aim is to evaluate the effectiveness of the anomaly detection algorithm (RQ2). We analyze the detected failures across various signals (RQ2.1) and examine their detection performance with different lead times (RQ2.2). We utilize the results obtained by the LSTM+CNN model in Stage 1.

Starting from predicting signals one hour in advance, Table 3 presents the TP, FP, and FN results obtained using information from each signal independently acquired from stage 1. Here, TN is considered when no failure is predicted and no failure actually occurs, corresponding to the rest of the time not included in the previous measurements. The table also shows the specific failures that have been correctly identified with each signal. For instance, $F1$ corresponds to the failure indicated as 1 in the Table 1, and similarly for each identifier used. We can see several signals that detect a significant number of faults (a TP = 15 indicates that it identifies the 15 faults we want to find), but on the other hand, any of these models have a high number of false positive predictions (FP).

It is important to optimize both values to the maximum extent possible, as we want to anticipate the maximum number of real faults (TP), but we also want to avoid continuously alerting about faults that are not actually occurring. To achieve a more robust model, our approach analyzes the different signals and only determines that there is a fault when at least three signals agree that an anomaly exists in that interval. Table 3 shows this information considering the intersection at the last row. It can be seen that in this case, all faults were detected, and the number of FP and FN was considerably reduced, making it very interesting to combine the information, especially in this context where we are already dealing with potential errors working with predicted signals rather than real ones.

Finally, Table 4 presents an example of a specific prediction execution at various time horizons. As the prediction time horizon increases, the number of detected true positives (TP) decreases. Additionally, the table displays the average values of Recall, Precision, and F-measure obtained from multiple executions. These results are competitive, considering that previous research analyzing similar outcomes [6] achieved a 33% F-measure, with the main limitation being a lack of anticipatory capability over time.

Table 4. Detection of faults using signal prediction with varying time horizons. An example and average values

Signal	Horizon	TP	FP	FN	Precision	Recall	F-measure
		An example			Average values		
Intersection	1 hour	15	7	0	0.7126	0.8197	0.7539
Intersection	3 hours	10	8	5	0.5630	0.8116	0.6605

5.3 Result Discussion

We have studied the outcomes of the initial stage of the proposal, which involves predicting the signal, and observed that the results had a low error, allowing for accurate signal prediction. In the second study, we used these predicted signals to detect anomalies in the future data and aggregated results across different signals to make a decision. In this scenario, we achieved results demonstrating high fault detection rates with minimal false positives, utilizing a one-hour lead time.

We can note that: 1) the proposal detects a high number of faults. Specifically, all faults published alongside the dataset [5] have been identified. Additionally, many of the faults determined in the work [6] are also detected. 2) The number of false positives is remarkably low, ensuring that issues are not mistakenly identified when they do not exist. This aspect underscores the reliability and accuracy of the fault detection system, contributing to its effectiveness in practical applications. 3) We manage to anticipate in time, a crucial factor in PdM problems to optimize the use of systems as much as possible. Moreover, it is feasible to easily extend the prediction time, providing even greater flexibility and foresight in maintenance operations. With these findings, we can confidently assert the effectiveness of our proposal (RQ3).

6 Conclusion

The paper proposes an approach for forecasting in advance failures to solve a very relevant problem in the field of PdM. It involves discovering problems as early as possible to increase the overlap between prediction and ground truth. In this way, in the case study being conducted, the problem could be addressed without causing disruptions to the service. The proposal shows strong performance with a lead time of one hour and maintains promising results even with a lead time of three hours. Future work will involve analyzing the relationship between signals to enhance the performance of the proposal in both time series prediction and anomaly detection. Exploring various methods to correlate these signals could provide valuable insights into the different types of faults they represent and their interrelationships. Additionally, the study has examined two time horizons. It would be interesting to analyze the anticipatory time window at which the proposed framework significantly degrades and to seek solutions that optimize fault detection as effectively as possible.

Acknowledgements. This research was supported in part by the TED2021-132702B-C22 project of Spanish Ministry of Science and Innovation, by the ProyExcel-0069 project of the Andalusian University, Research and Innovation Department, the European Regional Development Fund and by the own research plan 2023 of the University of Cordoba.

References

1. Baptista, M., Sankararaman, S., de Medeiros, I.P., Nascimento, C., Jr., Prendinger, H., Henriques, E.M.: Forecasting fault events for predictive maintenance using data-driven techniques and arma modeling. Comput. Ind. Eng. **115**, 41–53 (2018)
2. Barros, M., Veloso, B., Pereira, P.M., Ribeiro, R.P., Gama, J.: Failure detection of an air production unit in operational context. In: Gama, J., Pashami, S., Bifet, A., Sayed-Mouchawe, M., Fröning, H., Pernkopf, F., Schiele, G., Blott, M. (eds.) ITEM/IoT Streams -2020. CCIS, vol. 1325, pp. 61–74. Springer, Cham (2020). https://doi.org/10.1007/978-3-030-66770-2_5
3. Chen, Y., Tong, S., Lu, X., Wei, Y.: A semi-supervised railway foreign object detection method based on GAN. In: Proceedings of the 5th International Conference on Computer Science and Application Engineering, pp. 1–5 (2021)
4. Davari, N., Veloso, B., Costa, G.d.A., Pereira, P.M., Ribeiro, R.P., Gama, J.: A survey on data-driven predictive maintenance for the railway industry. Sensors **21**(17), 5739 (2021)
5. Davari, N., Veloso, B., Ribeiro, R., Gama, J.: MetroPT-3 Dataset. UCI Mach. Learn. Repository (2023). https://doi.org/10.24432/C5VW3R

6. Davari, N., Veloso, B., Ribeiro, R.P., Pereira, P.M., Gama, J.: Predictive maintenance based on anomaly detection using deep learning for air production unit in the railway industry. In: 2021 IEEE 8th International Conference on Data Science and Advanced Analytics (DSAA), pp. 1–10. IEEE (2021)
7. Divya, D., Marath, B., Santosh Kumar, M.: Review of fault detection techniques for predictive maintenance. J. Qual. Maint. Eng. **29**(2), 420–441 (2023)
8. Esteban, A., Zafra, A., Ventura, S.: Data mining in predictive maintenance systems: a taxonomy and systematic review. Wiley Interdisc. Rev. Data Min. Knowl. Disc. **12**(5), e1471 (2022)
9. Filios, G., Katsidimas, I., Nikoletseas, S., Panagiotou, S., Raptis, T.P.: An agnostic data-driven approach to predict stoppages of industrial packing machine in near future. In: 2020 16th International Conference on Distributed Computing in Sensor Systems (DCOSS), pp. 236–243. IEEE (2020)
10. García, S., Herrera, F.: An extension on "statistical comparisons of classifiers over multiple data sets" for all pairwise comparisons. J. Mach. Learn. Res. **9**, 2677–2694 (2009). http://www.jmlr.org/papers/volume9/garcia08a/garcia08a.pdf
11. Hajirahimi, Z., Khashei, M.: Hybridization of hybrid structures for time series forecasting: a review. Artif. Intell. Rev. **56**(2), 1201–1261 (2023)
12. Kang, G., Gao, S., Yu, L., Zhang, D.: Deep architecture for high-speed railway insulator surface defect detection: denoising autoencoder with multitask learning. IEEE Trans. Instrum. Meas. **68**(8), 2679–2690 (2018)
13. Kang, J., Kim, C.S., Kang, J.W., Gwak, J.: Anomaly detection of the brake operating unit on metro vehicles using a one-class LSTM autoencoder. Appl. Sci. **11**(19), 9290 (2021)
14. Kang, S., Sristi, S., Karachiwala, J., Hu, Y.C.: Detection of anomaly in train speed for intelligent railway systems. In: 2018 International Conference on Control, Automation and Diagnosis (ICCAD), pp. 1–6. IEEE (2018)
15. Manco, G., et al.: Fault detection and explanation through big data analysis on sensor streams. Expert Syst. Appl. **87**, 141–156 (2017)
16. Najjar, A., Ashqar, H.I., Hasasneh, A.: Predictive maintenance of urban metro vehicles: classification of air production unit failures using machine learning. Available at SSRN 4403258 (2023)
17. Nunes, P., Santos, J., Rocha, E.: Challenges in predictive maintenance-a review. CIRP J. Manuf. Sci. Technol. **40**, 53–67 (2023)
18. Samariya, D., Thakkar, A.: A comprehensive survey of anomaly detection algorithms. Ann. Data Sci. **10**(3), 829–850 (2023)
19. Shi, W., Lu, N., Jiang, B., Zhi, Y., Xu, Z.: An unsupervised anomaly detection method based on density peak clustering for rail vehicle door system. In: 2019 Chinese Control and Decision Conference (CCDC), pp. 1954–1959. IEEE (2019)
20. Song, H., Choi, H.: Forecasting stock market indices using the recurrent neural network based hybrid models: CNN-LSTM, GRU-CNN, and ensemble models. Appl. Sci. **13**(7), 4644 (2023)
21. Veloso, B., Ribeiro, R.P., Gama, J., Pereira, P.M.: The metropt dataset for predictive maintenance. Sci. Data **9**(1), 764 (2022)
22. Zhang, W.: Graph based approach to real-time metro passenger flow anomaly detection. In: 2021 IEEE 37th International Conference on Data Engineering (ICDE), pp. 2744–2749. IEEE (2021)

Author Index

H. Quintián et al. (Eds.): HAIS 2024, LNAI 14857, pp. 353–355, 2025.
https://doi.org/10.1007/978-3-031-74183-8

The manufacturer's authorised representative in the EU is Springer Nature Customer Service Centre GmbH, Europaplatz 3, 69115 Heidelberg, Germany. If you have any concerns regarding our products, please contact ProductSafety@springernature.com

Printed and bound by CPI Group (UK) Ltd, Croydon, CR0 4YY
30/09/2026
02225597-0014